Havana USA

Havana USA

Cuban Exiles and Cuban Americans in South Florida, 1959–1994

María Cristina García

UNIVERSITY OF CALIFORNIA PRESS

Berkeley / Los Angeles / London

University of California Press
Berkeley and Los Angeles, California

University of California Press, Ltd.
London, England

© 1996 by
The Regents of the University of California

Library of Congress Cataloging-in-Publication Data

García, María Cristina, 1960–
    Havana USA : Cuban exiles and Cuban Americans in South
Florida, 1959–1994 / María Cristina García.
        p.   cm.
    Includes bibliographical references and index.
    ISBN 0-520-20131-0 (alk. paper)
    ISBN 0-520-21117-0 (pbk.: alk. paper)
        1. Cubans—Florida.   2. Cuban Americans—Florida.
    3. Florida—Emigration and immigration—History—20th
    century.   I. Title.
    F320.C97G37   1995
    973'.04687291—dc20   94-46401
                                                                   CIP

Printed in the United States of America

9 8 7 6 5 4 3 2 1

To my family, those living and those who have passed on, who are examples of faith, courage, and perseverance

Contents

Preface

This book details three waves of migration from Cuba to the United States. As the book goes to press, a fourth is under way. This most recent wave began as a migration of *balseros,* people who cross the Florida Straits in small boats and homemade rafts. Since 1959, thousands of people unable to emigrate through legal channels have left the island clandestinely on these small craft, hoping to defy the odds and reach the U.S. safely. The *balseros* of 1994 are different, however, in the sheer number of people who have made the journey. In one five-week period alone, from August 5 to September 10, the U.S. Coast Guard picked up 30,305 Cubans at sea. These *balseros* are also different in that they left their homeland with tacit approval from the Castro government. In the past, the Cuban government actively dissuaded Cubans from leaving illegally; those caught were sent to prison, and only the most brave or desperate risked the venture. In 1994, however, the Castro government reversed this policy and began using the boat traffic to its advantage: it became a means of externalizing dissent and easing the domestic pressure caused by a disintegrating economy.

The arrivals of tens of thousands of *balseros* presented the United States with yet another immigration crisis. The Clinton government made several unsuccessful attempts to pressure the Castro government to end the boat traffic (see chapter 2). Finally, in September 1994, representatives from both countries met in New York, Washington, and Havana to negotiate a solution. The United States ultimately agreed to admit at least twenty thousand new immigrants from Cuba each year for an unspecified period, and Cuba agreed to prohibit the illegal boat traffic. Americans criticized the Clinton administration for giving in to the Cuban government, but these accords were the only viable means of controlling U.S. borders and U.S. immigration policy while still offering assistance to those trying to leave Cuba.

In May 1995, the Clinton administration made yet another controversial announcement: the administration agreed to admit 21,700 *balseros* who were being detained at the Guantánamo naval base. Unable to convince the *balseros* to return to Cuba, and unable to find homes for them in other countries, the administration decided that it was wiser to grant them immigrant status than to house them indefinitely at the base at the estimated price tag of $1 million a day. However, the administration also announced that in the future all *balseros* would be returned to Cuba, in the first application to Cuban refugees of the standard practice of deporting illegal aliens. Only those who made a persuasive claim of religious or political persecution would be granted temporary refuge in the U.S., pending review of their cases.

The Cuban emigrés in the U.S. have mixed feelings about this new wave of migration. For those who still have family on the island, the United States's new open-door policy provides them with the opportunity to bring their relatives to live with them in the U.S. For the more politically committed, however, who continue to work for Castro's overthrow, the migration diminishes the possibility of an internal uprising. Instead of staying on the island to fight for change, the dissenters are leaving, as they have over the past thirty-five years. At the same time, many in the community are disturbed by the Clinton administration's new policy of deporting those who arrive illegally. They argue that their compatriots should not be deported to face an uncertain future. They claim that the Cubans' case is different from that of the Mexicans, Haitians, Guatemalans, etc., who may also claim persecution and hardship if they enter the country illegally. As political refugees from a communist state, they argue, the *balseros* should be exempted from the standard policy.

This book focuses on the immigration and adaptation experience of the first three waves of the post-revolutionary Cuban migration. The experience of the fourth wave is yet to be written. Whether or not they will adapt is currently the subject of much speculation in south Florida. However, a few predictions can be made.

Each wave of Cuban immigration to the U.S., and specifically to south Florida, where the majority of Cuban exiles have settled, has revitalized Cuban culture in the U.S.; this fourth wave will be no different. The use of Spanish has been reinforced with each wave; cultural traditions have been perpetuated, adapted, or invented; ties to Cuba have strengthened. At the same time, new arrivals from Cuba remind the older, more established immigrants—and their children—just how "Americanized" they have become. It is a long ninety miles between Cuba and the United States. Dress, attitudes, and even rhythm of speech demonstrate that Cuban culture is evolving in different ways on opposite sides of the Florida Straits. The new immigrants who will settle in Miami will find the city familiar and yet alien. Miami is certainly not a Cuban city, but it is home to the second-largest Cuban population in the world, and new immigrants will find it enough like home to want to settle there—or return there, if things do not go well for them in other parts of the United States. Miami will serve as a prism through which to interpret the U.S., and hopefully a buffer to shield them from the harsher aspects of the adaptation process. They will be among *compatriotas* who know what it's like to leave one's homeland in search of better options.

This is not to say that there will not be conflict. Emigrés of the first wave (1959–62), disproportionately white and middle class, will find it difficult to relate to the new immigrants, whom they consider rough, poor, and uneducated. The fact that many of the new immigrants are black or of mixed racial heritage, and were once the faithful revolutionary proletariat, widens the cultural chasm. Already, the term *balsero* has become a pejorative among the older emigrés, a way of differentiating themselves from the new arrivals, just as the term *marielito* (for the Cubans of the third wave) acquired currency in the early 1980s for many of the same reasons. The arrival of more than twenty thousand new immigrants each year, most of whom will probably stay in south Florida, will also exacerbate ethnic tension in Miami. Maintaining peace will be a major challenge for the city's civic and religious leaders in the late 1990s.

The new immigrants, many of whom will have spent an entire generation in revolutionary Cuba and will have never traveled outside the country, will be amazed, frightened, and disillusioned by what they encounter. They will be amazed by the sheer abundance of products lining the shelves of supermarkets, the relative freedom to think and say what they want, and the opportunities available to them to rebuild their lives in the U.S.; but they will also be disillusioned by the difficulties of carving a niche in a capitalist society. They will encounter many of the problems they thought they had left behind, among them the feelings of alienation and frustration.

Nevertheless, south Florida will accommodate the new wave of immigrants, as it has all migrants from Cuba and elsewhere. Like their
predecessors, the new wave of Cubans will alter the cultural landscape
of south Florida, but they, too, will be changed in the process.

Acknowledgments

I am grateful to a number of people who assisted me in my research. At
the Special Collections Department of the University of Miami's Otto
G. Richter Library, Gladys Ramos and Esperanza B. de Varona (and
many student workers) helped me sort through the extensive Cuban
Exile Collection. Week after week, they brought me boxes of materials
that proved crucial to my study. I thank them for their cheerfulness,
interest, and encouragement during the many months I spent there. UM
reference librarians Ana Rosa Nuñez and Rosa M. Abella suggested
secondary sources and people to interview. I spent many hours talking
to Ana Rosa during my first trip in 1986. She is a highly regarded poet,
and her stories about her fellow artists and writers gave me insight into
the creative work of Cuban exiles.

I also wish to thank the librarians and archivists of the following
institutions: the John F. Kennedy Library; the Lyndon Baines Johnson
Library; the Jimmy Carter Library; Florida International University,
University Park; the Perry Castañeda Library and the Nettie Lee Benson
Latin American Collection, both at the University of Texas at Austin;
and the Miami-Dade Public Library, Downtown Branch. My research
was facilitated by grants from Texas A&M University and the University
of Texas at Austin. The Abba Schwartz Fellowship and the John F.
Kennedy Foundation also extended financial assistance for research during 1992–93.

I am grateful to the many people who spent hours talking to me about
their experiences. I have quoted from only a few of the interviews that
I conducted over the years, but all the stories were in mind as I wrote
these chapters. My interviewees are not responsible, however, for any
opinions expressed in this book. In particular I would like to thank Mirta
R. Vega, Bertha Rodríguez, Lutgarda Mora, Deborah Carrera, Candy
García, and Conchita Alonso.

I am grateful to my colleagues at the Department of History at Texas
A&M University for all the support they have offered. I would especially
like to thank Julia Kirk Blackwelder, Larry Hill, and Al Broussard. My

colleagues Cynthia Bouton, Harold Livesay, and Larry Yarak commented on all or parts of the manuscript, as did Benigno Aguirre of the Department of Sociology. Mario T. García of UC Santa Barbara read various drafts of this manuscript and I thank him for the feedback and encouragement. I would also like to thank the anonymous reviewers who offered valuable criticism that helped me revise the final manuscript.

Some of the research in this book was presented at various scholarly forums: the American Studies Association; the Organization of American Historians; the European Association for American Studies; the Caribbean Societies Post-Graduate Seminar, Institute of Latin American Studies–Institute of Commonwealth Studies, University College of London; and the Instituto de Estudios Cubanos. I would especially like to thank the scholars associated with the IEC, in particular María Cristina Herrera, Marifeli Pérez-Stable, Yolanda Prieto, and Lisandro Pérez, who encouraged my research in Cuban American studies from the beginning.

I would like to thank my editors at UC Press. Lynne Withey and Eileen McWilliam worked with me when I first submitted the manuscript. Barbara Howell, Erika Büky, and Evan Camfield worked with me through the final revisions and copyediting. I thank them for their patience, good humor, and expert editorial assistance.

Lastly, but not less important, I want to thank my family: Joe, Lydda, Victoria, Eddie, and in particular my parents, Chary and Clemente García, for their loving encouragement and good humor during the many years I worked on this book. I also want to thank the Vega family—Mirta, Osiris, and Beatriz—for allowing me to stay in their home in Miami for months at a time over the past several years, and Mrs. Amparo Vega, for offering me the hospitality of her home in Little Havana on various occasions. Beatriz never got to read the final manuscript. She died in March 1992, at the age of thirty-three, after an eight-year battle with a brain tumor. Physical pain forced her to put off her own academic career, but she never failed to offer me enthusiastic support. I thank her because her courage helped me put my own life and work into perspective. She is deeply missed.

A special debt of gratitude is owed to my grandmother, Rosario Argilagos Rodríguez. Like most women of her generation she never attended a university or pursued an academic career, and yet she was a self-taught historian. She taught her grandchildren to value our cultural heritage and to appreciate "todo lo cubano." I thank her for making sure I learned Spanish and Cuban history, and I thank her for dragging me to all those events in Little Havana that now, years later, I write about. She is present in every page of this study.

Introduction

Since the early nineteenth century, Cubans have come to the United States in search of political stability and economic opportunity. The upheaval of the wars of independence (1868–78, 1895–98), the struggling economy of the young republic, and the often radical shifts in government in the first half of the twentieth century all contributed to Cuban emigration; but by far the largest number of Cubans (approximately three-quarters of a million) emigrated after January 1959, when Fidel Castro's July 26th Movement overthrew the government of Fulgencio Batista.

The majority of the Cubans who arrived after 1959 came during three distinct periods: immediately after the revolution, from 1959 to 1962; during the "freedom flights" of 1965 to 1973; and during the "Mariel boatlift" of 1980. As with most revolutions, the first people to be affected, and thus to leave Cuba, were those of the middle and upper classes. With each wave, however, the migration became more representative of Cuban society, not just in socioeconomic status but also in race, ethnicity, and geographic distribution.

Over half of the Cubans settled in south Florida, especially in Dade County and its largest city, Miami. South Florida was close to Cuba, with the same climate, and the area was also attractive because it was already home to a small population of Cubans who had emigrated in previous decades. The new Cuban emigrés perceived themselves as exiles, not immigrants. They did not want to begin life anew as *norteamericanos*. Rather, they hoped to return to their homeland once a more tolerable government replaced Fidel Castro's. Because of the long history of U.S.

involvement in Cuban affairs, many believed it was only a matter of time before Castro fell. The Cubans arrived in the United States during the height of the Cold War, and for Americans they became powerful symbols of the clash between democracy and communism. The U.S. government drafted new immigration laws to accommodate them and devised the Cuban Refugee Program, the most comprehensive refugee assistance program in American immigration history, to welcome them.

As the Cubans waited to return to their homeland, they focused their energies on survival. They had to concern themselves with earning an income, educating their children, and other mundane aspects of day-to-day living. Despite the obstacles of language and culture, they integrated into south Florida's labor market. Building on the successes of earlier Cuban immigrants, they created a vibrant business community in south Florida that revitalized the local economy and drew other immigrants to the area. Two factors contributed to the Cubans' creation of a viable economic enclave: their middle-class values and entrepreneurial skills, which transferred readily across borders, and the Cuban Refugee Program, which pumped millions of dollars into the economy and facilitated the Cubans' adaptation through vocational and professional retraining programs. The economic enclave founded by middle-class Cubans in the early 1960s accommodated all subsequent arrivals from Cuba and served as a magnet for immigrants from all over Latin America.

The Cubans created a cultural enclave as well. Over the years, they tried to define what it meant to be Cuban in a country other than Cuba, and they struggled to define their relationship to both countries. Previous immigrants from Cuba had grappled with the same concerns, but for the refugees from Castro's Cuba, preserving *cubanidad* ("Cubanness," or Cuban identity) became a political responsibility. Feeling betrayed by Castro's revolution, they were determined to maintain a visible presence in south Florida, just ninety miles away from the regime they hated, as a symbol not just of *la Cuba de ayer* (the Cuba of yesterday) but of the Cuba that could be. A politically and economically successful community was the best revenge the *gusanos* (worms—Castro's term for the emigrants) could have. Since many of them hoped to return to their homeland one day, maintaining a sense of *cubanidad* in exile was crucial for the distant day when repatriation would become possible; in the meantime, it would ensure their survival as a distinct community.

With the large concentration of emigrés in south Florida, and its geographic proximity to Cuba, Miami became the symbolic center of *el exilio*. The most important exile organizations emerged in this city, as did the exile media, consisting of hundreds of periodicals and close to a dozen Spanish-language radio and television stations. Miami became the center of Cuban creativity in the United States, home to some of Cuba's most important artists, writers, and intellectuals, and Cuban culture found its most vital expression (outside Cuba) in Miami, where it took new forms. Miami was home to Little Havana and Calle Ocho, the Ermita de la Caridad, the *municipios*, and a host of cultural institutions that defined *cubanidad*.

It was also from south Florida that emigrés waged their war against Castro, a paramilitary and propaganda campaign to discredit the Cuban leader and undermine his government that at times received financial and institutional support from the United States government. However, the Cubans were as diverse politically as they were socioeconomically. While opposition to Fidel Castro's government was the raison d'être of the community, the Cubans had different political visions for their country's future. The emigrés all claimed to want "democracy" for their homeland, but they had different ideas of what democracy entailed, and their visions were shaped by the successes and failures of Cuban politics. Some favored an authoritarian, non-communist government that would establish social and economic order, modeled in part on the Batista government that Castro's July 26th Movement overthrew. Others advocated an open, multiparty electoral system, modeled after that of the United States or the parliamentary systems of other western democracies. In economics, some were free-market capitalists, while others favored some variation of socialism that would address the social and economic inequalities that had plagued *la patria* since the creation of the Republic. Some wanted to continue their country's symbiotic relationship with the United States, while others, more staunchly nationalistic, favored political and economic independence. Represented within the emigré population were supporters of the various political parties, factions, urban resistance groups, and guerrilla groups of pre-1959 Cuba, as well as literally hundreds of new political organizations that emerged in exile, each coalescing around either some charismatic individual or a particular political concern.

The debates between these different groups contributed to a heated and often violent political climate in south Florida. A segment of the emigré community even came to adopt a more tolerant view of the Castro government and dedicated its efforts to trying to ameliorate U.S.–Cuba relations. Ironically, the exiles' strong sense of responsibility toward Cuba contributed to their success in the American mainstream: whether trying to topple the Castro government or to cooperate with it, the emigrés learned to work within the American political system.

The purpose of this study is to provide a history of the post-1959 Cuban emigré community in south Florida, a history that not only chronicles the details of the Cubans' immigration and adaptation but also examines the cultural, political, and intellectual life of this community. There is a rich body of work on contemporary Cuban migration, almost all of it in the social sciences, but most of the work focuses on specific aspects of the Cuban experience, whether the formation of an economic enclave or the extremism of exile politics. I have tried to build on these works, using a variety of new research sources, to fill in some of the pieces of the Cuban story and provide an alternative interpretation. As a historian, I have tried to look at the overall picture, discussing not only the Cubans' economic and political life but other aspects of their culture: in short, the formation of community. The Cuban emigrés' case is in some ways unique, and one cannot completely understand their experience without understanding the Cuban exile psychology and the formation of identity. Whenever possible, I have tried to let the emigrés speak for themselves to provide a sense of the human drama of migration and to demonstrate the process of identity formation and cultural negotiation.

The Cubans' experience provides a fascinating case study in American immigration and ethnic history, not only because of the federal government's response to their arrival, or the role they have played in U.S. foreign policy, but because of their response to life in the United States. Few immigrant groups have assimilated structurally in so short a time and simultaneously forged a uniquely bicultural identity. While the Cubans' original goal may have been to preserve Cuban culture on American soil until they could return to their homeland, over time they have produced a uniquely Cuban-American culture. Recent arrivals from Cuba joke that arriving in Miami is like stepping back in time into the Cuba of the 1950s. All around are visible reminders of prerevolutionary Cuban society: schools, businesses, and organizations that shut down in Cuba reopened in exile. But closer examination demonstrates that Cuban culture has developed in different forms on opposite sides of the Florida Straits. As anthropologists and folklorists have pointed out, culture can never be passed on intact from generation to generation; rather, it is continually reinvented in the present. While the emigrés may have thought they were preserving Cuban culture (which was already somewhat Americanized), in fact they adapted their traditions and customs to meet the realities of life in the United States, much as their compatriots on the island redefined their culture to meet the social and political demands of the new state.

Many emigrés developed a dual identity as both Cuban exiles and Cuban Americans.[1] Staunchly nationalistic, they initially resisted naturalization, perceiving it as a betrayal of their homeland and a negation of the forces that propelled them into exile. Most emigrés eventually realized, however, that citizenship offered them legal protection and opened professional and commercial opportunities. Over time, they also developed strong emotional ties to the country that gave them refuge. As they bought homes, paid taxes, attended PTA meetings, and participated in civic affairs, they developed ties to Florida and the United States in spite of their original intentions. However, with Cuba less than one hundred miles away, and with the continual influx of new refugees, the emigrés remained as preoccupied with their homeland as with their new country. The war against Castro was just one manifestation of this reality. The Cubans adapted socially, economically, and politically to the United States and, at the same time, influenced the political realities in their homeland. They learned English while retaining Spanish, ultimately making bilingualism a necessity in the local labor market. They changed the cultural landscape of south Florida and at the same time became highly Americanized.

Visitors to Miami often claim that they feel they are in Latin America rather than the United States. Billboards dotting the highways advertise Latin American products; streets are named after Spanish and Cuban historical figures; and Spanish is heard as commonly as English in every setting. (Signs in some shops facetiously state "English spoken here.") This ambiance is what has made Miami so unique, and also what has earned it the most criticism. Only three decades ago, Miami was a resort town in the Deep South whose economy revolved around winter tourism. It is now a major international city, the so-called gateway to the Americas and the principal port of trade between North and South America. The Cubans have played a large role in this economic transformation.

The Cuban presence in south Florida is ubiquitous. According to the most recent census figures, over half of Dade County's population—or roughly one million people—identify themselves as Latinos or Latin American immigrants, and Cubans make up the majority of these. Commenting on this Latin American influence, journalist Joel Garreau compared south Florida to Hong Kong: an island independent of yet related to the mainland.[2] South Florida, however, is really a hybrid society, a border town connected to two mainlands: Cuba and the United States. While the Cubans are not, of course, the only immigrant group in south Florida, they are the most visible and influential group in Miami's political, economic, and civic life. Theirs is a community that continually redefines itself in relation to two nations and two cultures.

This larger theme of cultural negotiation lies at the heart of this study. The book is divided into two parts. Part I provides a history of Cuban migration following the revolution. The experiences of the emigrés varied from wave to wave. The first chapter focuses on those who arrived during the first two waves, from 1959 to 1962 and from 1965 to 1973. These are the Cubans who emigrated in response to the radicalization of Cuban society. As refugees from communism during the height of the Cold War, they received the sympathy and admiration of most Americans. Popular magazines such as *Life, Newsweek,* and *Fortune* portrayed them as the "model immigrants," celebrated their heroism and patriotism, and dubbed them the new Horatio Algers. The U.S. government rewarded them with a relief package and benefits program to assist in their adaptation to American society. It was these middle- and working-class Cubans who created the vital cultural and economic enclave in south Florida.

Chapter 2 focuses on the Cubans of Mariel, who are unique within both the Cuban immigrant experience and American immigration as a whole. Unlike the earlier emigrés, these Cubans came of age or lived most of their adult lives in Cuba's new revolutionary society. They were the so-called *hombres nuevos,* the New Men, or New Cubans, produced by the revolution. Many of them had no experience to which they could compare their lives under Castro; thus, their migration was prompted by a different reality. Among the 124,776 new immigrants who arrived in Key West were a sizable number of felons, whom the Cuban government expelled to discredit the emigré community and punish the United States. While the felons comprised less than 4 percent of the total number of immigrants, they commanded a disproportionate amount of media attention. Consequently, the Mariel Cubans became one of the most stigmatized immigrant groups in American history. They were not granted refugee status, nor were they celebrated for their patriotism and heroism. They were shunned by most Americans and even by their compatriots, who feared being stigmatized by association. Yet, in spite of the odds against them, over the next decade they demonstrated patterns of adaptation similar to those of the Cubans who arrived earlier.

It is important to note that this section of the book does *not* attempt to provide an evaluation of the Cuban revolution of 1959. There is a vast literature on the revolution, reflecting a variety of political perspectives and interpretations. A number of these works are included in the bibliography. While researching my book, I found that Americans disagree as to whether the emigrés were justified in leaving Cuba, and their views are usually determined by their interpretations of the revolution. Some perceive the emigrés to be heroes, patriots, and "freedom fighters" (to use a term popularized during the Reagan administration); others view them as Cuba's old guard, the corrupt bourgeoisie whose emigration was motivated by economic rather than democratic concerns. Both views are simplistic. Close to one million people left Cuba during this period, and their reasons for emigrating are as varied and as complex as the migration itself. I am not interested in judging the revolution or in evaluating whether the emigrés were justified in their reasons for leaving Cuba. It is sufficient that they considered themselves to have ample reasons. I am more concerned with analyzing their response to the exile experience.

Part II of the book explores larger conceptual issues: What does it mean to assimilate into American society? Can one maintain one's national identity and yet be a full participant in American society? What does it mean to be an American? These are not new questions. Every immigrant and ethnic group has struggled to define its identity within the larger society. However, these questions have particular relevance in the final decade of the twentieth century. Worldwide, the 1980s and early 1990s witnessed the emergence of the "new nationalism"; in the United States, this period saw the emergence of the "English-Only" movement, immigration reform, and the debate over multiculturalism. The debate over what type of society we want to have in the twenty-first century figures prominently in academic forums, the news media, and political circles. The Cuban community in south Florida provides the perfect setting in which to investigate some of these larger issues and questions.

Chapter 3 examines the issue of biculturalism, exploring how the emigrés defined and asserted their identity and altered the cultural landscape of south Florida, as well as how they were altered by the experience of exile. The chapter includes a discussion of exile organizations, the news media, religion, and education as institutions through which to understand this process of cultural negotiation.

Chapter 4 explores a much more controversial topic: exile politics. As a community of predominantly first-generation immigrants, with friends and family still on the island, the emigrés are as concerned with events in Havana as with those in Miami. Over the past thirty-five years, their mission has been to discredit and topple the Castro government. While emigrés' attitudes toward the Castro regime have not changed much, their methods have. As the emigrés became more and more involved in domestic politics, they applied the skills they learned in the American political arena to their war against Castro. The paramilitary groups of the 1960s were replaced by political action committees in the 1980s, and these were more successful in intensifying U.S. and international pressure on the Castro government.

Cuban exile politics are hardly monolithic, however. A segment of the community has come to favor rapprochement, supporting the normalization of U.S.–Cuba relations as a means of provoking democratic change in Cuba. Some emigrés have abandoned exile politics altogether and immersed themselves in local or ethnic politics. By 1992, Cubans dominated Miami's city commission; the city and county managers were Cuban; ten of the twenty-eight seats occupied by the Dade County delegation in the state legislature were held by Cubans; Cubans had been elected mayor of several cities, including Miami; and one emigré had been elected to the U.S. House of Representatives. (Another Cuban, Lincoln Díaz Balart—Fidel Castro's nephew—was elected later that year.) In addition, Cubans occupied top administrative posts in the key institutions of Dade County, from the *Miami Herald* to the AFL-CIO to local colleges and universities. Nevertheless, in Cuban ethnic politics a politician's success is more often than not determined by his or her views on Cuba. Residents of Miami joke that Florida is the only state in the union with its own foreign policy. (During 1982–83, for example, the Miami City Commission passed twenty-eight resolutions and ordinances that dealt more with foreign policy issues than with local interests.)[3] Whether involved in domestic or foreign policy, however, the emigrés' political activities provide another opportunity to study the process of accommodation.

Chapter 5 explores the intellectual and creative life of the emigré community. It is the intellectuals—the writers, poets, dramatists, scholars—who help shape the cultural and political debate in the emigré community. Many of them choose to live outside south Florida, but much of their work is written for—and in response to—the emigré community in south Florida. It is the writers who best exemplify the process of cultural negotiation that is taking place at a wider level in the community. Some are obsessed with their homeland, keeping it alive through characters and plots drawn from memory, or writing social commentaries on the present-day realities in Cuba. They perceive themselves to be Cuban writers, first and foremost, not immigrant Americans. Conversely, other emigrés write about the complexities of life in the United States. They explore issues of identity and the clash and mediation of cultures—issues relevant, of course, to other immigrant and ethnic writers. Whether in literature, art, or political commentary, these intellectuals struggle with issues of nationalism, adaptation, identity. The work of emigré scholars has also expanded the parameters of political discussion in this community. They have promoted scholarly exchange between *cubanólogos* (those who study Cuba) on and off the island, and thus encouraged diverse interpretations of Cuban history, the revolution, and the exile experience.

Many Americans see the Cuban emigré community as a community that refuses to assimilate. They are angered by the pervasiveness of Spanish as a public language and the role of Cuba in public debate. Some believe that abandoning exile politics altogether and concentrating entirely on domestic issues would be the truest sign of the Cubans' assimilation. As strong believers in the proverbial melting pot, they do not understand the Cubans' reluctance to become Americans. The emigrés are puzzled by these criticisms. They perceive themselves to have assimilated quite well. Even though they are a community of predominantly first-generation immigrants, their average income almost equals that of the national average. Their naturalization rates are among the highest of any Latino or immigrant group. They have high voter registration and voting rates and one of the highest school completion rates in the country. They have created the most lucrative Hispanic business community in the nation. They have a powerful political lobby in Washington. They do not understand why becoming "American" should require that they forget their homeland, their customs and traditions, and their language. These differences in perceptions of what it means to be American have contributed to social tension in south Florida, which over the years has expressed itself in riots, demonstrations, and a variety of political referendums.

Despite the uniqueness of their experience, the Cubans may present a realistic example of assimilation in the contemporary U.S. The nineteenth-century expectation that immigrant groups should relinquish their cultural ties to the homeland (except, perhaps, for a few quaint customs to be displayed at folklife festivals) and "melt" into some generic American culture has become unreasonable in today's society. Indeed, many scholars are now questioning whether the melting pot ever existed at all. Traveling through the United States, one is reminded that there is no such thing as one American culture. Each region, populated over generations by different native and immigrant groups, has its own unique identity and culture. As international borders become blurred in the late twentieth century and communication and travel between countries becomes easier, it is increasingly possible for immigrants to assimilate structurally and yet retain a distinctive cultural identity. At the same time, this cultural identity will be continually redefined, evolving in response to contact with other groups, the mass media, the public school system, and other influences. Like the Cubans, immigrants will change the character of the communities they move into—but they will also be changed in turn.

PART ONE

The Emigration

CHAPTER I

Exiles, Not Immigrants

Cuban Immigration to the United States,
1959–1973

From January 1, 1959, to October 22, 1962, approximately 248,070 Cubans emigrated to the United States.[1] The first to leave were those whose positions of power tied them to the old regime: political leaders, high government officials, and military officers of Fulgencio Batista's government. Associated with the corruption and abuses of the *Batistiato* (the Batista regime), these people faced a loss of position, property, and even life, and their only option was to leave Cuba until a less hostile government was in place. Many top officials had amassed great fortunes over the years, which they invested in foreign bank accounts, guaranteeing themselves a comfortable wait.

Not all who left during this first wave were affiliated with the Batista regime, however; thousands of people were negatively affected by the social and economic upheaval of the new revolutionary government. The migration followed a logical socioeconomic progression. Cubans of the upper class were the first to leave. Members of the middle class followed: merchants, business executives, and professionals such as doctors, lawyers, engineers, and teachers. By 1962, Cubans of the working class also began to leave: office and factory employees, artisans, and skilled and semiskilled laborers.

Those who left Cuba did so for a variety of reasons, political, social, and economic.[2] Many had opposed the revolution from the beginning, but others were Castro supporters who became disillusioned with the course *la revolución* ultimately took.[3] They had perceived Fidel Castro and the July 26th Movement as a democratic alternative to the corruption and terrorism of the Batista regime. Other political groups had emerged during the 1950s to challenge the government, but the July 26th Movement, led by the young, Jesuit-educated lawyer from Oriente province and his band of *barbudos* (bearded ones), had captured the imagination and allegiance of these future emigrés. Fidel was intelligent, witty, and charismatic, and his brand of nationalism appealed to Cubans who were resentful of foreign (U.S.) exploitation of their native resources and their economy. When Fidel took over, Cubans eagerly awaited the reimplementation of the liberal Cuban constitution of 1940, suspended under Batista, as well as new, progressive legislation that would ensure basic civil liberties. Instead, they witnessed the creation of a Marxist state.

The social upheaval of the first years of the revolutionary government fueled their ideological opposition. Cubans reacted in different ways to the new government's policies affecting ownership, management, production, and trade: some supported agrarian reform, for example, but not the nationalization of Cuban-owned businesses. However, it was the widespread violence, social indoctrination, and general climate of suspicion and harassment that proved to be the decisive factors causing many people to leave. They feared the *fusilamientos,* the mob-style executions of Batistianos and counterrevolutionaries. They resented the indoctrination in their children's schools, the Marxist propaganda, the imprisonment and harassment of religious clergy, the censorship of the news media, and the reduction in personal freedoms. They also resented the shortages in basic food staples and consumer goods brought on by the restructuring of the Cuban economy, and later by the trade embargoes imposed by several nations.[4] For those who left Cuba, the general feeling was that *la revolución* had been betrayed.

Most Cubans who traveled to the U.S. did so under the assumption that their stay would be temporary and that they would soon return to their homeland. Exile movements had always been a part of Cuban history, and these Cubans perceived themselves as the most recent, albeit largest, wave of people forced out of their country by changing political tides. Because of the Castro government's nationalization of American property—and because the United States had a long history of intervention in Cuban and Latin American affairs—most emigrés believed that it was just a matter of time before the United States intervened and a more conservative, and hopefully democratic, government replaced Castro's. In the meantime, the emigrés had to survive as best they could: they had to find jobs and housing, enroll their children in school, and, if possible, contribute in some way to liberating their homeland. Crucial to their identity was the belief that they were political exiles, not immigrants; they were in the U.S. not to make new lives for themselves as *norteamericanos* but to wait until they could resume their previous lives back home. In the meantime, they hoped to live in some peaceful community and, if lucky, to improve their economic standing.

Because of the pervasive American economic and cultural presence in prerevolutionary Cuba, the U.S. was not particularly foreign to the exiles, especially to the upper- and middle-class Cubans who comprised the earlier arrivals. Since the United States had been Cuba's principal trading partner, Cuban businessmen and politicians had traveled there frequently to negotiate transactions. Before the revolution, vacationing in Miami Beach or New York City was as popular for middle-class Cubans as vacationing in Havana was for middle-class Americans. Some private schools taught English as a second language, and families who could afford to do so sent their children to boarding schools or universities in the U.S. Cuban culture in general was highly Americanized: Cubans were consumers of Hollywood movies and the American mass media, and their language, dress, and even sports and recreational activities reflected the influence of their neighbor to the north.

For the middle to upper classes who made up the early migrations, then, the United States was the most logical place to go. More importantly, it was the only nation to have a fairly open immigration policy—at least with regard to the Cubans. Those who settled in other countries— Mexico, Spain, Venezuela, Puerto Rico—did so for other reasons. Some were simply unable to acquire seats on planes to the U.S., or were unable to meet immigration criteria. Others, particularly the wealthy landowners and *azucareros* (sugar producers), had property and investments in Latin America and chose to remain close to these investments. Still others wanted to live among fellow *latinoamericanos;* no matter how familiar they were with American popular culture, they felt more at home in a Spanish-speaking society. And yet others were motivated by nationalism. Though they admired American know-how, many Cubans resented the United States' interference in Cuban affairs. Pride and anger prevented them from turning to the U.S., which had propped up corrupt Cuban "presidents" in order to protect U.S. economic investments. The revolution, they believed, was an inevitable response to such policies.

Those who traveled to the United States regarded Florida as the most appealing place to spend their exile. Since the nineteenth century, Cubans had been migrating back and forth between the island and Florida in response to changing fortunes and politics, and the small Cuban communities there offered some stability and familiarity. By 1959, close to thirty thousand Cubans lived in Miami, many of them having come as exiles a generation or two earlier.[5] Key West and Tampa also had long-established Cuban communities: both had played a key role during the nineteenth-century wars of independence.[6] For homesick, snow-fearing Cubans, Florida's climate and topography were also important considerations; and as an added incentive, the plane ride from Havana to Miami was quick (fifty-five minutes) and inexpensive (approximately twenty-five dollars), making a return easy when conditions in Cuba changed. In south Florida, one could even pick up Cuban radio stations on a portable radio. Emigrés ultimately settled wherever they found jobs, however, even if it meant relocating to northern cities such as Chicago, St. Louis, or New York. Taking care of one's family was always the primary consideration. The majority of emigrés stayed in south Florida because, over time, the economic environment there accommodated them.

Since they perceived themselves as temporary visitors, few Cubans arrived with regular immigrant visas. Most arrived as "tourists," others came with student visas, and some had no visas at all. Until January 3, 1961, when the United States severed relations with Cuba, visas were secured at the American embassy in Havana or at the American consulate in Santiago; afterwards, "visa waivers" could be acquired through the Swiss embassy in Havana, which henceforth represented U.S. interests on the island. These waivers were granted to the parents, spouses, and minor children of persons already in the United States, as well as to children who were coming to the U.S. "for study" and to persons who had "urgent and legitimate business or personal affairs" in the United States.[7] By late 1961, the Immigration and Naturalization Service (INS) was receiving requests for visa waivers at the rate of twelve hundred per working day, of which two-thirds were normally approved. Once in the United States, the Cubans were granted "indefinite voluntary departure" or "parole" status.

To leave their country legally, Cubans had to acquire an exit permit from the Cuban Interior Ministry. Many emigrés stated that they were traveling to the United States as tourists to avoid harassment (or possible detention); the Cuban government kept up the charade, fully aware that most of these people would not return. Castro encouraged the departure of those who opposed his government, calling them *gusanos* (worms or maggots) and *escoria* (scum), but he also wished to halt the "brain drain"; the exit permits allowed the government to screen the emigrés and prevent individuals with certain technical skills from leaving the country. Those suspected of "crimes against the revolution" were also detained. Cubans who could not get exit permits, or who feared for their safety, took refuge in foreign embassies. Some stayed there for as long as two years, waiting for the embassy to secure their permission to travel. Others sailed clandestinely to the Florida Keys. Those eager to leave the country but unable to get on a plane to the U.S. had the option of traveling to a third country—if they were fortunate enough to acquire visas—and applying for U.S. immigrant visas at the American embassies there.

By the end of 1961, the exit process had become a long and tedious affair. Potential emigrés had to fill out numerous forms and submit to lengthy inquisitions. After 1960, airline tickets had to be purchased with U.S. currency; Cubans who did not have American dollars had to wait until friends or relatives in the U.S. sent them the proper currency by postal money order. Even after they received the money, there was a waiting list for seats on airlines. At the airport, members of the Cuban state police carefully inspected every piece of luggage and often subjected passengers to dehumanizing personal searches. Jewelry and other expensive goods had to be turned over to friends or relatives staying in Cuba or be confiscated by the police. The exit process, most emigrés believed, was a form of psychological harassment, which continued even as they boarded their flights: it was not uncommon for people to be removed from planes awaiting takeoff and detained for further questioning. Travelers knew that until the plane crossed over into U.S. air space, they could be recalled. A typical experience is described by this emigré, a fifty-year-old grandmother when she left Cuba:

> At the airport, the *milicianos* [the G-2, the state police] made us disrobe and they checked all our personal belongings. Everybody . . . even babies in diapers . . . even old people. They were so arrogant, those *milicianos*. But we didn't say anything because if we did, they wouldn't let us leave. On the plane everybody was quiet. You can imagine. . . . We were all heartbroken. Many people were crying; others just sat there staring off into space. We were leaving our country for who knows how long. We were leaving everything behind. Halfway into the flight the pilot announced that we were in U.S. territory . . . that we were now free . . . and then everybody started clapping and cheering. Some men started cursing Fidel Castro . . . and his mother.[8]

If the emigrés failed to return to Cuba within an allotted time, the government confiscated their remaining property. After 1961, Cubans were allowed to take only five dollars and thirty pounds of luggage per person out of the country. The most fortunate Cubans arrived in Miami and stayed with relatives or friends who assisted them in finding housing and jobs, or they took a train or a bus to cities where they knew people who could help them. Most exiles, however, arrived at Miami International Airport penniless, with no idea as to where to take their families, much less where to find a job.

"Every exile has his story," said one emigré to the author. Indeed, all the emigrés interviewed for this study tell poignant stories of their first years in exile. Bertha Rodríguez was ten years old when she arrived in Miami with her mother and two sisters. She recalls:

> My father was waiting for us in Miami. The day we arrived, he had a meal waiting for us. . . . He worked in a restaurant . . . in catering. But the very day we arrived, they dismissed him from his job. Afterwards he found work in a factory, he and my mother both. . . . We moved into an apartment, and on the second day, the caretaker, or the owner—whoever was managing the place—got drunk and threw us out. He said we had no right to be there. At that time we didn't know any English, so we didn't understand everything he said. But he was very nasty.[9]

Lutgarda Mora, who traveled with her daughter, remembered:

> Our luggage arrived from Cuba twenty-nine days after we did. The luggage was all wet and moldy. The clothes were all full of mold. It was a disaster. Since we arrived with nothing, my daughter had to go out and buy us a change of underwear. . . . Many people stayed in our apartment. They stayed with us until they found jobs. Cubans who arrived in Miami had our telephone number and would call us to see if they could stay with us until they found work. In the living room we had a sofa-bed especially for our friends. Our landlords never said anything . . . I guess they knew how needy we all were.[10]

Deborah Carrera remembers:

> I was a professional in Cuba. I had degrees in teaching and pedagogy. I felt compelled to give it all up and leave my country because I realized that I could never teach communism. It contradicts my Christian and democratic ideals. . . . When we got to Miami, the first thing [the immigration authorities] did was interview me. I declared myself to be against Fidel. That sealed my fate forever. I could never return because if I did I would be sent to prison.[11]

Another emigré, then twenty-six, married and with two toddlers, re-membered:

> We stayed in a fleabag hotel in Miami Beach. Now that place is a fancy hotel in the Art Deco district, but back then, only the poor stayed there. It cost us about five dollars a night. It was the only place we could afford. I would sit there every day and just look at the ocean. All I did was cry. The only thing that kept me going were the children. They depended on me. The hotel eventually threw us out because the neighbors complained that the baby cried too much. Everywhere we looked, the signs said "No children."[12]

During these first years, the Catholic Church became the major source of assistance for Cuban exiles in Miami. Since the overwhelming majority of Cubans were at least nominally Roman Catholic, they log-ically turned to the Church in their time of need. Parish priests directed them to the Centro Hispano Católico, a social welfare agency that Bishop Coleman F. Carroll established in 1959 to assist the Cubans.[13] Located in a remodeled wing of the Gesu parochial school in downtown Miami, the Centro offered services such as housing and job referrals, English classes, a day nursery, educational programs for children, an outpatient and dental clinic, home visits to the sick, and small loans to cover miscellaneous expenses such as eyeglasses and dentures, as well as food, toiletries, and used clothing. By December 1961, the diocese of Miami had spent $1.5 million in assisting the Cuban refugees.[14]

Voluntary relief agencies (VOLAGs) also opened up offices to assist the refugees. These included the Catholic Relief Services (a division of the National Catholic Welfare Conference), the Protestant Latin Amer-ican Emergency Committee (affiliated with the Church World Service), the International Rescue Committee, and the United HIAS Service (in cooperation with the Greater Miami Jewish Federation). Individual churches and synagogues also carried out their own relief efforts. By late 1960, representatives of these different VOLAGs met each plane coming from Havana to answer the emigrés' questions and to inform them about the resources available to them. The VOLAGs distributed blankets, clothing, food, and toiletries.

By the end of 1960, close to forty thousand emigrés had arrived in the United States, and their numbers were increasing by one thousand to fifteen hundred per week.[15] Most of them stayed in Miami, and Dade County residents understandably worried about this continuing migra-tion. South Florida's economy was dependent upon winter tourism and retirees, and the locals felt they could not accommodate this sudden population growth. To make matters worse, the Cubans arrived during a mild economic recession, when the city had an unemployment rate of over 6 percent. Cubans had to compete with an already large pool of unemployed, unskilled laborers as well as with the northern migrants who traveled south each winter in search of jobs.

Cubans of the middle class, in particular, experienced radical downward mobility during these first years in the U.S. Approximately 36 percent of the early arrivals were professionals (doctors, lawyers, engineers, and educators) or semiprofessionals (draftsmen, radio operators, aviators, designers) who were unable to practice their professions, because they did not meet the state licensing requirements, did not speak the language, or could not find jobs in their trades.[16] They worked at whatever jobs were available, in construction, maintenance, and service occupations. It was common to see doctors working as hospital orderlies, lawyers as dishwashers, architects as gardeners, teachers as janitors. Doctors and dentists often practiced illegally, making house calls or working out of their homes, offering their services only to their fellow Cubans and at much lower rates than American doctors.

Women found jobs more easily than men because employers paid them even lower wages.[17] These jobs were also unskilled or semiskilled and did not require experience or fluency in English, with limited contact with the general public. Women found jobs as seamstresses (many doing piecework at home), domestics, janitors, cooks, dishwashers, waitresses, cashiers, manicurists, and other service positions. Some were fortunate enough to find employment in Miami's expanding garment industry. Others found jobs sorting shrimp in warehouses by the Miami River, work so tedious and painful that they nicknamed it *la Siberia*. Still others found their first jobs as agricultural workers in *las tomateras,* the fruit and vegetable fields outside the city.

Local residents complained of losing jobs to Cubans, who were willing to work for lower salaries and thus depressed wages for Miamians as a whole. While the national news media celebrated the refugees' heroism and middle-class values (one *Newsweek* article enthusiastically told readers "They're OK!"),[18] letters to the *Miami Herald* and the *Miami News* revealed the frustration in the city that was forced to accommodate them. Most Miamians sympathized with the plight of the Cubans but could not understand why their community had to bear the burden of a crisis it did not create.

In October 1960, a Cuban Refugee Committee, composed of leading citizens from civic, charitable, and professional organizations in Miami, appealed to President Eisenhower for assistance. Concluding that resettlement was the only viable solution to Miami's problems, the president released $1 million from the contingency funds of the Mutual Security Act to assist in resettlement efforts. In invoking the Mutual Security Act, Eisenhower officially recognized that Cuba was a communist state and that Cuban exiles were political refugees. The president also appointed Tracy Voorhees, head of the 1956 Committee for Hungarian Refugee Relief, to study the Cuban refugee situation and make further recommendations.

Following Voorhees's report, on December 7, the Eisenhower administration established a Cuban Refugee Emergency Center in downtown Miami to coordinate the relief efforts of all the voluntary relief agencies and oversee the resettlement program. (The building was subsequently nicknamed "Freedom Tower.") Most of the financial burden continued to rest with volunteer agencies, however, since the federal funds were used specifically for refugee resettlement and did not cover food, clothing, medical care, or other miscellaneous forms of assistance. Private groups eventually established eight refugee centers in south Florida specifically for humanitarian assistance, among them the Centro Hispano Católico and the Protestant Latin Refugee Center, to meet the needs the federal government failed to acknowledge. During the Eisenhower administration, the federal government provided no direct financial help to the community, the churches, the relief agencies, or the Cuban exiles themselves.

The administration's limited commitment was not due to inexperience. After the Hungarian revolt of October 1956, the U.S. granted asylum to thirty-eight thousand Hungarians who had taken refuge in Austria. Congress passed emergency legislation to bypass the pre-existing immigrant and refugee quotas and allow the Hungarians to enter, and the government spent close to $50 million in relief efforts.[19] In the Hungarian case, however, the federal government controlled the immigration by establishing a strict quota. As the Hungarians arrived in the U.S., they went to Camp Kilmer, a military base in New Jersey, where they stayed until they found sponsors and jobs. Within a few weeks, all of the Hungarians had been resettled throughout the United States.

In the Cuban situation, by contrast, federal officials had to deal with a population that was already immersed within one community. They could only assist or keep track of those who registered at the Cuban Refugee Center, and for every seven refugees who registered, three did not.[20] There had been a finite number of Hungarians, but the Cuban refugee population kept growing; for humanitarian and political reasons, few Cubans were denied entrance into the United States. The Cubans also resisted resettlement outside the Miami area. They believed that democracy would soon be restored to Cuba and that resettlement to other parts of the U.S. would only delay their repatriation.

The Eisenhower administration's commitment to relief efforts may have been halfhearted, but it did establish the bureaucracy that allowed Cubans to enter the United States in the first place. In trying to explain why immigration laws were "bent, if not broken" for the Cubans, President Eisenhower emphasized the "uniqueness" of the Cuban situation.[21] This was the first time that the United States had served as the country of first asylum for a large group of refugees, he argued, and the Cubans' plight deserved a generous response. In reality, however, the administration simply regarded the Cubans as temporary visitors. In March 1960, on the advice of Vice President Richard M. Nixon, Eisenhower approved a CIA plan to train a military invasion force that would "resolve the Cuban crisis" once and for all. Thus, elaborate relief programs and strict quotas were unnecessary.[22] The Cubans were not to be assimilated but rather assisted until they could resume their normal lives back in Cuba.

This perception of the Cubans as temporary visitors was evident in federal policy. The Cubans' "parole" status permitted them to seek employment in the U.S., a right generally granted only to those seeking permanent residency. In resettling the exiles throughout the U.S., the federal government guaranteed their transportation expenses back to Miami once return to the homeland was possible.[23] The government justified this accommodation of the Cuban refugees as a humanitarian gesture that would ultimately benefit the United States: the refugees would one day return to Cuba to mold their country's future, and would establish more cordial relations with the U.S.

Beginning in 1961, the Kennedy administration became more active in refugee relief efforts, considering the Cubans to be victims of the Cold War and thus a national responsibility.[24] Through aid to the refugees, the administration hoped to prove "the resolve of this nation to help those in need who stand with the United States for personal freedom and against Communist penetration of the Western hemisphere."[25] Kennedy established the Cuban Refugee Program (CRP) under the umbrella of the Department of Health, Education, and Welfare (HEW), coordinated with the departments of State, Labor, Defense, and Agriculture.[26] Funds were provided not only for resettlement but for monthly relief checks, health services, job training, adult educational opportunities, and surplus food distribution (canned meat, powdered eggs and milk, cheese, and oatmeal, among other food products).[27] The government also provided partial funding to the Dade County public school system to help it accommodate the more than thirty-five hundred Cuban refugee children who attended public schools by January 1961. (Another three thousand Cuban children attended Catholic parochial schools, many on diocesan scholarships, but these schools did not receive financial assistance from the federal government.)[28] Over the next twelve months, the staff at the Cuban Refugee Center increased from fourteen to over three hundred; even State Department personnel evacuated from Cuba were temporarily reassigned to work at the center.[29] Federal funds for all these programs were initially provided by presidential discretion, but in 1962 the Migration and Refugee Assistance Act (P.L. 87-510) established permanent authority for the relief program.

By March 1961, the registration process at the refugee center had become quite elaborate. Cubans arriving at the center were given an identification card, interviewed, and classified as to job skills, the number of "employables" in the family, and friends and relatives in the United States. They then received a medical examination to check for tuberculosis or other infectious diseases; any necessary inoculations were given, and the seriously ill were transported to either the Gesu Medical Clinic or Jackson Memorial Hospital. Refugees were also interviewed by representatives of the VOLAG of their choice to arrange for possible resettlement. The Red Cross distributed personal articles, and the Florida State Welfare Department arranged for financial assistance, if necessary, as well as for food distribution.[30] Remarkably, assistance was provided even to those Cubans who were admitted as permanent residents under the Immigration and Nationality Act and were not technically parolees.[31]

The Kennedy administration also had to deal with the unaccompanied children who arrived from Cuba; by September 1963, there were more than fourteen thousand of them. Many parents in Cuba, unable to emigrate, sent their children ahead to the United States, hoping to be reunited at a later date. Some parents worried about political indoctrination in Cuban schools; others hoped to save their boys from military conscription; and others were motivated by rumors that the government was going to send Cuban children to the Soviet Union and the Eastern bloc for training. Consequently, more than half of the children who arrived in Miami unaccompanied were between the ages of thirteen and seventeen, and over two-thirds were boys. Many arrived with only an identification tag pinned to their clothing, or a letter in their pocket requesting assistance. Some came carrying infants and younger siblings. Bryan O. Walsh, a Catholic priest and director of the Catholic Welfare Bureau in Miami, assumed responsibility for their care, finding lodging for the children in school dormitories and homes around the city.

By April 1961, with the assistance of the U.S. government and the Catholic Church, an elaborate underground network developed to get children out of Cuba. This network, called "Operation Peter Pan," involved dozens of people, among them Ramón Grau Alsina and Leopoldina "Polita" Grau de Agüero, the nephew and niece of former Cuban president Ramón Grau San Martín, and James Baker, the principal of the elite Ruston Academy in Havana.[32] Employees of KLM and Pan American Airlines also assisted in the network. Walsh, who had become executive director of the Cuban Children's Program, secured blank visa waivers, five or six hundred at a time, and smuggled them to his contact in Havana, Grau Alsina. Staff at various embassies in Havana, particularly the British and Dutch, acted as couriers, transporting visa waivers, correspondence, money, and other materials between Miami and Havana; at times, even ambassadors served as couriers. Grau Alsina filled out the blank visa waivers with the names of children, and the Catholic Church sent him the funds needed to purchase airline tickets.[33]

The airlines had to provide the Cuban Interior Ministry with the names of all those scheduled to travel on each flight. They deliberately set aside a number of seats for unaccompanied children, reserving those seats under different names. Right before each flight, Grau Alsina provided the airline with the names of the children who would actually occupy those seats; the airline then informed the ministry that there had been some last-minute cancellations and that others would occupy the seats. The number of unaccompanied children on each flight was varied to avoid drawing attention to the practice: one flight might transport three children, another seven, another five. Since the Interior Ministry was fairly unorganized during the early 1960s, it never investigated.

The granting of visa waivers was left to Grau Alsina's discretion as long as he forwarded to Walsh the names of all boys over the age of fifteen. Grau also forged passports, changing birthdates to allow young men of military age to leave the country. On one occasion he altered the passport of a twenty-six-year-old man who was sought by the G-2. "We would also hide people, even in our own house," said Polita Grau. "[We] helped them get political asylum." Word of the network spread, and people came from all over the island to see the Graus. "In my terrace I had a candy dish with tranquilizers," said Ramón, "because the people who visited me . . . were desperate to get out of Cuba. I had a 'travel agency' that resembled a psychiatrist's office." Grau wrote up over twenty-eight thousand visa waivers for unaccompanied minors; half of the children—14,156—actually made it to Miami. (The rest either chose not to use the visa waivers or were unable to take advantage of them once the flights to the U.S. terminated in October 1962.) All the participants in this network in Cuba worked at great risk to their lives, and most were ultimately caught and sent to prison. "We all fell like oranges, one after the other," said Polita. "Very few were saved." Polita served fourteen years in prison, Ramón twenty-one, for these and other counterrevolutionary activities.[34]

With hundreds of children arriving each month, Walsh found it increasingly difficult to provide enough beds for them. When foster homes were unavailable, the diocese rented space in five different centers (Camp Matecumbe, Florida City, Kendall, Jesuit Boy's Home, and St. Raphael's Hall). The local news media, both English and Spanish, and the wealthier emigrés living in Miami sponsored fundraisers for the Cuban Children's Fund and raised thousands of dollars for their care. The Kennedy administration eventually assumed financial responsibility for the children and began resettling them to homes and institutions around the country. The government provided foster families and institutions with per diems, paid for the children's transportation expenses and for their winter wardrobes if they traveled to colder climates, and made special arrangements for children with mental or physical disabilities. The government also provided funds for language tutoring, as well as for psychological counseling to help traumatized children cope with the separation from their families. Under the federal program, children remained under foster care until they reunited with their families or reached majority age.

Not all accommodations were ideal. Officials reported some cases of physical and emotional abuse in foster homes and institutions.[35] There were a few cases of children being beaten simply for not speaking English. While the services of the Cuban Children's Program were comprehensive, its programs could not always ease the anxiety and depression the children felt at being separated from family, friends, and homeland. Children relocated outside south Florida had an especially difficult adjustment period. The children in Miami at least had some community support, but those sent to Baltimore or Albuquerque were thrust into a completely alien environment and had no familiar network to rely on. Thirty years after the fact, the views of the now-grown children on Operation Peter

Pan vary: some are grateful for the care they received, while others remember those years with bitterness.[36]

The Kennedy administration worked with the local community to resolve other problems as well, among them Miami's employment crisis. Skills and talents remained untapped within the largely middle-class refugee community because of the language barrier and the Cubans' inability to meet state licensing requirements for various professions. Because the Castro government prohibited teachers and other professional people from bringing diplomas or transcripts of university records to the United States, it was nearly impossible to verify their educational backgrounds.[37] Local community groups, with grants from the federal government, designed programs to help Cuban professionals prepare for their state licensing examinations or retrain for other types of employment. In January 1961, the University of Miami established the Post-Graduate Medical Program for Cuban Refugees, a sixteen-week intensive course, in Spanish, for Cuban doctors. Private corporations and agencies, such as Eli Lilly, Upjohn, Mead Johnson, and the American College of Surgeons, provided partial funding, and later the program received a grant from HEW. Over twenty-five hundred Cuban doctors eventually took part in the program, which was later expanded to include all foreign medical school graduates who wanted to practice in the U.S.

Many Cuban teachers also had difficulty finding employment, even if they were competent in English. Many teachers in Cuba had received their teaching certificates from normal schools, not universities, and thus were not qualified to teach in American schools. Even those with the proper academic credentials and language fluency lacked the certification to teach. To employ the hundreds of experienced—and aspiring— Cuban teachers in Miami, the Dade County public school system established a teacher aide program, in which Cubans assisted in special classes set aside for Spanish-speaking children. The assistants, most of whom were women, received practical experience in American classrooms, serving as monitors and as interpreters between teachers and students. Dr. Mirta R. Vega, who retired in 1992 after thirty-two years in the Dade County school system, found her first job in the U.S. working as one of the "Cuban aides":

> I started working as a Cuban aide in May 1962. I couldn't find work in my profession, of course—I was a pharmacist. I was desperately trying to find some type of job. My sister-in-law told me that they were hiring Cuban aides. I applied and was immediately accepted. I worked as an aide for two months, and they liked my work so much that the principal asked

me to return the following school year. We were poor and had no telephone, so the principal had to send someone to my house to offer me the job. My students were all Cuban refugee children and they were very frightened. Many of the American teachers were also frightened. I could understand that. Each day two or three or four new refugee children arrived at the school . . . every day. New classes had to be created all the time. Some of the teachers just couldn't handle it. One day, two American teachers came up to me and said, "Don't take it personally, but we've decided to take early retirement. The changes here are just too much for us."[38]

To meet the need for qualified teachers, the University of Miami, through a grant from HEW, initiated a Cuban Teacher Training Program in 1962. The first year, over two hundred candidates applied for the program and took an entrance exam, and thirty-two were chosen; Dr. Vega was one. The course lasted one year and afterward the trainees had to take the National Teacher's Exam, a certification exam so difficult that the Teacher's Union in south Florida had lobbied to eliminate it because of the low success rate among native-born Americans. That first year, however, all thirty-two of the Cuban aides passed the exam. The Cuban trainees were then allowed to teach their own classes, and to teach American children. Dr. Vega taught American junior and senior high school students:

> Despite all the positive evaluations I received, there were days, during those first months of teaching, when I honestly thought I would never make it. The anxiety was horrible. It was just so difficult to get up in front of a class of American children and try to teach them in a language that wasn't your own. To this day, whenever I drive by one of the schools where I first taught, the feelings of anxiety rush back. . . . Personally, I never experienced any rejection by the other teachers. In fact, most were very supportive. But I could tell that some did not like the situation. At first, whenever I walked into the faculty room, everyone would stop talking. You could tell that they had been talking about Cubans. I knew that I had been accepted when I could walk into the faculty room and everyone continued talking.[39]

Over the next few years, the rapidly growing school system hired most of the graduates of the UM program. Others—especially instructors of foreign languages—were relocated to school systems around the country. As late as 1972, Florida International University had a federally funded teacher-training program for Cubans. The Dade County school system did a remarkable job in accommodating both Cuban teachers and students; never has a school system had to take in so many children in so short a time. "If there's any institution in south Florida that helped the Cuban exile," said Dr. Vega, "it was the Dade County public school system."

The federal government extended assistance into higher education as well. By 1961, more than two-thirds of the faculty of the University of Havana reportedly lived in Dade County, and like many others they occupied jobs for which they were overqualified.[40] The Cuban Refugee Center compiled a roster of Cuban academics in Miami and made efforts to find lectureships for them in colleges and universities, or positions in the United States Information Agency. Through the Cuban Affairs Research Project at the University of Miami, the government also granted a limited number of research fellowships for the study of Cuba, Latin America, and the Caribbean, to encourage "the study of those problems that inevitably will confront the Cuban people upon the return of democracy to their nation."[41] The administration even considered the possibility of establishing a new university in south Florida to take advantage of this population of academics, though no action was taken.[42] In February 1961, HEW's Office of Education established a loan program for Cuban students, allowing college students to borrow up to one thousand dollars to continue their education. By 1966, the program had assisted more than fifty-five hundred students at 293 colleges in forty-three states, the District of Columbia, and Puerto Rico.[43]

Of all the professionals, Cuban lawyers faced the most difficult challenge. Apart from the difficulties with language and certification, lawyers had to learn the workings of a legal system based on English common law, which was substantially different than the Napoleonic codes on which Cuban law was based.[44] In March 1961, the American Bar Association established a special committee to help Cuban lawyers, judges, and legal scholars find employment as teachers, librarians, and legal counsel in corporations. But unless the Cubans returned to law school, they were unable to practice privately in any state. Only in 1973 did the University of Miami and the University of Florida create an intensive eighteen-month program specifically for Cuban lawyers that allowed them to graduate with an American law degree.[45]

Ironically, the federal government's larger role in Cuban refugee relief increased complaints in the Miami–Dade County area. It was much easier for local citizens to be sympathetic to the plight of Cubans dependent upon the charity of voluntary agencies and service clubs; as the amount of federal assistance increased—and surpassed the level of assistance available to U.S. citizens living in the state of Florida—resentment grew.

In 1959, Florida ranked thirtieth in per capita income and forty-seventh in welfare funds per inhabitant.[46] The maximum amount granted to the elderly per month was sixty-six dollars; to a family with dependent children, eighty-one dollars. The Cubans—foreign, non–English-speaking people claiming to be temporary visitors—received much more: a single person was granted seventy-three dollars per month, and a married couple, with or without children, received one hundred dollars. Although the relief offered to Cubans was far from enough to meet the basic necessities in Miami's recessed economy—the average rent was seventy-five dollars, for example—it was still far more than the average Dade County resident could receive.[47] Cuban refugees were also the first to receive government-surplus food; only later did state and local agencies extend this service to needy Americans. Local citizens had no job-training programs at this time, nor did the unemployed have the opportunity to resettle, all expenses paid, to areas where jobs were available.

As letters to local newspapers revealed, the financial assistance the refugees received was not the only thing that inspired resentment. Miamians complained that their Spanish-speaking neighbors were boisterous, rude, and disrespectful of American laws, especially traffic regulations. The Cubans, they said, used "horns for brakes."[48] Because of the housing shortage, many Cuban families temporarily moved into together, causing many Miamians to fear that property values would drop and slum districts similar to Spanish Harlem in New York City would be created. Signs reading "No Cubans allowed" became a common sight in apartment buildings throughout the city; others barred families with children from renting. Parents worried that their children would receive an inadequate education in the Dade County public schools, since educators readily admitted that in trying to accommodate the non–English-speaking Cubans they neglected their other students. Blacks watched in disbelief as Cuban black and mulatto children attended "white schools," prompting one local minister to write that "the American Negro could solve the school integration problem by teaching his children to speak only Spanish."[49]

The constant bickering among Cubans also baffled Miamians. Within the first few years, emigrés created literally hundreds of political organizations to lead a counterrevolution. The only thing the organizations held in common, however, was their hatred of Fidel Castro.[50] Emigrés fought constantly over what sort of government should replace Castro's, and more significantly over who would assume leadership. They accused each other of being Batistianos or *comunistas* and refused to work with each other for their common goal. The local media tried and failed to analyze exile politics. "We all know that when Americans talk politics, lifelong friendships are broken," commented one local television documentary. "But when two Cubans get together—within minutes you have a general and a mayor. Give them a national holiday, throw in a statue of the revolutionary hero, José Martí—and you have the makings of a riot."[51] Of particular concern to local residents was the Cubans' use of south Florida as a base from which to launch their war against Castro. Several political organizations carried out paramilitary maneuvers against the island (described further in chapter 4), and local authorities frequently confiscated large caches of munitions. Miamians feared for their security and resented being caught in the middle of someone else's war.

Throughout 1961, local newspapers and television and radio news shows produced highly charged stories on the problems of accommodating the Cuban refugees. Many of these programs were sensationalistic and angered the Cubans, who resented being resented. In order to counteract this negative press, the federal government stepped up its own propaganda efforts, trying to portray the Cubans in a more positive light. Government reports emphasized the Cubans' rapid adjustment to the U.S. as well as their gratitude at being welcomed into a democratic society. To downplay the financial costs of the CRP, the government released statistics on the number of Cubans who were turning down assistance, or repaying the government for the assistance they had received.[52] The director of the CRP and other officials of the Kennedy administration made frequent appearances before local civic groups, praising them for their efforts and encouraging further tolerance and patience. Increasing social tension, however, led the Subcommittee on Refugees of the U.S. Senate Judiciary Committee to hold hearings on Miami's refugee problems through most of December 1961. Local residents, both native and exile, testified before the subcommittee and discussed ways to address these problems. The discussions proved helpful in the formulation of future Cuban refugee policy.

A Turning Point:
The Failure of the Bay of Pigs Invasion

On March 17, 1960, President Eisenhower authorized the Central Intelligence Agency to organize, train, and equip Cuban refugees to overthrow Fidel Castro.[53] The CIA recruited close to fifteen hundred exiles to take part in the invasion force—or Brigade 2506, as the regiment came to be known—and over the next year trained these men at secret bases in Panama, Guatemala, and Nicaragua.[54] In Miami, the CIA chose a "government-in-exile" to replace Castro and his top officials, composed of exile leaders representative of the various political factions. From the very beginning, the CIA planned for the Cuban refugees to conduct the invasion themselves, with limited U.S. support. Misunderstandings over the nature of this support ultimately contributed to the invasion's failure.

The word "fiasco" has been used over and over to refer to the events that took place at the Bay of Pigs and Girón Beach on April 17–19, 1961. In retrospect, the invasion had little chance of succeeding. Information given to the landing parties was inaccurate because the landing area was not charted in advance; much of the equipment, including the military landing craft, was inadequate for the type of warfare planned; and the ships carrying most of the soldiers' supplies were either sunk or forced to flee far from shore by the Cuban air force. The underground counterrevolutionary groups in Cuba, on which the Brigade depended for military assistance, were never notified of the invasion. Most importantly, just hours before the invasion, President Kennedy, who had inherited and approved the CIA plans, canceled the use of American air cover for the landing force without informing the Brigade soldiers, leaving them highly vulnerable to the Cuban military.

Even without these tactical mistakes, whether the Brigade could have defeated the Cuban military is arguable. Information on the Brigade leaked to the press months before the invasion, giving the Cuban government ample time to prepare a formidable defense. *La Hora*, a newspaper in Guatemala City, printed a story about one of the training camps as early as October 1960; other reports quickly followed in the *Hispanic American Report* (Stanford University), *The Nation*, the *Los Angeles Mirror*, and the *St. Louis Dispatch*. In Miami, most exiles suspected that an invasion of Cuba was imminent, and exile periodicals published stories based on the numerous rumors circulating through the community. CIA recruitment centers were established around the city, including one at the University of Miami. Emigrés kept "disappearing" and yet their families were financially taken care of.[55] The upcoming invasion was a subject of discussion at every Cuban social gathering, and exiles made plans for their return home. Amid all the talk of revolution, the *Miami Herald* investigated and acquired evidence of plans for a U.S.–sponsored invasion. The editors chose to sit on the story so as to not jeopardize the mission, but when the *New York Times* published its story, including a map of the Guatemalan training base, the *Herald* quickly followed suit.[56]

The media attention, however, simply confirmed what the Cuban government already expected. A few years earlier the CIA had assisted in the successful overthrow of the Jacobo Arbenz government in Guatemala, and Castro knew that the U.S. government perceived Cuba to be a much more dangerous threat. Cuban officials did not debate if an invasion was imminent but when it would come.[57] As early as 1960, the Cuban military was on alert, preparing to deal with any invasion. Within two days of the Brigade's landing, an estimated twenty thousand Cuban troops surrounded the soldiers, with enough artillery and tanks for a long fight. The popular uprising the Brigade had hoped to catalyze never took place. During the invasion, the Castro government reportedly detained over one hundred thousand people suspected of supporting the American invasion, thus undercutting any possible internal uprising.[58]

On the day of the invasion, Cubans in Miami waited anxiously for news. Hundreds crowded into churches or met in parks for candlelight prayer vigils. Others gathered at bars, cafés, and newspaper stands to listen to the radio. Within forty-eight hours, they heard the crushing news that the Brigade had failed to maintain its beachhead. Over the next few days they would learn that some 120 men had died and 1125 soldiers had been captured and imprisoned. As news of the defeat spread through Miami, emigrés sent telegrams to President Kennedy pleading for U.S. intervention. A successful invasion was their only hope of returning to Cuba in the immediate future. When the U.S. failed to intervene, most Cuban exiles felt betrayed by President Kennedy.[59]

Throughout the rest of 1961 and 1962, the exile community tried to negotiate the release of the Brigade soldiers.[60] Five were executed as war criminals of the Batista regime, and seven others were condemned for political crimes, but Castro agreed to exchange the other prisoners for five hundred bulldozers, as indemnification for the damages caused by the invasion. The U.S. government refused to either finance the ransom or negotiate with the Cuban government directly, and so a bipartisan committee of private American citizens conducted the negotiations through unofficial channels. A Tractors for Freedom Committee, which included former First Lady Eleanor Roosevelt, Johns Hopkins University president Milton Eisenhower, and United Auto Workers president Walter Reuther, took on the responsibility of appealing for funds from the American public. The negotiations collapsed by mid-June 1961, however, when the committee, fearing that bulldozers could be used in military construction, insisted on substituting five hundred tractors. Castro's subsequent demand for one thousand tractors or $28 million in cash and credits in lieu of the bulldozers was rejected as too steep a ransom.[61]

After the soldiers were sentenced to thirty years in prison in March 1962, outrage in the exile community forced a new round of negotiations. Castro raised the ransom to $62 million: $25,000 to $500,000 per soldier, depending on his rank.[62] The Cuban Families Committee for the Release of the Cuban Prisoners of War, under the direction of New York attorney James P. Donovan (who also successfully negotiated the exchange of U2 pilot Gary Francis Powers for the KGB's Rudolf Abel in 1962), prepared a careful public relations campaign to raise the necessary funds. The committee kept the plight of the soldiers continually in the press, placing stories of their courage on the battlefield in popular magazines such as *Life* and *Reader's Digest*. To raise the necessary funds, the committee sold limited-edition "Freedom Medallions" for twenty-five dollars, each with the Brigade number of a particular soldier, and they enlisted Ed Sullivan to appeal for donations on his weekly television show. One of the largest single donations ($1 million) came from Richard J. Cardinal Cushing of Boston.[63] To counteract domestic political opposition and minimize the chance that Castro would change his mind, Christmas 1962 was set as the deadline for ransoming the prisoners.[64]

Castro agreed to lower his demands to $53 million in material goods. Almost all of the ransom was paid in baby food, powdered milk, medicines and medical equipment, pesticides (for both household and agricultural use), and other items in short supply in Cuba that Castro specifically requested. Donations were made to the Red Cross by private companies on a tax-deductible basis as charitable contributions.[65] Other items were purchased by the Red Cross with the funds raised. Transportation costs (air, sea, rail, and truck) were also donated by various companies. Despite the administration's desire not to negotiate with the Castro government directly, officials worked behind the scenes to facilitate the purchase and delivery of the ransom items.[66] Attorney General Robert Kennedy convinced U.S. manufacturers of baby food and pharmaceuticals to donate large quantities as a "humanitarian" effort. The Department of Commerce provided the permits necessary to export the large quantities of narcotic drugs.

Both the committee and the administration worked under intense pressure, knowing that at any time Castro could once again raise the amount of the ransom or dispute the market value of the shipments.[67] In light of mounting congressional criticism, paying a higher ransom was impossible; allowing the Brigade soldiers to remain in prison, however, was equally impossible, as Kennedy felt responsible for the invasion's failure. Talks resumed even after the Cuban Missile Crisis. Kennedy advisors felt that by ransoming the prisoners their historical image would be preserved: the Bay of Pigs would be remembered as an "operational failure" with few casualties rather than a "real tragedy where twelve hundred men died as a result of this operational failure."[68]

Finally, by late December 1962, all but seven of the soldiers were ransomed.[69] As his "Christmas bonus," Castro permitted thousands of the soldiers' relatives in Cuba to leave on the vessels that delivered the shipments of food and medicines. Donovan also arranged for the release from prison of twenty-seven Americans (many of them adventurers or mercenaries), including three CIA agents.[70] After several deliberate delays by the Cuban government, the first planeload of Brigade soldiers reached Homestead Air Force Base on the afternoon of December 23; the last of the soldiers arrived on Christmas Eve.[71] Each plane was met by INS and Red Cross personnel and by representatives from the Cuban Refugee Center; families and friends were not allowed at the base. According to administration personnel, the arrival of each plane was an emotional affair, with the soldiers crying and kissing the ground as they stepped off the plane.[72] After they were interviewed, fed, and given new uniforms, the men were transported by bus to Dinner Key Municipal Auditorium, where they were reunited with their families at a reception hosted by Miami mayor Robert King High and the Cuban Families Committee.

On December 29, 1962, forty thousand cheering and flag-waving emigrés gathered at the Miami Orange Bowl to hear President and Mrs. Kennedy address the soldiers and their families. On a platform set up at the fifty-yard line, Kennedy shook hands with the Brigade commanders and moved among the lines of soldiers to greet them and shake hands. At a highly emotional point in the ceremony, the officers presented the president with the flag of Brigade 2506, and then stood in silence as a band played the national anthems of the United States and Cuba.[73] Provoking speculation on the possibility of another invasion, the President surprised the audience by saying, "I can assure you that this flag will be returned to this Brigade in a free Havana." Kennedy finished his speech by saying, "Your conduct and valor are proof that although Castro and his fellow dictators may rule nations, they do not rule people; that they may imprison bodies, but they do not imprison spirits; that they may destroy the exercise of liberty, but they cannot eliminate the determination to be free."[74]

Surprisingly, normal commercial air traffic from Cuba to the U.S. continued after the Bay of Pigs invasion. The Cuban government still expected U.S. retaliation, however, and continued to tighten its control over the population. The number of Cubans who made use of their exit permits increased, as dissidents realized that they had better emigrate while they still had the opportunity. Rumors circulated that the government was going to shut off all commercial air travel between Cuba and the United States. The invasion "was the only hope we had to liberate Cuba," said one emigré who was living in Cuba at the time. "After that we lost all hope, and many people chose to leave."[75] Like the exiles in Miami, they realized that Castro's overthrow was not in the immediate future.

The flights out of Cuba continued until the Missile Crisis in October 1962, when the United States confronted the Soviet Union over the presence of nuclear missiles in Cuba. Castro immediately closed Havana's airport to all American planes.[76] For a few days Cuban exiles, like the rest of the world, anxiously prepared for the possibility of war. Many were hopeful that this confrontation might provide the necessary impetus for U.S. military involvement in Cuba and the overthrow of the Castro government.[77] Like many Americans, they were ignorant of the consequences of nuclear war. The emigrés' hopes for U.S. involvement in Cuba were dashed, however, by the negotiations that followed. The Kennedy-Khrushchev accords included a nonintervention clause: in exchange for the removal of nuclear missiles, the United States agreed not to invade the island.

1962–1965: A Breathing Spell

Many Miamians were relieved when the flights out of Cuba were suspended. In just three short years the city had undergone radical change as it absorbed over two hundred thousand "temporary visitors." The Cuban Refugee Center could now concentrate its efforts on assisting those Cubans already in the United States without worrying about five or six thousand potential additions to the relief rolls each month.

Despite the lack of communication between the U.S. and Cuba, many Cubans did manage to leave the island and travel to the United States. From October 22, 1962, to September 28, 1965, approximately fifty-six thousand Cubans arrived in the U.S.[78] The majority came via third countries, mainly Spain or Mexico. Many were given special visa priority because they were the parents or siblings of unaccompanied children already in the U.S. Another five thousand arrived on the ships and Red Cross planes that carried the ransom for the Bay of Pigs prisoners. Many Cubans also sailed clandestinely to the U.S. on small boats, rafts, and even inner tubes. By 1963, approximately four thousand men, women, and children had crossed the Florida Straits in such craft and either arrived at Key West or been rescued by the U.S. Coast Guard.[79]

Following the failure at the Bay of Pigs, aid to the Cuban emigrés increased, motivated in part by the administration's sense of guilt.[80] To ease the persistent tension in south Florida, the CRP continued to focus on resettlement. Officials enacted a comprehensive public relations campaign to find jobs and sponsors for Cubans outside of Miami. Brochures, "fact sheets," and information packages were sent to service clubs, chambers of commerce, business and industrial associations, and church and civic groups around the country, as well as to newspaper editors and television and radio personnel. The CRP mounted displays about the refugees at business conventions and loaned specially made films such as *We Shall Return* (Cari, 1963) and *Force of the Wind* (United International, 1962) to civic and community groups. These films and information packages were naturally designed to pull heartstrings, and the lists of sponsors multiplied.

The U.S. Employment Service compiled a list of job offers from around the country. Qualifications of individual refugees were matched against the requirements of the jobs and telephone interviews were arranged, though in most cases businesses were content to rely on the evaluation of the USES. Those who got jobs were immediately resettled. For refugees with limited work experience or none at all (as in the case of many women), training programs were arranged in conjunction with labor unions such as the Amalgamated Clothing Workers of America or the AFL-CIO. While a lack of English skills limited some refugees' chances of finding employment, the greatest barrier was age: hardest to place were those over fifty. Most American employers saw age not as a marker of experience but of limited productivity.

Cubans were still reluctant to leave Florida, but all efforts were made to convince them that resettlement was in their best interest. Whenever possible, Cubans were resettled in groups of three or four families of relatives and friends, and homes were found for them in close proximity. They were assigned a sponsor or contact in their new communities—in many cases, a church congregation—to which they could turn for counseling and direction. They were assured that they would be entitled to comparable welfare benefits should they lose their jobs. The CRP even appealed to their patriotism: they were told that they would be ambassadors of a democratic Cuba, informing Americans of the evils of communism. As in the early years, the Cubans were also promised that they would be returned to Miami once repatriation became possible.[81]

By June 1963, an estimated 35 percent of the 165,000 Cubans registered at the Cuban Refugee Center had found homes and jobs outside of Miami.[82] Resettlement efforts acquired an additional impetus in 1964, when the Johnson administration announced that financial aid would be cut off to unemployed Cubans in Miami if they refused to relocate to cities where jobs were available. As the CRP's director, John F. Thomas, explained, the new policy was "designed to encourage the refugee who is caught in a vicious web of uncertainty, dependency, and propaganda to face the realities of life."[83]

While Miamians continued to complain about the social and economic burden the Cubans posed, reports suggested that the problems were not as serious as local citizens believed.[84] Studies conducted by the Florida State Employment Service and the U.S. Department of Labor revealed that refugees were not taking jobs away from local citizens but rather creating new businesses and job opportunities. A report by the Miami Police Department showed that while crime had indeed increased during the past three years, the Cuban influx did not affect the crime rate. Tourism to south Florida increased, despite the emergency situation. Studies by the Miami Housing Authority and the Federal Housing Administration reported that while the housing shortage produced overcrowding, no slums had been created and the real estate market was booming. The millions of dollars channeled into the Dade County public school system through the CRP had improved the schools, despite the difficulties of accommodating thousands of new students. In addition, all the money pumped into the local economy by the federal government ($70 million just from January to May, 1963) had helped the economy to develop despite forecasts of a recession.

1965–1973: The Freedom Flights

On September 28, 1965, Fidel Castro surprised Cuba, Cuban exiles, and the United States government by announcing that all Cubans with relatives in the United States who wished to leave the island would be permitted to do so. Criticizing the United States for using those who escaped from Cuba on small craft as propaganda against his government, Castro remarked, "Now we shall see what the imperialists will do or say."[85] He designated the small fishing port of Camarioca, in the northern province of Matanzas, as a possible gathering place and point of departure. On October 10, he pledged "complete guarantees and facilities" to exiles returning to Cuba to get their families out.[86]

Within hours, the exile community flooded Cuba's Interior Ministry with telegrams requesting exit permits for their relatives. The State Department tried to discourage the exiles from sailing to Cuba—partly because of the physical danger, but also because it wished to control any migration—but many emigrés rented tugboats, yachts, shrimpers, anything that could float, and sailed for Camarioca to negotiate for their relatives there. The Coast Guard intercepted hundreds of boats and rescued dozens of stranded or sinking vessels off the Florida Keys, but from September 30 to November 30, more than 150 boats succeeded in crossing the Florida Straits, bringing back 2866 people.[87]

The Johnson administration announced that it was willing to accept more Cuban refugees into the United States, and on September 30 the State Department began the long process of negotiation with the Cuban government through the Swiss embassy in Havana. The crisis coincided with the passage of H.R. 2580, which amended the McCarran-Walter Immigration Act of 1952, abolishing the harsh national quota system in favor of a seven-category preference system. On October 2, 1965, in a ceremony at the base of the Statue of Liberty during which Johnson signed the bill into law, the president stated: "I declare this afternoon to the people of Cuba that those who seek refuge here in America will find it. . . . Our tradition as an asylum for the oppressed is going to be upheld."[88] In keeping with the new immigration law, Johnson also stated that immigration priority would be given to the parents, children, and spouses of Cubans already in the United States, as well as to those imprisoned for political reasons.

A month later, the government made public the terms of the "memorandum of understanding" negotiated between Cuba and the United States. Beginning December 1, chartered planes would travel to Varadero, outside of Havana, twice each day, transporting between three and four thousand Cubans each month. Relatives of those already in the U.S. received immigration priority. Although the State Department negotiated for the release of political prisoners and the transport of young men of military age (15–26), the Cuban government refused to include them, or those individuals whose professional and technical skills were vital to economic production. Both governments insisted on strict, impartial adherence to the terms of the memorandum. No exceptions were granted, even for special medical cases. Whenever some difficulty such as weather or mechanical trouble interrupted the schedule, the U.S. government added extra flights on the following days until the transport was on schedule again.[89]

Claiming a relative in Cuba was complicated. Exiles had to contact the Cuban Refugee Center and fill out the necessary forms. The list of requests, known as the U.S. Master List A, was sent to Cuba for screening, where it was compared with the Cuban Master List A, the list of Cubans who had requested permission to leave and had been cleared for emigration. These two lists were then edited into a Joint Consolidated List A. The Cuban Refugee Center notified exiles if their relatives were approved for immigration but was unable to inform them of specific travel dates. Their arrival could be a matter of days—or perhaps years, since Cuban officials made flight assignments randomly. A period of forced agricultural labor was sometimes required before Cubans were allowed to emigrate. Some families received letters from their relatives in Cuba providing their travel schedules, while others did not find out until their relatives landed in Miami. Local Spanish-language radio stations read the names of each day's arrivals.

These were anxious times for many emigrés. Despite assurances from both the U.S. and Cuban governments, many emigrés feared that Cuba would not live up to its end of the bargain. The flights from Cuba were the only opportunity they had to be reunited with their families, and they did not rest easy until their relatives were safely in the U.S. As one emigré remembered the 1960s, "Sofía used to call the airport every day and ask: 'How many flights do we have from Havana?' But the way she pronounced it, it sounded like she was asking about flies rather than flights. We were always awaiting someone's arrival. I also remember that the whole family would gather in the back yard each Sunday, but our celebrations consisted just of drinking a little Cuban coffee."[90]

The INS and other government agencies carefully screened the arriving refugees. Occasionally the government denied entry to some individual, but it then arranged for his or her emigration to another country. Resettlement remained a top priority during the "freedom flights," and more than half of the Cubans who arrived after 1965 were resettled around the country. Temporary barracks housing up to four hundred refugees at a time were set up at Miami International Airport;

the barracks were nicknamed the *Casa de Libertad*. Local businesses and churches provided them with clothes, blankets, food, and toys while they waited for their flights out of Miami.

Miamians were not pleased with the freedom flights. They realized that despite the resettlement effort a percentage of the Cubans would remain in or return to south Florida. One columnist at the *Miami Herald*, angered that the refugee ranks were swelling once again, complained that they were "up to [their] armpits with Cuban refugees."[91] Letters and telegrams flooded the local newspapers, Miami City Hall, and the White House, most expressing the usual concerns about employment, housing, language, and overcrowding in the schools. Other writers believed that Castro—and the Cuban exiles—were taking advantage of American generosity, and that the president was allowing them to do so. One woman wrote: "I sincerely think that our president is letting down his people again, sacrificing our welfare and security further for Cubans who will not appreciate it and . . . will stab us in the back every chance they get."[92] Other citizens were afraid that Castro might use the airlift to sneak communists into the U.S. to commit sabotage and "stir up racial trouble," perhaps as revenge for the Bay of Pigs invasion. A few Americans wrote to suggest that the government explore military alternatives. They regarded Cuba as a much more dangerous threat than Vietnam, and recommended that the government solve the Cuban refugee problem by "cleaning Cuba out."[93]

Many letters came from the black community in south Florida. African Americans, disproportionately poor, uneducated, and semiskilled, had suffered the most from the Cuban migration, since the two groups competed for the menial service jobs that required a minimum of education or training. Blacks watched in anger and amazement as the "temporary guests" became the beneficiaries of social and educational programs that the Civil Rights movement had long fought for. For most blacks, the refugee crisis proved yet again that they were second-class citizens in their own society. Many of them wrote the president to remind him of his responsibilities "towards the economically-oppressed of this community, [not just] the politically-oppressed of Cuba."[94]

Even schoolchildren wrote the president, prompted, perhaps, by teachers or parents. The children were among the most affected by the refugee population, for they experienced the overcrowding and the clash between cultures and languages on a daily basis in their schools. They respectfully chastised the president and accused him of being out of touch with the realities of life in south Florida. One seventh grader wrote: "I know that when you signed that bill you had put tremendous amount of thought into it. But, sir, you don't live down here and you don't know what it's like."[95]

While not all the letters sent to the White House were negative, most of the positive ones came from addresses outside south Florida. Many Americans sent checks and money orders to contribute to refugee relief. Others wrote to offer Cubans employment or to volunteer as sponsors, and these letters were forwarded to the Cuban Refugee Center. Requests came for construction workers, custodians, foreign-language instructors, sales attendants, factory workers, and gardeners. One Texas rancher wrote the president to offer jobs to "Cuban cowboys," and several American housewives requested domestic servants.

Many emigrés also wrote the president, mostly to express their gratitude for the freedom flights. One in Wisconsin wrote: "[We] never will forget [the American] people and [their] president. Each Cuban refugee feels very deeply indebted to you from the bottom of his heart and that he has with the United States of America an eternal debt of gratitude."[96] Cubans expressed their appreciation in many different ways. Some continued to send checks to repay the government for the financial assistance they received a few years earlier. Others thanked the president—or "his excellency," as a few addressed him—with paintings, dinner invitations, and even offers to landscape the White House grounds. A few letters were heartrending. Children wrote the president asking to be reunited with their parents; mothers asked that their sons be discharged from the Cuban military or released from prison; families requested that sick or dying relatives in Cuba be given first priority on the freedom flights. Under the terms of the memorandum of understanding, however, the administration could do very little to accommodate these pleas.

During this second wave of Cuban immigration, the local, state, and federal governments tried to work out the kinks in the refugee relief program. In 1965, the Florida legislature narrowed the gap between state welfare benefits and CRP benefits. (The gap was still substantial, however: while the maximum grant to families with dependent children was raised to eighty-five dollars a month, one hundred dollars was awarded to Cuban families.) Dade County public schools established various bilingual education programs that were so successful in integrating the Cuban students that they were later used as models for bilingual education programs around the country. New vocational training programs for adults helped retrain Cubans for the U.S. labor market. A program entitled Aprenda y Supérese, or Training for Independence, targeted Cuban women who found themselves alone in Miami and on relief. The program became mandatory: those women who refused to participate were denied any benefits of the Cuban Refugee Program. The participants also had to agree to resettle in another part of the country if jobs in south Florida were unavailable. The women received intensive English-language instruction as well as training in any of a number of skills: hand sewing, machine sewing, office machine operation, clerical work, nursing, domestic service, and even silk-screen art work. Also available to the women who took part were an excellent day-care system and a monthly check for nine dollars to cover transportation costs to and from the vocational training center. Aprenda y Supérese was so successful that it became a model for the amended Aid to Families with Dependent Children (AFDC) program in 1968.[97]

In November 1966, in order to help Cubans change their legal status in the United States, Congress passed the Cuban Adjustment Act (P.L. 89-732). This law allowed Cubans who had lived in the United States for at least two years to apply for permanent residency, thus removing them from the "parole" ranks. Under the quirks of earlier immigration laws, Cubans who sought to become permanent residents or citizens had to first travel to a third country—usually one of the Caribbean countries or Canada—to secure an immigrant visa and then reenter the U.S., and many who wanted to apply for permanent residency were unable to do so because they could not afford the trip, or because they were not granted visas to enter a third country. Because of staff limitations, U.S. consular offices in these countries were unable to process all the applications they received, so only a small percentage of those who actually traveled to a third country for the purpose of adjusting their status were ultimately successful.[98] The Cuban Adjustment Act eliminated all this red tape. The government also waived the thirty-five-dollar fee required by the Immigration and Nationality Act.[99] By enacting this law the government hoped to help Cuban professionals meet state licensing requirements and to assist the Cuban elderly in receiving benefits (such as Medicare) that were available only to U.S. citizens. More importantly, even though the Johnson administration articulated its "strong desire" that Cuba should "be freed from Communist domination," the administration hoped to encourage emigrés to establish psychological ties to the United States rather than cling to the hope that they would soon return to their homeland.[100]

The federal government also helped Cubans reunite with family members stranded in other countries. To hasten their departure from Cuba, many Cubans had traveled to Mexico, Spain, Venezuela, or other countries, and many were later unable to secure immigrant visas to the U.S. In 1966 the departments of State and Justice announced that the parents, spouses, and minor children of Cubans already in the U.S. would be granted admission without having to fulfill all the normal requirements for an immigrant visa.[101]

In August 1971, the Castro government interrupted the regularly scheduled freedom flights, at first for a few days and then for weeks. Finally the flights were stopped altogether. In December 1972, Castro permitted a partial resumption of the flights to rid the country of thirty-four hundred more *gusanos,* mostly elderly and infirm, but the flights ended permanently on April 6, 1973.[102] By this date, 3,048 flights had carried 297,318 refugees to the United States.[103]

The second wave of Cuban refugees was distinct from the first in several ways. First, both the U.S. and Cuba were able to exert more control over this migration: the U.S. limited immigration to the immediate families of those Cubans already in the country, thereby upholding its new immigration laws, while the Cuban government protected its own interests by thoroughly screening the emigrant pool, prohibiting the emigration of those with skills vital to the regime. Secondly, the refugees differed socioeconomically from the earlier emigrés. During the first wave, 31 percent of the Cubans who arrived in the United States were professionals or managers; by 1970, only 12 percent of the second wave were professionals or managers, and 57 percent were blue-collar, service, or agricultural workers.[104] As men of working age were the most likely to be held back by the Cuban government, women were overrepresented in this migration, as were the elderly.

By the end of the freedom flights, the emigré population included a substantial percentage of Cuba's Chinese and Jewish populations. The 1953 Cuban census found more than sixteen thousand Chinese living in Cuba, most of them in Havana province.[105] Many of them operated small businesses such as fruit stands, restaurants, and laundries, businesses severely affected by the revolutionary government's urban reform laws. By 1973, more than half of Cuba's Chinese population had emigrated and settled in Miami, New York, and upstate New Jersey. Like the Chinese, most of the Cuban Jews were merchants. Approximately fifteen thousand Jews lived in Cuba in 1959, most of them Ashkenazim whose families had come during the 1920s and 1930s from central and eastern Europe, and the majority eventually emigrated to the United States, Israel, or Latin America.[106] By 1990, an estimated ten thousand

Cuban Jews lived in Dade County, comprising the majority of four Jewish congregations.[107]

Of Cuba's various racial and ethnic groups, blacks remained the most underrepresented among the emigrés. While the 1953 census revealed that 27 percent of Cuba's population was black or mulatto, less than 3 percent of the Cubans in the United States in 1970 were black.[108] Since racial equality was one of the goals of the revolution, black Cubans were generally optimistic about the future in their country. As the poorest segment of Cuban society, they also stood to gain the most, and generally became enthusiastic supporters of the Castro government. Further, blacks were leery of the United States, with its history of racial segregation; during the early 1960s, photographs and news stories coming out of the U.S. showed a society in violent confrontation over the civil rights movement. The Cuban government actively encouraged such fears; an exodus of blacks from Cuba would have been too powerful an indictment of the government. The Cuban media frequently gloated over the hardships encountered by the emigrés, claiming that they were marginalized in a racist society,[109] and members of the radical Black Panthers were invited to Cuba to speak on violence and discrimination in the United States. Finally, U.S. immigration policy gave preference to those with relatives already in the U.S., thus favoring whites, who were the first to leave.[110] It was not until the Mariel boatlift of 1980 that a significant number of black Cubans emigrated to the United States. (Even in the 1990 census, however, only 16 percent of the emigré population identified themselves as black, Chinese, or of another race.) The few blacks who did emigrate during the first two waves settled mostly in the Northeast to escape the heightened racial tension in the South.

By the end of the freedom flights, the Cuban exile community was fairly heterogeneous. Cubans of every social class and profession were represented, as were various ethnic and religious groups. While the emigrés came predominantly from Havana province, Cuba's most populated region, all six provinces were represented among the emigrés (the westernmost more so than the poorer eastern provinces). Perhaps most significant were the political differences among them: the various political parties and factions covered a wide ideological spectrum.

By 1974, the CRP had resettled 299,326 of the 461,373 Cubans who had registered with the program. They were placed all over the country (as well as in Puerto Rico and the Virgin Islands), but the largest percentages went to New York (27.1 percent), New Jersey (19.8), California (13.2), Puerto Rico (8.5), Illinois (7.5), and Louisiana (2.8).[111]

By this time the CRP had dispensed over $957 million in relief and services, and a gradual phase-out of the program began.[112] Churches and voluntary agencies spent millions more, for which they were never fully reimbursed. John F. Thomas, the CRP program director, justified these expenses in all CRP literature. The benefits gained from accommodating the Cuban refugees had far exceeded the costs, he wrote; with so many Cuban professionals and skilled laborers now working in communities around the country, the United States had profited from Cuba's brain drain.

However, many Americans had long since begun to call for an end to the freedom flights. Editorials in the *Miami Herald* argued that the number of people wanting to leave Cuba was infinite, and the U.S. simply could not accommodate them all. While the editors celebrated the rapid economic adjustment of the Cuban exiles—whom they called the "cream of a nation"—they voiced the widespread concern that Cuba's cream had already been skimmed, and that the continuing influx of lower-class Cubans presented an economic burden to the United States. They also protested the prolonging of the CRP, which continued to provide these immigrants with more benefits than needy Americans received. (Resentment over the inequity became the subject of a 1969 film entitled *Popi*, directed by Arthur Hiller and starring Alan Arkin as a Puerto Rican New Yorker who in order to ensure a better life for his children moves to Miami and registers them as Cuban refugees.)

The end of the freedom flights did not halt Cuban migration to the United States. Several thousand more Cubans came to the U.S. over the next few years, mostly via third countries. Clandestine emigration continued, as desperate Cubans risked their lives on the Florida Straits to get to the United States. By September 1977, the total number of Cubans to arrive in the United States (since January 1, 1959) reached 665,043.[113] For the time being, however, the Castro government's official policy of externalizing dissent ceased.

CHAPTER 2

The Mariel Boatlift of 1980

Origins and Consequences

In April 1980, as he had fifteen years earlier, Castro announced that all who desired to leave Cuba would be permitted to do so, this time from the port of Mariel. Thousands of emigrés sailed across the Florida Straits in yachts, sailboats, shrimpers, and even freighters to pick up their relatives and any others who wanted to leave. Between April and October 1980, 124,776 Cubans arrived in the U.S., comprising the third wave of Cuban migration.[1]

Mariel provides one of the most fascinating case studies in recent immigration history, not only for the circumstances of the migration but for the controversy it engendered. The government's inability to control the migration raised important questions about President Jimmy Carter's leadership (as well as about the adequacy of American immigration policy) and ultimately contributed to Carter's electoral defeat in 1980. Few immigrant groups elicited as much negative response as the *marielitos*. Public opinion turned against them when the press revealed that Castro had used the boatlift to rid the island of "undesirables" and that among the new immigrants were hundreds, if not thousands, of criminals. Even the exile community turned against this new wave, afraid that their golden reputations as model immigrants would be tarnished by the criminal element. Unlike the earlier refugees, the *marielitos* encountered hostility and discrimination wherever they settled. Neither their homeland nor their host society wanted them.

1978–1979: The Origins of Mariel

While Mariel caught immigration authorities by surprise, the migration was understandable in light of the events of the late 1970s. In September 1978, during a press conference with Cuban exile journalists, Fidel Castro invited emigrés to a dialogue in Cuba to discuss several issues of importance to the exile community, including the fate of political prisoners and a possible family reunification program. Castro announced that upon the successful completion of the *diálogo* the government was prepared to release up to three thousand political prisoners.[2]

The invitation to the *diálogo* was a radical departure from Cuban policy, and it stunned the emigré community. Particularly surprising was the conciliatory tone of Castro's invitation, since over the past two decades he had rarely missed an opportunity to attack the *gusanos*. Only three years earlier, he told foreign journalists that although a reconciliation with the United States was possible, emigrés would never be forgiven for deserting the homeland and would never be allowed to return.[3] But political and economic circumstances now forced the government to extend an olive branch to the exile community. During the press conference, he carefully referred to the emigrés as "the Cuban community abroad" rather than the usual *gusanos, escoria,* and *apátridas* (people without a country) and publicly stated that perhaps he had "misjudged" the community.[4]

Castro's move was politically astute. There had been a gradual thawing in the tensions between the United States and Cuba since the Ford administration, culminating in 1977 in the establishment of limited diplomatic representation in the form of "interests sections."[5] By 1978, however, a number of issues had brought negotiations for full diplomatic relations and the lifting of the trade embargo to an impasse, most notably U.S. opposition to Cuba's military presence in Angola. Through the *diálogo,* Castro hoped to keep the lines of communication open. By appealing to the exile community, he sought to influence the segment of American society most opposed to renewing diplomatic relations, and he used the two issues of most importance to emigrés to bargain for support for his political agenda. Castro also hoped to improve his image abroad. In the 1970s, his government had lost international support because of its worsening human rights record. His vow to release thousands of political prisoners was a humanitarian gesture that promised to pacify critics, particularly among the European intelligentsia.

In reality, the Carter administration was partly responsible for Castro's about-face. Throughout 1978, as part of Carter's human rights agenda, members of the administration met with Cubans in New York and Havana to discuss a number of issues, among them the release of political prisoners. A preliminary agreement for the release of thousands of prisoners was reached as early as August 1978, but when the Carter administration refused to publicly acknowledge its role in the negotiations, the Castro government decided to use the scheduled prisoner release program as a public relations campaign to improve relations with the exile community.[6]

Exiles were unaware of the negotiations between the United States and Cuba, and consequently Castro's invitation spurred intense debate. A segment of the exile community reacted enthusiastically to the new developments, even praising the regime for its conciliatory gesture. Hundreds of emigrés sent letters and telegrams expressing their willingness to participate in the *diálogo*. Others, suspicious, criticized the invitation, arguing that if Castro were sincere in his concern for political prisoners and family reunification, he had the power to act; he did not need the counsel of *gusanos*. Editorials in the Spanish-language media warned that the *diálogo* was not an attempt to make peace with emigrés but rather a ploy to manipulate the community to Castro's political advantage: Castro was using a controversial issue to pit emigré against emigré, ultimately undermining the community's lobbying power in Washington. The truth of this argument was suggested when an official at the Cuban Interests Section in Washington warned that without the *diálogo* there would be no release of political prisoners, and that "any hesitation on the part of emigrés would be perceived as a lack of concern or interest."[7] The fate of thousands of political prisoners was left up to the emigré community—or so they thought. For the emigrés, it was a moral dilemma with no easy or satisfactory resolution.

Within weeks, enough emigrés had responded to Castro's invitation to permit the first *diálogo*. A committee of exiles was formed, nicknamed the Comité de los 75, headed by Miami banker Bernardo Benes.[8] Most were scholars, journalists, and businessmen from the United States, Puerto Rico, Spain, Venezuela, and México, leaders in their communities, skillful at communication and shaping public opinion, approved by the Cuban government for this very reason. All of them could eloquently represent Cuban interests within the exile community and in

Washington. The Comité arrived in Havana for the first *diálogo* in November 1978. They returned to Havana a month later for a second series of talks, joined by sixty-five other emigrés.[9]

Nothing in the past twenty years had divided the community as the *diálogo* did. Lifelong friendships dissolved as Cuban exiles debated the ethical and moral implications of "collaborating" with the Castro government. Thirty exile organizations publicly denounced the *diálogo*, including the Bay of Pigs Veterans Association, which expelled all the members who participated, in spite of the fact that eight Brigadistas were still imprisoned in Cuba and were among those considered for release. Editorials in the Spanish-language media called the *dialogueros* traitors, cowards, opportunists, *vendepatrias* (sellouts), *tontos útiles* (useful stooges), and *mariposas* (butterflies—that is, transformed *gusanos*).[10] They charged that the *dialogueros* were communists, because several of them had ties to organizations that were allegedly pro-Castro, such as the Grupo Areíto and the Brigada Antonio Maceo.[11]

Critics of the *diálogo* could not believe that anyone in the exile community would want to negotiate with the government responsible for the execution and imprisonment of so many of their compatriots. As one editorial in an exile tabloid stated: "We cannot forget the executions. . . . We cannot forget the thousands of children who were orphaned . . . the wives, sisters, sons and daughters. . . . We have a debt of honor with our dead."[12] To remind the community of this debt, various exile newspapers published photographs of *fusilamientos* (executions) and family snapshots of the dead.

One of the most vocal critics of the *diálogo* was Juanita Castro, Fidel's younger sister and an exile in Miami, who spoke on the radio and made public appearances to condemn all who participated.[13] *La Crónica*, a Spanish-language tabloid in Puerto Rico with a wide circulation in Miami, published the names, addresses, and telephone numbers of all the *dialogueros* so that angry emigrés could personally express their rage.[14] One organization urged a "campaign of repudiation and moral sanction" against them.[15] Militant extremists, working on their own or through secret organizations, used terrorist tactics to harass the *dialogueros* and their supporters. They bombed Miami's Continental Bank because its president, Bernardo Benes, traveled to Cuba. Orlando Padrón, owner of Padrón Cigars, became the target of a boycott after the *Miami News* published a photograph of him offering Fidel Castro one of his cigars; by 1982 his cigar factory had been vandalized or firebombed four times.[16] Militants in New Jersey harassed and threatened Father

Andrés Reyes, even during his celebrations of mass, forcing the Catholic Diocese of Newark to transfer him to another parish.[17] In New York, militants bombed the lobby of *El Diario–La Prensa*, one of the most popular Spanish-language newspapers in the country, because reporter Manuel de Dios Unanue took part in the *diálogo*.[18] Two *dialogueros*, Eulalio José Negrín of New Jersey and Carlos Muñiz Varela of Puerto Rico, were assassinated.

Among the critics of the *diálogo* were some of the political prisoners themselves. Calling it a "farce," 138 prisoners clandestinely signed a petition rejecting the *diálogo*. The petition was smuggled to Spain and later to the United States, where it was circulated by Of Human Rights, a nonprofit organization at Georgetown University.[19] The 138 prisoners were all *plantados*, considered the moral elite of political prisoners for their refusal to participate in the government's rehabilitation programs or wear the uniforms of common criminals (thereby remaining naked in their cells). Most had spent from thirteen to twenty years in prison, and by signing the petition they forfeited their chances of being released. The release of political prisoners, they argued, must be unconditional.

Not all political prisoners viewed the *diálogo* in the same light, however. Interviews conducted by *Miami Herald* reporters at the Combinado del Este prison revealed that many of them favored any talks that might help end their tenure at this repressive installation, one of dozens located throughout the island.[20] A few prisoners even wrote letters to the exile community urging them to put their animosities aside and help secure the prisoners' release.

The rallies, petitions, and violence failed to alter the course of events. The Cuban government considered the first *diálogo* a success, and on November 21 Cuban officials announced that they would release 3,000 political prisoners over the next several months, at the rate of 400 per month.[21] By August 1979, 2,400 political prisoners had been released; of the 1,463 who expressed a desire to come to the United States, 813 were approved for entry, along with 1,200 of their dependents.[22] Most of those who chose to emigrate elsewhere settled in Venezuela, Mexico, and other Latin American countries. Among the prisoners released in 1979 was Huber Matos, the former *comandante* of the Cuban revolutionary army, imprisoned since 1959.[23] Also included were four Americans accused of working for the CIA, who were released after the Carter administration agreed to commute the life terms of Lolita Lebron and three other Puerto Rican nationalists sentenced for the 1954 seige of the U.S. House of Representatives.[24]

Whatever doubts or reservations emigrés might have had regarding the *diálogo,* they could not argue with the results. It is difficult to say whether Castro would have reneged on his agreement with the Carter administration without the *diálogo,* but in any case more political prisoners were released in one year than in the previous twenty, and many perceived this as the victory of diplomacy and reconciliation over policies of hostility and aggression. In fact, by July 1980, the number of political prisoners released totaled almost four thousand, surpassing the government's initial agreement.[25] Opponents of the *diálogo,* however, continued to view the negotiations as a moral defeat. They argued that it was international pressure and the high cost of prison maintenance that forced the Cuban government to release the political prisoners, and they chastised the emigrés for allowing themselves to be manipulated by the Cuban government and for prostituting their values and convictions: they had bargained with the devil and lost their souls.

Another, equally controversial consequence of the *diálogo* was the "opening" of Cuba to emigrés. For the first time, Cuban government officials granted emigrés permission to return to the island to visit their relatives and witness firsthand the accomplishments of the revolution. One of the great ironies of 1979, therefore, was that as thousands of political prisoners traveled to the United States, thousands of their refugee compatriots returned to the island as tourists. By year's end, more than one hundred thousand Cuban exiles in the United States alone had taken advantage of the Cuban government's relaxed travel policy. They did so with some trepidation, however. The Cuban government required that all emigrés enter the country with Cuban passports regardless of their present citizenship; the emigrés feared they would not be allowed to return and sought some legal protection. INS authorities reported that applications for permanent residency rose to twice the normal monthly rate during this period, mostly due to the growing number of Cuban exiles who wished to travel to Cuba but wanted some assurance that both Cuba and the United States would permit them to return to their homes in exile.

The exile community became as divided over the "emigré tourism" as over the *diálogo.* Critics argued that as refugees and *exiliados,* Cubans could not morally travel to the country they had fled. Their trips would help finance Castro's exportation of revolution by providing the Castro government with the currency it so desperately needed. Wrote one editor of an exile tabloid: "It is sad to see Cubans today, supposedly exiles, giving money to the regime that humiliated them years ago and is now humiliating them by forcing them to return to their homeland as tourists."[26] Some exile newspapers tried to instill fear in those considering travel to Cuba by warning them that any benefits they received in the U.S., like Medicare and food stamps, might be canceled, and that they might not be allowed to reenter the U.S.[27] And the possibility of being harassed or even assassinated by militant extremists always lurked in the back of most emigrés' minds.

The chance to return to Cuba and see one's family after so many years was hard to refuse, however. If Castro had eased the travel restrictions a decade earlier, perhaps not as many emigrés would have responded. During the first years of exile, most emigrés swore that they would never return to Cuba as long as the Castro regime remained in power, and they were passionate enough about their politics to remain faithful to that oath. But by 1979 the many years of separation from family and homeland had tempered these views. The majority of those who chose to travel to Cuba had parents (some quite elderly), siblings, or children living on the island whom they had not seen in as long as fifteen or twenty years. When the Cuban government eased travel restrictions, these emigrés jumped at the opportunity. Many returned with their American-born children, so that they too could meet relatives they knew only from pictures and see the country whose nationality they claimed. After years of loneliness and separation, family now took precedence over political ideologies.

Undoubtedly, the Castro regime profited from its new travel policy, as it did from many of its humanitarian gestures. Cuba was burdened by a stagnant economy, an inefficient bureaucracy, and an unmotivated workforce; emigré tourism generated much-needed income. In preparation for the tourists, the government refurbished Havana's once-famous hotels and nightclubs. Package deals were prepared that included airfare, hotel accommodations, and meals, for which emigrés paid from a few hundred to a few thousand dollars. These tourist packages were immensely lucrative, since most emigrés stayed with their relatives and rarely used the services the government charged them for. The average emigré tourist also spent hundreds of dollars in Cuban stores buying gifts or needed goods for his loved ones. The economy further benefited from the many consumer goods emigrés brought from the United States, most of which were in short supply on the island: medicine, shoes and clothing, books and records, and even televisions, stereos, and other small appliances. So great was the quantity of emigré "luggage" that the Cuban government eventually imposed a limit of forty pounds per person. According to the *Miami Herald,* by April 1979 the Cuban government had already siphoned an estimated $150 million from the exile community.[28]

While emigré tourism helped to resolve some of the government's immediate economic concerns, it did not provide a long-term solution to Cuba's many problems, of course. The government ultimately paid a high price for its open-door policy, since the visitors undermined revolutionary fervor and fueled popular discontent. Some Cubans became confused and even resentful about the change in government policy. After twenty years of official rhetoric condemning the *gusanos* for betraying the revolution, the government suddenly welcomed them, giving them access to restaurants, stores, and hotels that few in Cuba were able to enjoy. As thousands of emigrés arrived each month, Cubans had ample opportunity to compare their lives with those of the visitors returning to the island with fashionable clothes and suitcases filled with the latest American gadgets, bestowing gifts on their poorer relations. The emigrés, foreigners in a "decadent capitalist society," seemed to have more opportunities available to them than Cubans did in their revolutionary socialist state.

The new ideas and perspectives that the emigré tourists brought with them had a profound effect on the island particularly among those born and raised in communist Cuba, whose contact with other countries was chiefly limited to the Soviet bloc. Cubans became aware of views of history, politics, and international relations that challenged the standard interpretations they had been taught. They also caught up with the latest developments in American popular culture through the records, books, and magazines the emigrés brought with them. These new perspectives, whether ideological or cultural, aroused curiosity and interest, and challenged the Cubans' most basic beliefs about their society as well as about life in the United States. As one Cuban, then fifteen years old, explained:

> Personally, we had no family in the United States, but our neighbors did. I remember when their cousins came to visit. . . . I think they hadn't seen each other in twelve years. I went over one evening out of curiosity, you see. They impressed me as very nice people. They weren't at all what I expected. You know how children's imaginations are. . . . But they were people just like us. They were funny and had some great stories about life in the U.S. and all the problems they had had to deal with. But, obviously, from the way they were dressed and the things they brought with them, things were going quite well for them. I remembered thinking that I wanted to visit the U.S. and see it for myself. So when my parents decided to leave Cuba [in 1980], I thought it was going to be a great adventure. . . . Boy, and what an adventure it turned out to be![29]

For those already discontented with Castro's communism, contact with the emigrés only exacerbated their resentment; for others, it provoked a serious reevaluation of their society, their evil, imperialist neighbor to the north, and the anti-American propaganda promoted in the media, schools, and workplace. Disaffection grew in many quarters of society. Political repression, underemployment, and chronic shortages of basic consumer goods frustrated even the most enthusiastic of supporters. Some found subtle but powerful ways of defying the government and expressing their discontent. Having few incentives at work, they performed their jobs inadequately and ignored production quotas. The black market flourished, despite Cuba's strict laws, with the import of new consumer goods from the U.S. Young Cubans, many of whom did not share their elders' admiration for Castro, found ways of expressing their discontent through "decadent," "bourgeois," "extravagant" behavior like taking drugs, reading or writing "subversive" literature, and wearing American designer jeans or hippie clothing. Many grew their hair and beards long; like the *barbudos* of the July 26th Movement, these young men and women used their physical appearance to express their open defiance of society's conventions. Twenty years after the revolution, such behavior was interpreted as counterrevolutionary.

What began, then, as an economic campaign to alleviate Cuba's sagging economy resulted in what some emigrés jokingly called the blue-jean revolution.[30] The Cuban government failed to provide many of its citizens with the necessary incentives to revitalize their former revolutionary zeal. Consequently, when the opportunity to leave Cuba presented itself in 1980, thousands of Cubans took it, and by then the government was more than willing to facilitate their departure. Popular discontent threatened the stability of the regime, and emigration once again provided a safety valve for Cuban society. The emigration of 1980, however, proved to be an embarrassing indictment of the Castro regime, a catastrophe from which the government never fully recovered. It also had long-term repercussions for the United States.

The Peruvian Embassy Crisis and the Mariel Boatlift

In May 1979, a few Cuban nationals began smuggling themselves into Latin American embassies to request political asylum. The Venezuelan and Peruvian embassies were the most popular choices.

By March 1980, close to thirty Cubans had crashed their vehicles through the entrances of these embassies and taken refuge in the compounds, sparking angry exchanges between the government of Cuba and those of Venezuela and Peru. On January 5, the Venezuelan government recalled its ambassador to protest "the heavy-handed measures used by the Cubans in dealing with forcible entries at its Embassy."[31] At the Peruvian embassy, the ambassador agreed to turn over twelve Cuban nationals—including children—who entered the compound illegally on January 21. The Peruvian government subsequently recalled him, and the twelve Cubans were returned to the embassy.

On March 28, six Cubans stole a bus and crashed through the Peruvian embassy gates. The Cuban guards stationed at the three entrances to the compound shot at the bus, even though the gate-crashers were unarmed; one of the guards was caught in the crossfire and killed.[32] The new ambassador refused to turn these gate-crashers over for criminal prosecution. On April 4, Good Friday, Castro pulled all Cuban guards from around the embassy compound and sent in steamrollers to tear down the embassy gates and barricades. In a radio broadcast later that afternoon, Castro stated that his government would no longer risk the lives of its soldiers to protect "criminals."[33]

As news of the event spread through the city of Havana, people left their homes and jobs and drove to the embassy to observe. Many left their cars by the side of the road and quietly walked into the embassy compound. One bus driver, in the middle of his daily route, simply got off the bus, told his passengers to wait for the next bus, and entered the compound. Within forty-eight hours, approximately 10,800 men, women, and children had taken refuge inside the Peruvian embassy.[34] These people were a cross section of Cuban society in age and occupation: students, housewives, factory and construction workers, writers, and even government bureaucrats. On Easter Sunday, when the compound was filled to capacity, Cuban police put up barricades all around the perimeter of the embassy—and for several blocks beyond—and prohibited anyone else from entering.

For days the fate of the refugees was uncertain. Rumors circulated that the police were going to arrest or shoot them, prompting some to change their minds and leave the compound; others simply could not tolerate the cramped conditions. The refugees at the embassy sent messages to the Vatican and to President Carter and other heads of state, requesting assistance in leaving Cuba. While they waited for international aid, conditions within the camp steadily worsened.[35] The Cubans were so densely packed inside the lot that many had to sit on tree branches, iron gratings, and the roof of the embassy building. Sleep was virtually impossible. Two babies were born in the compound (one of them was later named "Peru"). For almost a week, the refugees endured the rain and the hot tropical sun. With little food or water, they had to improvise: some ate the leaves of plants and shrubs, while others roasted cats and birds over small wood fires. Even the ambassador's pet parrot became one family's meal. Cuban officials eventually sent in cartons of food, but never enough to feed everyone, and fights broke out among the tired, frightened, and hungry "inmates." Portable toilets were eventually provided, but not before the lot became covered with mud, urine, and excrement. To impose some semblance of order, the refugees created their own governing body and elected twenty-one men and women to distribute food and bolster morale. The committee also helped break up fights, some of which were reportedly caused by the *provocadores* the government sent in.

Thousands of onlookers gathered around the compound each day. Some hoped to be allowed into the compound; others were there as an act of support for the government. *Granma,* the official state newspaper, called the refugees "delinquents, social deviants, vagrants, and parasites" and blamed them for all the ills that plagued Cuban society.[36] One article declared that crime had dropped 55 percent since the *gusanos* had entered the embassy. The government refused to perceive the situation at the embassy as either an act of defiance or an indictment of the revolution; rather, it was a temporary crisis that would ultimately strengthen Cuba's national character. With the nineteenth anniversary of the Bay of Pigs invasion a few days away, the government compared the Peruvian embassy crisis to the 1961 crisis, predicting that Cuba would triumph against this "army of delinquents" as it had against the forces of Yankee imperialism nineteen years earlier.[37] Pedro Ortíz Cabrera, the guard killed in the initial entry, became the martyr and symbol of this new moral campaign, and the state used his death to rally public support. Editorials in the Cuban press fueled the passions of loyal citizens. The Peruvian embassy became a symbol of everything that was wrong with the country, and many Cubans vented their anger against those who took refuge there. People taunted and insulted the refugees and threw stones and rotted food at them. The Cuban police participated in the harassment, beating those on the outer periphery of the compound, unleashing their dogs on them, and blinding the refugees with reflector lights at night.

Candelaria García, who lived a few blocks from the embassy and whose husband was one of the 10,800, remembered how tense those days were:

> People kept arriving with children and with bags full of food, and they would settle themselves on people's front porches hoping that the embassy would open once again. People came from the interior [of the island] on trucks. Many people were shouting "Down with Fidel," and I said, "Oh God, there's going to be a revolution." That's when the people from the *Comités* [Committees for the Defense of the Revolution] came out with clubs. I put a barricade on my door . . . because my husband was one of the people at the embassy and I thought that someone might break down the door, or whatever . . . because that's what they were doing to those who were against Fidel. With my husband at the embassy what were they going to think of me? One of the members of the *Comité* told me, "I saw you walk to the embassy with your husband," and I said, "Yes, but I didn't go in." The things that went on in Cuba were horrible. You tell the stories but they're hard to believe.[38]

As news of the horrible conditions in the compound reached Miami, Cuban exiles rallied in support of the refugees. They sent telegrams to the White House urging the Carter administration to intervene, and they organized food and clothing drives through their churches and civic organizations. In just one day, Spanish-language radio station WQBA in Miami raised over one hundred thousand dollars for the refugees' emergency care. Most of their supplies never reached the embassy, however; the Cuban government reportedly blocked all international relief efforts.[39]

The emigration plan that was eventually negotiated by the governments of Peru and Cuba required the assistance of several countries. Peru was unable to offer asylum to more than one thousand of the refugees, and so it appealed for help to the United Nations, the Organization of American States, and the member nations of the Andean Pact. The Carter administration authorized the acceptance of thirty-five hundred refugees,[40] and Costa Rica, Spain, Ecuador, Argentina, Canada, France, and West Germany pledged to accept a total of twenty-five hundred.[41] While four thousand refugees remained unaccounted for, Costa Rica agreed to accept them on a temporary basis with assurances from Peru and the United States that they would find homes for them. The U.S. eventually took in a total of sixty-two hundred of the embassy refugees.

The airlift negotiated by Peru provided Cuba with an acceptable solution to the crisis: the island was rid of eleven thousand dissidents at little or no expense to the Cuban government. Castro granted the refugees *salvoconductas,* or safe passage, so they could leave the embassy and wait for their exit permits at home. Most of the refugees accepted the offer and returned home to bathe and eat, and to say goodbye to their relatives and friends, though several hundred chose to remain at the compound, fearful that Cuban authorities would not honor their pledge and would arrest them once they left Peruvian jurisdiction. Their fears proved reasonable: a number of people who left the embassy were later denied exit permits and found themselves without homes or jobs.[42] The six original gate-crashers were among those denied exit permits.[43]

The airlift began on April 16. Under the terms of the negotiations, the refugees flew first to Costa Rica before continuing on to their final destination. Journalists from around the world converged at the Juan Santamaría Airport in San José to document the refugees' arrival. They filmed the refugees defiantly shouting "Freedom!" and "Down with Castro!" as they left their planes, or kissing the airport tarmac, or tearfully embracing. These simple yet powerful images ultimately did more harm to Castro's regime than any counterrevolutionary plot. After years of promoting an image abroad as the model socialist state, Cuba now appeared as a society in crisis. The government claimed that these were the bums and delinquents of Cuban society, but the journalists' interviews with the refugees suggested otherwise: these were ordinary citizens who said they preferred the isolation of exile to the repression in Cuba.

Castro abruptly suspended the flights to Costa Rica four days after they began, claiming that the United States and Peru were using the Costa Rican connection for "publicity and demagogic purposes." Henceforth, he announced, Cubans could only travel on flights that took them directly to their final destination. To counteract the negative publicity, the government staged a massive rally and parade to commemorate the nineteenth anniversary of the victory at the Bay of Pigs and granted visas to hundreds of foreign journalists to cover the events. Close to a million loyal citizens, including Ché Guevara's father, turned out to demonstrate their support. They marched in front of the Peruvian embassy for thirteen hours, chanting "¡Que se vayan!" (Let them go) and "¡Abajo con la gusanera!" (Down with the worms).[44] Cuban newspapers and magazines printed special issues to commemorate both the anniversary and the march, and *Granma* published letters of support from Cuba's allies in the Eastern bloc.

The rallies and marches continued over the next several weeks. One million people marched to the Plaza de la Revolución during the annual

May Day celebration. In a speech denouncing those who chose to emigrate, Castro reiterated his government's position: "We say to those who do not have the genes of revolutionaries, or the blood of revolutionaries, or who do not have the necessary discipline and heroism for a revolution: we don't want you, we don't need you."[45] Several heads of state, including Daniel Ortega of Nicaragua and Maurice Bishop of Grenada, attended the rally. Nobel prizewinning author Gabriel García Marquez of Colombia, among others, expressed support through letters and telegrams.[46] One month later, in yet another symbolic effort to strengthen national resolve, the Cuban government turned the Peruvian embassy compound into a historical museum—El Museo del Pueblo Combatiente (Museum of the People in Combat)—to honor their countrymen's courage during this crisis.[47] Exhibited in the new museum were the blood-stained clothes of Ortíz Cabrera and enlarged photographs of some of the embassy refugees' alleged criminal records.[48]

After the Costa Rican fiasco, the Cuban government focused all its hostility on the United States. The refugees were now portrayed as pawns in a Yankee imperialist plot. In mid-April, when U.S. armed forces staged military and naval exercises at Guantánamo Base, the government launched a vehement anti-American propaganda campaign.[49] At rallies and demonstrations, angry citizens burned American flags and hung Uncle Sam in effigy. They rallied outside the U.S. Interests Section and accosted any Cuban seen entering or leaving the offices. One especially brutal incident occurred on May 4, as state police attacked more than seven hundred Cubans lined up in front of the U.S. Interests Section to request visas. Dozens were injured, and up to four hundred took refuge inside the Interests Section, where they hid for days. *Granma* accused the Interests Section of provoking the incident;[50] in response, the Interests Section closed its visa offices, and they remained closed for the next five months. Anti-American sentiment became so intense on the island that Washington temporarily recalled seventeen diplomats and their families from Havana.[51]

At the time of the airlift's suspension, some seventy-five hundred Cubans had emigrated.[52] Three days later, Castro substituted a new plan to rid the island not only of the remaining asylum-seekers but of thousands of other dissidents as well—a plan partially inspired by emigrés in Miami. Back on April 19, several adventurous emigrés had taken advantage of the confusion and sailed to Cuba, where they successfully negotiated the release of their families (and forty-nine from the Peruvian embassy).[53] Realizing that other emigrés would follow, as they had in

1965, the Cuban government decided that a flotilla could be used in its best interests. On April 20, the government announced that all Cubans who wished to leave the island would be permitted to do so and urged them to call their relatives in the United States to come pick them up. The port of Mariel, some twenty miles west of Havana, would be the new emigration center. Camps were quickly set up around the port to process the thousands of Cubans expected to leave.

Most emigrés in Miami did not wait for their relatives to call. When news broke out that Castro had opened the port of Mariel, they rushed to the nearest marina to rent any available boat. By the end of the week, an estimated five hundred boats had sailed into the port, and hundreds of others followed over the next few weeks.[54] Some came from as far away as New York and New Jersey. To minimize their risks in the short but dangerous trip across the Florida Straits, emigrés teamed up and traveled in squadrons of up to fifty boats. Those who did not know how to sail found a large pool of sailors and fishermen in Key West willing to transport any number of Cubans for the right fee. Many of the emigrés who sailed to Mariel didn't even have friends or relatives in Cuba; they risked their lives and spent their life savings on the voyage because they considered it their moral obligation to assist anyone who wanted to leave the island. By May 4, more than one thousand boats had returned from Mariel with over thirteen thousand refugees. Thousands more arrived every day for the next few months.[55]

The U.S. Coast Guard, the INS, and other federal authorities tried to discourage the flotilla, warning the exile community that those who sailed to Cuba violated U.S. immigration laws and faced possible fines. As in Camarioca fifteen years before, however, these warnings did not deter the emigrés. Most were willing to pay any price to get their families out of Cuba. The government's warnings drew criticism from the exile community and even from some federal officials. "I want to see the guy who arrests some Cuban for picking up his parents," said one U.S. Customs agent. "Sometimes people forget this is America."[56] The Cuban government also criticized this policy and accused the U.S. government of hypocritically welcoming illegal immigration when it suited propaganda purposes and now turning away legitimate immigrants.

Emigrés were aware that there were risks in sailing to Cuba, but nothing prepared them for what they encountered at Mariel, or the "Bay of Fools," as the port was nicknamed. As each boat reached the port, the "captain" presented Cuban officials with a list of relatives he or she wished to take back to the United States. The boats then had to wait several days before receiving any response, and the port became so jammed with boats that newcomers had to dock out at sea. One participant in the flotilla commented that if all the boats had been lined up one behind the other, their relatives could have walked back to Key West. At night, Cuban gunboats patrolled the waters and police patrolled the coast, both to prevent any subversive activity and to prevent any Cubans from swimming out to the boats. As the emigrés waited, they ran out of fuel, food, and water, and had to buy them from the government—at up to ten dollars for a ham sandwich, fifteen dollars for a gallon of gasoline. Those emigrés who could afford to do so stayed at the Tritón Hotel in Havana, which was set aside for them by the Cuban government.

When their relatives finally arrived at the port, the emigrés were informed that they also had to transport anyone else the Cuban government told them to take. Those who refused to cooperate were prohibited from leaving. In many cases, Cuban officials forced emigrés to return to Key West with a boatload of strangers and no relatives at all. The returning boats were so overloaded with passengers that many of them broke down at sea and had to be rescued by the U.S. Coast Guard. Recalled one emigré:

> One of the most incredible cases involved a boat that was so overcrowded. . . . They ran into bad weather and a wave toppled them. Fourteen people died, I think, but many more have not been found [and are presumed dead]. Among the dead was an entire family—mother, father, two daughters, and a grandmother—who drowned. The only member of the family saved was a fourteen year old girl. . . . [The stories of Mariel] are all very sad stories that the world, I think, does not want to believe.[57]

By the end of May, the Coast Guard had conducted 989 search and rescue operations and rescued thousands of stranded passengers.[58] They had also recorded twenty-five fatalities.

Poet and novelist Reinaldo Arenas was one of the thousands who emigrated via the port of Mariel. In his collection of essays, *Necesidad de libertad,* he recounted the details of his migration, a process he compared to "livestock on stampede."[59] Arenas's experience was typical: he left the port of Mariel on a small boat called the *San Lázaro* whose captain, a Cuban emigré from Miami, risked financial ruin to sail to Cuba to pick up his relatives. Cuban officials forced him to crowd thirty strangers onto his boat, among them a psychotic patient from a state institution who was being forced to emigrate. When the *San Lázaro* was several miles out to sea it broke down from the weight, and the current took the boat further out into the Atlantic. They drifted aimlessly for three days, without food or water, until finally being rescued by the U.S. Coast Guard and taken to Key West. They arrived ill, sunburned, weak from thirst and hunger, but relieved to be in the United States. "There were thousands of us wanting to come to [Key West] and kiss the earth," said Arenas. "That day we became human beings."[60]

As in the previous Cuban migrations, a large and complex bureaucracy evolved to register and assist the new immigrants. The first arrivals were processed in Key West, but as their numbers increased two other processing centers were established in south Florida: one at Miami's Tamiami Park and another in the Opa-Locka barracks. There they were photographed, fingerprinted, and given medical tests. Volunteers helped the refugees fill out extensive questionnaires asking them about their families, employment history, political sympathies, and the types of groups and activities they had participated in back in Cuba. One volunteer at Opa-Locka recalled her experiences:

> Working at Opa-Locka was very tiring because it was a very large place, very noisy, and very hot. . . . We found that the people we interviewed were simple, modest, humble, understanding. They were all very tired. They had spent a terrible time at the camp they call "El Mosquito" [a holding camp outside Mariel] and they were eager to settle down and begin a new life. It was amazing how many children came and how many older people came. But it was also amazing to see so many young men alone . . . fourteen, sixteen, thirty years of age.[61]

Voluntary relief agencies provided the refugees with medical care, food, clothing, and toiletries. While they waited to be processed, released to relatives, or resettled, they were housed in churches, gymnasiums, recreation centers, hotels, National Guard armories, and even the Orange Bowl stadium, which the government leased until football season started. Two processing centers, Krome North and Krome South, were opened to house and process the Cubans, along with the growing number of Haitians who were also arriving in south Florida during this period. For a short time, Cubans were even housed in dog kennels that had been converted into emergency lodgings.[62] Officials worked around the clock to register the Cubans and release them to their families as quickly as possible. Those who had no families or friends in the United States were detained for longer periods of time;

without a sponsor (an individual or institution such as a church willing to assume responsibility for their care and supervision), the government could not release them into society. The government eventually had to build "tent cities" in parks and underneath expressways to house those with little chance of immediate sponsorship. The largest tent city was built underneath Interstate 95 on the eastern perimeter of Miami's Little Havana.

By May 6, the Carter administration had declared a state of emergency in Florida and released $10 million from the Emergency Refugee and Migration Assistance Fund to establish a processing camp at Eglin Air Force Base, Florida. Meanwhile, four hundred marines were sent to Key West to maintain order and assist the incoming refugees. The Federal Emergency Management Agency (FEMA), best known for managing crises caused by natural disasters, assumed responsibility for coordinating the work of the VOLAGs.[63] The federal government opened up three additional camps to house and register Cubans: Fort Chaffee, Arkansas (opened May 8), Fort Indiantown Gap, Pennsylvania (May 17), and Fort McCoy, Wisconsin (May 29). Almost half of the Mariel immigrants, 62,541 Cubans, waited for sponsorship in these camps. Some stayed a few days, others remained for over a year.[64]

People who interviewed and registered the Cubans heard astonishing tales of human rights abuses. The Cuban government encouraged *actos de repudio* (acts of repudiation) against those who applied to leave the country via Mariel, and gangs of thugs accosted them on the street and at work or school, or pelted their homes with rocks, bottles, and spoiled food during nightly rampages.[65] A volunteer at Opa-Locka recalls that one man arrived with both his arms broken, and many others had bruises, welts, and severe wounds.[66] Most Cubans had had to wait for days before Cuban officials transported them to the port, and in the meantime they lost their jobs and ration coupons, and in some cases their homes. At El Mosquito and other holding camps near Mariel they endured more insults. Few were given any food. Before they could leave the country, they had to sign documents confessing that they were social deviants and had committed crimes against the state. With one signature, decent, hard-working citizens established fictional records as burglars, arsonists, murderers, rapists, and CIA agents. At the pier, officials forced them to board any available boat, but not before taking away all their personal belongings: money, suitcases, jewelry, wedding rings, and even address books with the names and phone numbers of relatives living in exile. By the time they arrived at Key West, the refugees were sunburned, frightened, weak from illness or malnutrition, and without any personal belongings or documentation.

Many Cubans, knowing that the government expedited the exit papers of criminals, went to police stations to register as prostitutes and delinquents. Others were forced to leave whether they wanted to or not. "I had a neighbor whose husband was expelled via Mariel," said one Cuban, "and she never found out until he contacted her from the United States." She added:

> If you were willing to leave your house, all furnished, to the government, then sometimes they let you leave. I have some friends who had a very beautiful house. They told her that she had to leave. When she said that she couldn't, because her husband was in prison [as a counterrevolutionary], they told her that they were transporting her husband directly from prison to Mariel. They lied! She later had to purchase his freedom through Panama. They told her that so she would leave her house.[67]

A number of the refugees had either physical or mental disabilities. An estimated fifteen hundred had mental health problems or were mentally retarded; five hundred of these were judged to need long-term institutionalization, while another five hundred were eventually placed in halfway houses.[68] Exact numbers were hard to determine, since spouses and children often hid or covered for their mentally ill relatives for fear that they would all be sent back to Cuba.[69] An estimated sixteen hundred had chronic medical problems such as drug and alcohol abuse, tuberculosis, or cardiovascular disease. Four had Hansen's disease (leprosy). To meet the health care needs of the camp residents, each camp maintained hospital wards, including psychiatric care units.

Most distressing to U.S. officials, however, was the discovery that thousands of the Mariel emigrants—twenty-six thousand by the end of the boatlift—had criminal records. (One of the Cubans who arrived at Key West had been responsible for hijacking a U.S. airline *to* Cuba a few years earlier.) Estimates varied, but of these twenty-six thousand approximately two thousand had committed serious felonies in Cuba. Most of these were sent to the Federal Correctional Institution at Talladega, Alabama, for further screening and possible exclusion.[70] The majority of the offenders, however, had served time for lesser crimes. Under Cuba's *ley de peligrosidad* (law of dangerousness), Cubans could be incarcerated for such offenses as alcoholism, gambling, drug addiction, homosexuality, prostitution, "extravagant behavior," vagrancy, and dealing on the black market. Many of the "criminals" fell under this category; they had served terms ranging from a few months to a few years at a work farm. Others had served time for political crimes—longer terms, usually, some up to two decades in a maximum security prison. Still others had been jailed for refusing to conform to revolutionary norms: these included members of religious groups such as the Jehovah's Witnesses and the Seventh Day Adventists which discouraged military participation, as well as draft dodgers and conscientious objectors to the war in Africa.

Unfortunately, the American press focused an exaggerated amount of attention on those with mental disabilities and on the hardcore felons. While the latter constituted less than 4 percent of the total number of entrants, they commanded almost all of the media attention. Few journalists ever mentioned the fact that up to 80 percent of the Mariel Cubans had no criminal history, nor did they mention that many of those who had served time in prison did so for crimes not recognized in the United States. Instead, they focused on the disturbing details of Castro's plan to rid the island of undesirables. Newspapers printed story after story of how the Cuban government rounded up the criminals and "social deviants," transported them to Mariel, and forced them to board the boats. Most of the stories were highly sensationalistic and based on rumor rather than fact. The *Washington Post*, for example, including homosexuals in its list of "deviants," reported that up to twenty thousand of the Cubans were homosexuals (the actual number was closer to one thousand).[71] Such sensationalism gave Americans a warped view of the new immigrants, and the Cubans of Mariel ultimately suffered for it.

The shift in public perception of the Cubans came abruptly. Most Americans initially sympathized with the plight of the Cubans: stories of the refugees' courage at the Peruvian embassy provided the only heartening news in a year of gloomy headlines, and Americans applauded their defiance of the Castro regime. Around the country, editorials in the *Wall Street Journal*, the *Washington Post*, and other major newspapers urged the federal government to extend humanitarian assistance to the refugees and to grant them political asylum. The Carter administration shared this perspective. In a speech before the League of Women Voters in Philadelphia on May 3, President Carter reiterated his strong support for human rights in Latin America and declared that the United States would provide "an open heart and open arms" to the people fleeing from Cuba.[72]

This spirit of generosity waned as the boatlift dragged on for weeks. Over eighty thousand Cubans entered the United States in just one month—more than had come in any previous *year* of Cuban immigration.[73] Enthusiasm quickly faded as Americans comprehended the burden these refugees would place on state and federal resources, especially during the economic recession. Letters once again swamped the White House urging Carter to do something. While Americans applauded the Cubans' struggle for political freedom, they did not necessarily want the Cubans to exercise that freedom in the United States. The discovery of the criminal element, however, proved to be the principal factor in turning public opinion against the boatlift. Americans perceived the boatlift as an act of aggression against the United States. They resented being used as the dumping ground for Cuba's social deviants and called on their legislators to expel the criminals and end the boatlift once and for all.[74]

In south Florida, local residents had already witnessed the arrival of more than half a million Cuban refugees during the past twenty years, and they were unhappy with the prospect of thousands more. News of the criminal element only fueled the fear and anger in the community. A *Miami Herald* poll revealed that 68 percent of non-Hispanic whites and 57 percent of blacks in Dade County regarded the Mariel boatlift as detrimental to their community and to the United States.[75] The feelings of discontent became evident during the first week of May, when riots broke out in a predominantly black neighborhood in Miami known as Liberty City. Although the riots erupted as a result of the acquittal of the four white police officers responsible for the fatal beating of a local black businessman, the Mariel boatlift only heightened the racial tension. For many blacks, the boatlift proved yet again that their needs and concerns were secondary to those of foreign-born immigrants.

Oddly enough, though, some of the more extreme reactions came from parts of the country that had little or no contact with Cuban immigration. Colorado Governor Richard Lamm publicly announced that he did not want any Cubans resettled to his state, and Senator Donald Stewart of Alabama didn't even want Cuban detainees sent to the federal correctional institution at Talladega.[76] Families and church groups around the country canceled their offers of sponsorship, and some communities signed petitions to have resettlement camps banned from their city. Capitalizing on the hysteria, the Ku Klux Klan staged marches and demonstrations across the nation—most noticeably in Ft. Walton Beach, Florida, home to one of the temporary camps.

Americans accused the Carter administration of dealing ineptly with the crisis. How could a small nation like Cuba take such obvious advantage of the United States? And why did the federal government allow the emigrés in south Florida to dictate immigration policy? The issue of his leadership haunted the president later that electoral year. In all likelihood, the administration failed to deal decisively with the crisis during the first days of the boatlift simply because it did not know what to do. As one White House statement reported, "Our laws never contemplated and [did] not provide adequately for people coming to our shores in the manner that the Cubans . . . have."[77] Never before had a neighboring country imposed such a large-scale migration on the United States, and never before had thousands of Americans rushed out to help. In the first week of the boatlift, no attempt was made to block the boats going to Cuba; the administration did not want to cut off the Cubans' only opportunity for emigration. But as the boatlift entered its second week and the number of arrivals reached the tens of thousands, the government was forced to consider other options.

A tripartite group consisting of the United States, Costa Rica, and Great Britain tried to negotiate a more orderly migration.[78] The Carter administration proposed a new series of airlifts or sealifts similar to the freedom flights of the late 1960s lasting approximately twelve months. In order to weed out undesirables, Carter proposed that the Cubans be screened in Cuba, with preference given to political prisoners and close relatives of U.S. citizens, in line with current U.S. immigration policy. Beginning on May 15, the federal government established registration offices in Miami, where Cuban emigrés who were citizens or permanent residents could register the names of family members they wished to bring out of Cuba. Within the first twenty-four hours, close to ten thousand emigrés arrived at the various offices to register relatives.[79] The government chartered two large ships and stationed them in Key West, waiting for the Cuban government to give the go-ahead. On May 23, the Cuban government officially rejected the proposal, calling it "an international attempt to meddle in Cuba's internal affairs."[80]

Over the next several weeks, the U.S. continued to pressure the Cuban government, and in the meantime Carter called upon the Cuban emigré community to end the boatlift. The U.S. Coast Guard increased its patrol teams off the Florida coast and warned all captains of outgoing vessels that those caught transporting Cubans illegally would be prosecuted to the fullest extent of the law: their boats would be seized and they would be fined up to one thousand dollars for each Cuban brought to the United States without a proper visa. Warnings were also sent by radio to the ships already in Cuban waters, and although the Cuban government attempted to jam the marine frequency the messages got through on commercial radio stations, and some ships returned before the Cuban authorities could hold them and load them with passengers. While the warnings deterred some emigrés, others paid no heed. Many were willing to pay any price to get their families out of Cuba. They left spouses or children behind at Key West with cash in hand, ready to pay their fines once they safely returned home. Over the next few months, the U.S. Customs Service seized over one thousand boats, and the INS issued more than fifteen hundred notices of intent to issue fines.[81] One of the largest ships confiscated was the *Ruby Diamond*, a freighter of Panamanian registry chartered by Cuban Americans, which brought 731 Cubans to Key West. By the end of the summer, the stricter policy had reduced the flow from thirteen thousand a week to less than seven hundred.[82] The Cuban government finally closed the port of Mariel to further emigration on September 25 and the last boat arrived in Key West four days later, by which time more than 124,000 Cubans had made it to the United States.

Profile of the New Immigrants

The Cubans of Mariel were substantially different from those who arrived during the 1960s. They were about ten years younger, averaging thirty years of age. There were more blacks and mulattoes among them (from 15 to 40 percent, compared to 3 percent of the 1959–73 migration), and they reflected a wider geographic distribution.[83] This migration was also almost 70 percent male;[84] many of the new immigrants were men who had been prohibited from leaving Cuba during the 1960s because of military conscription. Despite these demographic differences, though, the Cubans of Mariel had much in common with the working-class Cubans of the freedom flights, especially in their occupational history: they were predominantly craftworkers and factory operators, or professional and technical workers.[85] In education they rated slightly higher, having completed more years of schooling than their earlier working-class compatriots.[86]

The Mariel migration was most distinctive, however, in the way it was perceived by the federal government and the larger society. Unlike the Cubans who immigrated from 1959 to 1973—and unlike the Cubans in the Peruvian embassy—the Cubans of Mariel were not considered legitimate refugees. Although the overwhelming majority cited political reasons for their emigration, and administration officials commonly referred to them as "refugees" in interdepartmental correspondence, the Carter administration determined that under the terms of the 1980 U.S. Refugee Act (which went into effect in March) the Cubans did not qualify for refugee status or the special assistance it entitled them to receive.[87] The U.S. government had traditionally defined refugees as persons fleeing from countries ideologically opposed to the United States; Mariel marked the first time since the Cold War began that the government denied refugee status to individuals emigrating from a communist state. Instead, the government labelled the Cubans with the rather ambiguous term "entrant," which allowed them to remain temporarily in the United States until a more permanent status—if any— could be defined.[88]

Political considerations weighed heavily in this new policy. The Mariel Cubans arrived during a time when Americans were generally less sympathetic to the plight of immigrants, having taken in over the past decade thousands of people displaced by war, revolution, or persecution in Southeast Asia, the Middle East, the Soviet Union, Central and South America, and the Caribbean. More significantly, the Cubans arrived during an economic recession, when news of oil embargoes, high unemployment, and high interest rates dominated the news. Most Americans viewed the Cubans as burdens on the national economy and as competitors for jobs, and they resented the money ($400 million by August) the government was spending to assist and resettle the Cubans and the Haitians arriving at the same time.[89]

Carter, whose popularity had dropped drastically in the polls, did not wish to alienate his constituents further in the middle of an election year. The Cubans' "entrant" status was a political compromise, a resolution that allowed the U.S. to symbolically uphold its open door policy while appearing to take a harsher stand against illegal immigration. However, while the Cubans were not entitled to benefits under the Refugee Act of 1980, limited financial assistance was authorized through other measures.[90] In October 1980, the Refugee Education Assistance Act, with an amendment introduced by Florida congressman Dante Fascell and Senator Richard Stone, allowed the Cubans to receive the same benefits as refugees under the Refugee Act of 1980. The Cubans became eligible for such federal programs as Aid to Families with Dependent Children (AFDC), Supplemental Security Income (SSI), the Comprehensive Employment and Training Act (CETA), and Medicaid and Food Stamps.

Under the Fascell-Stone amendment, the states were also eligible for 100 percent reimbursement for all social services, education, and health care benefits provided to the "entrants."

No amount of legislation could change public opinion, however, and the Mariel Cubans remained the most stigmatized group of immigrants in recent history. No articles or editorials praised their patriotism, their democratic spirit, or their Horatio Alger drive to succeed. Instead, they were described as troublemakers, criminals, and opportunists who took the place of more worthy immigrants.[91] Miami mayor Maurice Ferre complained that Castro had "flushed these people on to us."[92] The president's mother, Lillian Carter, said to reporters, "I'll tell you the truth, I hope they don't come to Plains." When the federal government announced that Fort Allen in Puerto Rico was to become a processing center for up to five thousand of the Cuban and Haitian refugees, Puerto Ricans responded angrily, and the White House had to assure the governor that the refugees would not be allowed to leave the camp and that they would not be resettled on the island.[93] Despite these assurances, Puerto Rico tried to block the move with various measures, including three civil lawsuits, a "cease and desist" order by Puerto Rico's Environmental Control Board, and a federal restraining order.[94] The issue was only resolved in November 1980, when the U.S. Supreme Court took action to allow the federal government to use Fort Allen. As a compromise, the government announced a month later that Fort Allen would be used only to process Haitian refugees.

The Cubans' image worsened during the summer of 1980, when Cubans rioted at three of the resettlement camps to protest their incarceration.[95] At Fort Chaffee, Arkansas, the site of the worst rebellion, some one thousand Cubans rioted, resulting in the injury of forty Cubans and fifteen policemen. Two buildings were burned, and police had to use tear gas to disperse the rioters. Eighty-four Cubans were subsequently arrested. The riots drew front-page coverage, and over the next several weeks many stories followed in the press about the criminal environment that had developed at the camps: gang fights, prostitution rings, rapes and stabbings, liquor stills and contraband, homemade firearms. People living near the camps organized themselves into vigilante committees to protect their communities. The press usually failed to mention, however, that the troublemakers were a small fraction of the camp population; those arrested for rioting and other incidents at Fort Chaffee, for example, comprised less than 2 percent of the eighteen thousand immigrants processed there. The negative publicity only heightened the animosity toward the Cubans, and diminished the pool of sponsors for those who remained in the camps—which, in turn, prolonged their detention and increased their frustration.[96]

By November, 1,769 Cubans—approximately 1.4 percent of the boatlift population—were being detained in federal correctional institutions to await exclusionary hearings.[97] In the minds of most Americans, however, the Cubans of Mariel were all "excludable." Offers of sponsorship came slowly, since most Americans feared bringing home a felon. While federal officials detained all those who posed an obvious threat to society, they readily admitted that the screening process was not infallible. To prevent large backups in Key West and at the processing centers, Cubans were not given as thorough an interview as ordinarily required under normal immigration procedures. The press reported at least one incident of a woman raped and murdered by the man she sponsored.[98] Thousands of Cubans reportedly roamed the streets homeless.[99] Some Cubans, unable to adjust to life in the U.S., turned to burglary and theft, and crime statistics rose in many communities where the Cubans settled. In Miami, crime rose 66 percent in 1980, and over a third of those convicted of murder were Mariel Cubans. Nine hijackings took place in August and September, six of them in one five-day period.[100] The White House eventually asked the Public Health Service and the INS to conduct follow-up investigations of the earlier arrivals who had been released to sponsors to determine if their criminal or mental health histories had gone unreported.[101]

Understandably, most Americans preferred not to endanger their families or their neighborhoods by sponsoring a Cuban refugee. The camp population would have been difficult to resettle even without the negative press, because they did not fit the typical refugee profile. Most Americans preferred to sponsor women, children, or entire families, but the majority of the camp residents were young single men, and over half were black. Many were unskilled and uneducated, with a history of vagrancy, and up to sixteen percent had spent some time in prison.[102] Their chances of finding and keeping employment during these hard economic times were slim, and most Americans did not want to be burdened with their financial care. In addition, the Cubans had to compete for sponsorship with immigrants from many other countries, including the more than fourteen thousand Southeast Asian refugees who were arriving in the United States each month.[103]

In many respects, the reaction of the Cuban emigré community paralleled that of the larger society. Emigrés were initially sympathetic to their compatriots, pooling their resources to assist the new immigrants in their adaptation to the United States. By the end of April, the emigré community of Dade County had raised over $2 million to assist the new refugees in their immediate needs, and the emigré communities of Puerto Rico, Union City, Chicago, Los Angeles, and Houston had established their own fundraising efforts. Spanish-language radio stations in Miami broadcast around-the-clock news updates on the exodus and organized *radio maratóns* to find jobs and sponsors for the Cubans. The Spanish International Network (now Univisión) followed suit with a nationally televised telethon. More significant were the personal demonstrations of concern and generosity. Every day emigrés arrived at the temporary camps with carloads of clothing, food, medicines, blankets, radios and television sets, cots, and mattresses; some emigrés even donated cars and house trailers. Local restaurants, hamburger franchises, and bakeries donated cartons of food, and families prepared large pots of *arroz moro* (black beans and rice) or *arroz con pollo* (chicken and rice) to serve to the Cubans in the camps. By May 1 more than two hundred doctors and nurses had traveled to Key West to volunteer their services,[104] and over the next few months, many more donated their time either in Key West or in the camps in Miami. The Little Havana Community Center provided the refugees with counseling and information on job training programs and housing.

Having been through their own problems of adjustment and accommodation years earlier, emigrés felt a moral duty toward the new immigrants. Currents of fear, however, ran beneath these feelings of obligation. Between the Mariel Cubans and those who had emigrated in the early days of the revolution lay twenty years of social and ideological differences, and the older emigrés worried that the Mariel generation, raised under a socialist and authoritarian regime, would never adapt to democratic institutions and free enterprise. The new immigrants, they feared, would never fit into their community; they were too different; they spoke and dressed differently. Some of them had Russian or Eastern European names. Some older emigrés even worried that the new immigrants might be spies. Over the past two decades, hundreds of intelligence operatives had reportedly infiltrated the emigré community to spy on anti-Castro activities and terrorize the community, and the boatlift provided Castro with the perfect guise under which to get more of his agents into the U.S.[105]

The emigrés' worst fears became reality when news of the criminal records of some of the refugees broke out—news which, like the rest of the nation, they accepted unquestioningly. Unlike many Americans, however, they did not call for an end to the boatlift, since the boatlift provided the only opportunity for family reunification. But the negative publicity affected their community, and ultimately their relationship with the new immigrants. The emigrés took great care to distinguish themselves from the new immigrants. They coined a special term for them—*marielitos*—which quickly became a pejorative in the community. As fear spread, emigrés became reluctant to sponsor the Cubans and even to offer them jobs. The new immigrants never expected such behavior from their compatriots, and many Cubans complained that they encountered more discrimination within the emigré community than from Americans as a whole.

The Cuban government took great pleasure in reporting the difficulties the "parasites" encountered in the United States. Each week, beneath the latest emigration statistics, *Granma* printed translations of stories from the Associated Press and United Press International about Americans' negative reactions to the immigrants.[106] *Granma* also printed accounts of the camps, the riots, and especially the hostility within the emigré community, gloating over the number of criminals the U.S. government detained and using these figures to support the government's claims that the emigrés were lumpen. By July, several dozen refugees had found life unbearable in the United States and had asked to return to Cuba, and the editors capitalized on this news.[107] While celebrating the departure of the lumpen, the Cuban government sought to discourage further emigration.

As Americans debated the pros and cons of Carter's immigration policy, thousands of Cubans waited anxiously in the resettlement camps for the government to determine their future.[108] Twenty-two nations agreed to assist the United States in finding homes for the Cubans, but by the end of 1980, only three countries—Venezuela, Argentina, and Australia—had taken in even a small number.[109] Attempts were made to resettle the Cubans around the country, but approximately 73 percent stayed in the state of Florida, and of these, 75 percent (or 54 percent of all immigrants) found homes and jobs in the Dade County/Miami area. New Jersey and New York, two states with large Cuban populations, ranked second and third in the number of resettlements, with 6 percent and 5.5 percent respectively.[110] California (4.3 percent), Illinois (1.5 percent), and Texas (1.2 percent) were next on the list. By mid-October 1980, there were still 8,516 Cubans awaiting resettlement at various processing camps, and they were ultimately consolidated at Fort Chaffee, where most remained for several more months.

The administration sent note after note condemning Cuba's dumping of hardcore criminals and requesting that Castro take back the detainees; all went unanswered. Forcible deportation was ruled out because it might provoke a military confrontation with Cuba and would ultimately make the United States appear weak. The Carter administration considered various options, including bringing action against the Cuban government in the World Court, confining the detainees on a remote U.S.–owned island or some "abandoned out-of-the-way" military facility, or housing the detainees at the Guantánamo naval base.[111] None were acted upon.

The Aftermath of Mariel:
The Next Fourteen Years

In 1984, the Reagan administration and the Castro government signed a new immigration accord. Beginning in 1985, up to twenty thousand Cubans per year could now immigrate to the United States; in return, the Cuban government agreed to take back 2,746 criminals and mentally ill detainees of the Mariel boatlift.

As expected, non-Cuban residents of south Florida were strongly against the immigration accords. Despite resettlement efforts, most Cuban immigrants had returned to live in Dade County. Over one hundred thousand Mariel Cubans settled in south Florida in less than five years, and during the same period tens of thousands of immigrants from Haiti, Nicaragua, El Salvador, Mexico, and Colombia also settled in the area. State legislators warned the Reagan administration that their state could not take in the new immigrants without massive federal assistance; the state did not have the jobs, schools, or social services to accommodate twenty thousand people each year. Furthermore, the federal government still owed the state over $150 million for social services provided in the wake of the boatlift.[112]

State leaders also warned that ethnic and racial relations would worsen under the burden of renewed immigration from Cuba. Anti-Cuban sentiment was already evident in November 1980, when voters repealed the Bilingual-Bicultural Ordinance (originally passed in 1973) and made it unlawful to use county funds "for the purpose of utilizing any language other than English, or promoting any culture other than that of the United States."[113] A disc jockey at a local radio station initiated a letter-writing campaign called SOS ("Save Our South Florida") to ask the president to repeal the accords. One of the most popular bumper stickers sold in Miami read "Will the last American out of south Florida please bring the flag?" The public outcry subsided in May 1985, however, when the Cuban government suddenly suspended the immigration accords. Infuriated by the Reagan administration's installation of Radio Martí (discussed in chapter 4), Castro retaliated by refusing to take back any more prisoners. By then, only 201 Mariel detainees had been repatriated to Cuba.

The situation called attention to the state of limbo in which Mariel detainees still lived. Cubans who had had their immigration parole status revoked were held in federal custody indefinitely to await deportation. By March 1986, federal authorities held close to two thousand Cubans in the Atlanta federal penitentiary and another seven hundred in prisons and detention centers around the country.[114] Of these, 1,769 had been detained upon arrival, but the rest had committed crimes in the U.S. and had had their parole status revoked. Another five thousand Cubans were serving terms in local jails and state prisons, and upon the completion of their sentences they were scheduled to be handed over into federal custody to await deportation. Some were detained for minor offenses like drunkenness, trespassing, failing to pay traffic tickets, violating the rules of their halfway houses, even food stamp fraud. The majority, however, had committed serious crimes in the United States, from drug trafficking to assault and armed robbery.[115]

The Cuban population at the Atlanta federal penitentiary already demonstrated dangerously high stress levels; nine homicides, seven suicides, four hundred "unsuccessful but serious suicide attempts," and more than two thousand attempts at self-mutilation had been recorded among them.[116] With little chance for freedom either in the United States or in Cuba, the Cubans felt increasingly hopeless. The U.S. government was spending up to $40 million a year to keep these individuals detained. Civil rights activists charged that holding the Cubans indefinitely after their prison terms were completed constituted a violation of their civil rights. They filed lawsuits on the detainees' behalf and urged the Justice Department to begin a case-by-case review of their records, if not for humane reasons then for prison control. In 1981, Atlanta Federal Judge Marvin H. Shoob ruled that the Cubans could not be indefinitely detained and were entitled to due process. The federal government disagreed, however, claiming that since the Cubans had arrived in the United States without proper papers they were not in the United States legally and therefore were not entitled to due process. The Eleventh Circuit Court of Appeals ruled in support of U.S. policy,[117] and in 1986 the Supreme Court agreed, stating that aliens convicted of crimes in the United States were not entitled to constitutional due process.

Further lobbying continued over the next two years, bringing together an unlikely coalition of activists from the American Civil Liberties Union and the conservative Cuban exile community. Friends and families of the detainees created their own organizations, such as the Comisión Pro Justicia para los presos Cubanos del Mariel, to lobby on their relatives' behalf and to mobilize the emigré community. The latter proved especially difficult, however. While emigrés readily defended the human rights of political prisoners in Cuba, most preferred to remain ignorant of the prison conditions in Atlanta. Still reeling from the boatlift's damage to its image, the community preferred not to become embroiled in controversy once again, or to become too closely associated with the riff-raff in the prisons.

To increase pressure on the Reagan administration, the ACLU charged the United States with human rights abuses and petitioned the Organization of American States to intervene on the prisoners' behalf.[118] By 1987, several legislators had rallied to the cause and had succeeded in persuading the Justice Department and the INS to begin hearings on a case-by-case basis.[119]

The problem became critical in November 1987, when the Cuban government once again agreed to accept the Mariel detainees. On November 21, one thousand Cuban inmates rioted in protest at the federal detention center in Oakdale, Louisiana. The inmates set fire to four buildings, injuring dozens of prison employees and inmates, and took twenty-eight people hostage. Two days later, three hundred detainees at the Atlanta federal penitentiary followed suit, setting fire to three buildings and taking ninety-four people hostage. The inmates at both prisons demanded that they be allowed to remain in the United States and that their cases be reviewed individually before a parole board.

During the following week, federal officials tried to negotiate with the Cuban inmates. The situation was tragic: a group of foreign, non–English-speaking inmates, imprisoned in the Deep South, holding hostages to guarantee an uncertain future in the United States. Hundreds of people mobbed the entrance to the prisons each day. Relatives held nightly prayer vigils outside the gates and spoke to their loved ones through loudspeakers. From time to time, the inmates at the Atlanta penitentiary allowed news reporters inside the compound to interview prisoners and hear their demands. Photographers and cameramen with zoom lenses captured poignant scenes of inmates standing at the barred windows, waving small American flags and holding banners that read "Please let me stay in America."[120]

The inmates' willingness to remain in prison rather than return to Cuba won for them the support of the emigré community, since it provided yet another opportunity to discredit the Castro government. After seven years of apathy, the community now rallied to the prisoners' side. Prominent Cuban exiles, including Xavier Suarez, the mayor of Miami, traveled to Atlanta and Oakdale to assist in the negotiations. Cuban exile spokesmen argued that the *marielitos* should not be sent to Cuba against their will.

Of all the people who became involved in the negotiations, only one person secured the trust of the inmates: Rev. Agustín Román, the Cuban Auxiliary Bishop of the Archdiocese of Miami. Oakdale inmates specifically demanded that Bishop Román represent their interests and suspended all talks until Justice Department officials granted him a role in the negotiations.[121] Over the next several days, Román traveled from city to city acting as mediator, interpreter, priest, and confessor. Finally, on November 29, the Oakdale inmates threw down their homemade weapons and released all their hostages. The following week, Román succeeded in convincing the inmates at the Atlanta penitentiary to lay down their weapons as well, earning him ABC News's designation of "Person of the Week."

As part of the negotiations, the Justice Department agreed that no reprisals would be made against the inmates who took part in the siege and promised them a "full, fair, and equitable" consideration of their pleas to remain in the United States. The government established a special panel to review each case, and Cuban American leaders formed a coalition, headed by Román, to defend the inmates' interests over the course of the deliberations. The nine hundred Cubans approved for parole before the riots erupted were released over the next few months, and the government began a review process for the others, which dragged on for several years. As it reviewed each case, however, the INS carefully dispersed the detainees to dozens of prisons around the country to prevent another riot.[122] By 1991, approximately sixteen hundred prisoners had been paroled and four hundred deported. Amazingly, the Cuban government gave these returning *gusanos* a hero's welcome and released them into the general population.[123]

The prison riots were just part of a series of events during the 1980s that focused more negative publicity on the Mariel immigrants. Crimes involving Mariel Cubans usually drew heavy media attention. The television and film industries capitalized on anger and resentment, portraying Cubans as drug dealers, pimps, and psychopaths. Nowhere were the stereotypes plainer than in Universal Studios' 1983 remake of *Scarface,* directed by Brian DePalma, in which the mobster made famous by James Cagney became a *marielito* cocaine king, played by Al Pacino. Cubans in Miami expressed their outrage even before the movie was filmed; City Commissioner Demetrio Pérez tried (unsuccessfully) to get the city government to prohibit DePalma from filming in Miami. To combat the negative images that now dominated the media, emigrés in Miami founded Facts about Cuban Exiles (FACE) in 1982. Like the NAACP, LULAC, and other minority rights groups, FACE's goal was to educate Americans about the emigré community through conferences and publications and to celebrate the Cubans' accomplishments.

Fear of another boatlift was a lasting legacy of Mariel. South Floridians lived with the knowledge that Castro could at any moment allow another large-scale migration, and rumors of a new boatlift periodically circulated in Miami. Throughout the 1980s, the *Miami Herald* regularly interviewed sociologists and political scientists for their "migration forecasts": analyses of social and economic conditions in Cuba that might foster another migration.[124] In 1983, the federal government and the state of Florida compiled a list of emergency procedures called Operation Distant Shore to follow in case of such an event.[125] The plan called for, among other measures, a naval blockade by U.S. warships of the south Florida coast to prevent another boatlift.

By the early 1990s, another boatlift seemed very possible. Following the "Velvet Revolution" in Eastern Europe and the dismantling of the Soviet Union, Cuba found itself isolated politically and economically. Its former Latin American allies now pressured the Castro government to institute democratic reforms, and the United States tightened its trade embargo with the passage of the Cuban Democracy Act. More significantly, a number of human rights and dissident groups emerged on the island to call for reforms, and even members of Castro's own government began advocating reform. With Cuban society in crisis, the Castro government sought ways to ease domestic pressure.

The number of Cubans who emigrated clandestinely on rafts and small boats increased dramatically. In 1990, 467 *balseros* were picked up by the Coast Guard; but every year the numbers multiplied.[126] An emigré organization called Hermanos al Rescate (Brothers to the Rescue) was founded specifically to patrol the Florida Straits by helicopter and assist the Coast Guard with rescue missions.

From January 1 to August 15 of 1994, more than sixty-two hundred rafters were picked up.[127] After a series of anti-government demonstrations in Havana in mid-August turned violent, an angry Fidel Castro announced that the government was considering allowing another mass emigration.[128] The Clinton administration quickly warned Cuba that the U.S. would not permit another boatlift like that which occurred in 1980, and warned that the U.S. was prepared to impose a naval blockade of the island if Castro tried to launch another boatlift. At the same time, federal officials warned the emigré community that another boatlift would not be permitted. Cuban American leaders cooperated with federal government and advised the community to be prudent, reminding them that another boatlift would only help Castro stay in power.

The Cuban government was then forced to change its game plan: the Cuban Coast Guard was instructed not to detain those who left on the rafts. The government could not lure emigrés to transport people off the island, but it could encourage the discontented to leave by their own means. As rumors spread through the country that they were free to leave, thousands of Cubans set off on homemade rafts from Cojímar, Mariel, and other beaches and ports. The change in Cuban policy was calculated to ease domestic pressure but also to bring the United States to the bargaining table. Cuban officials hoped that Americans would reevaluate the legitimacy of their thirty-two-year-old trade embargo against Cuba; at the very least, the crisis might force the Clinton administration to negotiate another immigration accord.

In a reversal of three decades of U.S. policy, on August 18 the Clinton administration announced that Cubans picked up by the U.S. Coast Guard would no longer be brought to the United States. Rather, they would go to the Guantánamo naval base in Cuba or other safe havens around the Caribbean. They had no chance for parole status and would remain at these camps indefinitely until they were accepted by a third country or Castro allowed them to return. This announcement, however, did little to dissuade the *balseros*. Two days later, in order to pressure the Cuban government to restrict illegal emigration, the administration announced that the sending of U.S. dollars to relatives on the island was once again prohibited, and charter air traffic from Miami to Cuba was canceled. (Both were important sources of income for Cuba in the post–Cold War era.) Still, the *balseros* kept coming. By the end of August, over 17,000 Cubans had arrived.

Beginning on September 1, 1994, representatives of the U.S. and Cuban governments held a series of meetings in New York, Washington, and Havana to try to resolve the crisis once and for all. Despite the Cuban representatives' attempts to negotiate an end to the U.S. trade embargo, the U.S. government refused to concede. Finally, on September 9, the governments reached an agreement: the U.S. would accept a minimum of twenty thousand new immigrants each year, not including the immediate relatives of United States citizens, and in turn the Cuban government agreed to restrict illegal emigration. As an additional measure, the United States agreed to accept during the next one-year period all qualified Cuban nationals in Cuba currently on the immigrant visa waiting list, and Cuba agreed to continue to discuss the return of Cuban nationals excludable from the United States.[129] The Cubans held at Guantánamo and Panama had the option of either returning to Cuba and applying for visas at the U.S. Interests Section or relocating to safe havens around the Caribbean. In the fall of 1994, then, a fourth Cuban migration was under way.

PART TWO

The Emigrés

CHAPTER 3

Defining an Identity
in the United States

The Cubans who emigrated during the 1960s left one
society in transition to enter another. They settled in during the age of
Camelot and the Great Society, the counterculture, protests over the
draft and the Vietnam war, the feminist and civil rights movements.
Within a society seeking its own definitions, these emigrés tried to define
their identity and culture: what did it mean to be Cuban in a country
other than Cuba? Could a Cuban exile culture thrive in a society that
celebrated ethnic pluralism and yet rewarded (in Milton Gordon's term)
anglo-conformity?[1] Could one be both a Cuban exile and an American
citizen? These and other questions became increasingly important with
each year of exile, as returning to Cuba seemed less probable. Maintaining a sense of *cubanidad* in the United States became crucial for these
emigrés, not just for some distant day when repatriation would become
possible but to maintain the cultural boundaries that would allow them
to survive as a distinct community in the United States. Just as their
compatriots on the island were redefining Cuban identity within the
context of a political and cultural revolution, the emigrés had to redefine
what it meant to be Cuban within the context of exile in the United
States.

To maintain a sense of *cubanidad* meant to preserve those customs,
values, and traditions that they associated with being Cuban, and the
emigrés created numerous cultural organizations to promote and reinforce these values in exile. In preserving and expressing their *cubanidad*,
they asserted an identity that was political as well as cultural. Despite their
condition as refugees in a foreign land, they were still—and always would

83

be—Cubans; complete assimilation would be a rejection of their past and of their heritage, as well as a negation of the forces that propelled them to the United States.

In the long term, oddly, *cubanidad* eased their adaptation to the United States. By giving their hardships a larger meaning, it psychologically empowered them to deal with exile. Starting over was difficult for this first generation. Many had already been successful back in Cuba and were settled into career, family, and home, but they now had to adapt to a new society and a new way of living. When life in the United States seemed overwhelming, these Cubans took some comfort in the fact that they were actors in a complex world struggle between authoritarianism and democracy, between communism and free enterprise. They were victims—"martyrs"—of a political cause. Consequently, they resisted being called "immigrants," particularly those who arrived during the first decade of exile, and many continue to resist the term even today. *Immigrant* implies a choice, and most Cuban emigrés believed that they had no choice; they had been pushed out of their country by the social, economic, and political chaos of the Castro regime. When the Cubans called themselves "exiles," it was a powerful political statement, a symbol of defiance that at the same time distinguished and isolated their experience from that of other immigrants. Preserving *cubanidad* became not just a nostalgic attempt to live in the past, then, but a political responsibility. They had to be symbols of Cuba's political alternatives: symbols of *la Cuba de ayer* (the Cuba of yesterday) and of the Cuba that could be.

Maintaining a sense of *cubanidad* was easier in Miami than elsewhere simply because of numbers. Despite the resettlement efforts of the Cuban Refugee Program, cultural isolation prompted thousands of exiles to return to south Florida throughout the 1960s and 1970s. Wages were higher up north, but they preferred to endure hardships in Miami than to live in the cold climates far from their relatives and news of Cuba. Census figures showed that 299,217 Cubans lived in Dade County in 1970, but by 1980 the number had almost doubled to 581,030,[2] and more than 52 percent of the 803,226 Cubans in the United States lived in the Miami–Ft. Lauderdale area alone; the only city with a larger Cuban population was Havana.[3] The Cuban population had dropped somewhat by 1990, as Cubans moved to neighboring cities, but at 563,979 they comprised 29 percent of Dade County's total population.[4]

Exiles found it easier to establish cultural boundaries in south Florida. With such a large Cuban support network, the pressure they felt was to differentiate rather than to assimilate. The most important Cuban exile organizations emerged in Miami, and it was in Miami that the "Cuban success story" unfolded. Cubans who relocated to distant cities, on the other hand, with few or no compatriots nearby, had neither the social nor the economic support networks that were valuable to structural assimilation.[5] As one Cuban told me, "In the Midwest one feels even more in exile."

The area that attracted the second largest percentage of Cubans was the Union City / West New York area of New Jersey, where approximately 20 percent of the refugees, mostly working class, settled. First settled by Germans and later by Irish and Italians, Union City attracted Cuban immigrants as early as 1940, most of them factory workers from Fomento in central Cuba who left their hometown to seek economic opportunities in the lucrative garment industries of the Northeast. By 1959, over two thousand Cubans lived in Union City, and this small community, as well as the job opportunities in the area, attracted thousands more during the sixties. Union City became known as "Havana on the Hudson." By 1975, Cubans comprised over two-thirds of Union City's residents and almost half of the residents of the neighboring city of West New York. The Cubans provided most of the workforce in the local industries and created a vital commercial business district along Bergenline Avenue, which runs for roughly 90 blocks from Union City into North Bergen, West New York, and Guttenberg. Today the majority of businesses on Bergenline Avenue are Cuban-owned.

In many ways, Union City became a satellite of Miami. Cubans traveled back and forth between the two cities, visiting relatives and friends. Among the most lucrative businesses in Union City were the private bus lines that transported Cubans to and from Miami. Miami merchants advertised in Union City newspapers, and candidates for political office in Union City often campaigned in south Florida (a tactic learned from Puerto Rican merchants and politicians who promoted themselves both in New York City and San Juan). Successful entrepreneurs operated businesses in both cities. Spanish-language radio stations in New Jersey carried news of Miami and vice versa.

During the 1980s and early 1990s, Union City lost many Cuban residents who either retired to south Florida or moved to North Bergen, West New York, or various suburbs to avoid congestion: with fifty-eight thousand people living on 1.4 square miles, Union City was the most densely populated area in the country. At 25 percent of the population (15,084), however, the Cuban presence there remains unmistakable.[6]

Creating Little Havana

Cubans who came to Miami during the early 1960s settled primarily within a four-square-mile area southwest of the central business district, an area now known as "Little Havana." This area attracted emigrés for several reasons: a small Cuban neighborhood already existed here, and Cuban or Latino-owned drugstores, *bodegas* (grocery stores), and shops catered to the new exiles' needs; low-rent houses and apartment buildings were available; and public transportation gave easy access to the employment opportunities in the central business district, as well as to the Centro Hispano Católico and the Cuban Refugee Center. Until the emigrés moved in, the area, like much of Miami, came alive only during the winter season, when northeasterners came south to escape the ice and snow. Cubans renovated the old buildings and established their own businesses along Flagler Street and Southwest 8th Street (Calle Ocho), important thoroughfares that run through the heart of Little Havana. Local residents were initially concerned that the area would become a ghetto, but the Cubans in fact turned an economically depressed area into a lucrative commercial and residential district. By 1970 about 14 percent of the total Cuban population in the U.S. resided in Little Havana,[7] but as the enclave became increasingly concentrated, Cubans moved west and south into other residential areas. "All of Miami is now a Little Havana," remark many emigrés enthusiastically.

The emigrés settled in adjoining cities in Dade County as well. Hialeah drew many Cubans because of the jobs available at Miami International Airport and the Hialeah race tracks. By 1970, Latinos comprised 42 percent of its population; by 1980, 74 percent. Some local residents called West Hialeah "Little Marianao," after the working class suburb of Havana. The city of Sweetwater also grew with the Cuban migration, and by 1980 its Latin population was 81 percent.[8] It became the first city in south Florida to elect a Cuban-born mayor. Coral Gables and Miami Beach also attracted Cubans, especially those with higher incomes. Little Havana, however, remained the symbolic center of the exile community in south Florida and in the United States.

The exiles slowly changed the character of Miami and Dade County. The local economy grew and diversified as the Cubans purchased homes, appliances, and automobiles and paid taxes. The Cubans set up all types of small (and not so small) businesses: restaurants, groceries and supermarkets, gas stations, drugstores, photography studios, department stores, factories, theaters, bars, and nightclubs. While the major banks would not lend money to Cuban entrepreneurs without collateral— which only the wealthier emigrés had—the smaller banks in the area (usually Cuban- or Latino-owned) lent applicants money on the basis of their "character."[9] Cubans who had a solid history of entrepreneurship in Cuba, or who had strong personal references, usually qualified for these loans. By the late 1960s, Cuban entrepreneurs also had access to loans from the Small Business Administration.

Some entrepreneurial women created businesses catering to the needs of women who entered the workplace: day-care centers, housekeeping and delivery services, laundries and dry cleaners, home ateliers and dress shops, beauty parlors, and even driving schools. Cubans discovered that any business that made life easier for the working woman had a good chance of flourishing. Some of the most successful businesses founded on this principle, for example, were the *cantinas:* subscription home-delivery food services that brought hot meals of *lechón asado, boliche, arroz con pollo,* and other Cuban specialties every evening to homes throughout the city. Women with little time or energy to prepare large family meals gave their patronage to the *cantinas,* permitting them to spend time with their families while enjoying traditional, familiar meals. Over time, as more and more women went into the workplace, these and other Cuban-owned businesses thrived and became permanent fixtures in the community, reminders of the impact of emigration on women's roles.[10]

Many U.S. companies, particularly in the garment and textile industries, relocated to south Florida to take advantage of the large, nonunion labor pool. By 1980, workers of Spanish origin (mostly women) comprised the overwhelming majority of workers in the garment industry. Corporations also established headquarters in Miami, eager to take advantage of a large middle class adept at doing business with both the U.S. and Latin America. By the 1980s, Miami had developed into an important banking, trade, and commercial center. Miami was outgrowing its image as a tranquil winter resort and retirement haven and becoming a major American metropolis.

The Cuban presence permeated the city. Small Cuban-owned businesses lined all the major thoroughfares. Spanish-language services were scheduled at churches and synagogues. Radio programs played *danzones* as well as Top 40. Statues of saints and la Virgen de la Caridad were visible on front lawns, as were *bohíos* (thatched roof huts, symbols of

Cuba's indigenous past) in backyards, beaches, and picnic areas. Cuban little league teams competed against other city teams. Street vendors sold *guarapo* (a sugarcane drink) and *granizados* (snow cones). The "foreign" smells of *puros* (cigars), *pasteles* (pastries), and *café cubano* filled the air. Cuban and Latin American brands lined the shelves of groceries and supermarkets: Café Estrella, Frijoles Kirby, Mariquitas Banana Chips, Malta Hatuey, Galletas Wajay, Theresa Guava Paste, Dulce de Coco Ancel. Outside city limits, small farmers harvested vegetables important to the emigrés' diet: *malanga, boniato, carambola, yuca,* and *calabaza.*

While the economic transformation of Miami meant more jobs all around, non-Cubans had mixed feelings about the changes. With close to three hundred thousand new residents in just one decade, Dade County became one of the fastest-growing areas in the nation, and as such had to deal with the problems of growth: a lack of adequate housing, schools, utilities, and sewer systems, as well as increases in taxes, traffic, and crime. Non-Cubans accused the exiles of consciously trying to take over their city. The Cubans "have created their own comfortable Latin culture in Miami," wrote a reader to a magazine editor, ". . . which they will leave willingly only for the real Havana."[11] The social and demographic changes produced a "white flight" to cities north of Dade County. (Blacks were more likely to remain in Dade.)[12]

Non-Cubans were particularly disturbed by what they perceived to be a refusal to speak English and a rejection of American ways. Department store clerks, hospital emergency room staff, telephone operators, and city personnel all complained that the Cubans expected everyone to speak to them in Spanish. Some Cubans did refuse to learn English, obstinate in their belief that they would never need the language once they returned to their homeland. For others, particularly the elderly, it was difficult to learn. Like countless other immigrants to the United States before them, they found that wanting to learn a language did not always mean that one *could* learn. Fortunately for this segment of the exile community, the large Cuban presence in Dade County prevented them from becoming isolated and made it easy to survive without understanding English. They could shop in stores owned and operated by Cubans, read and listen to the Spanish-language media, and live and work alongside their compatriots. Employees, friends, and children were always nearby to serve as interpreters when necessary. As the Spanish-speaking population grew, it became increasingly possible to live and die in Miami without ever having learned to speak English.

Most exiles, however, realized that competency in English was a prerequisite for better-paying employment and a criterion for success within the U.S. mainstream. Many Cubans had at least some familiarity with the language, since English was taught in many Cuban schools, but of course understanding the basics of grammar was not the same as fluency. Enrollment in language courses increased. Schools throughout the city, among them the English Center in downtown Miami (founded in 1962), established evening classes to accommodate those who wanted to learn.

As Miami became a major trade center linking the two continents, bilingualism became a professional asset whether one worked for a multinational corporation or in the retail and tourism industries. Even so, English never surpassed Spanish in importance for the emigrés—at least for the first generation—since Spanish was so crucial to *cubanidad*.[13] Spanish never became a private language, spoken only at home and in hushed voices far from "Anglo" ears; rather, it was used in both private and public places, in all social and business interactions with fellow Cubans and other Latin Americans. By the mid-1980s, one study reported that more than half of Cubans spoke Spanish at work and over 70 percent used it in social situations.[14] Spanish was commonly heard in the halls of city government, in the corridors of local schools and hospitals, in banks and corporate headquarters.

In recognition of the importance of bilingualism, the Dade County public school system experimented with bilingual education as early as 1963, long before bilingual education received a federal mandate. Instead of using Spanish as a transitional language—that is, as a means of conducting classes only until the Cuban students learned enough English to be incorporated into mainstream classrooms—Dade County's bilingual education programs encouraged the retention of Spanish language skills as well as the learning of Spanish by native English-speakers. By the 1970s, Dade County's bilingual education program served as a model for bilingual education programs around the country.

To many non-Cubans, these changes showed that the Cubans refused to assimilate. They could not understand why the Cubans refused to dissolve into the proverbial melting pot as (according to family lore) their own grandparents had. The sheer number of Cubans meant that Spanish was heard just about everywhere, and it was an irritating reminder to non-Cubans that their city was changing. Cubans insisted, however, that they were in fact adapting, but without relinquishing an essential element of their identity. When department store clerks angrily demanded that they "speak American," they shrugged it off as American ignorance and provinciality. If the Cubans were successful it was because they had a strong sense of who they were—and language was part of that identity. They did not understand how Americans could expect them to sever such an essential part of themselves.

Reinforcing *cubanidad* became an obsession for many emigrés, particularly during the 1960s and 1970s. Life in exile made them nostalgic and introspective, even depressed, and they looked for ways to remember and celebrate the past, reinforce their feelings of nationalism, and stress their identity. They did this through a variety of cultural activities that served to rally, inform, and entertain the community. Exile organizations sponsored lectures and seminars in schools and community halls throughout Little Havana. With names such as "Añoranzas de Cuba" (Longing for Cuba) and "La Cuba de Ayer" (The Cuba of yesterday), these courses provided their hundreds of participants with the opportunity to study their homeland in depth, often for the first time. As one course for elderly Cubans advertised, "We will encourage the exchange of anecdotes and memories with the aim of, perhaps, preserving them before the years take their toll."[15]

Numerous cultural organizations emerged during the 1960s and early 1970s. The best known of these was the Cruzada Educativa Cubana, founded in 1962 by Dr. María Gómez Carbonell, which fostered the study of Cuban history and tradition through literary contests, awards, and cultural pageants. Cuban-owned bookstores organized *peñas literarias* (literary circles) for artists, writers, and poets. Cultural organizations such as the Sociedad Pro-Arte Grateli and Teatro Bellas Artes staged productions of Cuban and Spanish works. Local colleges and universities also contributed: the University of Miami's Koubek Memorial Center, for example, sponsored a Cuban Culture Program of seminars and exhibits on the art, music, literature, history, and folklore of the island. Miami-Dade Community College and the new Florida International University (founded in 1972) also sponsored art exhibits, theatrical productions, and lectures by distinguished emigré artists, writers, and scholars.

Of particular concern to the emigrés was the second generation, those born in the United States or who came here as children and knew little about Cuba or their heritage. How would their children fare in Cuba once they returned to their homeland if they could not speak Spanish or understand the basics of Cuban history and culture? Equally important, in a city in which residents frequently shunned or criticized Cubans because of their foreignness, how would these children develop a sense of pride and self-esteem? In a society overrun with drugs, sexual promiscuity, hippies, and leftists, how would they resist the pressures to "Americanize"?[16]

To help parents educate their children on the essentials of *cubanidad,* schools and churches established after-school programs. San Juan Bosco Church in Little Havana, for example, opened its Escuela Cívico-religiosa in 1967, offering grade school and high school students religious instruction as well as courses on Cuban history, geography, and culture after school each day.[17] A more intensive Cuban education was available at the dozens of small private schools that emerged in Miami and Hialeah, nicknamed *las escuelitas cubanas* (the little Cuban schools). By 1990 some thirty such schools existed, among them the Conchita Espinoza Academy, Miami Aerospace, La Luz, Lincoln-Martí, La Progresiva, and José Martí School.

Several of Havana's best private schools, such as LaSalle and Loyola, reopened in exile. To obtain state accreditation these schools modeled their curricula after their American counterparts, but they retained much of their original staff and faculty from Cuba, offering some cultural continuity. Parents who sent their children to these schools could be assured of a quality education that would prepare them equally well for life in Cuba or the United States. The most renowned of these private schools was Belén Jesuit, founded in Cuba in 1854 by Isabel II of Spain; its alumni include distinguished statesmen, scholars, scientists, clergy, and Fidel Castro.[18] When the Cuban government confiscated Belén's classrooms and libraries and expelled the foreign-born Jesuits, the school reopened in Miami, first at the Centro Hispano Católico, later on Flagler Street in the heart of Little Havana, and finally in the southwest Miami suburbs.

Also active in the cultural mission to preserve *cubanidad* were the *municipios,* the first of which were founded in 1962. Prior to the revolution, Cuba was divided into 126 *municipios* (townships) in six provinces, and each Cuban belonged to a particular *municipio* simply by residence. The *municipios* in exile, however, were social organizations similar in some ways to the Mexican American and Puerto Rican *mutualistas* or the Immigrant Aid Societies of the Northeast. Eventually 114 *municipios* were established in Miami, each self-governing but united under an umbrella organization known as the Cuban Municipalities in Exile. The *municipios* were immensely popular: one—Bayamo—

consistently had a membership of over eleven hundred during the late 1970s and early 1980s.[19]

Over the years, the *municipios* carried out a variety of functions. During the 1960s, they served as clearinghouses of information on practical matters such as housing and employment as well as on local residents. Cubans who arrived in the city for the first time could contact a *municipio* (usually the one named after their township in Cuba) for information on the whereabouts of old friends and neighbors. Many *municipios* kept detailed lists of former residents now living in exile. Each *municipio* also funded a treasury with its modest dues and provided financial assistance to members for funeral expenses and small personal loans. Some *municipios* sent medicines and clothing to needy people back in Cuba. A few even maintained building funds to be used for any construction or renovations needed in their townships when they re-turned to the island. Their principal function, though, was to provide comradeship and guidance, and most of the members were from the working class, people who were more apt to feel alienated in the United States and to need assistance.

The *municipios* provided cultural and recreational opportunities as well: musical and historical programs, *tertulias* (conversational gather-ings), dances, *ferias* (fairs), and picnics. Their headquarters also func-tioned as small-scale museums, full of photographs and memorabilia of their township. Many of the *municipios* published their own newspapers, newsletters, or magazines, which included articles on the history and folklore of the township; photographs of life in Cuba, in sections called *Rincón del recuerdo* ("Memory Lane"); short biographies of *cubanos ilustres* (noteworthy Cubans); essays and poems contributed by mem-bers; and social news on baptisms, first communions, *quinceañeras,* weddings, and deaths (particularly of those who died in Cuba). Direc-tories at the back of these publications listed the names of members who offered professional or commercial services—doctors, lawyers, ac-countants, mechanics, beauticians, landscape gardeners, plumbers—encouraging members to do business with their own.

In this politically divided community, the *municipios* in exile aspired to create a sense of brotherhood that would be retained once a return to the homeland was possible. "It is the only group in exile that has united Cubans," said the founder of one *municipio*. "It is the ideal vehicle to help us arrive united in Cuba."[20] In theory, these organiza-tions hoped to overcome the petty ideological squabbles among Cu-bans by appealing to the cultural bonds they shared. These ideals were never fully realized, however, since the *municipios* were by their very nature political creations, the products of revolution and exile. Hence, every social gathering and every cultural function became a forum for a political discussion of what was going on in Cuba. The *municipios* reminded exiles that they were Cubans, not Americans, and that their ultimate responsibility was to work for the liberation of the homeland. They compared themselves to the late nineteenth century *liceos* (lyceums) and chapters of Martí's Cuban Revolutionary Party in Tampa, Key West, and New York that had worked for Cuba's independence from Spain.[21] Over the years, to hasten the "war of liberation" against "Castro-communism," the *municipios* lent their support to different exile political groups, causing rifts within the organizations. Despite their idealism, they were not exempt from squabbles and infighting.

Many lucrative businesses grew out of satisfying the Cubans' cultural needs. The first Cuban exile bookstores and publishing houses emerged during the 1960s, ensuring that the community could read the works of the Cuban greats as well as present-day exile writers and ideologically correct intellectuals. The first eight-volume *Encyclopedia de Cuba* (now fourteen volumes) was published in the early 1970s and advertised as "indispensable in every Cuban home." "We are selling nostalgia," said the publishers. "We are selling a piece of Cuba that anyone who misses it dearly can have in their living rooms."[22] The exiles could see *zarzuelas* (Spanish operettas) and the serious works of well-known dramatists in local theaters, as well as the irreverent, often slapstick plays known as *vodevil* or *teatro bufo*.[23] The business of nostalgia sometimes bordered on kitsch: local businesses sold wax busts of José Martí, oil-on-velvet paintings of Havana's El Morro fortress, and even plastic placemats with photographs and trivia questions about Cuba circa 1950. Variety shows were also common, and they served the double function of entertaining the masses while raising funds for one political group or another. In 1961, for example, a show entitled *Cuba canta y baila* (Cuba sings and dances) was staged at Dade County Auditorium to raise money for the ransom of the Brigade 2506 prisoners, and in 1966 the political groups Alpha 66 and Second Front of the Escambray sponsored a show entitled *Balas para la libertad* (Bullets for liberty) to raise funds for their counterrevolutionary activities.

Cuban exiles realized that their identity was dependent upon a continuity between past and present, and between Cuba and the United States, but they tried to duplicate the past so exactly that Cubans who arrived in Miami during the Mariel boatlift of 1980 often joked that they had entered a time warp and stepped back into the Cuba of the 1950s. Spanish-language radio stations imitated their prerevolutionary counterparts, with fiery news editorials, soap operas, and reruns of old comedy shows such as *Tres patines* and *La tremenda corte*. Commercial establishments took the names of popular businesses in Cuba, whether the original owners managed them or not. Medical clinics modeled after Cuba's *quinta* system flourished long before HMO legislation was passed in Florida. Professional organizations and labor unions were reestablished in Miami, some with "in exile" added to the title.[24] Cuban Jews established their own cultural centers and religious congregations, such as the Círculo Cubano Hebreo and the Cuban Sephardic Hebrew Congregation, modeled after the Chevet Achim in Havana.[25] Even the activities of Cuba's upper classes were recreated in Miami, in restrictive country clubs, elaborate balls and dances, social registers, and numerous charitable events.

The emigrés also tried to establish a symbolic continuum between their experience and the nineteenth-century revolutionary heritage. In Miami, they named parks, monuments, streets, and businesses after long-dead heroes of Cuba's wars of independence. They commemorated Cuban national holidays with rallies, parades, concerts, and religious services.[26] The annual José Martí parade in Hialeah (down West 29th Street, or "José Martí Boulevard") has attracted thousands of spectators since it was first held in 1969. Wherever large numbers of Cubans settled—in Houston, Union City, Chicago, Los Angeles—they built some permanent marker in a public area to celebrate their *cubanidad,* usually a bust or statue of Martí, Antonio Maceo, Carlos Manuel de Céspedes, Félix Varela, or some other hero of the nineteenth century struggle for independence. These markers and celebrations were not representative of the Cuban exile experience at all, of course. Apart from a monument on Calle Ocho in Miami to honor the soldiers of Brigade 2506, few symbols or markers spoke to the experience of the post-1959 emigrés, at least during the first two decades of exile. The community was too politically factionalized to rally around any current symbols, so instead they chose nineteenth century heroes and events to honor, which provoked no controversy and symbolized the idealism and patriotism the community hoped to emulate. Cuban exiles drew parallels between the heroic efforts to liberate Cuba from Spanish dominion and their own war against another form of tyranny.

The Cuban culture that the emigrés strove to preserve was already somewhat Americanized. Americans had been constantly visible on the island following Cuba's independence, and Cuban speech was littered with American words and expressions. Just as the United States incorporated Cuban cultural forms into its popular culture, particularly in music and dance (the *mambo,* the *cha cha cha,* for example), Cuban sports, entertainment, television, and advertising absorbed American influence. Still, in trying to maintain Cuban culture intact, the emigrés further altered the culture they were trying to preserve. Cultural traditions never pass intact from generation to generation; rather, they are always symbolically reinvented in the present.[27] The emigrés were selective in the customs and values they chose to hold on to, and some traditions were adapted to meet the realities of life in the United States. Social customs such as the chaperoning of young women before marriage were largely abandoned under the Americanizing pressures of the mass media and the public school system. The celebration of the Epiphany (January 6), the traditional holiday on which children receive gifts from the Magi, shared equal billing with or was replaced in importance by a visit from Santa Claus on December 25. Sunday afternoon meals of traditional Cuban foods with one's extended family became irregular events as distance and career pressures prohibited such gatherings. Children forced many accommodations: the older generations may have been concerned with the proper ways of retaining and teaching *cubanidad,* but their children did not always share their ideological passion. They were thoroughly immersed in the non-Cuban world at school, on the playground, and while watching television. They were the most susceptible to the overwhelming pressures to adapt and fit in. Customs and traditions were adapted to fit their needs. Cultural compromises were forged.

In south Florida, as multiple cultures met and sometimes clashed, new traditions were invented, created out of present-day needs and realities. In the early 1980s, for example, the Little Havana Kiwanis Club (itself a cultural compromise) organized the annual Festival de la Calle Ocho, a week-long celebration of Latino food and music, in response to the growing tension between the various Latino groups in Dade County. Modeled loosely after Cuba's annual *comparsas,* the festival celebrated not only *cubanidad* but *hispanidad,* and it became a meeting ground for various groups in south Florida, both Latino and non-Latino. Since then, the festival has become a vital part of community life; it is nationally televised and attracts millions of visitors, more than Miami's other famous institution, the Orange Bowl parade.

Other community traditions were invented in response to events in Cuba. In 1971, for example, when Cuban exiles in Miami learned that

Castro had banned all celebrations of the Epiphany on the island because it interfered with the sugarcane harvest, they responded by organizing the Parada de los Reyes Magos, or the Three Kings Day Parade. The parade has since become an annual celebration, is nationally televised, and is an integral part of community life.

Some of the Cubans' cultural traditions provoked controversy—in particular *santería,* a centuries-old Afro-Cuban syncretic religious cult whose rituals included animal sacrifice.[28] *Santería* practitioners (*santeros*) were highly secretive, even in Cuba, excluding nonpractitioners from their rituals. Some Miamians came to suspect that it was a satanic cult. Whenever the carcasses of dead animals appeared on beaches or in trash bins, residents blamed the *santeros* and complained to police and the local news media. Animal rights activists pressured the local government to ban *santería* rituals as cruelty to animals, while others argued that the improper disposal of animal remains posed a health threat to the county. Race and class also played a role in the public debate. White, middle-class Cubans practiced *santería,* but supporters were more common among blacks and mulattoes of the working class. Emigrés who criticized *santería* tended to be the white elite, who were embarrassed and resentful of the negative attention. When the first official *santería* church, *Lukumi Babalú Aye,* opened in Hialeah in 1987, the city council (with a Cuban majority) passed ordinances forbidding animal sacrifice, essentially shutting the church down. *Santeros* took the city to court, claiming that the ordinances violated their constitutional right to freedom of worship, and after several years of hearings and appeals the U.S. Supreme Court finally ruled on the church's behalf in November 1992.[29]

Also controversial, but for an entirely different reason, was the celebration of *quinceañeras,* a Latin American tradition in which upwardly mobile families celebrate a young girl's fifteenth birthday with a special party that serves as a symbolic rite of passage as well as a "debut," a coming out into society. In front of family and friends, the young woman dances the traditional *vals* (waltz) with her father; afterwards, she dances with her date, accompanied by fourteen other couples (consisting of friends, siblings, and cousins of approximately the same age). Afterwards the guests feast and dance until late in the evening. In Miami, however, the *quinceañera* sometimes assumed exaggerated—and comical—proportions. To show off their new wealth, some families threw lavish affairs costing hundreds of thousands of dollars that were later profiled in the Spanish-language press. These new *quinces* adopted special themes; expensive, Hollywoodesque props and costumes were required. Themes might range from Spanish Colonial to Roaring Twenties to nautical, depending on the whims of the family. Instead of being escorted by her father into the ballroom, as was the custom, a young woman might be carried in on a horse, or in a vintage automobile, or inside a huge clam shell. Instead of wearing the traditional floor-length ball gown, she might dress as Queen Isabella, or a flapper, or a mermaid.

New businesses emerged in Miami to cater to these special events. Choreographers staged and rehearsed dance numbers with the same care as if they were presenting a variety show; seamstresses designed special costumes; musical directors chose and prepared the appropriate music. Non-Cubans (as well as many emigrés) were amazed by the lavishness and absurdity of many of these parties. The majority of *quinceañeras* continued to be celebrated in the traditional conservative fashion, but these "Hollywood" events became most associated with the term in the public consciousness. Not surprisingly, the *quinceañeras* were heavily satirized in Cuban American theater and literature.[30]

Preserving *cubanidad,* then, resulted in both the adaptation and invention of tradition. These customs, rituals, and pageants served a larger ideological purpose, since the raison d'être of the exile community was its political opposition to the Castro government. Celebrations, gatherings, and cultural functions were rich in political symbolism, reminding Cuban exiles of who they were and why they were in the United States. From the playing of the Cuban national anthem at ballgames and ballet recitals to the costumes and floats at the Three Kings Day Parade, every public event reminded the exiles of their distinct cultural identity.[31]

Even manifestations of religious faith were not completely divorced from politics. In 1962, 12,500 people attended the ordination of the first emigré priest in a demonstration of both religious sentiment and political solidarity.[32] Catholic parishes established Spanish-language services not only to accommodate the monolingual and those who preferred to worship in their native tongue, but also to suit a style of worship. At a "Cuban" Mass, emigrés sang the hymns they sang in their parish churches back home, and the priest—usually an exile like themselves—discussed issues important to emigrés in the homilies. The ability to worship in a familiar style offered the emigrés solace but also an opportunity to assert their cultural identity. Catholic lay groups such as the Caballeros de Colon (Knights of Columbus), the Cursillistas (Cursillo Movement), and the Movimiento Familiar Cristiano (Christian Family Movement) were established in Miami both as an expression of faith and because they offered cultural continuity. Throughout the 1960s and 1970s, Cubans gathered in churches and parks for candlelight prayer vigils to pray for political prisoners, or for their loved ones back home, or for Castro's overthrow. On May 31, 1961, for example, thousands gathered at Miami's Bayfront Park to pray for the children of Cuba facing communist indoctrination, as well as to pray for their compatriots in exile who were becoming "apathetic, resigned, and indifferent to the tragedy of Cuba."[33]

Cuban exile devotion to la Virgen de la Caridad del Cobre also exemplified this linking of religion and politics. Like Mexico's Virgen de Guadalupe, Cuba's Virgen de la Caridad (charity) had both religious significance as the mother of Christ and political significance as the symbol of Cuban society's hopes and aspirations.[34] Throughout their history, Cubans had prayed to la Virgen to protect their families and to help their country during periods of great political and economic strife. Now, in exile, they prayed to la Virgen to protect their homeland and to facilitate their return. Many Cubans carried with them a "holy card" of la Virgen, with the caption "Devuelvenos a Cuba" (return Cuba to us). In 1960, several hundred emigrés attended the first celebration of her feast day in exile at Saints Peter and Paul Church in Little Havana. The following year twenty-five thousand attended the mass, which Bishop Coleman F. Carroll celebrated at Miami Baseball Stadium.

Cuban exiles built a shrine in Miami to house a statue of la Virgen that was brought out of Cuba in September 1961.[35] Bishop Carroll proposed the idea for the shrine, the Ermita de la Caridad, during the annual mass in 1966,[36] and the Catholic diocese later donated land on Biscayne Bay, next door to the diocese-owned Mercy Hospital. Over the next seven years, the exile community collected hundreds of thousands of dollars for the shrine's construction. The *municipios* played a crucial role in this fundraising, and the park surrounding the shrine eventually came to be known as *el parque de los municipios*. The new chapel was finally dedicated in December 1973, coinciding, poignantly, with the termination of the freedom flights. As one Cuban exile told me, "That year, we needed the shrine more than ever."

The shrine itself is a study in political symbolism. Underneath the main altar is a large foundation stone molded out of sand and rock from Cuba's various provinces as well as from ocean water taken from a raft on which several Cubans had sailed clandestinely to the United States (a voyage that took fifteen lives). Behind the altar is a sepia-colored mural by Teok Carrasco. It took twenty-four months to complete and occupies more than 747 square feet. It depicts the history of Cuba from the pre-Columbian era to the Castro revolution. The golden cone-shaped roof has six sides, representing Cuba's six provinces prior to the Castro revolution. On the grounds are various symbols of the Cuban heritage: busts of heroes surrounding the chapel, a large Cuban flag outlined on the ground with blue, red, and white stones, *bohíos* surrounding the property, offering visitors shade from the tropical weather. Even the shrine's location is symbolic: like the Statue of Liberty, the Ermita is a distinctive beacon, overlooking the ocean that thousands of Cubans crossed to come to the United States.

Like the shrine of El Cobre in Cuba, where the original statue is housed, the Ermita de la Caridad is the destination of pilgrimages. Cuban exiles go there to light candles for their friends and relatives back in Cuba. The Ermita is one of the first places a Cuban immigrant visits when he arrives in Miami, and political prisoners just released from Castro's prisons celebrate thanksgiving Masses there. Apart from the baptisms, marriages, and funerals that are part of everyday parochial life, the Ermita hosts special masses to commemorate Cuban national holidays; hundreds turn out to hear their priests speak on the timely, difficult virtues of patience and forgiveness.

The most popular event at the shrine, however, is the annual flotilla procession, held since 1960, which celebrates the feast-day of la Virgen de la Caridad del Cobre on September 8. On this day, the statue of Mary is temporarily removed from the Ermita and placed on an elaborately decorated boat, which is then escorted by a procession of yachts and sailboats, also festively decorated, across Biscayne Bay to Miami Marine Stadium. Once the statue arrives at the stadium, an outdoor mass is celebrated. Like other cultural pageants in Miami, this one is also politically charged: the audience waves Cuban flags, sings the hymn to la Virgen de la Caridad (sung to the music of the Cuban national anthem), and recites special prayers for the liberation of Cuba. The guests of honor include former political prisoners, heads of exile organizations, and local elected officials. It is a celebration through which emigrés reaffirm their faith in God, their faith in themselves, and their hope for Cuba's future.

The Exile News Media

A vital news media of Spanish-language periodicals and radio and television stations developed in south Florida to keep Cubans informed on issues that were important to them. Before 1959, only one newspaper, the Nicaraguan-owned *Diario las Américas,* provided news in Spanish to Dade County's Latino community; by the early 1970s, the emigrés published literally hundreds of newspapers, tabloids, and magazines. Though most were centered in Miami, others were published by emigrés in Boston, New Orleans, New York, Union City, Houston, Los Angeles, Wilmington, San Juan, Caracas, Madrid, and even as far away as Luxembourg.

The emigré periodicals focused their news almost entirely on Cuba: emigrés could read about economic shortages on the island, Cuban-Soviet relations, Castro's diplomatic trips, the plight of political prisoners, and Cuban trade, technology, and agricultural production. Articles and editorials were written by some of Cuba's leading journalists in exile, who reestablished the Colegio de Periodistas (College of Journalists), with *en el exilio* appended to the name. The periodicals also relied on reports from UPI and AP, as well as on transcripts from the emigré-run Miami Radio Monitoring Service, which recorded and transcribed transmissions from Cuba's three largest radio stations, Radio Rebelde, Radio Liberación, and Radio Progreso.

Some of the exile periodicals lasted only one issue, while others circulated for over twenty years. Most were available only at newsstands or at Cuban-owned restaurants, bars, and supermarkets. Some charged a nominal price while others were distributed free of charge, the costs of publication underwritten by some exile organization or by advertisers. A number of the periodicals, such as *Alerta, El Mundo, Bohemia, El Avance Criollo, El Imparcial, Isla,* and *Occidente,* had been first published in Cuba; others were the products of exile.

Among the first to begin publication in exile were *Patria* and *Bohemia* (also known as *Bohemia Libre*). First published in 1959 by Ernesto Montaner and Armando García Sifredo, *Patria* reflected the political agenda of the Batistianos. The editors praised the accomplishments of the Batista years, vehemently attacking the new government and all who had aligned themselves—even fleetingly—with the revolutionary process in Cuba. "Our goal is to defend the Cuba of yesterday," wrote García Sifredo, ". . . the pre-Castro Cuba." The editors' hard line against the revolution earned *Patria* the support of Fulgencio Batista, who reportedly financed the newspaper during its first years of operation. The tabloid eventually became self-supporting, however, financed by advertisements for Cuban-owned businesses, some of them owned by Batista supporters.[37] During the 1960s, *Patria* was a vocal critic not only of the Castro regime but of the numerous political groups that emerged in exile. Early on, the editors accurately predicted that political unity in exile would be impossible given the extremes in ideological perspectives.[38]

The news magazine *Bohemia,* on the other hand, targeted those who had supported political change but became disillusioned by the extremism of the revolution. Founded in Havana in 1908 by the Quevedo family, *Bohemia* had once been regarded as the most prominent weekly of the Spanish Caribbean.[39] The magazine became a vocal critic of the Batista government in the 1950s and published editorials in support of Fidel Castro's July 26th Movement. By June 1960, however, after the revolutionary government had taken a more radical turn, Miguel Angel Quevedo, the paper's editor and publisher, began writing editorials critical of communism, which naturally made him unpopular with the new government; he was ultimately forced to seek asylum in the Venezuelan embassy. Soon after his emigration, Quevedo began publication of *Bohemia Libre,* first in New York, later in San Juan, Puerto Rico, and finally in Caracas, where it became the forum for his angry editorials against the Castro regime. During the early 1960s Quevedo encouraged support for the anti-Castro guerrilla forces in the Sierra del Escambray, publishing reports and photographs of their activities. Quevedo's enthusiastic support of Fidel Castro in the 1950s earned him the lasting enmity of the Batistianos; on one occasion, upon hearing that Quevedo was visiting relatives in Miami, the editors of one tabloid encouraged their readers to "pay him a visit" and "render him the honors that were due him."[40] Quevedo remained the publisher of *Bohemia* until 1969, when he committed suicide. After his death, the magazine continued under the direction of Armando de Armas.

The emigré periodicals were as diverse as the emigrés themselves. Civic, cultural, religious, and professional organizations published their own newspapers and *boletines* (newsletters), as did some labor unions, fraternities, and *municipios.* Emigrés also published entertainment and sports magazines, literary and historical journals, and a number of "women's publications" giving advice on child-rearing, housekeeping, fashion, and health. As more and more Cuban women entered the workplace—50.5 percent by 1970—these periodicals also provided them with useful information on the workplace as well as advice on juggling employment, family commitments, and housework.

The most popular—and the most controversial—periodicals were the political tabloids, nicknamed the *periodiquitos* (little newspapers).

Hundreds of them emerged in south Florida, most as propaganda vehicles for the various political organizations in Miami. Newspapers such
as *Girón* (published by the Bay of Pigs Veterans Association), *Alpha*
(Alpha 66), *Guerra* (Movimiento de Recuperación Revolucionaria),
R.E.C.E. (Representación Cubana en el Exilio), and *Trinchera* (Directorio Revolucionario Estudiantil) provided emigrés with updates on the
war against Castro and informed them of upcoming rallies, demonstrations, marches, letter-writing campaigns, boycotts, and lobbying efforts.
Organizations involved in paramilitary actions against Cuba published
photographs of their secret camps or gave detailed accounts of their
military maneuvers to boost morale in the community, and to increase
financial contributions.

The *periodiquitos* varied in style. Some provided serious news coverage, relying on international news wires and respected journalists;
others were sensationalistic, inflammatory, and libelous. Editors of the
latter doctored photographs, misquoted interviewees, and blantantly
labeled all those who did not agree with their political views "communists"; all was fair in the war against Castro. Although all the *periodiquitos*
maintained an anti-Castro, anti-Soviet, anticommunist stance, each interpreted *la problematica cubana* through a distinct political prism. The
editors of *Página,* for example, claimed to represent the interests of the
true Batistianos. In an angry editorial, they said that they had a moral
responsibility to publish their tabloid because all other tabloids were
controlled by those who had "helped the communist system . . . ex-
tinguish all civil liberties."[41] *Trabajo,* on the other hand, claimed to
represent the interests of the Cuban working class: the revolution, they
argued, had betrayed the worker, and the editors articulated a workers'
vision of an egalitarian society.[42]

The rhetoric and symbolism in the *periodiquitos* were powerful. With
names like *Conciencia* (Conscience), *El Clarín* (The bugle), *Centinela
de la Libertad* (Sentinel of liberty), and even *El Gusano,* the *periodiquitos*
played on their readers' emotions and their sense of nationalism. They
referred to Cuba as *la patria sangrienta* (the bleeding nation) and
nuestra patria esclava (our enslaved homeland); the exile community
was referred to as *el pueblo libre de Cuba* (the free people of Cuba). Their
mottos were battlecries: *¡Con Cuba, contra los traidores!* (With Cuba,
against the traitors!); *¡En defensa de nuestros valores tradicionales!* (In
defense of our traditional values!); *¡Sin unidad no hay regreso!* (Without
unity there will be no return!). One editor always ended his essays with
the dateline "Miami, año ____ de la entrega de Cuba a los Rusos"

(Miami, year _____ of Cuba's deliverance to the Russians). Photographs of Castro always showed him at his worst: unshaven and unkempt, scowling, or with a finger up his nose. When Ernesto "Che" Guevara, Castro's friend and fellow revolutionary, was killed in Bolivia, the *periodiquitos* published graphic pictures of el Che's cadaver. Political cartoons ridiculed Castro and his cronies or made poignant comments on the effects of Castro-communism on the homeland.

The *periodiquitos* kept *la causa* in the public consciousness. They published photographs of the Cuban martyrs—those executed by the regime—and printed interviews with their families. They kept the community informed on the increasing number of political prisoners in Cuba as well as on the conditions in the prisons. They published letters from anonymous sources discussing the deteriorating conditions on the island. Concerned about the growing political paralysis in the community, the editors incited their readers to take an active role in the war against Castro. "If you are the type of Cuban who prefers a stroll or a television program to working for your country, then don't waste your time," stated one tabloid, ". . . but if you are one of the valiant and heroic Cubans who follows the path that only has two ends—Death or Liberty—then keep on reading. Meditate on what you read, pass it on, and prepare yourself for the decisive moment."[43] The *periodiquitos* always claimed that Castro's fall was "imminent."

Most *periodiquitos* lasted only a few years, sometimes just a few months. Advertisements usually didn't generate the revenues necessary to cover printing costs, forcing publishers to cut down on paid staff and rely almost entirely on volunteers. Like the paramilitary soldiers, the writers and editors of the *periodiquitos* were totally committed to *la causa*. They put in long hours—often after a full day of work—to ensure that their papers reached the newsstands, diners, and *bodegas*. As one editor wrote, "Only a minority of our compatriots understand our work and our struggle to keep these newspapers circulating. They don't understand that our publications are generated by our patriotism and our indomitable faith in the struggle to defeat Castro and his scumbags. I repeat, our newspapers are not supported by either the FBI or the KGB or Castro's G-2.[44]

The *periodiquitos* elicited a variety of responses in the community. Some, like author Gastón Baquero, called them "heroic journalism" because they promoted and defended *la causa cubana*. Others blasted them for their biased news coverage and vitriolic editorials and turned instead to the American news media or the *Diario* for more objective interpretations. To those who criticized their obsession with Cuba, one tabloid editor responded:

> We realize that many are put off by the fact that we are constantly talking about Cuba. But what else are we going to talk about? What else are we going to write about if we have a responsibility to the cause? . . . We realize that many get upset when you talk to them about Cuba. But what do we care? We do not know how to talk about anything else, nor do we want to talk about anything else.[45]

Of the various newspapers and tabloids that emerged in exile, only one appealed to emigrés of all political persuasions: the humor magazine *Zig-Zag*. Originally founded in Havana in 1941, *Zig-Zag* began publication in Miami in 1962 under the direction of José Manuel Rosenada.[46] *Zig-Zag* provided a few news articles and human-interest stories, but emigrés read the magazine mostly for its political cartoons, anecdotes, jokes, riddles, and puns, which were written and drawn by a large staff of political satirists, among them the famous Silvio (Silvio Fontanilla). *Zig-Zag* poked fun at both the Castro government and the United States: Cuba was spelled "Kuba," Castro was portrayed as a fat and unkempt woman smothered by a lustful Khrushchev, and Uncle Sam was an aging and bewildered figure outwitted by conniving world leaders. The cartoons also satirized such aspects of life in exile as discrimination in housing and employment, the language barrier, and the growing generation gap. By 1966, *Zig-Zag* had a paid circulation of over thirty thousand, and exile political organizations, knowing the value of humor in ideological warfare, air-dropped additional copies (fifty thousand by 1966) into Cuba.[47] *Zig-Zag*'s nonpartisan nature was largely responsible for its success; instead of supporting a particular political faction or leader, the magazine poked fun at Castro, their common enemy. Its success also reflected the emigrés' ability to laugh at themselves despite their predicaments.

The Nicaraguan-owned *Diario las Américas* remained the most popular Spanish-language newspaper, daily or otherwise, in south Florida. It expanded its operations during the 1960s, hiring more journalists and staff, mostly Cuban, and increased its coverage of news relating to Cuba, thereby increasing its circulation not just in Miami but in San Juan, New York, and other cities where emigrés resettled. In the highly politicized milieu of the Cuban exiles, objective news was hard to come by; the emigrés trusted the *Diario* to give them just that. While the publishers were clearly anti-Castro, the *Diario* straddled Little Havana's political fence, careful not to side with any particular faction in the exile community, and it provided a forum for the discussion of opposing political views.

Hoping to corner part of the Spanish-language market, the *Miami Herald* in March 1976 began publication of an insert entitled *El Herald:* the first Spanish section in a major American newspaper. During the 1960s, the *Herald* had expanded its news coverage of Cuba and Latin America in order to appeal to the emigré community, even publishing a few token articles in Spanish, but the emigrés did not subscribe in the anticipated numbers. The editors hoped that *El Herald* would augment the paper's circulation, not just among emigrés but among the growing community of immigrants from the Spanish Caribbean and Latin America.

During its first years, *El Herald* was merely a translation of the parent paper, but it helped to fill the void in serious news coverage. By 1979 *El Herald* was delivered to over thirty-six thousand households. Circulation doubled over the next five years, but the editors remained dissatisfied with the numbers. Part of the problem lay with how the *Herald* was perceived in the exile community: while the newspaper was staunchly anti-Castro, it took a strong stand against many issues important to exiles—criticizing, for example, the commando raids and the political intimidation practiced by the exile media and many exile organizations. The more conservative element of the community nicknamed the newspaper the "Moscow Herald." Many emigrés also felt that the newspaper tended to portray Cubans in a negative light.

In December 1987 Knight-Ridder, the publisher, revamped *El Herald* again, turning it into an independent newspaper, *El Nuevo Herald.* Delivery of the *Miami Herald* included *El Nuevo Herald* if requested, but it was possible to receive the latter separately. Under its new mandate, *El Nuevo Herald*'s staff expanded its local, national, and international news coverage and published articles by prizewinning Latin American journalists. Over the years renowned intellectuals such as Jorge Luis Borges, Guillermo Cabrera Infante, Carlos Fuentes, and Mario Vargas Llosa contributed op-ed pieces. The newspaper included translations of *Miami Herald* news articles, but the majority of the articles and editorials were independently produced. Politically, the paper's editorial positions on Cuban issues were moderate, similar to those of the *Miami Herald,* but compared with the other Spanish-language newspapers in the city, including the *Diario, El Nuevo Herald* was fairly liberal.

By 1990, *El Nuevo Herald* had a daily circulation of 102,289 and a Sunday circulation of 118,799. That same year, *El Nuevo Herald*'s publisher, Roberto Suárez, whose first job in exile was as a bundler in the *Herald* mail room for $1.56 an hour, was appointed president of the Miami Herald Publishing Company.[48]

Of the various Spanish-language media in south Florida, radio had by far the largest audience and the greatest influence. As early as 1963, three local radio stations in Miami allotted a few hours each day to Spanish-language broadcasts, usually in the evening or after midnight. These stations hired popular Cuban radio personalities and modeled their programming after old radio shows in Havana. One, WMIE-AM, became the first station in Miami to broadcast completely in Spanish, renaming itself WQBA, "La Cubanísima" (the most Cuban). In 1965, WQBA was joined by another Spanish-language radio station, WFAB, "La Fabulosa." The first Cuban-owned station, named WRHC-Cadena Azul after an old Cuban station, went on the air in 1973, eventually transmitting in Spanish twenty-four hours a day. Several other stations followed in the next two decades.

Spanish-language radio became an integral part of the day-to-day life of the exiles. "*La radio* is an institution in Miami," wrote Heberto Padilla, ". . . a vice like smoking or playing dominoes, something that Cubans in Miami cannot live without."[49] During the 1960s, Cubans tuned in to Radio Reloj each morning to hear news from around the world, just like they had back in Cuba. In their cars, at work, and at home, they listened to passionate editorials, interviews with civic and political leaders, musical and comedy programs, an occasional soap opera. For those who spoke no English, radio served as an important link with the American world. Radio announcers provided information on community services and answered questions about taxes, health care, education, the legal system, and even the weather. Interpreting the new and often hostile environment for the emigrés, they tried to tell emigrés what to think, or reinforced what they already believed.

Cuban radio reflected the more conservative views in the community. Editorials were staunchly anti-Castro and anticommunist, opposing a political rapprochement with Cuba and the lifting of the U.S. trade embargo, and supporting the emigrés' paramilitary campaigns against the Cuban government. The radio announcers developed a style all their own, becoming known for their dramatic delivery of the news. The various radio personalities—almost all of them men—developed loyal audiences, over whom they exerted much influence; they could organize marches and demonstrations at a moment's notice and rally hundreds of their listeners to action. As early as 1965, the Federal Communications Commission fined WMIE (WQBA) and reprimanded two other stations for "incit[ing] local Cuban refugees to riot."[50] Twenty years later, such charges were still common: in 1986, a Cuban DJ was arrested for inciting a riot between emigrés supporting the Nicaraguan Contras and demonstrators from the South Florida Peace Coalition who were protesting U.S. policy in Nicaragua.[51]

The commentators frequently resorted to name-calling when their views were challenged, accusing politicians, intellectuals, and community leaders of "dubious politics" and of being *comunistas,* or questioning their sexual orientation. Because emigrés trusted the radio commentators, their accusations often had serious consequences; individuals attacked on the radio often found themselves harassed or accosted by listeners or had their businesses boycotted. In the 1970s and 1980s, the FCC received dozens of complaints from radio listeners who accused Cuban commentators of rudeness (djs often hung up on callers who disagreed with their views), political bias, racism, libel, and slander.[52] Others, particularly non-Cuban Latinos, were distressed by the obsession with Castro and Cuba. As one Puerto Rican listener told me, "You'd think that damn island was the center of the universe."

By the late 1980s, some ten Spanish-language radio stations broadcast in south Florida, four of them predominantly news stations: WQBA, WAQI, WRHC, and WOCN. WQBA consistently had the largest audience of any station in south Florida.[53] The news stations became very sophisticated in their programming, hiring well-known political analysts and intellectuals to offer commentaries on Cuba and Latin America. Radio personalities interviewed local and national politicians on the air and played taped broadcasts from Nicaragua, Angola, and other troubled areas connected in some way to Cuba or the exile community. The stations created various gimmicks to compete for listeners: trivia contests, call-in shows debating the issues of the day, and free advertising segments during which callers advertised services, second-hand items, and even jobs. Over the years, the Cuban stations also sponsored *radio maratónes* to raise money for scholarships, local charities, community service projects, and refugee aid, and sometimes for political organizations and the war against Castro. Perhaps the best indication of Cuban radio's influence is the fact that the Castro government repeatedly tried to jam their signals to prevent them from being heard on the island.[54]

By 1970, emigrés in south Florida also had their own Spanish-language television station, WLTV-Channel 23, an affiliate of the Spanish International Network (later renamed Univisión), which provided viewers with a steady fare of soap operas, community service programs, documentaries, and newscasts. During the 1960s and 1970s, the station began and ended each day's broadcast with the Cuban national anthem and a minute-long film of familiar landmarks such as El Malecón, El Parque Central, and La Habana Vieja. The quality of WLTV's programming, like that of the radio stations, improved with time and experience. By the 1980s, Channel 23 received higher ratings than any other station in Dade County, including the local affiliates of ABC, NBC, and CBS. In 1986, WLTV took twenty-three Emmy nominations—more than double the number of any other station in south Florida.[55] Two other Spanish stations emerged in south Florida in the 1980s: Channel 51, the Miami affiliate of the Hispanic Broadcasting Network (now Telemundo), and an independent station, Channel 40, known as TeleMiami.

The Emergence
of a Cuban American Identity

As early as the 1970s, there was evidence of a shift in the emigré community, as Cubans began to perceive themselves as permanent residents rather than temporary visitors, as immigrants rather than refugees. This shift in consciousness—attributable, in part, to the termination of the freedom flights, which forced many emigrés to come to terms with their status in the United States—was especially evident in three areas: the economic success of the Cuban community in south Florida; the growing number of exiles seeking naturalization; and their new involvement in domestic politics and civic affairs.

As the Cubans bought homes, built businesses, paid taxes, and sent their children to school, they established ties to their communities in spite of their original intentions. In south Florida they created a thriving economic enclave that absorbed each new wave of immigration from Cuba as well as from elsewhere in Latin America.[56] By 1980, emigrés in Dade County generated close to $2.5 billion in income each year. Forty-four percent of the nearly five hundred thousand Cubans living in greater Miami were professionals, company managers, business owners, skilled craftsmen, or retail sales and clerical personnel, and eighteen thousand businesses were Cuban-owned. Sixty-three percent of emigrés owned their own homes.[57] The figures improved with each year, and by the early 1990s over twenty-five thousand businesses in Dade County were Latino-owned, making south Florida home to the most prosperous Latino community in the United States.[58] In both the 1980 and 1990 censuses, Cubans also exhibited the highest income and educational levels of the three major Latino groups, levels only slightly below the national average—a notable accomplishment for a community of first-generation immigrants.[59]

The Cubans' success could be attributed to several factors. Cuban women had a high rate of participation in the labor force; as early as 1970, they constituted the largest proportionate group of working women in the United States.[60] Women expanded their roles to include wage-earning not as a response to the feminist movement or the social currents of the 1960s but to ensure the economic survival of their families. The structure of the Cuban household, with three generations living under one roof, also ensured success because it encouraged economic cooperation.[61] The elderly contributed to the family's economic well-being both directly, with salaries, refugee aid, and Social Security checks, or indirectly, by raising children and assuming household responsibilities. These factors, along with the Cubans' low fertility rates and high levels of school completion, facilitated the family's structural assimilation.

In the community, the Cubans created prosperous businesses, built with the skills and capital of the middle- and upper-class emigrés who comprised the first wave of immigrants. The wealthy elite had money invested in American banks at the time of the revolution, and when they settled in Miami they invested that capital in new business ventures. The middle-class emigrés lacked that kind of capital, but they did have the skills and business know-how with which to create lucrative businesses. They identified the needs in the community and built businesses catering to those needs, with the assistance of loans from local banks or the Small Business Administration and long hours of work by family members. As their businesses expanded, these emigrés took on additional employees, almost always their compatriots. Thus, south Florida became home to a thriving business community that provided job opportunities for the new immigrants who arrived each year, easing their assimilation into the economic mainstream.[62]

The Cuban presence attracted international investment and helped convert Miami into a major trade and commercial center linking North and South America. By 1980, thirteen major banks and over one hundred multinational corporations had established regional offices in the Miami area. Between 1977 and 1980 the port of Miami, which had already replaced New Orleans as the chief port of trade with Latin America, tripled its ship passenger traffic. From 1975 to 1980, air passenger traffic at Miami International Airport increased 100 percent and air cargo traffic 250 percent, making it the ninth busiest airport in the world in passenger traffic and sixth busiest in cargo traffic. During the same period, exports and imports increased by close to 150 percent.[63]

As early as the 1960s, the national news media, particularly popular magazines such as *Life, Fortune,* and *Newsweek,* celebrated the Cubans' business acumen and mythologized the "Cuban success story." Articles with titles like "To Miami, Refugees Spell P-R-O-S-P-E-R-I-T-Y" and "Cuban Refugees Write a U.S. Success Story" proclaimed the Cubans to be "golden immigrants" and the newest Horatio Algers.[64] In an era of social upheaval and disillusionment, when Americans questioned and discarded old values and perspectives, the Cubans seemed to prove that the American Dream was strong and intact. News of the Cubans' apparent success helped ease any misgivings Americans might have had about giving these people asylum or spending millions of taxpayers' dollars on refugee aid.

The "Cuban success story," however, overlooked the fact that many Cubans did not share in the community's wealth, as well as the fact that their success, while substantial, was less spectacular than the rags-to-riches stories promoted by the popular media.[65] Despite the large middle and upper classes and the comprehensive federal assistance pumped into the community, Cuban income still remained below the national average (albeit slightly) and a significant percentage of Cubans lived in poverty.[66] Working class emigrés, like other Americans, struggled for better wages, benefits, and working conditions, as well as job security, particularly if they were women. Black Cubans experienced discrimination from both their white compatriots and the larger society, and as late as 1990 their income lagged behind that of white Cubans by almost 40 percent.[67] As one editorial in an exile newspaper said:

> Many think that all exiles are rich; and it's not that way. . . . Ninety percent of exiles in Miami work in the factories or other such workplaces. They are all workers—some at a higher rank—but they are all workers. It is for these people that we publish our newspaper, so that they will learn

American laws and realize that they don't have to be exploited . . . and many of them are exploited, especially by Cuban bosses.[68]

Nevertheless, the Cuban success story enjoyed wide circulation within the exile community: the Cubans made the story an essential element of their collective identity. Rather than focusing on those who had not assimilated economically, they focused on those who had—and there *were* plenty Horatio Algers in the community. To do otherwise would have been to give Fidel Castro propaganda to use against them. They wanted to prove to their compatriots back home what could be accomplished. That the community had accomplished so much in so little time, they argued, was a testimony to the old-fashioned values of thrift, hard work, and perseverance, and a symbol that God was on their side. The U.S. news media celebrated the Cubans' adoption of the Puritan work ethic, but for the emigrés it was simply the exile work ethic. Their strong anticommunism and their economic prosperity were the two characteristics they took the most pride in and promoted about themselves. Their success within the American mainstream was an indictment of the revolution, the best revenge a *gusano* could have.

But not all Cubans were comfortable with the community's success. Some emigrés accused their countrymen of sacrificing *la causa cubana* for the comforts of exile: if they had invested as much time in assisting the counterrevolution as they had in climbing the economic ladder, went the argument, they could have all returned to Cuba within a matter of years. "The dollar sign has destroyed the patriotic values of many," lamented one editorial.[69] Another warned that economic success was "prostituting the combative spirit of the exile community . . . distracting our youth from working on behalf of our slave country."[70] Yet another editor wrote, "We exchanged the committed, militant exile of [1961] for the present apathetic exile, committed only to dances and festivities."[71] For these and other exiles, the economic success of the community signified a denial of their responsibilities toward Cuba.

Nowhere was the theme of national allegiance more evident than in the debate over naturalization, a debate carried out in homes and offices, in newspapers and on the radio, throughout the 1960s and 1970s. Many Cubans were completely opposed to the idea of applying for U.S. citizenship. Some even resented that their children were forced to swear allegiance to the American flag at school. Many Cubans believed that becoming an American citizen meant assuming a new identity, emotionally erasing any memory of life prior to taking the oath of citizenship.

The oath was a symbolic act by which they renounced allegiance to their homeland, their heritage, and their people; as one individual wrote, "How can I ever forget my language, my customs, my folklore? How can I honestly forget my past?"[72] Becoming a citizen meant that they had failed *la causa cubana* and compromised their ideals. They would no longer be exiles but rather ethnic Americans. In an effort to remind exiles of their responsibilities, the *periodiquitos* dedicated a number of issues in the early 1970s to defining the concepts of *patria* (nation) and *cubanidad*.

College students were particularly caught up in this debate over identity and national allegiance. Many had left Cuba as teenagers, and they were acutely aware that they straddled two cultures. At the University of Miami, Miami-Dade Community College, the University of Florida at Gainesville, and other universities around the country, Cuban students joined organizations such as the Federación de Estudiantes Cubanos and the Agrupación Estudiantil Abdala (known more commonly as Abdala)[73] to discuss issues of nationality, identity, culture, and their responsibilities toward Cuba. They tried to define *cubanidad* for themselves. "Young people who wish to identify themselves as Cuban face many difficulties in exile," wrote one student in *Antorcha*, the Cuban Students Federation publication at the University of Miami:

> I am not referring to the obvious problem of having to choose whether one is Cuban or American, but rather to a more subtle (and perhaps more dangerous) conflict, which is distinguishing between *cubanía* and being Cuban-like. It is one thing to be concerned about the people who share one's language and origin, to be genuinely concerned with Cuba. It is quite another thing to think that one is Cuban simply because one likes *arroz con frijoles* or reads a Spanish-language newspaper in the afternoons. It is best to do both.[74]

Some students became more staunchly nationalistic than their parents, and they castigated the community for forfeiting its ideals. One editorial in *Antorcha* challenged its readers: "We must ask ourselves why we came to Miami. To contribute to its growth? To become involved in its politics? To make money? Did we leave Cuba as emigrants? . . . While we should be proud of being Cubans we should be ashamed of not having a country."[75] Others appealed to their compatriots' sense of *cubanidad*, warning them that the traditions and values they took most pride in would eventually die in the United States. "The Cuban family will be destroyed on foreign soil. . . . It is only in Cuba that we can preserve her."[76] Not surprisingly, many students, particularly those affiliated with Abdala, became more deeply involved in the war against Castro.

Many Cubans, however, saw no contradiction in being both exiles and citizens of the United States. Tangible legal, professional, and economic benefits could be derived from U.S. citizenship; Cuban professionals in particular realized that in order to practice their careers they had to meet state licensing requirements, and permanent residency or citizenship was always a prerequisite. But it was more than just economic considerations that led many Cubans to apply for citizenship. As they resigned themselves to a lengthy stay in the United States, they developed a sense of loyalty to the country that gave them refuge, and citizenship seemed a logical step.

The *Miami Herald* reported in 1974 that approximately two hundred thousand Cubans had sought U.S. citizenship.[77] In late 1975, Cuban professionals, led by media personality Manolo Reyes, initiated a citizenship drive, the Cubans for American Citizenship Campaign, with the goal of registering ten thousand new citizens in celebration of the United States Bicentennial. Members of the steering committee recruited exiles, helped them fill out the necessary papers, and taught courses in schools to help them prepare for the examinations. The campaign surpassed its goal: on just one day—July 4, 1976—more than sixty-five hundred Cubans swore the oath of citizenship, and by the end of the year 26,275 exiles had become U.S. citizens.[78] The campaign continued throughout the late 1970s. By 1980, 55 percent of the eligible Cubans in Dade County were American citizens, compared to just 25 percent in 1970.[79] Even with their new legal status, however, these new citizens continued to regard themselves as Cuban exiles— and they would always maintain this dual identity. Their ties to Cuba were unseverable.

During the 1970s, the local news media, and in particular the *Miami Herald,* monitored the sentiments of the exile community. In the aftermath of the Civil Rights Movement, the media tried to reflect the concerns of ethnic minorities and to study the relationships between the different groups in the community. The *Herald* commissioned various polls and surveys to determine how well the Cubans were adapting to life in the United States. Did they feel accepted? Did they want to return to Cuba? Did they object to the reestablishment of diplomatic relations with the Castro government? Many of the surveys yielded surprising results: a 1972 poll revealed that while 97 percent of the

Cubans interviewed felt that they had been accepted in Miami, 62 percent were less satisfied with their lives in the U.S. than with the lives they had led in Cuba.[80] The termination of the freedom flights, however, proved to be a turning point in the exiles' attitudes toward Cuba and the United States. A study by sociologists Clark and Mendoza in 1972 showed that close to 79 percent of the Cubans interviewed wanted to return to Cuba once Castro was overthrown, but two years later, less than half expressed the same desire.[81] Another study by Portes and Mozo yielded similar results: in 1973, 60 percent of those interviewed reported plans to return to Cuba once Fidel Castro fell, but by 1979 less than one-fourth wanted to return.[82]

The Cubans' growing involvement in civic affairs and local politics also revealed a shift in consciousness. In 1965, seventeen Cuban businessmen created the Cámara de Comercio Latina (Latin American Chamber of Commerce), or *CAMACOL,* to lobby on behalf of Dade's Latino business community before the Metro–Dade County Commission and the state legislature. In 1970, emigrés created the Cuban National Planning Council to study domestic (U.S.) issues that were important to Cubans, including language, education, health care, and employment. A Cuban ran for the mayoral seat as early as 1967, two ran for the city commission in 1969, and another five ran for various public offices in 1971. All were unsuccessful, but in 1973 two veterans of the Bay of Pigs invasion were elected to public office, Manolo Reboso to the City Commission and Alfredo Duran to the Dade County School Board. The city of Sweetwater also became the first city in south Florida to elect a Cuban-born mayor.

Another example of the Cubans' growing influence in Dade County was the Bilingual-Bicultural Ordinance of April 1973. The resolution designated Spanish as the county's second official language and called for the establishment of a Department of Bilingual and Bicultural Affairs, the translation of county documents into Spanish, and increased efforts to recruit Latinos to county jobs.[83] The passage of such an ordinance by a board comprised entirely of non-Latinos demonstrated a recognition of the role Cubans and other Latinos were playing in the local community, and would play in the years to come. As the resolution declared, "Our Spanish-speaking population has earned, through its ever increasing share of the tax burden, and active participation in community affairs, the right to be serviced and heard at all levels of government."[84] (The resolution was repealed in 1980 in the aftermath of Mariel, but reinstated in 1993.)

Over the next decade, the Cubans' political accomplishments were even more impressive. Cubans came to occupy positions in the local, state, and national government, as well as key positions in the key institutions of Miami and Dade County. At the same time, they continued to be actively concerned with the political affairs of their homeland just ninety miles away. Whether they called themselves Cuban exiles or Cuban Americans, it was clear that the emigrés had carved a niche for themselves in their country of refuge and were satisfactorily resolving the question of identity—at least for themselves.

Redefining the Exile Identity in the 1980s and 1990s

The Cubans who arrived in 1980 via Mariel had a profound impact on the emigré community culturally. As these new immigrants struggled to define their own identity in exile, the stories they told, the questions they asked, and the experiences they had in the United States forced the more established emigrés to redefine what it meant to be Cuban in a country other than Cuba. The Cubans of Mariel, with their slightly different accents, their sometimes "foreign" names (Vladimir, Ivana, Milos), and their very different perceptions of Cuba and the revolution, reminded them that, over the course of a generation, Cuban culture had developed in different ways on opposite sides of the Florida Straits.

While the older emigrés at first feared and resented the new arrivals for the negative media attention they attracted, over time they developed a grudging respect for their compatriots. Despite the tremendous odds against them, the Cubans of Mariel made modest economic gains over the next decade and revealed the same democratic and entrepreneurial spirit as those who arrived earlier. The courage and passion they demonstrated at the Peruvian embassy, at El Mosquito holding camp, and in confronting the *actos de repudio* were now channeled into forging a new life for themselves in the United States. By 1986, more than one-fourth of the immigrants were self-employed, and in the three-year period from 1983 to 1986 their unemployment was halved, from 27 percent to 13.6 percent. By 1990, only 5.6 percent were unemployed, a rate comparable to that of the rest of the nation.[85]

The children of Mariel exhibited the most astounding success of all.[86] More than eleven thousand children enrolled in Dade County schools in the wake of the boatlift, and while none of them spoke English when they arrived, by 1987 only 8 percent required instruction in the bilingual education program known as ESOL (English for Speakers of Other Languages). In 1987, Cubans of Mariel presented the valedictory speeches at two Dade County high schools, and the number of *marielito* high school students going on to college was comparable to the rate for emigrés who arrived earlier. As one writer noted in the *Miami Herald*, the children of Mariel duplicated the success of the previous waves of refugees with only half of the benefits.[87]

A survey in April 1990, sponsored by the *Herald* and WTVJ–Channel 4 on the tenth anniversary of the boatlift, revealed that the *marielitos* were much like their compatriots politically as well. They advocated continuing international pressure on the Castro government as a means of bringing about democratic reforms, and thus opposed ending the U.S. trade embargo against the island. Like the Cubans who arrived earlier, they also strongly identified with the Republican Party, since the latter's foreign policy agenda was perceived to be more staunchly anticommunist. They had not exercised any political leverage, however: few Mariel Cubans had voted, since less than five percent were naturalized.[88]

The Mariel Cubans were to some extent a liberalizing influence on the emigré community. The earlier exiles generally supported traditionally "liberal" issues such as universal health care and a woman's right to abortion, but the *marielitos* did so in even greater numbers.[89] Having lived in a socialist economy for twenty years, they had a different perception of the responsibilities of the state and thus tended to favor government intervention. The Mariel Cubans also promoted a more balanced interpretation of the revolution that acknowledged both its accomplishments and its failures. While they readily complained about the lack of civil liberties in Cuba, they also acknowledged the benefits of *la revolución,* particularly widespread access to education and health care. The Cubans of Mariel were equally vocal in their evaluations of U.S. society. While the older emigrés, for ideological reasons, tended to shut their eyes to the limitations of a capitalist democracy, the Cubans of Mariel were more likely to weigh its pros and cons against those of Cuba. Life in Miami shocked many of them, and they criticized their compatriots for their selective memories. Some emigrés accused the new immigrants of being indoctrinated—but others were compelled to rethink their views of Cuba and the United States.

The Cubans of Mariel also brought a new energy to the community. They exhibited great pride and solidarity in the face of public hostility. They revitalized the cultural landscape, strengthening the use of Spanish in the community and reintroducing various customs and traditions. They created their own organizations, such as the Casa de la Cultura Cubana, the activities of which included a yearly "pilgrimage" to Key West to commemorate their migration.[90] They published their own magazines, such as *Revista Mariel* (later renamed *Mariel Magazine*), which became a vehicle for their literary talents. Several of Cuba's leading artists, musicians, writers, and intellectuals came to the United States via Mariel, sparking a renaissance in Cuban arts and letters and giving voice to a new generation of exiles. The presence of Reinaldo Arenas, Roberto Valero, Juan Abreu, Miguel Correa, Carlos Alfonzo, Andrés Valerio, Víctor Gómez, Eduardo Michaelsen, and others, in some sense validated this migration: they proved to both American society and the emigré community that the boatlift population was also comprised of Cuba's most creative and talented individuals. Ten years after the boatlift, *marielito* had ceased to be a pejorative, and many of the new immigrants now used the term as a symbol of pride and defiance to distinguish themselves from the earlier emigrés, whom they regarded as corrupt or too Americanized. Artists and writers, in particular, used the term to symbolize their unique experience, identity, and even style.

Contact with the Cubans of Mariel (along with the "family reunification trips") forced many emigrés to come to terms with their estranged relationship with Cuba. Many realized that the Cuba they remembered no longer existed and that their future role in their homeland was uncertain. Consequently, some propelled themselves more energetically into the campaign to topple Castro, while others further immersed themselves in—or resigned themselves to—life outside of Cuba. Increased contact with the new Cuba also forced them to reexamine their ties to the United States. Many ceased to refer to the U.S. as *el exilio:* now more than ever, it was home.

Of course, for the generation raised in the United States, it had always been home. While they feel a connection to Cuba, the members of this generation are not, for the most part, as passionately committed to Cuba or *la causa* as their parents. They are bilingual, but English is the language of choice.[91] One emigré who left Cuba as a child articulated a common view of her generation: "My roots are here. I am always happy to come back [to Miami]. I went to school here. I've been here since I was ten years old. I remember vaguely about Cuba, about my house, the street where I lived, the places I went . . . but if you left me in Havana, forget it. . . . It would be like leaving me in a foreign country."[92] The press calls this generation the Yucas: Young Upwardly-mobile Cuban Americans. The older generation, however, jokes that they are as bland as the vegetable from which they take their name. "Despite all our efforts," said one elderly emigré, ". . . our children are more American than Cuban. Their lives are different from mine. Sometimes I don't understand them at all. . . . And *their* children don't speak Spanish at all. It's a shame."[93]

As early as the 1970s, a bilingual television comedy entitled "¿Que Pasa, USA?" was shown on many affiliates of PBS, poking fun at the growing generation gap in the Cuban family. The sitcom revolved around three generations living in the same household and the social, cultural, and linguistic tensions between them. Although the family was Cuban, Latinos of all nationalities and age groups easily related to the problems of this household, and non-Latino viewers learned to empathize with the problems of their neighbors and co-workers.

Cuban exiles and Cuban Americans of all generations have come to realize that their community has some of the best elements of both countries. They are able to express their cultural values—their *cubanidad*—in a politically stable environment that offers numerous social and economic opportunities. The first-generation exiles were forced to leave their homeland and adapt their customs and traditions to the realities of life in the United States, but in the process they forged a hybrid society, a uniquely Cuban-American culture. *Marielitos* found the emigrés to be too Americanized, but Cuban Miami was still familiar enough to accommodate them, along with the thousands of other emigrés who chose to resettle there in the middle and late 1980s. Miami had become Havana USA: the border town between Cuba and the United States.

During the 1980s and 1990s, the emigrés learned to view their experience within a broader historical context. While they perceived themselves and their migration as an essential component of Cuban history, they came to realize that they were an important part of U.S. history as well, and a movement emerged within the community to document their experience in the United States. Emigrés expanded the Cuban exile archives at the two major universities in south Florida; they founded a Museum of Cuban Art and Culture in Little Havana to celebrate not only the art and history of the homeland but emigré culture as well; and they lobbied for the preservation of buildings important to their history, among them Freedom Tower. The emigrés renamed streets in Miami after their own present-day heroes, such as baseball star José Canseco, entertainer Gloria Estéfan, and salsa performer Celia Cruz. More and more Cubans distinguished themselves in U.S. politics, sports, and the entertainment industry, serving also as symbols around which the community could rally. Emigrés no longer had to rely on dead heroes from the nineteenth-century wars of independence. They had their own story to tell.

CHAPTER 4

The Evolution
of Cuban Exile Politics

The political culture of the exile community in south Florida evolved in response to events in both Cuba and the United States. Cuban emigrés engaged in both exile politics and ethnic politics: as exiles, they tried to shape the political reality in the homeland, and as immigrant citizens they tried to shape their local environment.

In some ways, the post-1959 emigrés were not unlike the Cubans who immigrated in the nineteenth century. The Cubans who came after 1868, for example, zealously contributed to their homeland's struggle for independence while at the same time joining the U.S. political and economic mainstream. The post-1959 Cuban exiles also assumed this dual role. In their struggle to liberate Cuba from communism, they considered themselves to be the twentieth century equivalents of the earlier emigrés, and they tried to establish a symbolic continuum between the two independence efforts. At the same time, the emigrés have become an active part of the political and economic culture of south Florida. Many emigrés might ultimately choose to return to Cuba one day, but many others will remain in the United States, as earlier emigrés have. They have invested time and energy here; some have spent more years living in south Florida than in Cuba. Cuba is the homeland, but Miami is home.

The line between Cuban exile politics and Cuban ethnic politics was often blurred. During the 1960s, Cubans were almost exclusively concerned with overthrowing Castro and with returning to the homeland, a campaign that at times received U.S. financial support. Their paramilitary campaigns earned south Florida a reputation as the cold war capital of the United States. Any tactic was justified in the war against

Castro; the exile community was often as repressive and authoritarian as the government they sought to overthrow. There was little tolerance of those who favored an accommodation of the Castro government. Each passing year, however, made returning to Cuba less probable, and the emigrés eventually focused more and more attention on improving their lives in the United States. Involvement in local, state, and national politics increased, and the Cubans demonstrated high voter turnouts in political elections. The emigrés never completely abandoned their war against Castro, but they did alter their tactics in ways that reflected their growing adaptation to the United States. They sought to influence Cuban affairs but more and more they did so as Americans, working within the U.S. political system. The commitment to *la causa cubana* meant not that they necessarily wanted to return to Cuba but that, like the Jews, the Irish, the Hungarians, and countless other immigrants in the United States, they felt an emotional commitment to their country of origin.

Like other cultural expressions, emigré politics in south Florida became a hybrid, reflecting both Cuban and American elements. Emigrés became quite adept at getting bills passed through Congress and lobbying for tougher economic sanctions against the Castro government. An aspiring emigré politician in south Florida learns how to conduct an effective election campaign *a la americana*—hiring strategists, public relations and media representatives, pollsters, and fashion consultants. But the passionate delivery of his or her speech (in both English and Spanish), and the style of the rhetoric itself, is very Cuban. Emigré politicians, like other ethnic politicians, are chameleons who can change personas depending on their audience. But all these tactics are for naught if their views on Cuba are out of line with those of the community: a suspected Castro sympathizer has little chance of being elected to any office in Dade County, even the school board. In a community of largely first-generation immigrants for whom the memory of revolution is an open wound, Cuba plays a tremendous role in public debate and consciousness.

A number of sociologists have written that the political solidarity of the community, as expressed in its opposition to the Castro regime, contributed to the success of the Cuban enclave.[1] Certainly, as noted in chapter 3, the emigrés' identification as exiles and their commitment to *la causa cubana* strengthened them psychologically and encouraged them to succeed in the United States. The politics of Cuban exiles and Cuban Americans were hardly monolithic, however; a broad range of political perspectives coexisted within anti-Castroism. The emigrés differed in their visions of a post-Castro Cuba, and they differed in the tactics they considered legitimate in the war against Castro. A segment of the community abandoned the war altogether, preferring instead dialogue and negotiation as a way of encouraging meaningful change in Cuba. The Cuban exiles are usually stereotyped as conserva-tive, but the Latino National Political Survey conducted by Temple University in the early 1990s revealed that 45.5 percent of naturalized Cubans identified themselves as "moderate" or "liberal."[2] And those who favor a hard line against Castro are often liberal on domestic issues, further blurring the political categories.

Eisenhower, Kennedy, and the Exiles' War Against Castro

Before the end of 1959, attempts to overthrow the rev-olutionary government had already begun. Groups such as the Segundo Frente del Escambray and the Directorio Revolucionario Estudiantil, which had fought along with Castro's July 26th Movement to overthrow Batista in the 1950s, now turned their wrath against their former com-rades in arms over the perceived betrayal of the original goals of the revolution. New groups joined the fight, such as the Movimiento de Recuperación Revolucionario and the Movimiento Revolucionario del Pueblo, comprised of former supporters or members of the revolutionary government. These groups established an underground rebel force that conducted a campaign of violence and destruction in both rural and urban areas, hoping to weaken the new government and pressure the population to support a counterrevolution. Their chief target was the Cuban econ-omy, and they bombed or torched important sugar and tobacco mills, factories, seaports, and other centers of economic activity. They raided police and government offices, jails, and military installations, destroyed water mains and farm machinery, and sabotaged railways and bridges. Bands of guerrilla fighters once again emerged in the Escambray moun-tains, this time to take on Castro's new revolutionary army.[3]

The Cuban underground extended across the Florida Straits to Mi-ami. Throughout Cuba's history, from the 19th-century wars of inde-pendence to the revolution of the 1950s, rebel groups had received their financial and moral support from exiles living in the United States, particularly in Florida, and the new counterrevolutionary groups were no exception. They sent representatives to Miami to garner support for their cause, and they received much of their food and armaments from expatriates, who flew clandestinely over the Escambray mountains to drop the necessary supplies, or smuggled them into the country by boat.

The counterrevolutionary activities conducted on the U.S. mainland violated U.S. neutrality, and the U.S. government cracked down on several operations.[4] However, as U.S.–Cuba relations deteriorated during late 1959 and 1960, and as Cuba aligned itself ideologically and economically with the Soviet Union, China, and the Eastern bloc countries, the Eisenhower administration began exploring ways of using the counterrevolutionaries to rid the hemisphere of the "Cuba problem." On March 17, 1960, President Eisenhower officially approved CIA plans to recruit and train a Cuban exile army to invade the island and overthrow the Castro government with the help of the Cuban underground. The CIA established recruiting offices in south Florida, most notably at the University of Miami, and volunteers were sent to training camps in Guatemala, Nicaragua, and other points around the Caribbean to prepare for an invasion tentatively scheduled for early 1961.

The CIA tried to form a provisional government out of the myriad of political groups that emerged in exile, each plotting Castro's overthrow, several of them operating underground in Cuba as well.[5] The CIA realized that it would have to unify at least some of these different factions if the invasion was to be successful.

Broadly speaking, there were three political leanings in the exile community. The right wing wanted a conservative, authoritarian government like that of the Batista dictatorship of 1952–58; the political center favored a return to the democratic process as guaranteed under the constitution of 1940 and included many supporters of the Grau San Martín and Prío Socarrás administrations of 1944–52; and the left wing consisted of those who supported social, economic, and political change, including former supporters of the July 26th Movement and other rebel groups. Within these general political groupings, various factions coalesced around either some charismatic individual or some pressing issue or concern; hence, by 1960, there were close to fifty different political factions, and the numbers continued to increase.[6] The CIA contacted the more popular of these groups and persuaded them to put their political and personal differences aside to unite under a common front, from which a provisional government in Cuba might eventually be formed. Such a front had to offer a viable alternative to the Castro regime—one that would appeal to those who had supported the revolution but were concerned about Marxism—and so the exiles were urged to restrict membership to those of the Center and the Left. While the brigade that was to carry out the invasion included former Batistianos, the exile front was told to exclude them.[7]

Emerging as the principal leaders of the Frente Revolucionario Democrático were Manuel Artime Buesa, former official of Castro's Institute for Agrarian Reform (INRA) and now the representative of the Movimiento de Recuperación Revolucionario (MRR) in Miami; Justo Carrillo, former president of the Agricultural and Industrial Development Bank (BANFAIC) under Castro and head of the anti-Batista and now anti-Castro Asociación Montecristi; Manuel Antonio Varona, prime minister during the administration of Carlos Prío Socarrás and now head of the Movimiento de Rescate Revolucionario (or simply Rescate), a splinter group of the Auténtico party, the official party of the Grau San Martín / Prío Socarrás administrations; José Ignacio Rasco, university professor and leader of the Movimiento Democrático Cristiano; and Aureliano Sánchez Arango, former minister of education under Prío Socarrás and head of the Frente Nacional Democrático, also known as the Triple A. Varona became the official coordinator of the Frente, Artime the military leader and the group's principal link with the CIA.

While the Frente was created essentially as a provisional government to replace Fidel Castro's, it failed to evoke much enthusiasm in the exile community or even among the soldiers whose duty it was to install this government. Batista supporters were naturally angered by the exclusion of members of the Batista government. The Batistianos ridiculed the Frente, calling its members *fidelistas arrepentidos* (repentant Fidel supporters).[8] Others in the community questioned the presence of members of the Prío government, which had been overthrown by Batista in 1952, in the coalition, arguing that they represented the corruption and abuses of the old guard. Still others felt that the Frente's ties to the CIA compromised the nationalist ideals of the revolution, and thus Cuba's future. The Kennedy administration, which inherited the invasion plans in January 1961, saw the Frente as lacking the leadership necessary to provide a "strong, vigorous liberal government."[9] It was an "uncomfortable coalition" of organizations, said one State Department official, joined together in a "shot-gun marriage."[10] Disagreements and arguments were common among coalition members as each group jockeyed for control. Each continued to plan its own separate missions in Cuba while at the same time trying to present the image of a unified front. More than a few soldiers left the Brigade because of political differences with one Frente leader or another. Sánchez Arango eventually resigned and withdrew his organization from the Frente as well, angered by both Varona's role as coordinator and by the CIA's dictatorial control.

Some of his closest advisors feared the international repercussions from U.S. involvement, but President Kennedy decided to go ahead with the planned invasion of Cuba, now scheduled for April 1961. However, the administration decided to create a new exile organization that it hoped would more adequately represent its vision for Cuba and inspire more trust among exiles and Cubans on the island. Administration officials realized that the United States had become so thoroughly identified with the corruption of previous Cuban administrations that any alternative government that the U.S. supported would immediately be suspect in Cuban eyes; thus, they needed to identify themselves with progress, change, and the original goals of the Cuban revolution by supporting the dissident liberal voices who provided a challenge to Castro's Marxism. By March 1961, the Kennedy administration had a wider pool of individuals to choose from, as more members of Castro's own government had defected to the United States, still committed to the ideals of the revolution but disillusioned with the communist alignment. Some of these men were brought into the coalition to tilt it further to the Left and ensure broader popular support.[11] Joining Varona, Carrillo, Artime, Carlos Hevia, and Dr. Antonio Maceo in the new Consejo Revolucionario Cubano (Cuban Revolutionary Council) were José Miró Cardona, who had been the first prime minister of the revolutionary government. After much negotiation, Manuel Ray, former minister of public works, and his organization, the Movimiento Revolucionario del Pueblo (MRP), also joined.[12] Miró Cardona was elected head of the CRC.

Not all applauded the new changes, of course. The Right and many who considered themselves centrists regarded the MRP and its leaders Ray, Felipe Pazos, Ramón Barquín, and Raul Chibás as too radical.[13] The MRP's platform followed that of the July 26th Movement more closely than did any other exile or guerilla group's, and critics complained that it was *Fidelismo* without Fidel.[14] The CIA also considered Ray and the MRP unacceptable, preferring to deal with the more conservative groups. Even with these new voices, though, it took some negotiation before the CRC's platform communicated the liberal vision the Kennedy administration had in mind. An early draft of the CRC manifesto prompted one Kennedy advisor to write, "If this manifesto represents what our group really believes . . . then this crowd simply will not be able to meet the problems of Cuba, because it obviously doesn't understand what the problems are."[15] However, by the time of the invasion, the organization had been molded into a provisional government that the Kennedy administration could live with.

The failure of the Bay of Pigs invasion in April 1961 should have signaled the end of the unofficial war against Castro; instead, the war escalated. Over the next two years, the Kennedy administration adjusted its foreign policy—and the role of the Cuban exiles in that foreign policy—to challenge Castro's perceived threat to the hemisphere. The administration's official line was that while the U.S. was not planning to intervene militarily, it reserved the right to do so if Cuba became a military threat to the U.S. or any republic in the hemisphere. The immediate goal became containing Castro's influence in Latin America. Plans were drawn up to provide various nations with technical help such as radar to spot incoming planes, counterpropaganda assistance through the USIA, and economic assistance, particularly through the "Alliance for Progress." Investigations of the Castro government's alleged covert activities in the U.S. increased.[16]

The administration also plotted ways to isolate the Cuban government diplomatically and economically. The U.S. trade embargo was tightened in February 1962. With U.S. pressure, the Organization of American States (OAS) voted in January 1962 to limit Cuba's participation in the various organizations of the inter-American diplomatic network and to place an embargo on arms shipments to Cuba (an embargo that was eventually extended to other trade items as well). The Kennedy administration pressured Latin American nations to break with Cuba, and by 1963 fourteen Latin American countries had severed diplomatic relations.

Behind closed doors, the administration continued to plot the overthrow of the Castro government.[17] The CRC was kept on the government's payroll, receiving an estimated one to two hundred thousand dollars a month to continue its various activities,[18] and the Department of Defense enacted a program to enlist able-bodied Cuban refugee males in the U.S. armed forces "against the day when they might be needed."[19] By late 1961, the government was covertly involved in Operation Mongoose, a six-phase program under the direction of General Edward Lansdale designed to bring about open revolt in Cuba by the end of 1962. The emigrés played a vital role in Mongoose. Phases one and two consisted of gathering intelligence within Cuba and conducting raids and acts of sabotage, and the CIA used emigrés, the Cuban underground, and its own agents for these purposes. The final stages were to involve limited U.S. military participation. The CIA canceled the program, however, in the wake of the Cuban Missile Crisis.

As part of the Kennedy-Khrushchev accords following the Missile Crisis, the Soviet Union agreed to withdraw its missiles from Cuba, and in turn the United States promised not to invade Cuba.[20] Unofficially, the U.S. goal continued to be Castro's elimination. Beginning in early 1963, the administration's "new" Cuba policy focused on provoking revolt from within rather than through an invasion. The CIA concentrated on strengthening the groups working covertly within Cuba. Exile groups were again enlisted to infiltrate men and equipment into Cuba and commit acts of sabotage. To give the impression that the U.S. was not involved, these exile groups moved their bases of operation to other countries, such as Costa Rica and Nicaragua, and the CIA channeled funding for their activities through the governments of those countries. When asked by the media how the raiders were supported, the government flatly denied any involvement and suggested that they received support from "generous Americans sympathetic to their cause."[21]

The Kennedy administration attempted to carefully monitor and control foreign policy towards Cuba, but the exile community was a wild card, testing, threatening, and sometimes even dictating that policy. The CIA found it difficult to control the groups on its payroll; raids canceled by CIA personnel in Miami were frequently carried out anyway by the impatient emigrés. Exile groups independent of CIA control conducted their own paramilitary operations. Frustrated by what they perceived to be the United States' half-hearted commitment to overthrowing Castro, they performed raids, established their own intelligence networks, and infiltrated their own guerrillas into Cuba. Many operated out of Miami or the Florida Keys, but others had bases outside the United States to avoid fines or prison terms for violating U.S. neutrality laws. The Bahamas, with its hundreds of uninhabited islands, some as little as forty miles from the Cuban coast, served as a perfect hiding place for their arsenals and as a launching pad for their expeditions. Guns and ammunition were purchased with donations from the exile community or from private groups who had a vested interest in Cuba: the John Birch Society reportedly financed one raid,[22] and others were funded by wealthy individuals with ties to various U.S. corporations.[23] By sea or air, these commandos bombed military camps, refineries, electric plants, sugar mills, railroad lines, and cargo ships. After their raids, they frequently held press conferences in Miami or Washington to give detailed accounts of their exploits.

One five-month period in 1962 saw five separate raids. On September 10, a five-man crew from the exile group Alpha 66 fired upon a Cuban vessel near Cayo Francés. One month later, a ten-man crew from the same group raided a military camp at Isabela de Sagua, causing an undetermined number of casualties. On October 12, a six-man team from the Comandos Mambises machine-gunned and sunk a Cuban vessel off the port of Cárdenas. On December 4, raiders from the Segundo Frente del Escambray (SFE) fired upon military installations in the port of Caibarién. But the raid that received the most media attention during this period, and which perhaps best illustrates how many of these raids operated, was the first, involving the Directorio Revolucionario Estudiantil (DRE).[24]

On August 24, a group of twenty-three young men, many of them students with no military or navigation experience, set sail from the Florida Keys on two newly purchased boats, carrying one twenty-millimeter cannon and a few rifles and shotguns. Following reports from the DRE's underground that Soviet officials stayed at a certain hotel on the coast and that Castro often joined them for a late-night drink, one of the boats sailed within two hundred meters of shore (the other stationed itself farther out, keeping watch for the Cuban/Russian coast guard) and fired upon the hotel for approximately six minutes. While they failed to assassinate Fidel Castro, they did damage the hotel and startle the Soviet delegation. The DRE returned to a hero's welcome in Miami.[25] Raids like this were the only good news exiles received in the wake of the Bay of Pigs invasion.

While the Justice Department questioned the value of the "pin-prick raids" and "flea-bite operations"[26] the exile community saw them as links in a long chain of events that would ultimately topple Castro's regime. As the Irish Republican Army used bombings to try to force Great Britain to relinquish its control of Northern Ireland, the exile groups sought to use paramilitary raids to turn Cuba into a liability for the Soviet Union. "We are sure that in the not too distant future Cuban exiles will be able to return to the country lost by the cowardness of some compatriots and the naive and exaggerated tolerance of Uncle Sam," said one 1963 editorial in an exile tabloid.[27] The Kennedy administration may have been embarrassed by the exiles' press conferences, but it realized these raids served a purpose within the larger U.S. foreign policy: they harassed the Cuban government, undermined the Cuban economy, and perhaps distracted Castro from "exporting revolution" by forcing him to commit his military to domestic defense. Just as important, these raids served as an outlet for an anxious exile community uncertain about its future.

It became difficult to distinguish raids sanctioned by the CIA from those that were not. The U.S. government denied all knowledge of the raids, and exile groups denied any connections to the U.S., but the Cuban government blamed everything on the United States government, which, even if it did not organize or fund the raids, did little to deter them. Castro threatened retaliation. On two separate occasions in early 1963, Cuban MiGs fired on American targets, one a shrimp boat forty miles off the Cuban coast, the other a five-thousand-ton motorship twenty-five miles off Key West. In September, MiGs fired on a U.S. Navy vessel. At the same time, the Castro government intensified its crackdown on the Cuban underground, breaking up various networks in Havana, Santiago, and other towns and cities and sending thousands of troops into the Escambray to break the guerrilla movement once and for all. Hundreds of counterrevolutionaries were rounded up and executed, or sentenced to prison terms of twenty or thirty years.

It was difficult to determine how much damage the exile raids actually inflicted, since both the Cuban government and the exile groups often distorted the details of the attacks. The Cuban news media played down the damage, highlighting instead the courage and tenacity demonstrated by the Cuban army and militias in combatting the raiders,[28] while the exile groups often exaggerated the success of their missions to increase their stature in the exile community, and perhaps to attract the patronage of the CIA. Since the groups competed with each other for funding from limited sources, it was also common for them to take credit for one another's hit-and-run missions. Publicity meant an increase in donations.

The exile groups did not limit themselves to Cuban targets. Cargo ships from the various countries that traded with Cuba—particularly the Soviet Union—were considered fair game. On March 18, 1963, a joint raid by Alpha 66 and the SFE at the harbor of Isabela de Sagua resulted in damage to the Soviet freighter *Lgov,* and one week later raiders from the group Comandos L attacked the Soviet freighter *Baku* in the port of Caibarién, also causing substantial damage.[29] Attacks on Soviet property and citizens prompted angry warnings from the Kremlin—which, more than any other factor, forced the U.S. to crack down on the independent raids. In a joint statement by the departments of State and Justice on March 30, the administration announced that it would "take every step necessary" to make sure that these operations were not "launched, manned, or equipped on U.S. territory." The exile community was warned that such operations could have effects opposite to those intended: they might "strengthen the Soviet position in Cuba rather than weaken it, tighten Communist controls rather than loosen them."[30]

The United States wanted to avoid a full-scale war with Cuba and the Soviet Union at any cost, but some Kennedy advisors suspected that a war was just what the exile groups were trying to provoke. Many emigrés believed that they would never return to Cuba unless the United States committed itself fully to the "liberation" of Cuba and that such commitment was unlikely without military provocation.[31] Despite Washington's new rhetoric, few groups abandoned their activities: they were too committed to the struggle. Many also doubted the sincerity of this new rhetoric, since the CIA continued to assist its protégés, and the exile community knew that the Kennedy administration was as anxious to be rid of Castro as they were. The administration had for so long denied any role in the war against Castro that few exiles believed that there could ever be a change in policy.

But the administration *did* begin to crack down. The administration cut off all funding to the CRC. The Coast Guard, the INS, and Customs agents were put on alert, as were every "deputy, sheriff, and game warden in the Florida Keys."[32] Agents of the FBI and CIA infiltrated several exile groups, compiled lists of members and patrons, and informed police of the dates of planned raids and the locations of arsenals. More and more raiding parties were intercepted and munitions confiscated, prompting an angry response from the exile community. Editorials in the exile press argued that the U.S. could back out of the war against Castro if it wanted to, but it should not prohibit emigrés from trying to win back their homeland. Despite the FBI's recommendations that the exile commandos be prosecuted to the fullest extent of the law as an example to the emigré community, both the president and Attorney General Robert Kennedy hesitated.[33] By the end of the year, most charges had been dropped. The few individuals prosecuted were given only token fines. Mixed signals and inconsistency became the hallmark of the dealings with the emigrés not just by the Kennedy administration but by those that followed.

The 1960s: The "Industria de la Revolución"

A popular joke in Miami in the 1960s said that if you put two Cubans in a room with a political problem to solve, they would come up with three organizations. By 1963, there were so many exile political organizations that the departments of State and Justice were unable to keep track of them all.[34] Even the exile press ridiculed the *industria de la revolución*—the revolution industry.[35] The majority of these organizations were in Miami, but others emerged wherever emigrés settled: Union City, Chicago, New York, Los Angeles, San Juan, Caracas, Madrid, Mexico City.

The best-known of these organizations, by virtue of the attention it received from both the Kennedy administration and the press, was the Cuban Revolutionary Council. Even after the failure of the Bay of Pigs invasion the CRC stayed on the government payroll, and its leaders met frequently with top administration officials to discuss Cuba policy. José Miró Cardona reportedly met with the president himself on at least four different occasions after the invasion. As in the original Frente, however, political and personal differences threatened the integrity of the organization from the beginning, and there were several defections following Bay of Pigs: in May 1961, Manuel Ray and the MRP withdrew, angered by the CIA's mishandling of the affair; in September, Justo Carrillo followed; and in 1962, a faction of Artime's MRR defected as well.

The CRC eventually fell out of favor with the Kennedy administration. In April 1963, Miró Cardona, angered by the crackdown on raids by exile groups, resigned from the Council, but not before publicly criticizing the administration.[36] His claims that Kennedy reneged on his promise to organize a second invasion forced the State Department to hurriedly issue a statement denying any such promise.[37] Within weeks, the government stopped financing the CRC. Throughout the next year, the Council tried to maintain its position as the provisional government. Dr. Antonio Maceo became head of the organization, but he too resigned two months later. Manuel Antonio Varona assumed control and expanded the Council to include over a dozen new members from other exile organizations, but the lack of funding, together with the community's increasing lack of regard, led to the CRC's dissolution in 1964. The stigma associated with the Bay of Pigs fiasco was simply impossible to overcome.

Other organizations tried to fill the power vacuum. By the end of 1963, there were at least four different "provisional governments" in Miami. The Junta Revolucionaria de Liberación Nacional, headed by Aureliano Sánchez Arango, claimed to represent more than one hundred exile groups; it tried to organize another invasion, and failed. The Asociación de Magistrados Cubanos en el Exilio organized a government-in-exile under the leadership of former Supreme Court justice Dr. Julio Garcerán de Vall y Souza.[38] The Christian Civic Military Junta, claiming to represent the fifteen largest underground groups in Cuba, sent a telegram to President Kennedy announcing that Dr. Mario García Kohly was the provisional president of the "Cuban government in arms in exile."[39] Even former president Carlos Prío Socarrás announced that he too, as the last popularly elected president of Cuba, had organized his government-in-exile.

Former members of the CRC continued their own personal crusades against Castro. Two in particular, Artime and Ray, attracted media attention for their paramilitary activities. In 1963, with the assistance of the CIA, Manuel Artime and the MRR moved their operations to Central America, where they organized a number of raids against Cuba. No other exile organization received as much financing as the MRR: during their years of operation they reportedly received between $3 million and $6 million from the U.S. government to train and equip an army of two hundred men. The MRR occupied five camps in Costa Rica and Nicaragua, owned four boats and a half-dozen planes, and published a biweekly tabloid (*Tridente*) to keep the community informed of its exploits. Families of its "commandos" received generous monthly stipends.[40]

Artime announced that 1965 would be Cuba's "year of liberation," but the MRR fell out of grace with the CIA before then. The CIA became anxious to rid itself of its protégés in the MRR: they "talked too much," drawing attention to their covert activities and thus to the United States.[41] The MRR was also strikingly inefficient, conducting fewer raids than independent exile groups in Miami operating on less than a tenth of its budget. A series of scandals—among them that right-wing Costa Ricans were training in the exile camps to overthrow the Costa Rican government—provided the final blow, and the CIA closed all the camps in Central America. The MRR continued to operate for a few more years without CIA backing, but their raids eventually ended.

Manuel Ray and his new organization, the Junta Revolucionaria Cubana, also attracted publicity and controversy. Founded in Puerto Rico in September 1962, the Junta, like its counterpart, the MRP, was similar in platform to Castro's July 26th Movement and thus attracted as many enemies as supporters. The Junta's budget was never as extravagant as that of Artime's MRR; the CIA had never shared the Kennedy administration's enthusiasm for Ray and the MRP.[42] Ray announced that his "army of liberation" would land in Cuba by Cuban independence day

(May 20) of 1964. Though his group did set off from Puerto Rico, they were intercepted by a British destroyer in the Bahamas and never made it to Cuba.[43] Little was heard from the organization after that.

Not all exile political organizations conducted paramilitary operations. The majority of the groups that emerged during the 1960s were simply propaganda organizations trying to discredit the Castro government in the international arena. They published reports and essays in journals and newspapers around the world, pressured Congress, the United Nations, and the OAS to enact more punitive policies towards the Castro government, and used demonstrations, marches, boycotts, petitions, and rallies to call attention to human rights abuses and the plight of political prisoners in Cuba. It was the paramilitary groups, however, that commanded the most media attention. These groups tried to present an image of being well manned, but in fact most conducted operations with just a few dozen volunteers: most emigrés preferred to contribute to *la causa cubana* in less dangerous ways. The commandos were unusual men. They were the true believers, men totally committed to their idea of Cuba who sacrificed their careers and incomes, their family life, and their safety for their political beliefs. Their commitment was not defined by class, age, or race; as many came from the working class as from the middle class. Some had been professional soldiers in Cuba; some were laborers or professionals; others were idealistic students. They saw themselves as actors in a holy war against communism. "We are going to war even if they call us crazy," said one commando in the tabloid *Guerra:* "Let us forget those who are waiting for secret formulas, marvelous continental alliances, or fairy-tale invasions; one day they will be judged by the homeland and they will be found guilty of high treason against Cuba and the world."[44] For the true believers, pacifism was a form of treason,[45] and those compatriots who sat by and did nothing for Cuba were traitors.

Women were excluded from the paramilitary organizations and from some propaganda organizations. Politics was considered a male domain. Most women were also too preoccupied with domestic and economic responsibilities to be full-time advocates of *la causa cubana*. If men were able to dedicate time to their political activities, it was usually because women carried more than their share of the domestic burdens—raising children, providing additional income, managing household resources to make ends meet. Women were just as concerned about their homeland, but tradition cast them into a marginal and supportive role. They could always be counted on to do the thankless and tedious work of sewing or painting banners, preparing food for protesters at demonstrations, writing letters and making phone calls, and marching in demonstrations. "The men did all the planning," said one woman, "but we always did the work." Women were periodically called upon to boycott products from countries that traded with Cuba—as one exile newspaper put it, to serve as "economic guerrillas." Women did not don military garb and train in the Everglades, and they seldom shared in the political decision-making, but they provided the community support structure vital to the campaign.

There were exceptions. A handful of political organizations exclusively for women emerged, among them the Unión de Mujeres, the Cruzada Femenina Cubana, the Movimiento Femenino Anticomunista de Cuba, and the Organización de Damas Anticomunistas Cubanas. These organizations, however, offered no real political alternatives. Rather, they functioned as auxiliaries, providing moral and financial support to different men's organizations by participating in their rallies and fundraisers, organizing public relations campaigns and membership drives, and even sponsoring memorial services for the men who died for *la causa*. The women's political organizations drew little attention, but they served an important purpose in providing women with a forum in which they could seriously and freely discuss questions and ideas, as well as their hopes and fears about life in exile. Through these organizations women exercised their political voice and offered support to the campaign against Castro.

During the Johnson administration, the CIA concentrated more and more attention on Southeast Asia.[46] The CIA maintained connections with some exiles, hiring them for missions in Cuba, the Congo, and other sensitive areas—and it continued to monitor the Cuban community, fearing that the exiles' zealousness to topple Castro would provoke an international incident[47]—but its chief focus became Vietnam. The exile community never quite understood this obsession. While agreeing that communism had to be defeated on many fronts, emigrés didn't understand why Americans traveled half a world away to fight it while ignoring communism on their very doorstep.[48]

During the rest of the 1960s, the exile paramilitary groups continued their war against Castro and tried to avoid detection by U.S. authorities. They hired lawyers to advise them on how to get around international neutrality laws. They held their meetings in church halls. They raised money to buy their equipment by selling "liberation bonds" (redeemable once Castro was overthrown), advertising in *periodiquitos*, and organizing rallies, dinners, and variety shows. When desperate, some sold their blood or resorted to petty (and not so petty) crimes.[49] As funding dwindled, they formed alliances and pooled their resources: one group would provide the vessels, another the gasoline, yet another the munitions, and so forth. Since groups of men on small boats immediately aroused suspicion, they devised ingenious plans to get past the Coast Guard. Several small boats, for example, holding three or four men each, would set sail at different times from the Florida Keys as if going on a fishing expedition. They would later rendezvous on a remote island in the Bahamas (then a British colony), board a larger vessel, pick up the machine guns, bazookas, and other firearms they had stashed away on the island, and set sail for Cuba. If they accomplished their objective and avoided capture by the Cuban navy, they repeated these steps on their way back to the United States.[50]

With each year, however, it became more difficult to elude the authorities. Even if they escaped the U.S. Coast Guard, they ran the risk of being caught by the British navy, the Bahamian police, or the other international forces that began collaborating with U.S. federal agencies. As the Castro government consolidated its military power, the raids became increasingly dangerous. Many men died, and many more were captured and sentenced to lengthy prison terms. Cuban spies posing as emigrés sometimes infiltrated the commando groups in Miami and Puerto Rico and reported their plottings to Cuban authorities; when the commandos arrived in Cuba, they found the military waiting for them.

The cause seemed to be lost, but exile groups continued their propaganda and paramilitary war against Castro. One of the greatest challenges was to unite the politically fragmented exile community. Castro remained in power, they argued, because the exiles were too divided; if the hundreds of exile groups overcame their political differences and joined forces, they could present a truly formidable threat to the Castro regime. The exile community placed much of the blame for its disunity on the U.S. government, which by supporting some groups and not others—indeed, each government agency involved in Cuba policy had its own preferred group—exacerbated distrust, aroused jealousies, and pitted one group against the other. More realistically, the reason emigrés failed to unite in a common front was that their visions of a post-Castro Cuba—and who would control it—were fundamentally different.

Perhaps the most ambitious attempt to unite the community and coordinate propaganda and paramilitary activities occurred in 1964, when the rum millionaire José "Pepín" Bosch of the Bacardí Company financed a referendum that allowed the emigrés themselves to choose the leaders of a new exile front. The referendum reportedly polled over seventy-five thousand exiles in the United States and abroad who registered with the Comité Pro-Referendum. The men elected to head this new exile front, the Representación Cubana del Exilio (RECE), were civic, political, military, and labor leaders, among them Ernesto Freyre, of the Cuban Families Committee; Erneido Oliva, second in command of Brigade 2506; Vicente Rubiera, of the Federation of Telephone Workers in Exile; Aureliano Fernández-Díaz, president of the Association of Public and Private Accountants in Exile; and Jorge Mas Canosa, Brigade veteran and head of the student group Juventud Cubana. The military leaders included Oliva, José Morales Cruz, and Hugo Sueiro Ríos, all former Brigadistas.[51]

One of RECE's first acts was to take a "military census" in cities with large exile populations to determine the number of potential troops available for military action.[52] RECE also established a treasury, or "banco de la revolución," to collect funds for its campaigns.[53] The leaders traveled around Latin America trying to rally moral and financial support to their cause, and they organized conferences to generate enthusiasm for la causa. By April 1967, more than fifty exile organizations, including the municipios, had lent their support to RECE. Together they sponsored fundraisers—ballet recitals, musicals, and "grandes veladas artísticas" (great artistic events) with well-known Cuban entertainers— to raise money for their propaganda and military campaigns.[54] RECE published its own newspaper to keep the community informed of its activities and accomplishments, and in some cities it even had its own radio programs.

At first, RECE financed the paramilitary operations of certain groups. Later, its own paramilitary wing carried out joint military operations with the Comandos L, the Pinos Nuevos, the Movimiento Revolucionario 30 de Noviembre, and the Veterans Association of Brigade 2506.[55] In November 1965, one of these joint forces sailed off the coast of Cuba and fired upon the G-2's eighth precinct in Havana, "a symbol of Communist repression and terror."[56] In other raids they fired upon the Hotel Riviera, where Soviet delegations reportedly stayed, and on the private residence of Cuban president Osvaldo Dorticós. Like most paramilitary groups, however, RECE's effectiveness was short-lived. The FBI infiltrated the organization, the Coast Guard curtailed more and more of its raids, and the organization lost the enthusiasm of its supporters. Although it continued its propaganda efforts for over twenty years, by the mid-1970s RECE had ceased to be the unifying force in the community that it had set out to be.

The 1970s: A Transition Period

During the 1970s, the exile community in south Florida seemed to be developing along parallel courses, one of adjustment and acceptance, the other of increasing militance and desperation. It was a decade of social and economic progress. The number of emigrés seeking American citizenship increased. The Latino business community of Dade County became one of the most productive in the nation. Emigrés became involved in domestic politics: by 1976, they comprised 8 percent of registered voters in Dade County and occupied important elected offices in city and county governments. There was an indication that some Cubans were developing an ethnic (as opposed to purely national) identity, as seen by their growing membership in pan-Latino organizations such as the League of United Latin American Citizens (LULAC) as well as in the creation of groups such as the Cuban National Planning Council, the Spanish American League Against Discrimination (SALAD), and the National Coalition of Cuban Americans, which focused on voting rights, employment, housing, education, health, and other domestic concerns. All signs seemed to indicate that the emigrés had psychologically unpacked their bags and settled into their new society.

Alongside newspaper headlines celebrating the emigrés' success, however, was news that the war against Castro had taken a menacing turn. Propaganda and paramilitary groups decreased in number in the late 1960s, victims of a lack of funding and growing apathy in the community—an apathy generated, in part, by suspicions that many of these political groups were embezzling funds. But at the same time, new, more militant organizations emerged, committed to overthrowing Castro at whatever the cost. Most had no specific political vision for Cuba, no particular leader they wanted to see occupy the presidency; their goal was simply to eliminate Castro. As these groups became desperate their tactics became more radical, drawing international attention to the exile community in south Florida and polarizing emigrés further.

A shift in American foreign policy catalyzed this radicalism. Under the guidance of Secretary of State Henry Kissinger, the Nixon and Ford administrations adopted a policy of detente. Negotiations concentrated on the Soviet Union and China, but the U.S. government also turned its attention to improving relations with Cuba. In 1973, both countries signed an antihijacking treaty. In 1975, the United States supported the OAS's vote to lift the eleven-year-old embargo of Cuba. For the first time, the U.S. government also allowed subsidiaries of U.S. corporations in foreign countries to trade with the island.

During the Carter administration, the United States and Cuba moved further towards rapprochement. The countries negotiated a fishing rights agreement and a maritime boundary agreement. The U.S. lifted its ban on transferring American currency to Cuba as well as on using an American passport to travel there. In April 1978, the first commercial flight between Miami and Havana in sixteen years departed from Miami International Airport, and the federal government also granted visas to Cubans to come to the U.S. on a temporary basis.[57] An unprecedented number of scholars, artists, writers, and scientists traveled to and from Cuba in the interest of cultural and scholarly exchange. The Cuban government also allowed a group of fifty-five young Cuban exiles of the Brigada Antonio Maceo to witness first-hand the accomplishments of the revolution—the first exiles since the revolution to be permitted to return to the island. The most important development, however, was the creation of American and Cuban "interests sections," which provided limited diplomatic representation.

Many emigrés of course were enraged by this new climate of tolerance. Polls conducted by the *Miami Herald* showed that more than 53 percent remained opposed to reestablishing diplomatic and trade relations with Cuba and felt betrayed by the U.S. government.[58] Emigrés expressed their anger in the exile news media and staged rallies and demonstrations in Miami, Union City, Washington, and other cities. A "Congress Against Coexistence" was held in San Juan, Puerto Rico, in 1974, attended by representatives from some seventy exile organizations. When the OAS announced that member nations would debate the lifting of sanctions against Cuba, emigrés traveled to the meeting as a protest lobby, and in Miami emigrés destroyed the Torch of Friendship, a monument to hemispheric solidarity at Bayfront Park. When the sanctions were finally lifted a year later, in 1975, exile organizations organized a "Liberty Caravan," a thousand-car parade through Little Havana culminating in a boisterous rally at the Orange Bowl condemning the OAS's action.[59]

At the same time, polls indicated that a growing number of emigrés supported some type of rapprochement with the Castro regime. A 1975 *Herald* poll, for example, revealed that 49.5 percent of Cuban emigrés were at least willing to visit the island; a surprising revelation to hardliners in the community. Letters to newspaper editors revealed that some favored reestablishing diplomatic and trade relations—not for the idealistic goal of furthering world peace but for more practical considerations: the normalization of relations would allow them the opportunity to visit their family and friends in Cuba. Many questioned the value of the U.S. embargo, which instead of weakening Cuba's revolutionary fervor only seemed to tighten its ties to the Soviet Union. Polls revealed a generational difference in attitudes: Cubans raised and educated in the United States were more likely to approve of some form of rapprochement than their elders were. While they shared their parents' suspicion of—perhaps even their contempt for—the Castro regime, they tended to favor a diplomatic solution to the problems in Cuba rather than continued military or economic aggression.

A handful of organizations emerged during the 1970s to lobby for the diplomatic approach, among them the Cuban Christians for Justice and Freedom, the National Union of Cuban Americans, and the Cuban American Committee. In 1979, the latter group sent a petition with over ten thousand signatures to President Jimmy Carter requesting that the United States normalize relations with the Castro government.[60] A few individuals established careers as advocates of a new diplomacy, the most controversial being the Reverend Manuel Espinosa, pastor of the Evangelical Church in Hialeah. Espinosa, a former captain in Castro's military and a former member of several anti-Castro organizations, used his weekly sermons to preach reconciliation and to advocate the normalization of diplomatic relations with Cuba.

The number of emigrés that joined these organizations, or who supported these activists, was not significant enough to serve as an effective lobby—at least during the 1970s. Those who favored the normalization of relations kept silent, for the most part, because they feared being branded *comunistas*. In this politically conservative community, such a tag inevitably affected careers, businesses, relationships, and even lives. Espinosa's activism brought him a severe beating at the hands of militant Cuban exiles in 1975, and other activists had their businesses boycotted, their homes vandalized, their families harassed, and their reputations ruined.[61]

Many emigrés believed that an accommodation of the Cuban government was an endorsement of Castro-communism. They could not understand why *exilados* would even speak to the individuals who had tortured, imprisoned, and executed tens of thousands of their compatriots. As one exile wrote, "Those who speak of coexistence demonstrate that they have forgotten our language.''[62] Another had harsher words: "Those who physically or intellectually support the Castro regime are traitors, as are those who support a *fidelismo sin Fidel,* a nationalist communism, or who surreptitiously plant the idea of coexistence. Those who forgive, accept, or befriend the traitors are also traitors. Yes, one can be a Cuban by birth, but if one's heart is not Cuban one is a traitor."[63] When Manuel Espinosa publicly admitted (years later, in 1980) that he was an agent for the Cuban government, most emigrés were not surprised; his admission simply confirmed the popular belief that active supporters of renewed relations with Cuba had to be in some way connected to the regime.

Even the shipment via third countries of medicine and food parcels to Cuba was considered by hardliners to be an accommodation of the Castro government.[64] Radio talk show hosts attributed Castro's continued hold on Cuba to the "economic subsidies" Cubans received in the form of packages from the exile community—estimated at hundreds of thousands of dollars a year. If exiles stopped sending their relatives food, clothing, and medicines, they argued, discontent on the island would grow and ultimately lead to Castro's overthrow. For those emigrés who had elderly relatives or children in Cuba, though, maintaining a hard line against Cuba came at great personal and psychological cost. Those who sent packages to Cuba preferred to keep it secret, to avoid censure.

Angered by the new developments in American foreign policy and what they perceived to be a growing complacency in the exile community, the militant extremists escalated the war against Castro. As one militant explained: "It is to be expected that after eighteen years in exile a frustrated generation would emerge whose impatience would lead them to use extreme methods."[65] Their methods were so extreme that even the exile community feared to speak out against them. Groups such as El Condor, Comandante Zero, Movimiento Neo-Revolucionario Cubano-Pragmatista, Coordinación de Organizaciones Revolucionarias Unidas (CORU), Poder Cubano, Acción Cubana, M-17, the Frente de Liberación Nacional de Cuba, and Omega 7 bombed Cuban embassies and consulates around the world, murdered Cuban diplomatic employees, harassed and threatened individuals and institutions alleged to have ties to the Castro government, and placed bombs aboard planes heading for Cuba.

1976 was a particularly violent year. As thousands of emigrés celebrated the U.S. Bicentennial by taking the oath of citizenship, others waged war against Cuba. In April, commandos attacked two Cuban fishing boats, killing one fisherman, and bombed the Cuban Embassy in Portugal, killing two persons. In July, bombs exploded at the Cuban mission at the United Nations, at the offices of the British West Indian Airways of Barbados (which represented Cubana Airlines, the national airline), and inside a suitcase that was about to be loaded onto a Cuban jet in Kingston, Jamaica. Later that summer, two employees of the Cuban Embassy in Buenos Aires disappeared; the Cuban consul in Mérida, Mexico, was almost kidnapped; and a bomb exploded in the Cubana Airlines office in Panama. In October, bombs exploded on a Cuban jet minutes after it left Barbados; all 73 passengers died. In November, a bomb destroyed the Madrid office of Cubana Airlines.[66] The violence increased further in 1977 and 1978 as a result of the Carter administration's new policies towards Cuba and the *diálogo*.[67]

While the paramilitary organizations of the 1960s had limited their actions to Cuba and its allies, the militant extremists targeted all those they perceived to be their enemies, including members of their own community, and many did not care how many innocent victims got in the way. They bombed Little Havana travel agencies, shipping companies, and pharmacies that conducted commercial transactions with Cuba. They harassed and threatened all who favored political coexistence. Extremists bombed the offices of *Réplica*, a popular Spanish-language news magazine, because its editor, Max Leznick, advocated lifting the trade embargo.[68] They harassed and ultimately murdered crane operator Luciano Nieves and Hialeah boatbuilder Ramón Donestevez because of their suspected ties to the Castro government.[69] In 1973, they assassinated Cuban exile leader José de la Torriente, who was suspected of embezzling funds from a liberation effort he had established, the Plan Torriente.[70] From 1973 to 1976, more than one hundred bombs exploded in the Miami area alone, and the FBI nicknamed Miami "the terrorist capital of the United States";[71] but the groups also operated in (and out of) New York, Union City, Los Angeles, Madrid, Santo Domingo, Mexico City, and Caracas. During the late 1970s, a Cuban exile tabloid in Puerto Rico, *La Crónica*, published interviews with the controversial leaders of these militant groups, whose identities were disguised. They warned the exile community to watch their backs.

Many emigrés spoke out against the terrorism of their compatriots, condemning these acts not only as immoral but also as tactically stupid. "They are politically and militarily incapable of producing a change in the regime," wrote a former member of the CRC of the terrorists: "[They] will] cost human lives, create immense anxiety in the community, and, more importantly, discredit the exile community before U.S. public opinion. . . . Whether one likes it or not, these acts do not serve the liberation cause but, rather, serve subversive Marxist elements in this country."[72]

Sadly, many who spoke out against the terrorism became victims themselves. In 1976, extremists murdered José Peruyero, president of the Brigade 2506 Veterans Association, because he condemned the participation of Brigade veterans in terrorist activities.[73] Journalists became popular targets; they were frequently threatened and their homes and offices vandalized. Three months after Peruyero's death, a bomb exploded in the car of WQBA news and program director Emilio Milián. Milián, who denounced acts of terrorism on his radio program *Habla el pueblo,* miraculously survived the explosion, but he lost both his legs. A few weeks later, he courageously returned to his job at WQBA and resumed his critical editorials, but a year later he was fired by the station because his editorials were allegedly too incendiary.[74]

A joint committee of local, state, and federal agencies investigating these terrorist acts learned that membership in the terrorist groups interlocked—that is, those who committed acts of violence often worked on behalf of three or four different groups. Organizations frequently disbanded and their members created splinter groups, giving the impression that there were more terrorists than there actually were. When a congressional subcommittee asked the Dade County Public Safety Department to identify the number of groups operating in the Miami area, one investigator revealed the frustration of tracking these organizations: "I can say that we have more than 10 militant groups with hard core militants. . . . those 10 groups may be 12 tomorrow, and next week there may be 50. And then week after next it may be [down] to eight, because there is a constant change in the staffing of these groups and there is constant exchange."[75]

While the terrorist groups received some funding from sympathetic individuals in the community, more often than not they resorted to extortion, threatening wealthier emigrés with death or property damage if they did not supply the necessary funds.[76] A few militants received financial assistance from foreign agents—agents who later used the Cubans in their own domestic plots. The Chilean state police, for example, reportedly hired Cubans to assassinate the former Chilean ambassador Orlando Letelier in Washington in 1976.[77]

Investigations were made especially difficult by the Cuban intelligence network in Miami. American law enforcement agencies had to determine whether the violence and terrorism were actually committed by emigrés or by *infiltrados* who tried to destroy exile organizations by framing them. The Castro government had reportedly infiltrated hundreds of spies into Miami, most of them arriving in the U.S. as small-boat escapees, "fence-jumpers" at the U.S. base at Guantánamo, or immigrants arriving from third countries.[78] So extensive was this network that Castro's spies often served as the FBI's informants on the emigrés' illegal activities: when Alpha 66, for example, hired a gunman to assassinate Fidel Castro during a planned speech at the United Nations, Cuban spies uncovered the plot and notified American authorities.[79] Interviews in the Cuban press with emigrés who defected back to Cuba also revealed the inner workings of the top militant groups operating in south Florida.[80]

Emigrés hotly debated who was responsible for the wave of terror. Most preferred to interpret it as a Castro plot to divide and demoralize the community,[81] arguing that these acts of terrorism were too professional to be done by the "weekend warriors." Castro also stood to gain the most by the campaign of intimidation, which divided and silenced his opponents. In the meantime, while Justice Department officials tried to track down the culprits, emigrés with unpopular views or in visible positions took extra precautions. The exile press carried advertisements for security devices, including remote-control gadgets that could start cars from a distance of one hundred meters.

The FBI eventually tracked down fifteen terrorists associated with the New Jersey–based Omega 7, regarded as the most dangerous of the organizations; all fifteen were ultimately convicted. The FBI also arrested dozens of other militants, including five emigrés accused of assassinating Letelier.[82] Many cases, however, remain unsolved.

The wave of violence that rocked the community during the 1970s arose in part out of the secret war of the 1960s. Several of those convicted for terrorism and government espionage were former CIA protégés. The skills they had learned to destabilize and overthrow the Castro government were now used against their own community and their host society. According to some newspaper accounts, some of the Cubans involved in organized crime in south Florida, particularly in drug trafficking, also had CIA connections. Three of the Watergate burglars, Bernard Barker, Virgilio González, and Eugenio Martínez, were Cuban exiles with ties to the CIA.[83]

Some in the emigré community regarded the extremists as heroes and *patriotas*. One editor of a *periodiquito* wrote:

> I know there are many Cubans who don't like these tactics and criticize them, but I have to ask myself, "What have these compatriots done all these past years, and what has been their contribution to the struggle for

liberation?" Most of them have simply enjoyed the comforts of living in the land of liberty. . . . No, my friends. A Cuban is not merely someone who was born in Cuba. A Cuban is someone who thinks about the seven million compatriots who are living as slaves.[84]

A well-known journalist wrote, "The realities of world politics leave no alternative but to use violence. Only when the exiles destroy the lives and interests of our enemies will Washington, Moscow, the OAS, or whoever take our views into account."[85]

Some exiles raised funds to help the militants in their cause—and later in their legal defense.[86] In 1974, Cuban radio stations in Miami helped raise over twelve thousand dollars for the families of two militants associated with the Frente de Liberación Nacional de Cuba who had been injured while constructing a bomb.[87] In 1978, *La Crónica* printed an advertisement for the Cuban Defense League, Inc., which raised funds for the legal defense of "Cuban political prisoners in the United States, Mexico, and Venezuela."[88] That same year, a New York–based publication entitled *Desde las Prisiones* began publishing articles by or in support of the "Cuban freedom fighters." The White House and the Department of Justice frequently received letters and petitions asking the government to commute sentences. In August 1979, for example, a Chicago exile coalition called the Federación de Organizaciones Cubanas de Illinois wrote Attorney General Benjamin Civiletti on behalf of ten men detained for various acts. "Now that the Cuban Communist authorities are releasing political prisoners," they wrote, ". . . we believe the United States Department of Justice should also grant benevolent concessions to the exile patriots incarcerated in this country, who acted according to the best interest of what traditionally has been a struggle to restore freedom and democracy in Cuba."[89]

The most famous militant was Orlando Bosch, a Miami pediatrician who in 1968 was sentenced to ten years in prison for firing on a Polish freighter with a bazooka. Released on parole after four years in a federal penitentiary, Bosch fled the country in 1974 when he became a chief suspect in the assassination of Cuban exile leader José Elias de la Torriente. Over the next two years, he served as leader of the militant group Acción Cubana, which claimed responsibility for the bombings of several Cuban embassies and consulates throughout Latin America. In 1976, the government of Venezuela charged Bosch with conspiracy in the Cubana Airlines bombing that killed seventy-three people, including the entire Cuban national fencing team. Although a Venezuelan judge found insufficient evidence to charge him in the bombing, Bosch remained in prison while his case was reviewed in civil and military courts.[90] Although he was acquitted two more times, he was not released from prison until 1987.

Over the years, Bosch's supporters staged marches and demonstrations to protest his incarceration. They organized exhibitions of his drawings in art galleries in Little Havana, Tampa, Union City, Chicago, and New York City to raise money for his defense and to assist his family. Miami mayoral candidates, hoping to garner a few votes, even visited Bosch in prison in Caracas. The emigré press in particular rallied to his defense. "[Bosch] has done some things which the U.S. government could call terrorism," said WQBA news director Tomás García Fusté, "but he is fighting for the liberation of our country. It is not terrorism but self-defense. We, the Cubans, are at war with Fidel Castro."[91]

Not all emigrés regarded Bosch as a hero, of course. When Miami City Commissioner Demetrio Pérez introduced a resolution in 1983 for an Orlando Bosch Day, both his office and the *Miami Herald* were swamped with letters, as many opposed to the motion as in favor of it. "I am a Cuban, and proud of it," wrote one woman, ". . . but I do not support someone whose idea of patriotism is to attack a Polish freighter, who has violated parole in the United States, and who has been accused of killing 73 innocent people."[92] The federal government was also unsympathetic. When Bosch returned to the United States in February 1988 following his release from prison, he was arrested by U.S. marshalls for having violated his parole. Deportation proceedings were begun, but the Justice Department was unable to find any country willing to grant Bosch entry. Finally, in late 1990, he was placed under house arrest.

For many emigrés, the wave of violence posed a moral dilemma that forced them to seriously reconsider their heroes as well as the methods they considered acceptable in the war against Castro. They learned that the line that divided revolutionary activities from terrorist activities could be a very thin one. The violence of the 1970s, then, led some emigrés to disassociate themselves completely, in fear or disgust, from exile politics. For others the negative media attention focused on the community, plus the realization that even the militant groups were impotent in bringing about change, forced them to reevaluate strategy, and slowly they realized that if they wanted to evoke meaningful change in Cuba they had to work within the political machinery of their host country. The war against Castro took a new direction in the 1980s, and the election of Ronald Reagan facilitated that redirection.

The 1980s: Working within the System

Any hopes for a peaceful coexistence between the emigré community and the Castro government were shattered by the Mariel boatlift. Many of those who favored rapprochement changed their views in anger and disillusionment; at the least they became less vocal. During the early 1980s, the community's militant opposition to Castro once again appeared monolithic.

Ronald Reagan's election in 1980 pleased the hardliners and rekindled their hopes for Castro's overthrow. For the first time in many years, Americans had elected a president whose views on communism (and Cuba) were compatible with those of the emigrés. With Reagan in the White House, there was little chance of rapprochement, and emigrés began to press for even more punitive policies toward the Castro government.

The emigrés' growing clout in domestic politics is what allowed them to influence foreign policy. During the past decade, Cubans had registered to vote as soon as they became naturalized, and their voter-participation rate exceeded that of the general population.[93] In Dade County, Cubans made up 20 percent of registered voters by 1983, up from 8 percent in 1976, and their high turnout made theirs a crucial swing vote.

Overwhelmingly, Cubans voted Republican—more consistently so than any other ethnic group. Democratic administrations had been responsible for the Cuban Refugee Program and the freedom flights, but the Republican Party was perceived to be more staunchly anticommunist (notwithstanding the accommodationist views of the Nixon and Ford administrations).[94] In 1980 and again in 1984, Cubans in Miami voted for Reagan by an overwhelming ninety percent. Even outside of south Florida, in communities where Cuban political attitudes were influenced by contact with more liberal Latino groups, Cubans voted mostly Republican (65 percent in New York, 68 percent in Chicago).[95] The Cuban community provided some of Reagan's most loyal supporters, and they were rewarded with various appointments in the administration.

Still, the Republicans knew that they could not take the emigrés for granted. A tough-talking Democratic candidate could lure away this valuable swing vote. On the local and state level, emigrés voted as readily for Democrats as for Republicans, taking into account not only candidates' views on Cuba but their positions on domestic issues affecting day-to-day life: health care, social security, education. Cubans helped reelect such Democrats as congressmen Dante Fascell and Claude Pepper, and later the Cuban-born mayor of Miami, Xavier Suárez (who eventually listed himself as an Independent). The emigrés, then, were in a position to be taken seriously.

To take advantage of the new conservative climate in the country, in 1981 a group of wealthy Cuban businessmen in Miami, many of them Brigade veterans, founded the Cuban American National Foundation (CANF), a nonprofit organization whose principal goal was to help the Reagan administration formulate a "realistic" foreign policy towards Cuba.[96] The organization established its principal base in Washington, D.C., not Miami, revealing just how politically assimilated emigrés had become. "We had to take the fight out of Calle Ocho and Miami Stadium and into the center of power," said the chairman, Jorge Mas Canosa. "We had to stop the commando raids and concentrate on influencing public opinion and governments."[97]

CANF concentrated its efforts on influencing congressmen through its political action committee, the Free Cuba PAC. Modeled after Jewish lobbying groups that influence U.S. policy toward Israel, most notably the American Israel Public Affairs Committee (AIPAC), the Free Cuba PAC rewarded senators and congressmen who supported a tougher policy toward Cuba with substantial donations to their reelection campaigns. From 1983 to 1988, the Free Cuba PAC contributed over $385,000 to congressmen of both political parties, among them Democrat Lloyd Bentsen and Republican Dan Quayle, both of whom became vice-presidential candidates in 1988.[98] According to one CANF member, the organization prided itself on being able to change votes through political contributions.[99]

An important tool in CANF's strategy against Cuba was Radio Martí, the proposed addition to the Voice of America broadcasting system. CANF became the principal lobbyist for Radio Martí on Capitol Hill. To assist in its lobbying efforts, the organization awarded a grant to the Center for Strategic and International Studies, a think tank at Georgetown University, to conduct a study analyzing the potential impact of radio transmissions on Cuba.[100] A heated debate ensued in Congress, in the press, and even within Reagan's cabinet. Some critics condemned the project as an overt act of hostility against a sovereign nation. Others argued that the station would only duplicate information already available to the Cuban population through commercial Spanish language radio stations in Florida and accused President Reagan of pandering to the passions of his Cuban American constituents. Still others criticized the financial burden of Radio Martí—an estimated $10 to $12 million per year—during a time of growing concern about the national deficit. The bill passed Congress anyway and was signed into law. President Reagan appointed several emigrés, including Jorge Mas Canosa, to the station's board of directors. Radio Martí beamed its first broadcast to Cuba from Marathon Key, Florida, on Cuban independence day, May 20, 1985.[101]

Many critics of Radio Martí were surprised by the quality of the station's broadcasts. The *New York Times*, which had published editorials critical of the station, later admitted that it had been wrong in its initial assessment: "Contrary to our fears last year, [Radio Martí] has avoided propaganda and supplemented, not duplicated, commercial Spanish-language broadcasts from Florida."[102] Over the next few years, the station provided analytical news coverage on a variety of topics and issues: the Third and Fourth Communist Party Congresses in Havana, AIDS, the defection of high-ranking military and government officials, and news stories from around the world, especially the Soviet Union, Nicaragua, Angola, Namibia, and South Africa. Listeners also heard readings of suppressed literature, interviews with former political prisoners, and philosophical discussions with various religious leaders, from Catholic priests to *santería* practitioners. Some of Radio Martí's more popular programs, according to recent emigrants, were the *radionovelas* (soap operas), the musical programs featuring Top 40 hits, and vintage radio shows such as "La tremenda corte," which Cubans reportedly taped and sold in the black market.

Despite the Cuban government's initial attempts to block Radio Martí's transmissions on AM and shortwave frequencies, the station was heard clearly in many parts of the island, and many of its news stories had an immediate effect. The station's series on AIDS forced the Cuban government to begin addressing this important health issue.[103] The number of attempted boat escapes also increased, and many of those who made it to the United States claimed that news of others' successful escape attempts had helped them decide to take the risk.[104] Less obvious, however, was the station's effect on Cubans' worldview, which would only be noticeable over time, and which the Cuban government reportedly feared. In retaliation, Castro suspended the 1984 immigration accords. Members of the Cuban government readily admitted that Radio Martí was Castro's greatest defeat in three decades.[105] As dissident

Marxist and human rights advocate Ricardo Bofill (then in Cuba) wrote to the station's director, Ernesto Betancourt, "There will come a time, with respect to the Cuban situation, when we will have to talk about the time before and after Radio Martí went on the air."[106]

The station was considered so successful in the ideological war against Castro that in March 1990 Congress voted to add a new component to the Voice of America: "TV Martí." These television broadcasts were even more controversial. Critics argued that the proposed transmissions would be of poor quality (signals were to be beamed from a balloon tethered over the Florida Keys) and could be easily jammed. Others opposed spending millions of dollars to broadcast Spanish-dubbed sitcoms like *Alf* to the Cubans. The transmissions were condemned by the National Association of Broadcasters and the International Telecommunications Union, which feared a broadcasting war. The Cuban government, of course, condemned the operation as a form of military aggression and threatened retaliation.[107] Once again, however, the bill passed Congress: it was a sure way for congressmen to demonstrate to their constituents that they were tough on communism. The station now beams various news and entertainment programs to Cuba, although these are not received clearly throughout the island.

CANF's Cuba policy focused on other issues as well, but all of them were in some way connected to Cuba and *la causa cubana*. Hoping to counteract Cuba's influence in the Third World, the organization lobbied for U.S. support for Jonas Savimbi and the UNITA forces in Angola and for aid to the Nicaraguan Contras. CANF pressured the Reagan and Bush administrations to tighten the trade embargo against Cuba. In 1982, American tourists were once again prohibited from traveling to Cuba, with the exception of scholars, journalists, and emigrés wishing to visit their relatives on the island. In 1989, Congress passed legislation prohibiting ships traveling to or from Cuba from stopping in American ports, and in 1992, after intensive lobbying, Congress passed the Cuban Democracy Act, which imposed penalties on American corporations whose foreign subsidiaries traded with Cuba.

Part of CANF's success lies in its financial base. The organization counts on contributions from over fifty thousand members, many of them from Miami's wealthy business community. Some donate ten thousand dollars or more a year, depending on their rank within the organization, but the majority of members donate more modest amounts. As one eighty-year-old retiree in Little Havana told me, "I give Mas Canosa about ten dollars every year. It takes some saving, but we need to get Castro out of there. I trust *la Fundación*." By 1986, CANF had a working budget of $1.5 million.[108] Some members cannot vote in U.S. elections because they still have not sought citizenship; Mas Canosa himself only became naturalized in the early 1980s. Interestingly, most members admit that their homes are in the United States, not Cuba; they may be working for Cuba's liberation, but they do not necessarily want to return to Cuba. They do, however, want to play a role in Cuba's political and economic reconstruction.

Some CANF board members work as lobbyists themselves. Many are former *brigadistas* with a long history of anti-Castro activities: Mas Canosa, for example, is a former student resistance leader, a Brigade veteran, and former propaganda director for RECE. Unlike professional lobbyists, CANF members feel a personal and emotional imperative to do this work, and after twenty years of waging war against Castro they know which strategies brings results and which do not.

Over the years, CANF has provoked its share of controversy, much of it surrounding chairman Jorge Mas Canosa—the man the *Miami Herald* called the most powerful exile in America—whose name has become synonymous with the organization. Like the Cuban leader he seeks to depose, Mas Canosa has both loyal supporters and angry detractors. He is perceived as charismatic or dictatorial, shrewd or conniving, idealistic or opportunistic. Critics call him "Señor Mas y Mas" ("Mr. More and More"), "the Godfather," or simply a caudillo. He once reportedly challenged a Miami city commissioner to a duel.[109] Over the years, more than a few members have resigned from CANF or Radio Martí because of personality differences with the chairman.[110] Supporters, on the other hand, regard him as the most important and influential leader to emerge in over thirty years of exile. Not surprisingly, Mas Canosa is politically ambitious: he readily admits that he would like to be president of Cuba, and many of his supporters in Little Havana already call him "Señor Presidente." While his name is not a household word in Cuba, recent defectors report that many Cubans have at least some knowledge of his activities from Radio Martí.

Most of the controversy surrounding CANF, however, revolves around its alleged abuse of influence. In 1987, critics accused the organization of using the Pan American Games in Indianapolis as a propaganda tool. Knowing that the 1991 Pan Am games would be in Havana, CANF distributed anti-Castro literature at the 1987 games, hired airplanes to fly over the stadium with anti-Castro banners, and scheduled press conferences with former political prisoners, who talked about human rights abuses on the island. The Cuban delegation even accused CANF of contacting athletes to convince them to defect.[111] In 1989, CANF allegedly used its influence to get the State Department to revoke visas for members of Cuba's famous Orquesta Aragón, which was scheduled to perform at a Chicago music festival.[112] That same year, CANF was also accused of arranging the arrest of Miami book publisher and art collector Ramón Cernuda on charges of buying Cuban paintings in violation of the U.S. trade embargo.[113]

In 1989, the foundation also drew fire for one of its projects, a Cuban Studies institute at Miami's Florida International University. CANF succeeded in getting a bill introduced in the Florida legislature to appropriate $1 million to the proposed Cuban American National Foundation Institute. Under the bill, the CANF institute would be partially funded with public money and would enjoy the prestige of FIU, but it would be governed by an independent board of trustees chosen largely by CANF. In addition, CANF was to have veto power over the institute's director and researchers, and the institute was to be exempt from most public records laws.[114] The bill immediately ignited a public outcry: the chancellor, the board of regents, and most of the faculty at FIU (including their leading Cuban Studies scholars) condemned the bill and mobilized educators around the state into an opposing lobby. FIU's president, Modesto "Mitch" Maidique, who served on CANF's advisory board, also withheld his support. Newspapers around the state lashed out at Florida legislators for even considering using state monies to fund a PAC-controlled institute and warned that such an institute would compromise the academic integrity of the university. One political cartoonist for the *Miami Herald* had perhaps the best comment: with CANF on campus, FIU would become an acronym for "Fidel Is Ugly."

Under fire, Mas Canosa withdrew his proposal for a CANF institute at FIU. The Florida House and Senate did, however, vote to allocate $1 million in the 1989–90 budget to the foundation for an independent research entity on Cuba and the Caribbean. Despite this "defeat," the entire incident proved yet again just how powerful the Cuban American lobby had become.

CANF came under fire again in 1992, when both the Inter-American Press Association and the human rights group Americas Watch condemned the Miami exile community for growing violations of civil liberties.[115] Both agencies put much of the blame for the climate of censorship on CANF, which they claimed used its political and financial clout to intimidate more liberal voices. Just a few months earlier, Mas

Canosa had accused the editors and reporters of the *Miami Herald* of being propagandists for the Castro regime when they published an editorial against the proposed Cuban Democracy Act. CANF plastered the city with billboards saying "Yo no creo en el Herald" (I don't trust the Herald) and threatened to organize an advertising boycott of the newspaper. Needing little encouragement, exile extremists vandalized *Herald* vending machines throughout the city, covering them with feces and graffiti. *Herald* offices received bomb threats, and several reporters received death threats.[116] Although CANF criticized such actions, the Inter-American Press Association blamed the foundation, condemning it for its "lack of tolerance" and "irrational charges" that were "damaging to the cause of free speech."[117]

Despite these controversies, CANF is by far the most popular organization in the exile community today. No matter how much negative media attention CANF may attract, it has the undying loyalty of many in the community, who feel that the organization has done more for *la causa* than any other organization of the past thirty years. "CANF has shown the world that the exile community is a force to be reckoned with," said one Little Havana resident. "People used to ridicule our raids . . . but who's laughing now?" Those who donate money receive monthly bulletins reporting on the organization's activities. Inside, photographs show Mas Canosa, looking very presidential, alongside world leaders such as Russian President Boris Yeltsin. Such evidence demonstrates to the community that its donations are having tangible results.

CANF's humanitarian projects have also earned it loyalty and praise. Beginning in 1983, the foundation sponsored the Cuban Exodus Relief Fund, headed by Bishop Agustín Román. The fund raises money to assist Cuban exiles living in third countries, many of whom have been prohibited from seeking employment in those countries and wait to be reunited with their families in the United States. By 1987, the fund had provided grants, rent payments, tuition scholarships, and meals to thousands of families in Costa Rica, Peru, Spain, and Panama.[118] (One of CANF's 1986 fundraising efforts for the fund was a musical record entitled "Yo vuelvo a ti" [I return to you] performed by over fifty emigré artists.) By 1991, the organization had helped to bring in more than eighty-six hundred Cubans living in third countries. In 1992, after Hurricane Andrew destroyed much of south Florida, CANF established an emergency center to assist supporters who had lost homes or businesses.[119]

While other organizations competed with CANF for political influence in the exile community and in Washington, none was able to match its success. One that came close—at least in community support—was Cuba Independiente y Democrática, or CID. Founded in Caracas, Venezuela, in 1981 by former political prisoner Huber Matos, CID established offices in major cities in Latin America and the United States, including Washington and Miami. It operated seven radio stations throughout the Caribbean that together beamed news to Cuba twenty-four hours a day. "Instead of infiltrating ten guns and explosives into the island, we inform Cubans," said Matos.[120] Like CANF, CID relied on *cabildeo,* or lobbying, to promote its political interests. The organization lacked an effective political action committee in the U.S., however, and instead relied on more traditional methods such as press conferences, meetings, and dinners. CID published *News Cuba,* an English-language newsletter that was distributed to senators and congressmen, the press, colleges and universities, and labor unions. CID also published a Spanish-language newspaper, with a circulation of over fifty thousand, which served as a forum for Matos's views on national and international affairs.

Unlike CANF, CID was not a Cuban American political organization but a multinational one. CID sought to unite the Americas in a common front against Castro so they could effectively challenge Cuban-Soviet aggression in the region.[121] Although the organization claimed to have a counterintelligence component that monitored Cuba's spy network, CID did not advocate military action against Cuba. "[While in prison] I realized that the infiltration method, as well as the Bay of Pigs method, always let Fidel survive because he could always command more forces than could be gathered abroad," said Matos. Instead, the organization encouraged rebellion from within; its propaganda efforts, especially the radio broadcasts, were designed to inform the population on political alternatives and spur them into action.[122]

CID's influence can be attributed to Huber Matos; as with Mas Canosa and CANF, it is doubtful that the organization could have acquired as strong a presence in exile politics without such a figure. A former commander of Castro's rebel army and former military governor of the province of Camagüey, Matos became one of the first victims of his own revolution. He was arrested in 1959 and tried for "antipatriotic and antirevolutionary conduct." He spent the next twenty years in prison, sixteen of them completely isolated, often in a concrete box two and a half by three meters. To diminish his popularity on the island and erase him from all public consciousness, Castro had Matos's face airbrushed out of the official portrait of the rebel army that appears on the Cuban peso.[123] He was finally released from prison in 1979 at age sixty, and shortly thereafter he founded CID to try to unite emigrés living in the United States and abroad.

Like Mas Canosa, however, Matos provoked controversy. Many, particularly the Batistianos, could not forgive him for his role in the July 26th Movement, particularly for the executions that took place under his command.[124] "Huber Matos has neither the authority nor the moral character to lead the exile community," wrote one critic. "It is insolent on his part that he now wants to tell us what we need to do to liberate our country. . . . Cuba only wants to shake off the communism that nursed those who now wish to pass themselves off as tame doves."[125] Others were more willing to forgive Matos; they felt that he, like most exiles, had been deceived by Fidel Castro. Whatever his crimes, they argued, Matos had fought against Batista to create a democratic society,[126] and he was one of the few emigrés who could truly challenge the Castro government. "There is no other Cuban who has the potential to discredit Castro-communism," wrote newspaper columnist Carlos Alberto Montaner. "He is the one who enjoys the most credibility abroad and the only one who has acquired international renown."[127]

Organizations such as CANF and CID succeeded in the 1980s because of the nationwide shift to the right; simply put, their political agenda was compatible with Washington's. The Reagan administration paid special attention to the Cuban exile community. The president visited Miami four times between 1983 and 1987, even dining in Little Havana. During the 1983 visit, sponsored by CANF, more than seventy thousand people lined the route of his motorcade, and when he spoke at the Dade County Auditorium the predominantly Cuban audience interrupted his speech thirty-two times with cheers and ovations. Reagan granted personal interviews to radio commentators from Miami's Spanish-language stations and even invited Tomás Regalado, Jr., then WQBA's general news editor, to travel to the 1985 Geneva summit aboard Air Force One. Reagan invited the Brigade 2506 veterans to a special ceremony at the White House commemorating the twenty-fourth anniversary of the Bay of Pigs invasion, and in 1987, when the Veterans Association inaugurated la Casa de la Brigada 2506, its new headquarters and museum in Little Havana, the president sent U.N. ambassador Jeanne Kirkpatrick as his personal representative. One *municipio* newspaper in 1984 published Reagan's photograph on the front page with the caption "The best of all your friends";[128] another newspaper gushed, "This sure is a president!"[129] A street in Little Havana was named for him in the late 1980s.

Cuban emigrés applauded Reagan's commitment to the Nicaraguan contras; they saw the conflict in Nicaragua as an extension of their own political struggle. A *Miami Herald* survey in December 1983 revealed that 87 percent of Cuban emigrés supported U.S. military intervention in Central America in order to stop the spread of communism.[130] The emigrés were particularly opposed to abandoning the contras, since they knew firsthand the experience of being promised military assistance and then denied it.

The emigré community rallied to the contras' support. Miami radio station WRHC, "la Cadena Azul," sponsored a letter-writing campaign in support of Reagan's contra policy and sent 106,000 letters to the White House.[131] The Brigade 2506 Veterans Association, CANF, CID, and the Junta Patriótica Cubana (a coalition of two hundred civic organizations) lobbied extensively for aid to the anti-Sandinista forces. The local press reported the "reemergence" of secret military training camps near the Florida Everglades where Cuban and Nicaraguan exiles trained to assist the contras.[132] Several Brigade veterans served as tactical advisors in the contra camps in Central America, most notably Félix Rodríguez, a counterinsurgency expert and Vietnam veteran who was later implicated in the Iran-contra scandal. Groups of emigré doctors and nurses flew to secret camps in Honduras and elsewhere to operate on wounded soldiers. Television news reporter Leticia Callavo of Miami's WLTV–Channel 23 organized a "toy campaign" to collect Christmas gifts for "los niños contras" (the contra children) in Honduran refugee camps. By 1986, the exile community had donated $1.5 million for medical supplies, food, clothing, and other miscellaneous items.[133] Popular comedian Guillermo Alvarez Guede even donned a military uniform and entertained contra troops in secret Central American camps—the Cuban Bob Hope.

Cuban emigrés were supportive of the president when news of the Iran-contra scandal broke out. They did not care that Reagan officials broke the law or that the administration violated the trust of the American people: "It's the theory of the greater evil," explained Jorge Luis Hernández of Miami radio station WOCN. "Any violation of the law that goes against the greater evil—communism—[the emigrés] see as justified."[134] When Reagan needed a public relations boost, he naturally went to Miami, where his staff staged a three-hour support rally with the assistance of various exile groups. Three thousand Cuban and Nicaraguan exiles attended the rally, cheering and waving American flags, while White House communications director Patrick Buchanan attacked the president's congressional critics and the "liberal press." In his speech, of course, Buchanan carefully emphasized the contra component and not the sale of arms to Iran. "It was like striking matches in a room full of explosives," commented one news reporter covering the event.[135]

George Bush inherited the Cubans' good favor in the 1988 presidential election, garnering 85 percent of the emigré vote in south Florida. In turn, he faithfully maintained Reagan's hard line toward Cuba. Bush was initially opposed to economic sanctions against foreign subsidiaries that traded with Cuba, but he signed the Cuban Democracy Act as a concession to his loyal Cuban supporters during the 1992 electoral year. The ties between the Bush administration and the Cubans became a family affair: Jeb Bush, son of the president, relocated to south Florida and became the campaign manager for Ileana Ros-Lehtinen, who became the first Cuban American elected to the U.S. House of Representatives in 1989, occupying the seat long held by Democrat Claude Pepper. The younger Bush sought to capitalize on his father's Cuban supporters in the 1994 gubernatorial election, but despite Cuban support he was defeated by incumbent governor Lawton Chiles.

Political Prisoners and the Emigré Community

The only constant in Cuban emigré politics through the past three decades has been the emigrés' concern for political prisoners in Cuba. The issue was nonpartisan. While emigrés might have disagreed on the best way of dealing with the Castro government, their concern for human rights in Cuba transcended politics.

Estimates of the number of political prisoners in Cuba varied, depending on how different monitoring agencies defined the term. (Humanitarian agencies usually exclude persons who used or advocated violence, as well as draft resisters.) By the late 1970s, the National Council of Churches estimated that Cuban prisons held approximately ten thousand political prisoners, while the International Rescue Committee and the U.S. State Department put the number at twenty thousand.[136] Both Amnesty International and Americas Watch reported that Cuba had "the longest term political prisoners to be found in the world."[137] The exile community's estimates tended to be much higher, however, since emigrés included in their tallies both guerrillas and the *comandos* who had conducted paramilitary actions.

During the 1960s, emigrés were the prisoners' only advocates. In 1961, Dr. Elena Mederos, Castro's former minister of social welfare, established Of Human Rights at Georgetown University in Washington, D.C., to monitor human rights abuses in Cuba. Emigrés organized marches in Miami, Union City, and Washington and asked their lawmakers to intervene on behalf of the prisoners. Women played a crucial role in this campaign, since it was their husbands, fathers, and sons—and sisters and daughters—who were held prisoner in Cuba. They wrote letters and sent petitions to Amnesty International, Americas Watch, the International Red Cross, and the PEN clubs; they held press conferences; and they met with presidents, congressmen, and foreign dignitaries.

The cause gathered momentum during the 1970s, when leading European, Latin American, and U.S. intellectuals finally began to speak out against human rights abuses in Cuba. Writers such as Eugene Ionesco, Jean-Paul Sartre, Simone de Beauvoir, Octavio Paz, Juan Goytisolo, Ernesto Sábato, Mario Vargas Llosa, Fernando Arrabal, William Styron, and Norman Mailer protested the torture and imprisonment of artists and writers in Cuba. International organizations such as PEN (Playwrights, Essayists, Editors, and Novelists) publicized the cases of specific prisoners such as Armando Valladares, Pedro Valerio, Jorge Valls, and Angel Cuadra. The emigrés were often dismissed as reactionaries; but these intellectuals and international organizations gave legitimacy to their campaign.

The prisoners themselves became eloquent spokesmen for their own cause. They established a prison samizdat and smuggled their essays and poetry out of Cuba to family and friends, who published them in exile. Books such as Miguel Sales's *Desde las rejas* (1974), Cuadra's *Impromptus* (1977), and Valls's *Donde estoy no hay luz y está enrejado* (1974) and *Twenty Years and Forty Days* (1986) gave startling testimony of the violent and dehumanizing treatment of the men and women accused of crimes against the state.

No prisoner attracted as much worldwide attention as Armando Valladares. Arrested in 1960 at age twenty-three for discussing his opposition to communism at his job in the Ministry of Communications, Valladares spent the next twenty-two years in prison. During his incarceration, he wrote poetry and painted on tiny pieces of paper, often no larger than a postage stamp or a cigarette wrapper. He made paintbrushes from his own hair, and ink and pigments from whatever materials were on hand. His poems and pictures, rolled up inside suppositories, hairpins, and tetracycline capsules, were smuggled out of Cuba, and his wife, Martha, published and promoted his work in the United States and abroad.[138] His collected writings, published in the collections *Desde mi silla de ruedas, El corazón con qué vivo,* and *Cavernas del silencio,* received international attention. He was nicknamed "the wheelchair poet" because he was left paralyzed after a thirty-six-day hunger strike. Finally, after years of meeting with presidents, congressmen, and various foreign leaders, Martha Valladares succeeded in convincing French president François Mitterand to petition on her husband's behalf, and Valladares was released in 1982.

Valladares's most controversial book was published three years after his release from prison: *Contra toda esperanza* (1985; *Against All Hope,* 1986). In these prison memoirs, he graphically describes what he witnessed at various prisons throughout the island during his twenty-two years of incarceration: physical and mental torture of prisoners, firing squads, squalid living conditions, long hours of arduous labor, hunger strikes, and the feelings of total isolation that drove some prisoners to madness or suicide. Valladares's book has been published in ten languages and has done more to increase awareness of human rights violations in Cuba than anything else of the past twenty-five years. His account was all the more poignant because he was not a politician, *comando,* or counterrevolutionary but an ordinary civil servant who fell victim to the revolution. Despite the Cuban government's attempts to discredit him, the book was a devastating blow to Castro's reputation in the international community.

Other works focused attention on Cuba's human rights abuses. In 1984, Academy Award–winning cinematographer Néstor Almendros and filmmaker Orlando Jiménez-Leal produced the documentary film *Conducta impropia* (Improper conduct), which presented testimony from dozens of survivors of Castro's prisons, from homosexuals forced to undergo "rehabilitation" in the UMAP camps[139] of the 1960s to internationally acclaimed artists, writers, dramatists, and intellectuals who were imprisoned for "ideological diversionism" or "improper conduct." Filmed in Paris, New York, Miami, London, Rome, and Madrid, the film provided a powerful indictment of the Castro government. Although it was originally made for a French television series entitled *Resistance,* Almendros and Jiménez-Leal exhibited their documentary at film festivals in Europe and the United States; in 1984, *Conducta impropia* received the Grand Prix at the XII International Human Rights Festival in Strasbourg. The film was so well received that in 1988 Almendros and filmmaker Jorge Ulla produced *Nadie escuchaba* (Nobody Listened), which further chronicled the Cuban government's abuse of basic human rights over the past three decades and the indifference of the world community to what was happening in Cuba.

Unfortunately, the campaign to free political prisoners focused on the plight of two small groups of well-known prisoners, the former revolutionaries and the artists and writers around whom the intellectual community rallied. These men and women were important enough to make the front page of leading newspapers around the world and to merit distinction from groups like Amnesty International and PEN; but the overwhelming majority of the political prisoners in Cuba were not Huber Matos or Jorge Valls. They had not fought with Castro in the Escambray, did not write poetry, and were not chosen to be the monthly "Prisoner of Conscience" by a human rights group. They were ordinary citizens who were charged with "ideological diversionism" and thus they remained anonymous. Guillermo Cabrera Infante compared them to Dumas's man in the iron mask, whose identity was also hidden from the world.[140]

Women political prisoners received even less attention than the men. Women were tried for the same crimes as men, received sentences as harsh as men's, and were tortured as readily as men, but their plight remained largely ignored by the emigré community; the term *counterrevolutionary* automatically conjured up a male image. The roster of women who served time in prison for counterrevolutionary activities or ideological diversionism has never been fully tabulated,[141] and it was not until the late 1980s that the women's experience even began to be told in the exile press in Miami. Among the more well-known prisoners—because they lived to tell their tales in exile—were Dr. Martha Frayde, former Cuban ambassador to UNESCO, who in 1976 was sentenced to 29 years for attempting to leave the country illegally and for "consorting with dissidents"[142]; Pola Grau Alsina, released in 1978 after serving fourteen years of a thirty-year sentence for her role in various counterrevolutionary activities; and Hilda Felipe, who, with her husband, had published the Communist Party newspaper *Hoy,* and was sentenced to two years in prison and three years of house arrest for ideological diversionism.

By the late 1970s, negative publicity (together with an overcrowded prison system) forced the Cuban government to institute an amnesty program, and the government released more than five thousand political prisoners between 1978 and 1986. To take advantage of the new policy, emigrés frequently asked foreign leaders and international celebrities to intercede. In 1984, Jesse Jackson secured the release of twenty-six

Cubans and twenty-two Americans during his visit to Havana.[143] In June 1986, Senator Edward Kennedy's office helped free Ricardo Montero Duque, one of the last Brigadistas still in prison.[144] A few months later, Spanish prime minister Felipe González secured the release of Eloy Gutierrez Menoyo, one of the leaders of the Segundo Frente del Escambray. Castro released prisoners to Régis Debray, a former French guerrilla fighter and official in the Mitterand government, and to various U.S. congressmen.[145] Even undersea explorer Jacques Cousteau managed to free twenty-one political prisoners.[146] So many visitors to Cuba left with freed political prisoners that one exile newspaper joked that Cuba had the most unusual souvenirs in the world.

About half of the political prisoners granted amnesty by the Cuban government during this period emigrated to the United States, where they reunited with family and friends and encountered new challenges. Like all other emigrés, they had to find employment and learn to communicate with their non-Hispanic neighbors; but unlike their compatriots, they also had to adjust psychologically to life outside prison. They had to relearn basic skills, such as how to drive a car; they had to cope with household appliances they had never seen before; they even had to learn to adjust to the simple comforts of sleeping on a mattress. "When you first become free, you want to forget, to close your mind like a curtain, and begin to live again," wrote Miguel Sales, sentenced to prison for trying to smuggle his wife and daughter out of Cuba. "The simplest actions, like paying bills, putting gas in the car, ordering a meal, or writing a check, acquire great significance."[147] Many of the prisoners returned to families they had not seen in years; they had to reestablish intimacy with their spouses and build new relationships with children who were now grown and perhaps had children of their own. In some cases prisoners returned to find that their parents had died or their spouses had divorced them.

In its fight to discredit Castro's human rights record, the emigré community received the most assistance from the Reagan and Bush administrations, in part due to intensive lobbying by CANF, CID, and other exile groups. From 1987 to 1991, the U.S. government tried to have Cuba officially condemned by the United Nations Commission on Human Rights. A U.S. delegation traveled to Geneva in March 1987 to present its fourteen-paragraph resolution calling upon the Cuban government to guarantee fundamental freedoms to its citizens and permit the emigration of anyone who wished to leave the country.[148] Heading the U.S. delegation as special UN ambassador was Armando Valladares.

Although Valladares lived in Madrid and spoke little English, the United States had granted him citizenship so that he could represent the U.S. at the Palais des Nations. For several days, Valladares offered firsthand testimony of Cuba's human rights abuses and exchanged insults with the Cuban delegation, which accused him of being a CIA agent. Over a dozen former political prisoners also traveled to Geneva, their trips paid for by CANF and other emigré organizations; although under commission rules they could not testify, they met with delegates in the after hours to show physical scars as proof of the abuses in Cuban prisons.

After almost two weeks of hearings, the Commission on Human Rights voted, 19 to 18, not to debate the U.S. resolution, with six countries abstaining. A coalition of mostly Eastern bloc and Latin American countries voted against the resolution to prevent the "politicization of the human rights process."[149] The emigré community in Miami was outraged. Over the next several days, thousands of emigrés demonstrated in front of the consulates of countries that had voted against the U.S.

Instead of abandoning the issue, the emigré community intensified its lobbying. A coalition of organizations, including CANF, Alpha 66, the Junta Patriótica Cubana, the Cuban Municipalities in Exile, and Mujeres Cubanas Pro-Derechos Humanos (Cuban Women for Human Rights) initiated a publicity campaign entitled Derechos Humanos '88 (Human Rights '88) to focus attention on the 1988 UN hearings. Emigrés purchased full-page ads in the major newspapers around the world, staged marches and demonstrations in front of consulates and embassies, and tied yellow ribbons (symbolizing the demand that hostages be freed) all over their communities.[150] On the eve of the hearings, dozens of former political prisoners went on a hunger strike. The news reached Cuba via Radio Martí, and more than seventy political prisoners joined the hunger strike.[151] A number of emigrés—former political prisoners, heads of political organizations, civic leaders, journalists, intellectuals—traveled to Geneva to witness the proceedings. Throughout the hearings, the emigrés lobbied the delegates, held press conferences, and sponsored special screenings throughout the city of *Nadie escuchaba*.

Finally, to avoid what promised to be another stalemate, four Latin American delegations suggested a compromise: a United Nations team would travel to Cuba to examine the Cuban penal system. The Castro government accepted the compromise and agreed to grant the UN team "complete freedom" for five days.[152] Both the United States and Cuba claimed victory in Geneva; the emigré community was not as certain. Most emigrés doubted that the UN team would be able to conduct a comprehensive examination in such a limited time, and they doubted that Castro would grant access to government records. Indeed, the UN delegation, which spent nine days in Cuba (September 16–25, 1988), found no grounds for a condemnation of Cuba. In its thirty-thousand-word document, the delegation reported that Cuban citizens were denied basic civil liberties such as freedom of expression, movement, and assembly, but there was no evidence of disappearances or secret executions. While the United States claimed that there were over fifteen thousand political prisoners in Cuba, the delegation, citing Cuban government sources, reported only 121. The UN Commission on Human Rights eventually adopted a resolution thanking the Cuban government for its cooperation.[153]

Victory finally came in 1990. Following the demise of communism in Eastern Europe, nations that had once defended Cuba became some of its principal critics. Cuba itself witnessed the emergence of a dozen human rights and pro-democracy organizations that provided human rights groups in Miami with much of the information they needed to continue challenging the Castro government.[154] The Cuban Committee for Human Rights smuggled a four-hundred-page report to Miami, and Amnesty International published its own twenty-six-page report on the prisoners of conscience in Cuba.[155] Consequently, in March 1991, the UN Commission on Human Rights finally voted to appoint a human rights monitor for Cuba. Twenty-two nations voted in favor of the resolution, including former Cuban allies Bulgaria and Hungary; six nations voted against, and fifteen nations (mostly Latin American) abstained.[156] The Cuban delegation was stunned. Raul Roa Kouri, Cuba's chief delegate, said his government would not accept a "single letter or comma" of the resolution or "anything imposed on [Cuba] by the United States in this field or in any other."[157] The Cuban delegation could not deny, however, that its government had suffered its most serious defeat in decades. Both the emigré community in Miami and the human rights groups on the island finally had an important victory to celebrate.

The 1990s: A Turning Point in U.S.–Cuba Relations?

The 1990s began with an escalation of hostilities between Cuba and the United States. The Bush administration, having witnessed the collapse of communism in Europe and the defeat of the Sandinistas in Nicaragua, abandoned any plans it might have had of accommodating the United States' longtime foe in the Caribbean. By 1991, Cuba had already met many of the U.S. government's conditions for renewing full diplomatic relations, among them the withdrawal of its forces from Angola. Conservative political strategists argued, however, that diplomatic relations would only strengthen the Castro government at the very moment its collapse seemed certain. Instead, with the creation of TV Martí, the lobbying for condemnation of Cuba in the United Nations, and the reinforcement of the U.S. trade embargo, the administration hoped to force democratic reforms, and perhaps eliminate Fidel Castro once and for all.

Talk of returning to Cuba was all over the exile community. A popular political button selling in Little Havana showed Castro toppled by a series of dominoes, with the slogan "¡El próximo!" (The next one). One of the most widely read books in Miami was comedian Guillermo Alvarez Guedes's *El día que cayó Fidel Castro* (The day Fidel Castro was overthrown), and two of the most popular plays on Miami's *vodevil* circuit were *A Cuba me voy hoy mismo . . . que se acabó el comunismo* (I'm leaving for Cuba this very minute . . . communism is finished) and *En los 90 Fidel revienta* (In the 1990s Fidel expires). CANF, Alpha 66, the Junta Patriótica Cubana, the Cuban Municipalities in Exile, and other exile organizations began drafting versions of Cuba's new constitution and transitional government,[158] while Cuba's former political parties began planning their own courses of action.[159] Representatives from the AFL-CIO met with former Cuban labor leaders in Little Havana to plan the future of Cuba's unions. Several companies began drafting plans for the construction of hydrofoils to sail between the two countries, and airlines began charting routes to Havana. The Dade County police department formulated plans for crowd control for the day the Castro government fell; the *Miami Herald* proposed a city-wide festival at the Orange Bowl for the occasion. More significantly, Governor Bob Martínez established the Free Cuba Commission, an eighteen-member commission of business leaders, government officials, and academics, to study the challenges the state of Florida will face after the Castro government collapses.

After the collapse of communism in the Soviet Union, many political observers gave the Castro government only a few more months before it, too, fell; but the Cuban government defied the odds. In 1990, in an effort to speed up democratic reforms on the island, Cubans both on the island and in Miami began to call for a national dialogue (including the emigrés) to determine the country's future. Although Castro continued to insist that Cuba would never abandon Marxism, the reformers believed that the time was right to sit down with Cuban officials and negotiate for democratic reforms, perhaps even for multiparty elections. The chief proponent of the dialogue was the Cuban Committee for Human Rights, a Havana-based dissident group headed by Gustavo Arcos Bergnes, a former member of the July 26th Movement who had served more than ten years in prison for human rights activities.[160]

Not since the *diálogo* of the late 1970s had an issue roused such passionate debate. Once again, emigrés were divided into two camps: those who favored a *diálogo* and those who wanted nothing less than the unconditional overthrow of the Castro government. Armando Valladares, who had relied on the CCHR's reports for much of his testimony in Geneva, emerged as the principal spokesman for the hardliners in the community. He called Arcos Bergnes a traitor and broke contact with the organization, claiming that the call was a "betrayal of those who fought, died, and remain in prison for nearly thirty years."[161]

Three of the most powerful exile organizations, CANF, the Junta Patriótica Cubana, and CID, also opposed the dialogue, arguing that it was absurd to negotiate with the Castro government now that it was on the verge of collapse: the only logical course of action was to isolate the regime further until it fell. Toward this end, exile leaders met in Miami and Moscow with Soviet officials to encourage them to abandon their economic subsidies of the island,[162] and the emigrés continued to lobby Congress in support of the Torricelli bill (which became the Cuban Democracy Act). One hundred thousand people marched through the heart of Little Havana to protest the proposed dialogue, while more than ninety exile organizations, led by CANF, signed a document opposing the dialogue and pledging to work together to defeat Castro.[163] Miami's Spanish-language radio stations criticized the idea round the clock; WQBA even went so far as to fire two news commentators, Ricardo Bofill and Ariel Hidalgo, for their vocal support of Arcos Bergnes. The extremists also had their say: a bomb exploded outside Little Havana's Cuban Museum of Art and Culture, which hardliners perceived as a "den of *dialogueros*."

To judge from letters to local newspapers, however, many emigrés supported Arcos Bergnes. Former political prisoners and leaders of human rights groups came to his defense, and one group even nominated him for the Nobel Peace Prize. Showing the usual emigré propensity for creating political organizations, a series of new exile groups emerged in the 1990s to lobby in support of a national dialogue in Cuba that would lead to democratic reforms. The Cuban Liberal Union (led by newspaper columnist Carlos Alberto Montaner), the resurrected Cuban Christian Democratic Party (led by José Ignacio Rasco), and the Social Democratic Coordinating Center all called for a dialogue to work towards free elections in Cuba; to consolidate their lobbying efforts, the three organizations joined to form the Cuban Democratic Platform.[164] The Cuban American Coalition, on the other hand, led by José Cruz, and the Social Democratic Cuban Party, led by former political prisoner Vladimir Ramírez, called for reforms within the socialist system. Former Cuban revolutionary and political prisoner Eloy Gutierrez Menoyo organized his own group, Cambio Cubano (Cuban Change), to work for a peaceful political transition on the island. One fringe organization, the Puerto Rico–based Cuban Statehood Movement, even called for the annexation of Cuba by the United States.[165]

It is difficult to estimate the percentage of the community that the pro-dialogue organizations represented. Back in 1988, a poll conducted in Miami and Union City revealed that 41 percent of emigrés favored accords that would lead to better relations between Cuba and the United States.[166] A *Miami Herald* poll three years later, however, revealed that only 28 percent supported a dialogue with the Castro government.[167] If these figures are reliable, the change is explainable in light of political events: the collapse of the communist world and the belief that Castro's fall was imminent led many emigrés to abandon their accommodationist views, fearing that they would only perpetuate Castro's hold on the country. Whatever the actual figures, however, a segment of the community was vocally supporting some type of rapprochement for the first time since the volatile 1970s. Despite continued pressure from the hardliners, the more liberal voices were making themselves heard. Even those who were wary of establishing a dialogue with the Castro government were calling for rational discourse at least within the exile community. As one editorial challenged:

> Why have we Cubans insisted on living in a perpetual state of war? It is time that we demonstrate to the world, and especially to those who are living under the horror of tyranny, and above all to ourselves, that we have learned the lesson and that we are going to exile from our thoughts and actions the gratuitous intransigence and the absurd pretension that we are the sole possessors of the absolute truth.[168]

Among the emigrés who supported better relations with the Castro government were those who had families in Cuba. They wanted to travel to their homeland on a regular basis without having to spend a fortune on inflated air fares, visas, and taxes. The Cuban government already allowed only a few flights per week between Miami and Havana. Arguing that the family reunification trips provided the Castro government with needed American dollars—an estimated $200 million per year—CANF pressured the U.S. government to restrict these trips further and to curtail any direct assistance to the Cuban population in the form of food and medicines.[169] Emigrés with families on the island, however, opposed such measures. The Cuban American Committee for Family Rights and other lobbying groups pressured the U.S. government to keep these channels of communication open, limited though they were, and the group Jewish Solidarity organized shipments of food and medicine to the island. When WAQI (Radio Mambí) in Miami condemned the sending of food and money to Cubans on the island, demonstrators picketed the station.[170] "You don't want to help Fidel, but you feel sorry for your family and you don't want them to have to suffer," said one emigré. "It's like you are torn between two desires."[171] The moral dilemma intensified further in 1993 when the Castro government relaxed currency and travel restrictions, making it easier for emigrés to travel and spend money in Cuba—and to feel guilty about it.[172]

Poll findings varied, but the pro-dialogue Cubans were certainly a minority. However, the fact that journalists, financiers, intellectuals, and other prominent leaders in the community as well as ordinary folk were openly and vocally supporting an unpopular position suggested that the numbers might grow. A passionate debate was under way in Miami, and unlike that generated by the *diálogo* of the late 1970s, this was not a debate about the moral implications of collaborating with the enemy. The stakes were now much higher, because any course of action taken by the emigrés might tilt Cuba one way or the other. Various groups fought to dictate not only the tone of the debate but actual foreign policy. In the ten years since the first *diálogo*, however, the more liberal voices had gained strength.

A number of demonstrations against powerful exile institutions showed that emigrés were rebelling against their reactionary reputation and the institutions that had promoted this reputation. In April 1991, during the annual commemoration of the failed Bay of Pigs invasion, one group of former *brigadistas* caused a commotion by insisting that the Veterans Association honor not only the Brigade soldiers who died but the Cuban soldiers as well.[173] A number of new magazines (*Contrapunto*, for example) that articulated the views of more politically liberal emigrés began circulating. In 1993, as an alternative to the conservative hegemony of the Cuban American National Foundation, liberal emigré businessmen, academics, and other professionals formed the Cuban Committee for Democracy, with ties to dissident groups on the island, to work for a "peaceful transition in Cuba and healthy U.S.–Cuba relations."[174] With offices at the Brookings Institution in Washington, the CCD has sponsored symposiums and press conferences on U.S.–Cuba relations and held various congressional briefings.[175]

A new radio station and a new radio program emerged in south Florida in the early 1990s, each trying to provide an alternative to the Castro-bashing operations that dominated the media. WWFE (Radio Fe), whose general manager was Emilio Milián, took a conservative position against the Castro regime but did so without the sensationalism and bias that characterized the older stations. (The Cuban Committee for Democracy had its own radio show, "Transición," on Radio Fe on Saturday mornings.) Radio Progreso, transmitted for a few hours each week via WOCN–Union Radio, was a particularly controversial program. Operated by Francisco Aruca, owner of Marazul Tours, which arranged flights between Miami and Havana, Radio Progreso broadcast news, sports, and music taped from radio stations in Cuba and aired commentaries critical of the conservative powerbrokers of Miami. The program called itself "El nuevo idioma de Miami" (Miami's new language), and its motto was "Porque queremos informarlo y motivarlo pero no volverlo loco" (Because we want to inform and motivate you but not drive you crazy).[176] Although the program was named after Havana's Radio Progreso, the former news director of Cuba's Radio Progreso became a vocal critic of Aruca and his program after defecting in 1991, calling it a propaganda tool for the Castro government. Extremists used a variety of tactics to try to shut down both Radio Fe and Radio Progreso, including intimidating advertisers and damaging property. By 1994, Radio Progreso had shut down, but the more moderate Radio Fe remained in operation. The fact that the latter had a loyal audience revealed a growing desire in the community for open forums. By 1994, a few of the older, more conservative stations had begun to hire news commentators who were more moderate and conciliatory in their editorials.

The hardliners, of course, refused to give ground: CANF's campaign against the *Herald* was only one example of their fear of losing power. Conservative exile groups successfully blocked Clinton's nomination of emigré and Wall Street lawyer Mario Baeza to the State Department's senior Latin American post on the grounds that he would be soft on the Castro government.[177] In April 1994, a group of emigrés returning from a conference on emigration in Havana sponsored by the Castro government was met with heavy criticism, boycotts, and even death threats.[178] In August, the hardliners won their most important victory in years when, in response to Castro's refusal to stem illegal boat traffic from the island, the Clinton administration made it illegal to send U.S. dollars to friends and relatives on the island and cut off all charter air traffic to Cuba—two measures that CANF and other exile organizations had been pushing for years.

By 1994, then, the exile community seemed to be at war with itself: while some adopted a more liberal position towards Cuba, others dug in their heels. Outsiders observing these events might have easily concluded that the Cuban emigrés in south Florida had not adapted to life in the United States, that they remained locked in the past. But the facts prove otherwise. By the early 1990s, members of this community of largely first-generation exiles and immigrants had been elected to government at the local, state, and national levels. Cubans occupied positions in city commissions around the state of Florida, held seven seats in the Florida house of representatives and three in the state senate, and had served as mayors of several cities, including Miami, West Miami, North Miami, Sweetwater, and Hialeah. Two emigrés (Ileana Ros-Lehtinen, the first Hispanic woman elected to the House, and Lincoln Díaz-Balarat, the nephew of Fidel Castro) occupied seats in the U.S. House of Representatives. In addition, emigrés held top administrative posts in the key institutions of the county: one was president of the Miami Herald Publishing Company, another was superintendent of Dade County public schools, another president of Florida International University, another president of the South Florida AFL-CIO. Even the state chair of Florida Democratic Party was a Cuban emigré.

It was clear that a significant percentage of this community planned to remain in the United States regardless of what might happen in Cuba. At the same time, Cuba played—and would always play—a large role in public debate. With the island less than one hundred miles away, and with the continual influx of new emigrés to south Florida, it could not be otherwise. Whether they perceived themselves to be Cuban exiles or Cuban Americans, they would continue to try to shape Cuban affairs.

CHAPTER 5

Cuban Writers
and Scholars in Exile

The diversity of the Cuban emigré community is reflected in the creative and intellectual work of its members. By the late 1970s, the list of intellectuals who had gone into exile was long and varied. Among the more renowned authors, poets, and dramatists in exile were Guillermo Cabrera Infante, Enrique Labrador Ruiz, Eugenio Florit, Severo Sarduy, Lino Novás Calvo, Lydia Cabrera, Matías Montes Huidobro, and Eduardo Manet. Many had been supporters of the revolution, and a number had served in the Castro government's cultural agencies or in the foreign service until disaffection forced them to choose exile. Cuba's emigration policy in the late 1970s and the Mariel boatlift of 1980 sent more dissident authors into exile, and the arrival of Heberto Padilla, Reinaldo Arenas, Belkis Cuza Male, César Leante, Andrés Reinaldo, Manuel Serpa, Carlos Victoria, Reinaldo García Ramos, and Miguel Correa, among many others, revitalized emigré arts and letters, providing new insight into the lives of both exiles and Cubans under the revolutionary government.

By the late 1980s, the exile creative community had expanded to include a new generation of writers, among them Roberto G. Fernández, Elías Miguel Muñoz, Ana María Simó, Iván Acosta, Dolores Prida, Gustavo Pérez-Firmat, Ricardo Pau-Llosa, and María Irene Fornés. They constituted a distinct generation not so much because of their age—many were first-generation immigrants themselves—but because of their thematic concerns. Unlike the exile authors who considered themselves Cubans writing outside of Cuba, writers of this new generation saw themselves as both Cuban and American. Most spent their

formative years in the United States and were truly bilingual and bicultural in their orientation. While the exile authors wrote largely in
Spanish, the Cuban American authors wrote in both Spanish and English, sometimes within the same text. Their creative work responded
largely to the interaction of cultures in the U.S. rather than to events in
Cuba and Latin America. Some explored race, gender, and sexuality
and how these influence identity and experience. Such themes are to
some extent universal, but since these authors wrote as immigrant minorities living in the U.S. they were labeled "ethnic" writers rather than
Cuban or Latin American writers. Their quest to define *cubanidad* for
themselves, however, links them to generations of Cuban authors
equally concerned with defining a national identity.

A discussion of Cuban exile and Cuban American writers requires
looking beyond south Florida. While some authors live among their
compatriots in Miami, others have chosen to live elsewhere—some to
avoid the petty intrigues and squabblings of exile politics, others because they have academic appointments in colleges and universities
around the country. Still others prefer to live in vital cultural centers
such as New York, Los Angeles, Paris, Rome, Madrid, or London,
where networks of artists and writers offer support and inspiration. A
few writers must live outside the United States because they have been
denied immigrant visas, reportedly due to their earlier connections to
the Castro government.[1] But wherever emigré writers settle, Miami
serves for them as both mirror and lightning rod: reflecting the best and
worst of Cuban culture, it both attracts and repels them. Many write for
and in response to the exile community, celebrating and satirizing *el
exilio* as well as their compatriots in Cuba. Their most loyal—and sometimes most hostile—audience is in Miami, and while they may try to
distance themselves from *el politiqueo* (exile politics), they cannot remain unaffected by it.

The work of these writers articulates *la problematica cubana,*
whether from the perspective of a Cuban exile or a Cuban American.
They express the concerns most emigrés have about Cuba or about life
in the United States. They write essays and articles for exile literary
magazines and the exile press. They appear at lectures, exhibits, and
cultural festivals and on television and radio news programs in south
Florida. They do not limit their audience to Cuban exiles, of course,
but because of their elite status within the culture they act as speakers,
whether consciously or unconsciously, for different segments of the
exile community.

Cuban Exile and Cuban American Literature

Few novels and short stories by Cuban exiles were published in the U.S. during the 1960s. Emigrés wrote almost exclusively in Spanish, which limited their audience in the United States. Editors at mainstream U.S. publishing houses were only interested in the work of internationally acclaimed authors such as Cabrera Infante. Most writers sent their manuscripts to publishing houses in Mexico or Spain, where they had better luck, but more often than not they ended up paying for the publication of their work themselves. In the wake of the revolution most of Europe and Latin America idealized the "Cuban experiment" and regarded Cuba to be the model socialist state, and few wanted to read the views of the *gusanos*. Fame did not always guarantee publication: some of Cuba's best writers, including Enrique Labrador Ruiz, Lino Novás Calvo, and Lydia Cabrera, had to finance publication of their works during their first years in exile.[2] By the early 1970s, a few publishing houses, most notably Editorial Universal, had been founded by Cuban exiles in Miami, New York, and San Juan for the specific purpose of publishing the work of emigré authors.

The work produced during the 1960s and early 1970s was of mixed quality. The more established authors, poets, and playwrights continued to experiment and produced some of their best work in exile in the United States and Europe. As Cabrera Infante commented, "I think that exile has made my work better. . . . I have not been able to return to Cuba, so I had to invent an Havana for myself, out of words, which has been a celebration."[3] These authors wrote about what they knew best: Cuba and Latin America. They continued to explore what literary critics have termed *lo real maravilloso* (the magic realism) of the Latin American experience: the geography, folklore, and exchange of cultures in Cuba, the Caribbean, and South America. Their plots and characters evolved within a Cuban or Latin American setting.

A number of "antirevolutionary" novels were written in the 1960s by lesser-known authors. The first such was Andres Rivero Collado's *Enterrado vivo* (Buried alive), published in Mexico in 1960, and it was followed by a host of others, by such writers as Angel A. Castro, Emilio Fernández Camus, Ramiro Gómez-Kemp, René G. Landa, Orlando Nuñez, Manuel Cobo Sausa, Raul A. Fowler, Miguel F. Márquez y de la Cerra, and Luis Ricardo Alonso.[4] Most of these novels are valuable more as sociopolitical documentary than as literature. They are stories about the revolution and the displacement it caused. These authors give graphic and often autobiographical accounts of the abuses of the revolution: the imprisonment and execution of government opponents, the general climate of suspicion and harassment, the repression of civil liberties.

For many, writing these antirevolutionary novels served as a means of exorcising personal demons and venting their hatred of Fidel Castro, but the vitriolic, dogmatic tone of the writing is unsettling, forcing the non-Cuban reader to question the truth of the information. Hence, non-Cubans generally dismissed their work as propaganda tracts. Since some of the writers had ties to the Batista government or to previous administrations, their tales of abuses were dismissed as the fantasies of the corrupt and vengeful bourgeoisie, and thus these novels had only a limited circulation and lifespan. Today they are available only from a few dozen libraries around the country. Thirty years after the revolution, however, they help to explain the mindset of one segment of the early exile community and shed light on the reasons for their disaffection.

By the late 1970s, many emigré authors began focusing their creative energies on the United States rather than on Cuba, reflecting the general trend in the community itself. For those who came of age in the United States, Cuba was a beautiful and stirring memory, but they were more and more bound to North American society. The cultural revolution of the 1960s and early 1970s encouraged this creative shift, as the civil rights movement and the counterculture focused new attention on "minority" experiences and thus on minority art and literature. Young Cuban American writers, like other Latinos, had opportunities to develop and showcase their creative work: grants gave them time to write, journals recruited their work, academic appointments offered institutional support. They were sometimes labeled fascists and counterrevolutionaries by their more left-wing colleagues and critics for their views on Cuba, but since their work focused on the more neutral themes of identity and accommodation, they avoided the censure that many exile authors encountered.

The distinction between Cuban exile literature and Cuban American literature was sometimes a subtle one, and some authors alternated between the two, refusing to be pigeonholed. The principal concern of Cuban American literature was the issue of identity. What does it mean to be Cuban? Can one retain one's national identity despite overwhelming pressures to conform and "Americanize"? Conversely, what does it mean to be an American? How does one maintain a balance between the two worlds? How do race, gender, and sexuality shape identity and experience? In trying to answer these questions, Cuban American authors produced an exciting body of work and provided us the best understanding of the psychology of the Cuban exile experience.

The works of Roberto G. Fernández, the most renowned of this new generation of Cuban American writers—*La vida es un special* (1981), *La montaña rusa* (1985), and *Raining Backwards* (1988)—are composed of satirical vignettes about life in exile. Among his targets are the older Cuban emigrés who cannot or will not adapt to the United States. They complain constantly about life in the U.S. For them, Cuba is the most beautiful country, with the finest people; the U.S. can never compare. A character in *Raining Backwards,* for example, insists that the sand of Cuba's beaches was made out of grated silver and diamond dust, with a texture "finer than Mennen's Baby Powder. . . . Everyone knows that Varadero was the most beautiful beach, not only in the world but in the whole universe. The waters were forever changing colors . . . the breezes were always warm but never hot. So how dare you say that Cancun or Sanibel are better and more beautiful. Liar! Communist!"[5]

The exiles' nostalgic memory is selective, of course. Many emigrés ignore the social and economic problems that encouraged the revolution. For them there was no racism, no poverty, no terrorism. In casual conversation, emigrés—particularly those who had been upwardly mobile in Cuba—often exaggerate how much property and wealth they owned in Cuba and subsequently lost to the revolution, distinguishing for themselves their experience from that of their compatriots. According to one popular joke in south Florida, if Cubans had had as much land prior to the revolution as they said they had, Cuba would have been the size of the Soviet Union. Fernández and other authors satirize this propensity: in *Raining Backwards* one character insists that her mother's cocoa plantation "would have put the Ponderosa to shame"—although in fact there were no cocoa plantations in Cuba.[6] A character in Omar Torres's *Fallen Angels Sing* (1991) insists that Cuba never had as many flies as the United States and that no one ever died from cancer there. "That's an American illness," she says.[7]

If older emigrés indulge in excessive nostalgia, it is because they feel alienated and marginalized. Their lives have been turned upside down. They have had to uproot themselves from their jobs, their homeland, their friends and neighbors, and in some cases their families, and they have had to adapt to a new language, a new social and economic status, a new lifestyle. Despite their attempts to recreate in south Florida the society they left behind, life can never again be what it was. In *Fallen Angels Sing*, Ana insists on being buried in Cuba when she dies. When asked what difference it makes where she is buried, she answers, "It makes a lot of difference. I don't belong here. We don't belong here." Her relatives agree: "We'll never be Americans," says Mario. "We'll never be anything," says Elena.[8] In Elías Miguel Muñoz's *Crazy Love* (1989), Julián and Johnny believe that their mother should never have left Cuba; American society is too complicated, too threatening, and it terrifies her. "Take a plant or a fruit tree that only grows in the tropics and plant it in a cold land," says Julián. "It will die, or go crazy, turn poisonous."[9]

In Virgil Suárez's *Latin Jazz* (1989), the elderly grandfather, Esteban, is the only member of his family who has not adjusted to life in Los Angeles. While his daughter and son-in-law complain about how hard they must work to make it in the United States, they manage to earn a modest living operating an ice cream truck in L.A. Esteban spends his time doing odd jobs around the house, but mostly he reminisces: he "has never forgotten the past, for in the past he lost, as he says, his identity, dignity, his respect for humanity."[10] The Mariel boatlift provides him with the opportunity to fulfill at last his wife's wish to return to the homeland. With his friend Domingo he digs up his wife's remains, cremates them in a pit, and then travels to Key West, where they rent a boat to take them to Cuba to scatter her ashes. Domingo ultimately decides to stay in Cuba, but Esteban, surprisingly, returns to the U.S., realizing that he now has as many ties to the U.S. as to Cuba. Back home he learns that his son, a political prisoner, has escaped and reached Key West. Esteban finds a new purpose for his life in helping his son rebuild his own.

Elías Miguel Muñoz also explores the emigrés' obsessive nostalgia. One of his poems, "Grandfather," tells how a family must lock an old relative in his room each day: "Because according to my grandfather / you need only cross / the door's threshold / to arrive in Cuba."[11] The reader is left to ponder whether the old man's nostalgia for Cuba caused his senility, or vice versa. The line separating obsession and madness can sometimes seem thin.

The alienation felt by immigrants and the clash between cultures are central themes in Cuban American literature (as in most ethnic literature). Despite the American cultural presence on the island before the revolution, the average working-class Cuban had little social contact with Americans, and in exile the emigrés find Americans puzzling, their customs alien. American idiomatic expressions make no sense; the American lifestyle is too fast-paced; American morals are found lacking. "We should never have left," says one character in *Raining Backwards*. "This country changes people. I think it's the water. It makes them crazy!"[12] When Connie brings her American boyfriend to a family gathering, the relatives are all upset: "You know they don't even respect their parents," says one.[13]

In Leopoldo M. Hernández's play *Martínez* (1980), the title character complains to the audience that he cannot understand American colloquialisms. "I resent to be told that I do not understand English. What I cannot understand is the English that Americans speak. Back in my country I was taught the language of Shakespeare, which is not the same as the language of Frankie from the Bronx."[14] His accent gets him into all sorts of trouble: it is a lightning rod, attracting prejudice and discrimination. "An accent is like an illness," he says. "At least it hurts like one."[15]

Martínez is also unsettled by the pace of life in the United States, which he considers uncivilized. He tells the audience:

> You don't understand *la siesta*. Americans will never understand how back home you can rush from work at noon, take a battered bus with passengers hanging from the door like bananas, reach home forty-five minutes later, have a beer, soup, lots of french bread, a juicy steak with eggs and white rice and plantains and custard for dessert, go to sleep for exactly ten minutes and get so much rest in those ten minutes that you have the energy to jump back into a bus full of sweat and strange odors, make a pass or two at a female passenger who is forgotten immediately after, and reach the office to put four more hours in yelling over the phone. You will never understand that. . . . You would understand however to work downtown in Manhattan and live in Connecticut and take the car at 5:45 am and rush to the station to get the 6:45 on time and travel fifty-two miles standing while munching burnt toast, then take the subway to the final destination in which you work for eight hours with no siesta, get back into the subway and defy death while trying to get the 5:20 along with a tribe of cavemen and eventually reach home where your wife tells you that the plumber never came and then you remember that you have to pee in the patio like yesterday.[16]

Emigrés could not duplicate the lives they left behind, but they tried to establish a familiar routine and environment for themselves. Even the simplest act could have tremendous meaning and comfort. For an old man in Carolina Hospital's poem "The Old Order," a quick fix of Cuban food gives him the strength to go on: "Outside, now he tilts his cap and walks away with ease."[17] In another of Hospital's poems, "A Visit to West New York," her mother-in-law's house, with the statue of la Virgen de la Caridad on the dresser and the smells of Cuban coffee and burnt toast, offers a warm and familiar welcome, in contrast to the cold world outside the house.[18] Too strong a fixation on the past, however, can ultimately tear a family apart. In Miguel González-Pando's play *Once upon a Time,* Dolores's obsession with the past threatens the economic future of the family as well as her relationship with her children. She has been carefully saving her small salary as a seamstress for years for a lavish *quinceañera* for her daughter—but her daughter does not want the party. Although the family lives in near poverty, Dolores is obsessed with this ritual of the Cuban middle class. It is her link to the past and the status she once enjoyed.[19]

Since returning to a communist Cuba is not a viable option for most emigrés, they aim for the next best thing: Miami. In Ivan Acosta's play *El super* (1977; made into a film in 1979 by León Ichaso and Orlando Jiménez-Leal), Roberto, a super in a tenement building in New York's Upper West Side, is obsessed with moving to Miami. After eighteen years in the U.S. he still has not learned English, and he detests his job. From the windows of the cramped basement apartment he shares with his wife and daughter, he can see only people's feet on the pavement outside. The cold weather and the rudeness of New Yorkers only exacerbate his alienation. He longs for the sunny climate of Miami and the compatriots who are the only ones who can understand his pain. Roberto's obsessive nostalgia strains his relationship with his teenage daughter, Aurelita, who has adapted rapidly to American society—too rapidly, according to her parents, who fear that she will become as "loose" as American girls. And indeed, they learn that Aurelita may be pregnant. Together with the news that his mother has died in Cuba, this finally forces Roberto to act on his dream of moving to Miami. If he cannot return to Havana to save himself and his family, then he will settle for Little Havana.

Aurelita, of course, vehemently opposes the idea of moving to Miami:

> I don't know what the hell you're looking for in Miami. The people there still live in 1959, *la Cuba de ayer,* dad, that's all, *la Cuba de ayer.* . . . I have spent eighteen years hearing about that Cuba of yesterday. Don't these eighteen years count? No, it's as if they've never happened. I don't know about you people. That's what you're going to find in Miami. What

you're going to do is take a long trip into the past, eighteen years into the past. You make your plans and I'll make mine. Here is where the action is.[20]

Roberto blames his daughter's attitude on his wife, who failed, he claims, to properly instill in her a sense of *cubanidad*. "I always told you to teach her about Cuba. . . . she doesn't even know the national anthem. . . . that's why she is the way she is."[21]

Aurelita's reaction is not uncommon for her generation, raised in the United States. They do not share their parents' obsession with the past because it isn't *their* past. It has no hold on them. For the older emigrés Miami is mecca, because it is the closest they can get to Cuba, but the younger generation recognizes its limitations. The exile community nurtures and supports its own, but it also has the potential to suffocate. Behavior and political beliefs are dictated by the powerful institutions of the exile community, and those who go against the tide are marginalized. The community seems provincial and narrow-minded to the younger generation. Their elders see the world in black and white: one is either a communist or an anticommunist, and if one does not oppose Fidel (and in very particular ways) then one is a communist. Such simplistic reasoning contributes to the climate of censorship in south Florida that inhibits serious and sophisticated political discourse.

It is not surprising, then, that exile politics comes under heavy fire in Cuban American literature. Authors ridicule the political factions and the war games. The work of Roberto Fernández again provides some of the most humorous examples. In *La montaña rusa*, an advertisement for the C.A.A.F.D.P.C.P.M.P.B. (Cuban-American Alliance for Freedom and Democracy and for the Prevention of Communism and the Preservation of Moral Principles and Biculturalism) states, "We are an Affirmative Action / Equal Opportunity Organization, no communists nor similar degenerates need apply."[22] In *Raining Backwards*, a weekend warrior bombs the Cuban presidential palace in Havana with grenades dropped from a large homemade kite, which he maneuvers from his apartment in Little Havana thanks to a fast-moving cold front. He is subsequently arraigned before a federal magistrate for violating the Kennedy-Khrushchev accords—and the case remains pending for the next fifteen years. While he awaits his fate at the hands of the judicial system, Congress awards him a purple heart.[23]

In Acosta's *El super*, Roberto and his friends discuss politics at all hours of the night. Like many emigrés, they cannot believe that after so many years Castro still has a hold on Cuba. Pancho, the Bay of Pigs veteran, offers this explanation:

> You know what the problem is? No one cares about Cuba. Not the Americans, nor the Russians, nor the Chinese, nor the Martians, not one damn. The whole world focused attention on Solzhenitsyn, that Russian who defected, because he was Russian, an intellectual, and a Nobel prize winner. But who the hell cares about Huber Matos, Orlando Bosch, Gutierrez Menoyo . . . Nobody. No one cares about the Cubans' suffering. We are a tiny island with an egocentric lunatic who does things according to his whims . . . and we only have nine million people. Ah, *compadre,* but if we were 50 or 100 million, then we would really have fun.[24]

Other authors poke fun at what they perceive to be the emigrés' lack of political sophistication, despite their obsession with politics. The narrator of Torres's *Fallen Angels Sing* mocks emigrés who claim that they always knew Fidel Castro was a communist: "There weren't ten people in Cuba at the time who could tell a communist from a fascist; the only Marx they heard of was Groucho, and even him they didn't understand."[25] An itinerant evangelist in *El super* tries to preach to Roberto and his friends about the "need to be united in one mind"; Pancho accuses him of being a communist.[26] Emigré writers frequently satirize their compatriots' obsession with communism. A character in *Raining Backwards* compares bugs to communists: "This year with all this rain they are like the communists: everywhere. You think you have killed every single one, and bang, they pop in where you least expect them, just like the communists."[27]

Omar Torres is also intrigued by those who emigrated young who become embroiled in exile politics. The narrator in *Fallen Angels Sing* understands why older emigrés yearn to return to Cuba and work toward that end, but for younger emigrés, who left Cuba as children and had little time to establish strong connections, to be as obsessed is odd. The narrator concludes that these atypical younger emigrés are trying to invent a past for themselves. They are pulled to a "myth of a country": "It was nothing tangible or tactile; it was a nostalgic longing for something they never had, but wished they had had; it was a life they had been robbed of, even if that life was worse than the one they were living in the United States."[28] Like the older emigrés, their political ideology is sometimes vague and undefined. Their principal goal in life is to see Fidel's overthrow; they have no specific program to propose as an alternative other than a vague insistence on "democracy". "They were right-wing in their political thinking because the left had taken over their places; they abhorred communism because it had stripped them of all they had known as a normal way of life. Given the right circumstances they could, perhaps, be more liberal than any man, more progressive than any man, but not as exiles, not as pariahs."[29]

Uva Clavijo also explores the insanity of exile politics in her play *With All and for the Good of All* (1986). The characters in the play represent specific types in the community, among them Cheo Calleocho, the macho freedom fighter in camouflage fatigues; Sir Preterit Perfect, the aging Cuban senator trying to carve a niche for himself in exile politics; his wife, Madame Pains Cross Perfect, the former society matron; Hope Still, 25 years old, the only member of her family to survive a clandestine raft trip across the Florida Straits; Johnny Know-It-All, a middle-class, thirty-six-year-old Cuban American who came to the U.S. as a young child; and Witness All-Knowing, a forty-two-year-old journalist. The characters are brought together on a mission to Nicaragua to provide relief supplies to the contras. The plane makes an emergency landing on the island of Cutopia, and while the characters wait for a rescue party, they discuss—what else?—Cuba. Each has a different theory about why the revolution succeeded. Age and class differences contribute to the heated argument. Their discussion about Cuba, exile, and world politics is not unlike the conversations heard in cafés, parties, and meetings across Miami for the past thirty-five years.

Hope, who has lived in both revolutionary Cuba and the exile community, notes the consistency of Cuban society on both sides of the Florida Straits:

> There, they spend all the time speaking ill of Americans, exalting the Revolution, and if perhaps one feels some desire to know about the years before the Revolution, he manages to find out only that everything was bad. Here, it is the same, but upside down. They spend time speaking ill of the Communists, exalting one another and the glories of the republic. Now I understand why Cheo's uncle said that the Cubans will never be Aristotelians. We are people of extremes.[30]

Sir Preterit's praise of Cuban society and politics before the revolution sparks an angry rebuttal from Witness and Hope. Like other young emigrés, they question their elders' recollection of the past. "Can you truthfully tell me that the rulers in Cuba were honest?" asks Witness. "That there was no government corruption? . . . Castro's revolution had its reasons."[31] For Witness, it is not Castro who is to blame for the country's present problems but the society that produced him: "If we had to point out culprits, I believe one would have to condemn ninety percent of the Cubans. It was a collective fever."[32] Hope asks, "If Cuba was the marvel that it was, why was Castro able to triumph, and why did so many Cubans go away fleeing instead of defending that country that they love so much?"[33]

Sir Preterit, in turn, resents that the younger generation has it comparatively easy. They sit back and pass judgment on their parents, but their success is built upon the sweat of the first generation:

> You have been able to study your careers here, it goes well for you, you make money, you have success, you forget Cuba. You don't know what it's like to have dedicated all your life to create a republic and see it trampled. When I went into exile, I was already fifty years old. I did not know English. My life had been politics and Cuba. It was as if my whole world had died.[34]

Madame Pains comes under attack as well. For Hope she represents the corrupt and superfluous bourgeoisie; they quickly fled Cuba after the triumph of the revolution and now attempt to replicate the lifestyle they left behind. They have no understanding of politics, nor do they care about anything other than conspicuous consumption:

> I have not seen women more frivolous than the Cubans. They all die to get their picture in the newspaper, and spend so much on dresses for those balls supposedly for the benefit of charity. . . . If they'd give only half to the poor. . . . They are moved by the death of the son of Franco's niece, whose picture appears in *Hola!* or by the death of Grace Kelly . . . but they are incapable of shedding a tear for the victims of Armero, or Mexico.[35]

When their plane is finally found, the Cubans learn that the people of Cutopia have overthrown a despotic ruler and the country is in a state of civil war. A representative of the Cutopian army, named Don't-Have-A-Choice, asks the Cubans to stay and help them create a new society, for Cutopia is in need of teachers, doctors, engineers, and other professional and skilled workers, and the Cutopians need advice on how to create a democratic society. After twenty-four hours of debate, most of the Cubans decide to return to the United States. They cannot agree on how to establish a truly democratic society, and they all claim to have pressing business back in the States. Only Hope and Witness, the most idealistic of the group, choose to stay and help out. Clavijo implies that for all their talk of returning to Cuba when Castro falls, the majority of exiles will more than likely stay in the United States. Building the new Cuban society will require commitment and sacrifice, and most emigrés will not want to uproot themselves from their comfortable lives in the U.S. to deal with uncertainty and instability.

A number of authors have explored the question of whether one can ever really return home, a question of particular importance to the Cuban American generation, most of whom left Cuba as children or teenagers before gaining a clear understanding of who they were. The decision to leave Cuba was made for them by their parents, and their identity was defined later by the exile community and the larger American society. For many, particularly those who left as teenagers, the separation from Cuba was as traumatic as it was for their parents and grandparents. Says Miguel, the principal character in *Fallen Angels Sing:*

> Mine was a generation drifting among fading memories, uncertainties and a sense of not belonging. It was a generation wishing time would either stop in pre-Castro Cuba—1958—or, to the contrary, speed ahead full blast; wishing the Revolution had never taken place or, better still, that it would end tomorrow; wishing we were back in our homeland, in our hometowns, with our loved ones. We were exiles within an exile, having been caught in the middle: hearing the unchanging voices of our parents chanting songs of yesteryear; watching boys and girls our age living the lies of old; willing to give anything to have had a choice.[36]

The late scholar and poet Lourdes Casal, who left Cuba as a university student in 1961, also wrote of the uprootedness that she and her contemporaries felt: "Exile is to live where no house exists / in which we were children."[37]

As adults, Cuban Americans had to define for themselves who they were and where they fit—where "home" was. As the poet Gustavo Pérez-Firmat wrote in "Home," "let him step / on soil that's his or feels his, / let him have a tongue, / a story, a geography."[38] The search for home led many Cuban Americans back to Cuba. Lourdes Casal was among the first emigrés allowed by the Cuban government to visit, in 1973. As a result of her experiences in revolutionary Cuba, Casal concluded that her ties to Cuba were unseverable: "I live in Cuba / I have always lived in Cuba / even when I thought I resided / very far from the alligator of agony / I have always lived in Cuba."[39] The 1973 trip (and subsequent visits to Cuba) rekindled her revolutionary consciousness,

and amidst much criticism she became a vocal supporter of the Castro
government in the emigré community and an advocate of renewed
diplomatic and trade relations between the U.S. and Cuba. Suffering
from kidney disease, she fell ill during a trip to Cuba in 1979, was
hospitalized, and died there two years later. She was buried in the
Pantheon of Revolutionary Exiles, her tomb decorated by a wreath sent
by Castro himself.[40]

Most emigrés, however, were not allowed to visit their homeland
until the family reunification trips of 1979, when more than one hundred
thousand emigrés returned to Cuba to visit family. These trips gave them
the opportunity to define themselves both in their personal lives and in
their creative work.

Flora González Mandri's memoir "El Regreso" describes the author's return to Cuba after an eighteen-year absence.[41] The trip offers
her the chance to determine for herself the accomplishments and failures
of the revolution and to reestablish ties with the extended family she left
behind. The narrator is struck by how familiar and yet how alien Cuban
society seems: the old landmarks are still there, but after a tour through
the historic cemetery in Santiago to see the tombs of Martí and Estrada
Palma, she realizes that the interpretation of those landmarks and of
Cuban history have changed. Her compatriots raised under the communist system have a very different way of looking at the world, their
views affected by two decades of life in a revolutionary state. The Cubans'
day-to-day routines are starkly different from hers; and yet the Cuban
sense of humor and joie de vivre remain intact, offering a sense of
continuity. The narrator is impressed with many of the accomplishments
of the revolution, especially in education and health care, but she is
dismayed by shortages in basic consumer goods, by the ever-watchful
police, and by the revolution's inability to eradicate certain social attitudes, such as the sexism that women continued to experience.

She tries to pass as a regular Cuban citizen, but her clothes and speech
give her away. She feels like a "strange insect" in what she still regards
as her country. When someone comments that she speaks strangely she
is terribly disappointed: "At that moment my heart sank, for his com-
ment confirmed that I no longer belonged to this world."[42] At the time
she visits Cuba the narrator is involved in the lonely task of completing
her dissertation, presumably somewhere in the Northeast, and the Cubans' communalism makes her painfully aware of how isolated she is in
exile. She longs for the network of extended family and friends who long
ago provided a more nurturing environment. "The solitude of my work

made me forget the possibility of sharing disappointments. . . . Among
the people of [my relatives'] block, dancing with their arms outstretched,
I felt the warm affection that was so sorely lacking in the nation of great
opportunities."[43]

She had hoped to define her relationship to Cuba during her trip, but
instead of answers she leaves with more questions. She is certain only that
there is a great misunderstanding between the Cubans on opposite sides
of the Florida Straits. Each group fails to understand the sacrifices that
the other has had to make. "The stories they told me proved to me that
the survival instinct was as alive in Cuba as in exile, only that their
objectives lay on opposite ends of the rainbow."[44]

René R. Alomá's semiautobiographical play, *A Little Something to
Ease the Pain* (1979; originally titled *The Exile*), tells the story of a young
Cuban writer from Toronto who returns to Santiago to visit his brother,
grandmother, and assorted kin. Carlos, or "Paye," as his family calls him,
is estranged from his brother, Tatín, a committed revolutionary and
writer who resents his parents and siblings for abandoning their revolutionary ideals and going into exile. Paye hopes to reconcile with his
brother as well as to define his relationship to Cuba. Like the narrator
of "El Regreso," he returns to Cuba during a difficult period in his
life—writer's block is jeopardizing his career—and he seeks some type
of validation; but his visit only makes him more painfully aware of his
isolation in Toronto. From the moment he arrives at his grandmother's
house he realizes that he feels whole only in Cuba, for it holds his past.
The house itself symbolizes continuity for him:

> It is an old house, a Spanish colonial house, one of the oldest in the city
> of Santiago de Cuba. I was born in this house and I spent my childhood
> riding a tricycle on this verandah with assorted cousins—all boys! My
> grandparents' house has seen weddings and wakes, nine children, twenty-
> six grandchildren, fires, earthquakes, hurricanes, revolutions, departures
> and reunions.[45]

Paye also comes to realize that for all these years he has envied Tatín
his passionate idealism and commitment to something larger than himself. His own life seems empty in comparison. At the end of his week's
stay, he stuns his family, and most especially his brother, by announcing
that he is abandoning Toronto and returning home to live in Santiago.
During the argument that follows, Paye learns that Tatín is plotting to
leave Cuba. The revolution is no longer what it once was; the restrictions
once regarded as temporary security measures have become permanent

features of the state. Tatín has become a victim of his own idealism; his disappointment with the failures of the revolutionary state have made him suspect. It is only a matter of time before he is accused of ideological diversionism. In the end, Paye returns to Toronto to take up his writing once again and to help secure his brother's emigration. A part of him will always be back home, but his reconciliation with his brother makes him feel less fragmented.

Margarita Engle's *Singing to Cuba* (1993) is a fictional account of one woman's pilgrimage to Cuba to visit relatives. The narration of what she sees and does in Cuba is juxtaposed with the story of her great-uncle Gabriel, a peasant farmer in Oriente province, who was erroneously accused of assisting counterrevolutionaries and sent to prison. His story is told through a series of flashbacks that take the reader back to the early years of the Castro government.

Engle's narrator is far more critical of Cuban society than Alomá's Paye or González Mandrí's narrator. Her Cuba is "enchanted," but it is also "cursed" and "bewitched."[46] She condemns the Castro government for the writers and poets who disappear and are later found tortured and maimed in the bowels of some ancient prison; for the climate of paranoia and repression that inhibits Cubans even from confessing their sins to a priest for fear that he may be a government informant; for an inhumane economic structure that is dependent on tourism, providing visitors with all the amenities that Cubans do without.

The narrator finds that her own relatives live in a constant state of fear: of not having enough to eat, of being accused by their neighbors, of disappearance and death. Her cousin Miguelito, a composer, is afraid to sing his songs out loud because they might be considered counterrevolutionary, while his family worries that Miguelito will commit suicide, as his father and so many of the men in the family have. The narrator is enraged: "How profoundly [Castro] had wounded my family! He was even in the room, behind closed doors, listening from behind the door. He was even deciding which of Miguelito's songs he could dare sing in a neighborhood bristling with the pointed ears of spies. He had destroyed faith and trust and love. On his island skeptics were pariahs and the outspoken were condemned to dungeons."[47]

The trip to Cuba changes her forever—not because she finds some resolution in her relationship to Cuba, or with her family, but because guilt and sadness overwhelm her. Back in the U.S., when bulletins from human rights organizations arrive in the mail she hurriedly combs through them to make sure that Miguelito or some other relative has not been imprisoned. She has learned to see the United States through Cuban eyes, painfully conscious of the excesses of American consumerism. The narrator wants to sing for the cousin that has lost his voice, and to "sing for Cuba" to make people aware of what is going on in her homeland. Her subsequent presentations to civic groups are met with polite indifference. She is surprised by American ignorance about Cuban affairs despite the island's historic connection to the United States:

> When I returned from Cuba, I tried to tell people what it was like but my words sounded so strange and remote that nearly everyone stared at me blankly, as if I had chronicled a trip to Neptune. . . . Northerners said they couldn't imagine a land where people were afraid of their own brothers and cousins, where feeling unhappy was against the law, and wistful songs were considered dangerous. They said that they couldn't imagine the fear, the silence, the constant search for food, the storm of melancholy sweeping across an entire island, the loss of one's own voice, the loneliness.[48]

In the final pages of the book, Engle dispassionately lists the most recent (1992) news from Cuba, as if chronicling the final days of the Castro government. The novel ends on an upbeat note: Miguelito, the cousin whose suicide seemed imminent, has found his voice once again and is defiantly singing his songs out loud despite the risk. There is now someone to sing for Cuba in each of their worlds.

Cristina García also addresses the theme of returning to Cuba in *Dreaming in Cuban* (1992). The novel revolves around three generations of women of the Pino family. Celia, a committed revolutionary, lives in Cuba with her daughter Felicia and Felicia's three children. Celia's other daughter, Lourdes, an equally staunch counterrevolutionary, lives with her husband and daughter, Pilár, in Brooklyn, where they run the Yankee Doodle bakery, a gathering place for Cuban political extremists. Relations between the two families are strained by their political differences. Letters are their only communication, and even these are cursory. Lourdes sends her mother photographs of the bakery: "Each glistening éclair is a grenade aimed at Celia's political beliefs, each strawberry shortcake proof—in butter, cream, and eggs—of Lourdes's success in America, and a reminder of the ongoing shortages in Cuba."[49]

Pilár, though, does not share her mother's hatred of communist Cuba. She longs to return to see Cuba through her own eyes, and she especially wants to visit her grandmother, with whom she feels a strong psychic connection despite seventeen years of separation. Celia visits her in dreams and calls her back to Cuba. Celia in turn feels a strong connection to Pilár, who she knows will be the chronicler of family history, the keeper of the family's collective memories.

When the opportunity to travel to Cuba finally arises in 1980, Lourdes and Pilár return to visit their family. For Lourdes, the trip is an opportunity for a political statement: she spends her time in Cuba criticizing the revolution and mocking her compatriots. She dreams of assassinating Fidel Castro. For Pilár, the trip is a journey of self-exploration, an opportunity to fill in missing pieces. It is a transforming experience:

> I've started dreaming in Spanish, which has never happened before. I wake up feeling different, like something inside me is changing, something chemical and irreversible. There's a magic here working its way through my veins. There's something about the vegetation, too, that I respond to instinctively—the stunning bougainvillea, the flamboyants and jacarandas, the orchids growing from the trunks of the mysterious ceiba trees. And I love Havana, its noise and decay and painted ladyness. I could happily sit on one of those wrought-iron balconies for days or keep my grandmother company on her porch, with its ringside view of the sea.[50]

Pilár comes to realize, however, that her ties are to New York—but not instead of Cuba, just more than Cuba. She must find a way to maintain her connection to Cuba and her grandmother despite the distance.

Not all Cuban Americans are as reflective about their lives and about Cuba as these writers. While the older generation of emigrés may be too preoccupied with the past, some Cuban Americans have absolutely no connection to it. Cuban American authors may poke fun at the older generation, but they also ridicule the YUCAs whose lives revolve around acquiring wealth and power. For Miguel in *Raining Backwards*, a real estate developer currently converting the old Freedom Tower into luxury condominiums, José Martí is simply a boulevard in Hialeah.[51] He plans to call the condos "Kennedy Towers."

Within the same generation—even the same family—there are radical differences in attitudes toward Cuba, as well as in self-perception. An emigré who left Cuba as a teenager may share a generation with a younger brother or sister who was born and raised in the United States, but the two will have far different notions of their own identity. Elías Miguel Muñoz portrays a sense of this in his poem "Little Sister Born in This Land": "Each time you intrigue me / with your riddles / with your words / that will always be foreign / to our experience."[52] With "our experience" the speaker places himself in his parents' world rather than his sister's.

The language in which one writes, dreams, and communicates is naturally a concern for Cuban American writers seeking to define their cultural and artistic identity. From the moment they arrived in the United States they have been pressured to learn one language and retain another. To maintain connections to both cultures, both societies, they had to be truly bilingual. Spanish provides a link to the past, but English represents the future and an opportunity for a reinvention of self. Language, moreover, determines their audience and degree of exposure. While many of the Cuban American writers began their careers writing in Spanish, most made the transition into English, both to expand their audience in the United States and because English reflects their growing ties to North American society.[53] In the poem "Dedication," Gustavo Pérez-Firmat gives a sense of the difficulties of determining which language to use to express your voice:

> The fact that I
> am writing to you
> in English
> already falsifies what I
> wanted to tell you.
> My subject:
> how to explain to you
> that I
> don't belong to English
> though I belong nowhere else,
> if not here
> in English.[54]

Bilingualism represents adaptation. One Cuban couple in Fernández's *Raining Backwards* doesn't even know when they're being insulted, mistaking a harassing phone caller for a salesman. The caller declares open season on Cubans: "We are going to be hunting you down. We are going to purify this land of trash. You fucking Cubans." The Cuban responds: "Chi no jiar. Ron, number. Senquiu."[55] But Fernández also satirizes non-Cubans in south Florida who would eradicate the use of Spanish and impose monolingualism. In trying to turn back the hands of time, they mirror the emigrés they are trying to control. In *Raining Backwards,* the Supreme Court has decided that "speaking in any other tongue, and especially in Spanish, is a form of disglosia, a degenerative disease of speech centered in the brain." The White House promises to secure $100 million from Congress to establish education programs to help "curb the spread of the disease."[56] In Miami, the local "Tongue Brigade" enforces the speaking of English. Other measures are passed, further aiming to eradicate any sign of the Cuban presence: an ordinance in the neighboring city of Gables by the Sea prohibits the playing of dominoes and the wearing of colored underwear, and the Miss Calle Ocho beauty pageant is forced to require English fluency of its aspirants. Outside of Fernández's fictional world, the nativists in south Florida have not yet lobbied for the banning of dominoes or colored underwear—but they *have* tried to ban the use of Spanish in public settings. Some businesses and institutions prohibit the use of Spanish among employees, and Dade County's bilingual-bicultural ordinance was repealed between 1980 and 1993. Fernández's satire is all too real.

For this generation of writers, defining their relationship to the United States is as important as defining their ties to Cuba. For those who came of age during the 1960s, the Civil Rights movement and the counterculture radicalized their perception of society as much as—or even more than—the Cuban Revolution. They became concerned with race, class, gender, sexuality, and how these define their identity and experience. They became equally concerned with the problems of poverty, violence, war, racism, and sexism.

Playwright María Irene Fornés examined the effects of poverty in *Mud* and the cruelties of dictatorship in *The Conduct of Life*.[57] Dolores Prida explored gentrification and its consequences in her play *Savings*.[58] One of the more developed themes, especially among Cuban American women writers, is the role of gender, in particular the demands made upon women (and, to a lesser extent, men) and their attempts to define a life that is meaningful to them. Prida's one-act *Beautiful Señoritas* looks at the stereotypes of Latinas in both Latin American and North American culture and how these stereotypes affect the perception and treatment of women. The images of (among others) Carmen Miranda, "Cuchi Cuchi Charo," the black-shrouded, ever-suffering mother, and the beauty queen have been engraved in American popular culture, from Hollywood westerns to magazine advertisements, and they come back to haunt Latinas, who are often perceived either as docile and subservient or as sex-crazed bimbos.

The struggle to assert a realistic identity begins at birth. Prida's play opens with Don José awaiting the birth of his child, convinced it will be a boy. When he learns that the child is a girl, he storms off in anger and disappointment. The narrator, a young girl, addresses the audience:

> He's off to drown his disppointment in rum, because another woman is born into this world. The same woman another man's son will covet and pursue and try to rape at the first opportunity. The same woman whose

virginity he will protect with a gun. Another woman is born into this world. In Managua, San Juan, in an Andes mountain town, in the South Bronx. She is not just any woman. She'll be put on a pedestal and trampled upon at the same time. She will be made a saint and a whore, crowned queen and exploited and adored.[59]

Beautiful Señoritas is about the struggle to assert a realistic identity in society; Prida's play *Coser y cantar* explores the inner struggle within women caught between cultures. The play is a bilingual monologue between "Ella" and "She," two halves of the same person. Ella represents the woman's cultural heritage, while She represents her more acculturated, Americanized self; Ella is the woman who immigrated, She the American woman she has become. Their tastes in food and music are different, as are their personalities and worldviews. Language becomes a symbol of their differences: Ella, of course, speaks in Spanish, while She speaks in English. The two halves continually bicker, each trying to assume total control. When Ella insists that She is not all that important to her life, She responds, "But, if it weren't for me you would not be the one you are now. *No serías la que eres.* I gave yourself back to you. If I had not opened some doors and some windows for you, you would still be sitting in the dark, with your *recuerdos,* the idealized beaches of your childhood, and your rice and beans and the rest of your goddam obsolete memories."[60] Toward the end of the play, they come to realize how dependent they are upon each other for survival. Neither can make it completely on her own, and to symbolize this fact they both begin to speak bilingually.

During the 1960s and early 1970s, Cuban exile women were bombarded with contradictory messages in the popular media. On the one hand, they were expected to contribute to their family's economic well-being; on the other, they were warned that too much success would destroy their femininity and their marriages (or marriage prospects). Magazine articles and radio shows advised them on the proper way to dress, to keep their households, to raise their children, and to keep their husbands "interested." The mainstream American media, equally concerned with controlling women, gave similar advice. In one of Fernández's vignettes in *La montaña rusa,* a popular radio show advises women on the art of conversation. The host advises her female audience not to express opinions, particularly not in an "aggressive" fashion. "A woman should have a topic rehearsed in which she feels confident. For example: 'The beach certainly was lovely yesterday.' A woman should speak little since most of the time we talk and talk without knowing what to say. A woman should listen more and talk less in order not to commit the mistakes that lead one to lose one's male audience."[61] The radio host also advises women not to become involved in the "masculine" forum of politics: "Only in an unavoidable situation might you murmur 'Yes, communism smells like poop.'"[62]

In *Crazy Love*, Elías Miguel Muñoz explores the conflict that results when women adapt to new roles in a new society. While many Cuban women have found life in the United States to be liberating, allowing them to develop themselves in ways they might never have in Cuba, they must often deal with resentment from their spouses, parents, and even children. In the novel, Julián's mother has undergone a radical trans-formation, as life in exile has forced her to become more assertive and independent. Her upbringing in Cuba did not prepare her for the realities of U.S. life, and she is determined that her daughter, Geneia, will not be weighed down by outmoded cultural expectations as she was. But her own mother, Julián's *abuela,* has very definite opinions about a woman's role and a daughter's responsibilities:

> "What's gotten into her?" asks Abuela. "She used to be such a docile creature, never raised her voice, never talked back to me, always listened and took my advice." It's all because of this damned country, she says. This evil world has turned her darling daughter into a monster. Because Mami won't call her ten times a day, and she won't consult with her when a major decision has to be made, and she won't allow her to put ideas about femininity and little-girl-duties into [Geneia's] head. Because she fights her, and hangs up on her when Abuela starts telling her what to do.[63]

Julián's mother is not completely satisfied with the changes in herself. She has become more independent and assertive not out of choice but because her new environment has required this of her, and she some-times longs for the life she once had in Cuba: "Mother remembers, nostalgically, the days when making a living was the task and problem of the men; when she could get up in the morning knowing that the housework would be done by the maid; when she could have breakfast at her leisure, and stay in bed while she listened to the radionovelas."[64] Like other Cuban women, she goes to work to ensure the survival of her family, taking on jobs far beneath her former status. Years later, however, after her family no longer requires the additional income that her labor provides, she continues to work outside her home. Work helps her to forget the loneliness she feels: "'I have friends at work,' she says. 'If I didn't have that job, I'd never see anybody. I'd have no reason to buy new clothes or to get my hair done. I'd never leave the house. I'd have no place to be but inside these four walls.'"[65]

While women's roles have adapted to the realities of life in exile, men's roles have not changed accordingly, at least not among the older generation. The man of the house is still expected to be the principal breadwinner, or at least the one with the most desirable job and the highest income. Attitudes toward sexuality remain as rigid as they did in Cuba. A man who cheats on his spouse is forgiven more quickly than a woman who does the same. Homosexuality remains taboo. Of the Cuban American authors, Elías Miguel Muñoz best articulates the demands made on men and the intolerance of homosexuality within Cuban exile culture. In *Crazy Love,* Julián, a bisexual artist, tells how upon his first demonstration of artistic behavior his parents took him to the doctor for hormone shots. Afterwards his father checked his penis to make sure that it was developing properly. Julián envies his sister: "You're a lucky girl who knows only psychological torture: long silences, violent screaming and prohibitions."[66] In Muñoz's *The Greatest Performance* (1991), two childhood friends, Rosa and Marito, one a lesbian and the other a gay man, are reunited in California after years of separation. Exile took them to separate cities, and they had to come to terms with their identities, both cultural and sexual, on their own. Marito is dying from AIDS; Rosa becomes his caregiver. "After searching Heaven and Earth for a true love, for a generous homeland, for a family who wouldn't abuse us or condemn us, for a body who wouldn't betray our truest secrets, we found each other: a refuge, a song, a story to share."[67]

In trying to define their relationship to both Cuba and the United States, most Cuban American authors have come to accept their hybridity, while others have concluded that they don't fit anywhere. In the process, they have not only articulated the concerns of their generation but enriched the literature of their adopted country.

The Politics of Creativity

During the 1960s and 1970s, the Cuban revolution provoked heated discussion in intellectual circles around the world. The debate became highly politicized; different camps emerged among both supporters and opponents of the revolution. Cuban exile and Cuban American writers were caught in the middle of these polemics. Some intellectual circles ostracized them as political reactionaries, while others dismissed them as not truly Cuban, as if they had forfeited their nationality by going into exile. Once regarded as the elite of Cuban arts and letters, they became nonpersons in exile.[68] Many emigré authors kept silent about the situation in Cuba for many years—some because they feared that to speak out might jeopardize the careers they were trying to rebuild, but others simply because there were few forums for their views, apart from a small number of conservative journals and newspapers. Few wanted to hear about the cultural and political repression in Cuba.

Beginning in the 1970s, however, the opportunities for political commentary increased. In the wake of Heberto Padilla's arrest in 1971, many European and Latin American intellectuals who had once supported Fidel Castro now publically broke with the Cuban government.[69] Criticisms of the Castro government became more common, audiences became more receptive, and emigré writers and filmmakers suddenly found themselves in the spotlight.[70] José Mario, the former director of Editorial el Puente, spoke out about Cuba's "tropical gulags," the UMAP camps.[71] Guillermo Cabrera Infante condemned the censorship of the arts that had ultimately forced him and others to leave the country. Carlos Franqui, the former director of Radio Rebelde and editor of *Revolución*, was able to publish his powerful critique of Fidel Castro, *Retrato de familia con Fidel* (1981; *Family Portrait with Fidel*, 1984). Filmmakers Néstor Almendros, Jorge Ulla, and Orlando Jiménez-Leal received funding and critical acclaim for documentary films exploring human rights abuses in Cuba. Heberto Padilla recounted his experiences, including his forced confession and imprisonment, in the semiautobiographical novel *En mi jardín pastan los héroes* (1981; *Heroes Are Grazing in My Garden*, 1984) and later in his memoir, *La mala memoria* (1989; *Self Portrait of the Other*, 1990). The prison memoirs of recently released political prisoners Jorge Valls, Miguel Sales, Angel Cuadra, and Armando Valladares became bestsellers.

Writers became more actively involved in *la causa cubana*. The newly organized Comité de Intelectuales por la Libertad de Cuba (Committee of Intellectuals for the Liberty of Cuba, or CILC) sponsored "dissident congresses" for the discussion of political and economic affairs on the island and to protest human rights abuses.[72] The first congress, organized by dramatist Eduardo Manet, took place in Paris in 1979, but others followed in New York (1980), Washington (1982), Madrid (1986), and Caracas (1987). Emigré intellectuals championed the rights of political prisoners in Cuba, enlisting the aid of other intellectuals from Europe and Latin America as well as government leaders, celebrities, and international organizations such as Amnesty International, Americas Watch, and PEN. Among those they defended were the members of the Havana-based Comité Cubano pro Derechos Humanos (Cuban Committee for Human Rights), members of which were repeatedly persecuted and jailed for their protests against state policies. In 1991, when a group of intellectuals on the island (many of them members of the state-run UNEAC, the Writers and Artists Union) were harassed and imprisoned for issuing a declaration calling for democratic reforms, more than one hundred emigré intellectuals (and fifty European and Latin American intellectuals) rallied to their defense. In a letter of support, the signers applauded the Cubans' attempt to work within the system and urged "governments, the news media, cultural groups, and human rights groups to monitor their futures."[73]

While Cuban emigrés in south Florida had publicly criticized the Cuban government from the moment they arrived in exile, it was the political views of Cabrera Infante, Franqui, Padilla, Almendros, and other intellectuals that drew the most attention—in part because of their elite status in the culture, but especially because they had once been associated with the Castro government. Their initial support of the revolution, and their eventual disillusion and victimization, made their accusations more credible than others'. As Cabrera Infante said years later, he was like "the whore who got married and [was] now a respectable lady."[74]

Still, as late as the 1980s, Cuban exile writers complained that they were shut out from mainstream publishing houses and excluded from literary anthologies, theater festivals, and even academic appointments because of their political views. "The Cuban intellectual is forced to disappear two times," wrote Reinaldo Arenas in *Necesidad de libertad*. "First the Cuban state erases him from the literary map of his own country; afterwards, the preponderant and mighty Left, installed, of course, in capitalist countries, condemns him to silence. For those leftists of the West, who are tourists of socialist countries, being anticommunist is in bad taste. . . ."[75] Consequently, emigré authors spent much of their time trying to challenge the reactionary reputation of the exile community (while remaining firm in their anti-Castro views). Whenever they were excluded from some intellectual forum, they protested in a series of *cartas abiertas* (open letters or op-ed pieces). In 1982, for example, Reinaldo Arenas and Roberto Valero protested the publication of *Los dispositivos en flor,* an anthology of Cuban literature that ignored the most important work of exile authors. The anthology included as examples of Cuban literature five texts by Fidel Castro and two by Che Guevara but disregarded works critical of the regime. The editor included a few pieces by Arenas, Cabrera Infante, Sarduy, and Padilla, but apparently for political reasons: Cabrera Infante's piece critical of the Batista government was included, but not those critical of Castro, while Padilla's poems were included but juxtaposed with the signed "confession" of ideological diversionism extracted from him under torture.[76]

That same year, thirty emigré artists and writers signed a letter protesting the "pro-Marxist bias" in the *Review of the Center for Inter-American Relations*.[77] Of particular concern was an issue entitled "Literature and Exile," which completely ignored the works of Cuban exiles, including instead Latin American writers who reportedly shared the editors' sympathy towards the Castro government. "As intellectuals who appreciate the value (and price) of freedom for having endured one of the longest-lasting tyrannies in Latin America," stated the letter, "our struggle is for a world where art and creativity will not be the tool of propaganda for any party but rather a vehicle for the most profound expression of the human condition and its innate search and struggle."[78]

In 1984, eighty Cuban artists and writers wrote Joseph Papp to protest the exclusion of Cuban emigrés from his annual Festival Latino in New York City, which included music, films, and art exhibits from Cuba. Claiming that this was a "dangerous" demonstration of political censure, the artists wrote: "The Festival does not have the right to use Hispanics and their culture as a shield for ideological manipulations; nor does it have the right to present to the Hispanics of this city a partial view of their own culture."[79] The protest was successful: the following year, emigré actor Manuel Martín was invited to perform at the festival, and in 1986 Papp extended an invitation to the Teatro Avance in Miami.[80] Since then, Cuban exile theater has had representation in the festival on a yearly basis.

The obstacles they encountered in the production, reception, and exhibition of their work caused emigré artists and writers in the U.S. to establish their own networks of support. These networks were especially valuable for those who were not big names in Cuban arts and letters, who wished to develop their careers in exile. In Miami, artists, writers, and musicians gathered at places such as the SIBI Cultural Center on Calle Ocho for *tertulias* (literary gatherings), conferences, music recitals, art exhibitions, and drama productions.[81] Visual artists of the Mariel generation gathered at the Little Havana Arts Center, where they shared information about upcoming exhibitions and artistic opportunities and gave each other support and criticism. The Cintas Foundation, from the estate of Oscar B. Cintas, the former Cuban ambassador to the United States, established twelve-month fellowships in painting, sculpture, printmaking, architecture, music composition, and creative writing, specifically for young artists of Cuban citizenship or lineage living outside of Cuba.[82]

Emigrés established their own publishing houses to circulate their works before a wide audience. As early as 1965, Ediciones Universal, founded by Juan Manuel Salvat, published the literary and scholarly works of leading emigré intellectuals as well as classics of Cuban history, art, and literature. His bookstore, the Libreria Universal on Calle Ocho, serves as a gathering place for artists and writers of the community. Other publishing houses emerged during the 1970s and 1980s including Editorial SIBI, Ediciones HispanicAmerican Books, Mariel Press, Editorial Cernuda, Editorial Persona, Editorial Arcos, and Linden Lane Press. In Spain, publishing houses such as Editorial Playor, directed by journalist Carlos Alberto Montaner, Editorial Betania, directed by Felipe Lázaro, and Editorial Pliegos, directed by César Leante, distributed emigré works in Europe and Latin America.

Emigrés also produced their own literary journals. Among the first were *Exilio,* edited by Víctor Batista Falla and Raimundo Fernández Bonilla in New York (1967–73); *Revista Alacrán Azul,* published by Editorial Universal in Miami (1970); *Caribe,* edited by Matías Montes Huidobro at the University of Hawaii (1975–80); and *Escandalar,* edited by Octavio Armand in New York (1978–82). In the 1980s a new wave of artistic and literary magazines emerged, many of them produced by Cubans who arrived during the Mariel boatlift. In 1983, authors Reinaldo Arenas, Roberto Valero, and Juan Abreu began publication of *Revista Mariel* in Miami. (It later moved to New York.) The magazine published works by well-known emigré authors as well as Latin American and European writers, but more importantly it published the writings of authors who were silenced in Cuba and never received the recognition they deserved. *Revista Mariel* proved invaluable in preventing these authors from being permanently silenced. The magazine also played an important role in challenging the stereotypes of the Cubans of Mariel. Although *Revista Mariel* ceased publication in 1985 because of financial problems, it reemerged in Miami from 1986 to 1988, with Marcia Morgado as editor and with a new name: *Mariel Magazine.*

In 1982, poet Belkiz Cuza Male and her husband, Heberto Padilla, moved from Madrid to Princeton, New Jersey, where they began publication of *Linden Lane Magazine*. Included in its pages were interviews, critical reviews, short stories, poetry, and essays written by and about emigré authors as well as leading artists, writers, and filmmakers from Europe and Latin America. *Linden Lane Magazine* became one of the most respected literary magazines produced by Cuban emigrés and an important showcase for new and established writers. Other literary journals that emerged during the 1980s included *El Gato Tuerto,* edited by Carlota Caulfield in San Francisco; *La Nuez,* edited by Rafael Bordao in New York; *Lyra,* edited by Lourdes Gil and Iraida Iturralde; and *Dramaturgos,* edited by Matías Montes Huidobro and Yara González Montes.

Although they encountered common obstacles in the reception and promotion of their work, emigré artists and writers were not always supportive of their own, especially in the politicized environment of Miami. Artists, writers, and musicians who were perceived as too friendly to or supportive of the Castro government were vehemently criticized and even blacklisted. In 1986, thirty-one artists and writers protested the production of Dolores Prida's play *Coser y cantar* at Miami's first annual Festival of Hispanic Theatre. Prida, a vocal supporter of the revolution, a participant in the 1978 *diálogo,* and a member of the Cuban American Committee, was one of three Cuban dramatists selected to present their work at the festival, along with René Ariza and Matías Montes Huidobro. Spanish-language radio stations called her "an enemy of the Cuban people," a "communist," and a "Castro agent,"[83] and emigrés wrote angry letters to the *Miami Herald* and to the festival's organizing committee demanding that she be removed.

The protest sparked yet another angry debate in Miami. Many residents of the city, including the editorial staff of the *Miami Herald,* objected to what they perceived as a violation of Prida's civil liberties and charged that the emigrés were trying to deny her the very rights of self-expression that they themselves left Cuba to enjoy. *Herald* columnist Carl Hiaasen was less kind, calling the Cubans "drooling zealots."[84] Many emigrés were offended by Prida's presence, however, and considered it an insult to produce her play in the same amphitheatre as one by René Ariza, who had been a victim of Castro's prisons. "No one would find it strange if a Jewish cultural institution were to vehemently protest the presence of anti-Semitic writers in these halls," wrote Carlos M. Luis of the Cuban Museum of Art and Culture. "But if a group of Cuban exiles denounces the participation of a known *procastrista* in a theatre festival, then the 'liberals' shout bloody hell and accuse them of being fascists."[85] Luis and others also charged that the "Prida affair" had been staged.[86] The festival organizers knew that Prida was persona non grata in the emigré community; by including her in the program they ensured controversy and, hence, ticket sales. Whatever the reason, the Prida affair fueled passions in an already polarized community. A bomb threat eventually caused Teatro Nuevo, the Miami theatre group that was to perform *Coser y cantar*, to bow out. Prida was forced to present her play in workshop form, and under heavy police guard, at Miami Dade Community College.

Another major controversy surrounded the Cuban Museum of Art and Culture in Little Havana.[87] In 1987, the museum sponsored an auction of Cuban art as a fundraising effort. It was a huge success, raising over thirty thousand dollars in commissions, and the museum planned another auction for the following year. However, among the works scheduled to be auctioned in 1988 were paintings by four Cuban artists who had not broken with the Castro regime.[88] Miami's exile media accused the board members of being communist sympathizers and began a campaign of harassment to force the museum to eliminate the works of the "compromised" artists.[89] The board (by a vote of nineteen to eighteen) decided to proceed with the auction as planned, and it too was a success. More than seven hundred people attended, even though a crowd gathered outside the museum to insult those who attended. During the course of the evening, one of the controversial paintings, purchased for five hundred dollars, was burned outside the museum.

Several days later, a bomb exploded just outside the museum, causing some property damage. An emergency meeting of the board was called; some members urged those who had organized the auction to resign. When they refused, seventeen board members resigned in protest and created the Cuban Museum Rescue Committee. The Miami City Commission, under pressure from the Rescue Committee and various exile groups, began to investigate the museum, and over the next eighteen months it audited the museum three times in search of financial irregularities (it found none).

The harassment continued. The remaining board members were accused by the exile media of being *infiltrados* (spies) and received death threats at home and at work. The auction's chief organizer, art collector and human rights activist Ramón Cernuda, became the principal target.[90] Led by U.S. District Attorney Dexter Lehtinen (whose wife Ileana Ros-Lehtinen was running for Congress), the federal government launched an investigation of Cernuda—the first of many. In 1989, he was arrested by Treasury Department officials on charges that he had violated the embargo against Cuba by bringing in artwork from Cuba, and officials confiscated 260 paintings. In November 1989, two months after he was cleared of those charges, immigration authorities confiscated his documents after a trip to Canada on the grounds that they were forged. The documents were returned three months later with no explanation or apology. In February 1990, immigration authorities raided his workplace; again, no irregularities were found. In March 1990, the Department of Labor investigated him for alleged violation of labor laws; he was cleared. In June 1990, he was audited twice by the IRS in a fifteen-day period, and again they found no irregularities.[91] Another board member, attorney Alfredo Durán (the former head of Miami's Democratic Party), was brought up on charges of irregularities in his law practice by the U.S. attorney, but the charges were eventually thrown out by a federal judge.

By 1992, the museum's future seemed uncertain. The city's attempts to evict the museum from the city-owned property failed when a federal judge ruled that such an eviction would violate the civil rights of the board members, but the museum's financial base had eroded because of the controversy. Many former patrons cancelled their pledges, and the Florida state legislature cancelled its annual $125,000 grant. Other museums were pressured not to lend any works to the Cuban Museum.[92] The museum, however, endured, and with funding from the Ford Foundation it organized a number of successful exhibitions over the next two years.

The Cubanólogos

Writers, poets, and dramatists were not the only emigrés to shape the intellectual discourse on Cuba. During the 1960s and 1970s, students and scholars of Cuban origin on various university campuses across the United States carried out their own analyses of *la problemática cubana*. They gathered formally, under the auspices of student organizations such as the Cuban Students Federation and the Fundación de Estudios Cubanos, or privately in homes and businesses to discuss issues of identity, nationalism, and culture.

Like Cuban American writers, these students and scholars were trying to forge an identity in exile. They had emigrated as teenagers or young adults, and they felt the shock of exile very strongly. From one revolutionary state they entered another: a society grappling with the counterculture, the Vietnam war protests, the feminist movement, and the civil rights movement of blacks, Chicanos, and Native Americans. When the young Cubans questioned their identity, they had ample company.

The radicalized milieu encouraged introspection and rebellion. Some students and scholars, outraged at the human rights abuses on the island, concluded that they had a moral responsibility to work for Cuba's liberation and joined student groups such as the DRE and Abdala, which sought direct confrontation with the Castro regime. Others developed a more tolerant view of the revolution, interpreting it as an inevitable stage in Cuban history and politics, and some even came to support the Castro government itself.

Many young Cubans turned to writing as a means of exploring themes of identity and culture and their relationship to the homeland. They founded journals (reflecting a variety of political positions) such as *Nueva Generación, ¡Cuba Va!, Nuevos Rumbos, Joven Cuba, Krisis,* and *Areíto* to discuss issues relating to Cuba and its people both on and off the island. Students and scholars from exile communities around the globe contributed essays and articles on Cuban history, the revolution, the sociology of exile, art, music, theater, and folklore. They also contributed poetry, short stories, photography and artwork, and book and film reviews.

Published largely in Miami and New York, these journals targeted Cubans like the editors: the student generation and the young professional and working class. The editorial staff took cultural concerns seriously, and they were as idealistic as the names of their journals suggest. They believed that as the "Young Cuba" and the "New Generation" they could have an impact on their homeland, even from exile—just as the exiles of the nineteenth-century revolutionary wars had influenced the intellectual and political climate in Cuba a century earlier. Students and young professionals had always played a key role in shaping Cuban politics (best exemplified in the "Generation of the 1930s," which inspired a reformist movement on the island that culminated in the Castro revolution), and they perceived themselves as part of this reform tradition.

These journals became vehicles to analyze their feelings, define their opinions, and explore new perspectives. As one editorial in *Joven Cuba* stated:

> We the young people did not choose to leave Cuba. That was a decision made by our parent's generation. . . . We are not going to discuss the correctness of that decision now. . . . But it is now time for us to study

Cuba and the revolution, and to form our own opinions. We did not know *la Cuba de ayer*. Cuba and the rest of the world have changed much during the course of our formative years, and our views have inevitably evolved differently from those of our parents.[93]

Weary of the biased and often libelous exile news media in Miami, the editors strove to make their journals a forum for objective discourse. They were willing to analyze both the accomplishments and failures of the revolution—a radical idea in a community where anger and resentment at the revolution colored all political discussion. As one editorial in *¡Cuba Va!* stated, "Objectivity does not mean ignoring truths which we do not wish to confront, or which will force us to assume difficult positions."[94] They turned a critical gaze towards the emigré community as well. The editors criticized the exile community for its *panfletería* (pamphleteering) and "terrorism of ideas"—"symptoms of the same disease that plagued the homeland."[95] "For our compatriots, the world, along with their capacity to reason, froze the day they left the island," wrote one editor of *Nueva Generación*.[96] Acting as the conscience of the community, the journals scolded emigrés for becoming materialistic, intolerant, and undemocratic in the name of anti-Castroism and urged them to redefine their ideals. Issues of *Joven Cuba* included a section called "Trapos Sucios" ("dirty rags"), where the editors blasted their compatriots in Miami for their bourgeois lifestyles and their attempts to duplicate the corrupt society that had contributed, in part, to the revolution.

Through these journals, writers tackled their *crisis de identidad*. As immigrants to the United States, trying to adapt to a new language and society, they felt marginalized, and as exiles, they felt disinherited and cut off from their roots. The years in exile only reinforced their anxiety, and the essays published in these journals reflected an urgency to define a relationship with the homeland. They came to many different conclusions. The editors of *Joven Cuba*, whose audience was the emigré community of the Northeast, concluded that their destiny lay in the United States, as ethnic Americans. While they adopted the name of the revolutionary group founded by Antonio Guiteras in the 1930s and referred to themselves as Cuba's "Generación de los '70s", this "Joven Cuba" adopted a more accommodationist stance. The editors urged their fellow emigrés to work with other Latinos and minorities to address common issues and concerns such as racism, poverty, and unemployment.

The editors of *¡Cuba Va!*, on the other hand, refused to see any cultural differences between the Cubans on the island and the Cubans in the United States, despite their geographic separation and their separate political cultures; they saw all Cubans as one people, with one identity, one literature, one culture, one language.[97] The contributors to *Areíto* reached the most radical conclusion of all. They concluded that they were bound to Cuba as participants in the revolutionary process: "Our path inevitably compels us towards an encounter with *la Patria* and its revolutionary destiny, even though we go wearing our Adidas."[98]

Some journals were more conservative than others, especially in their interpretation of the revolution. Both *¡Cuba Va!* and *Krisis* rejected the revolutionary process in Cuba, arguing that it was "slow and rheumatic" and had failed to create a more just society.[99] As writers and scholars, they considered it their responsibility to correct misinformation about Cuba, especially among other students from Latin America, who tended to idealize Castro and the revolution. Other journals, such as *Joven Cuba* and *Nueva Generación,* were more supportive of the revolutionary process. While the writers and editors were troubled by certain character- istics of the new society (the state-imposed censorship, for example), they asserted the Cuban people's right to choose their own destiny. They advocated lifting the U.S. and hemispheric trade embargo and rejected any foreign meddling in Cuban affairs, whether by the United States or the Soviet Union. These views earned them criticism from the exile news media, but they articulated the political tolerance in some segments of the exile community.

Of the various journals published during the 1960s and 1970s, *Areíto* was by far the most radical and controversial. Beginning in 1972, a group of young and radical emigrés, mostly from the New York area, began meeting to discuss their views of the revolution. Among those who attended the meetings was Lourdes Casal, a member of *Nueva Gene- ración.* In 1973, when Cuban diplomats contacted the staff of *Nueva Generación* and invited them to travel to Cuba and witness the accom- plishments of the revolution for themselves, Casal accepted. She re- turned from Cuba marvelling at what she had seen, and shortly thereafter the group began planning the publication of *Areíto* as vehicle through which to celebrate the revolution. The first issue came out in early 1974, and its radical position prompted the defection of several sponsors.[100]

The writers and editors of *Areíto* were outspoken in their support for the Cuban government, which they claimed had created a more egal- itarian society.[101] They disputed U.S. propaganda against the Cuban state, arguing that reports of human rights abuses were greatly exag- gerated. They criticized emigrés for their "bourgeois lifestyles" and the exile news media and the self-professed leaders of the community for encouraging political intolerance, racial bigotry, and sexism. They also ridiculed their fellow emigrés for believing that they were the true Cubans and the sole custodians of Cuban culture when in fact their obsessive nostalgia had fostered intellectual paralysis. Miami and Union City, they wrote, had become artistic and cultural wastelands.[102]

Like the contributors to the other journals, they struggled to define their identity. Those associated with *Areíto,* however, concluded that "without Cuba there is no *cubanía* [Cubanness]."[103] They realized that they had to relate not to *la Cuba de ayer,* which no longer existed, but to the Cuba of the present. As they accepted the "inevitable and unalterable destiny of Cuba," they realized that they were not *exiliados* but simply *cubanos* living in the United States. To prevent themselves from becoming a *generación perdida* (lost generation) they had to serve as a *generación puente,* a "bridge" between Cubans in the two countries.

In 1978, several of those who comprised the Grupo Areíto recounted their personal and political formation in the anthology *Contra viento y marea* (Against wind and tide), which was published by Havana's Casa de Las Américas. They recounted their emigration experience as children and teenagers who left Cuba not of their own free will but to follow their parents' wishes. They spoke of their alienation within American society, and "how against wind and tide, and contrary to all expectations and probabilities, they identified with Cuba, from the very cradle of exile and in the middle of North American society."[104] *Contra viento y marea* gave voice to a particular segment of the emigré community that until *Areíto* had remained voiceless. In 1978, Cuba awarded the anthology its most distinguished literary award, the Premio Casa de las Américas, in a gesture that was probably as much political as honorary.

To no one's surprise, *Areíto*'s editorial views encountered a great deal of hostility. In 1974, over a hundred emigré students from ten different universities, including Harvard, Georgetown, and the University of Florida, sent the editors a lengthy rebuttal, arguing that Cuba's human rights record challenged the myth of Cuba as an egalitarian society.[105] The exile press was less diplomatic, calling Grupo Areíto communists, spies, drug addicts, and *vendepatrias* (sell-outs). One editorial in *Abdala* said, "It doesn't surprise us that such detestable beings should exist: people who have the opportunity to choose between fighting for the liberation of their country or opposing tyranny should choose to follow Castro for reasons that only their unbalanced minds could explain. Traitors have always played a role in a country's history."[106]

In the middle and late 1970s, the editorial staff was targeted by militant extremists. Lourdes Casal was constantly harassed. Bombs were placed in the homes or offices of several members.[107] Other editors and contributors were harassed by phone or accosted on the street. In the 1980s, when *Areíto* criticized those who left Cuba via Mariel, Reinaldo Arenas called them "the official organ of the Cuban state police in New York."[108]

Despite the unpopularity of its views, *Areíto* survived for over a decade, well into the 1980s, while other journals ceased publication because of financial difficulties or loss of interest. For many emigrés, *Areíto*'s solvency was further proof that the journal had to be funded by the Cuban government, though the editors claimed that subscriptions allowed them to survive. In later years, the editors expanded their range of topics to include the revolutionary movements of all the Americas, especially the struggles in Chile, Nicaragua, and El Salvador; and for a brief period, they published an English-language insert to attract young Cuban Americans who might not be fluent in Spanish, as well as North Americans. *Areíto*'s circulation averaged some three thousand subscribers of various nationalities. By the mid-1980s, however, the journal folded. In 1989 the journal resumed publication, albeit irregularly, edited by Andrés Gómez in Miami.

Loosely affiliated with *Areíto* were the Círculo de Cultura Cubana and the Brigada Antonio Maceo. The New York–based "Cuban Cultural Circle" was an organization comprised largely of artists and university professors of various cultural backgrounds who wanted to network with colleagues on the island. The organization acquired films and publications for distribution in the United States and served as a clearinghouse of information on revolutionary Cuba. The Antonio Maceo Brigade, founded in 1977, modeled itself after the Venceremos Brigade, which sponsored trips to Cuba for young North Americans in defiance of the government's ban on travel to the island.[109] The Maceo Brigade's trips, however, were organized for young emigrés of all backgrounds and were meant as voyages of self-discovery. Emigrés returned to Cuba for several weeks to visit family and friends, travel through the island, and evaluate the success of the revolution for themselves. Like the Venceremos Brigade, the Maceo Brigade was also expected to contribute to the revolutionary process. The students and young professionals assisted in construction projects. Since several contributors to *Areíto* were involved in the creation of the brigade, the first group was comprised heavily of *Areíto* members.[110]

Like *Areíto,* the Círculo de Cultura Cubana and the Maceo Brigade drew harsh criticism from the emigré community. The exile press even criticized the brigade for naming the organization after Antonio Maceo, the nineteenth-century revolutionary hero, who—unlike this group, they argued—represented democratic ideals. One *brigadista* and participant in the *diálogo* of 1978, Carlos Muñíz Varela of Puerto Rico, was assassinated by militant extremists in 1979. Angry protesters frequently disrupted the brigade's meetings. In 1982, when the brigade scheduled a press conference in Miami to discuss a joint venture with groups supporting the Sandinistas and the Salvadoran guerillas, dozens of protesters turned out and forced the press conference's cancellation; the rescheduled meeting at a northwest Miami church also had to be cancelled because of hecklers. A few days later, the Miami City Commission unanimously approved a resolution calling upon the U.S. Attorney General to require that the Maceo Brigade register as a "foreign agent of the government of Cuba."[111]

The presence of *Nueva Generación, Joven Cuba, Areíto,* and the others, as well as organizations such as the Círculo de Cultura Cubana and the Brigada Antonio Maceo, added an important dimension to the intellectual discourse on Cuba. In some ways they were as obstinate in their political posturing as the traditional exile media on the opposite side of the ideological spectrum; but collectively they provided alternative interpretations for those who wanted to study the revolutionary process in Cuba.

Other journals and organizations emerged for the scholarly community. In December 1970, with institutional support from the University of Pittsburgh Center for International Studies, emigré scholar Carmelo Mesa Lago edited the first issue of the *Cuban Studies Newsletter,* dedicated to the promotion of scholarly exchange and dialogue among *cubanólogos,* or those who study Cuba. The newsletter provided current information on research projects, publications, academic programs, library acquisitions, and microfilming projects related to Cuban studies.[112] By 1975, the newsletter had evolved into a journal entitled *Cuban Studies / Estudios Cubanos,* which published articles, in both Spanish and English, by leading scholars from around the world.

Another forum for emigré scholars emerged in 1969. Scholars from the United States, Puerto Rico, and Latin America, representing various institutions and academic disciplines and covering a wide ideological spectrum, came together in Washington for the first Reunión de Estudios Cubanos, a series of workshops, presentations, and roundtable discussions on Cuba. The meeting was also open to nonacademics, making the Reunión the first attempt to gather a heterogeneous group of emigrés for a scholarly discussion about Cuba. The papers presented at this meeting were later published in the 1969/1970 edition of the journal *Exilio*. The gathering led to a second *reunión* in 1971, and during this meeting scholars discussed the idea of creating an Instituto de Estudios Cubanos to oversee future meetings. The IEC was officially incorporated the following year under the direction of María Cristina Herrera, one of the driving forces behind the first Reunión. Members of the IEC have since met every year for either a conference or seminar in cities including Caracas, Miami, San Juan, Cambridge, and Orlando.

From the beginning, the IEC differed from other exile organizations. As an academic forum, it was open to all who wished to study Cuba "in a serious and responsible fashion, no matter what their political orientation."[113] Members ranged from conservatives to Marxists, but most could be called "center-to-left": they did not support Castro's communist government, but as scholars they were willing to establish a dialogue with other scholars on the island and to study the revolutionary process without political bias. Several members participated in the *diálogo* of 1978, and others have carried out research projects on the island. In 1980, the IEC sponsored one of its seminars in Havana. Cuban scholars from the island are regularly invited to participate in the annual meetings, though the U.S. State Department at times refuses to grant them visas.

While a commitment to pluralism is the hallmark of the IEC, it has provoked much hostility. Hardliners called the IEC members collaborationists, and many conservative scholars refused to attend its conferences, claiming that the presence of Marxist scholars (both from Cuba and the United States) was ample proof that it is a pro-Castro organization. After the *diálogo* of 1978, militant extremists targeted members, in particular María Cristina Herrera, who had to have round-the-clock police protection for three months in 1979 because of threats on her life.[114] The "communist" tag persisted into the 1980s: in 1983, a guest commentator on WQBA announced to his audience that he had ample proof that Herrera was a communist, leading her to file a complaint with the FCC and threaten to sue WQBA. The station was ultimately forced to make a retraction. In 1988, when the organization sponsored a seminar in Miami on the pros and cons of reestablishing diplomatic relations with Cuba, extremists placed a bomb in the garage of Herrera's home. Through it all she has remained un-daunted:

> Our institute affirms, in its existence and its work, fundamental pluralist and democratic values that are important both for the U.S. and for all Cubans who came here as exiles. We condemn and reject any efforts by the Cuban government to prevent free expression and discussion. Like-wise, we condemn and reject any efforts at intellectual intimidation to prevent free expression and discussion in Miami about Cuba or Cu-bans.[115]

Many within Cuba's scholarly community also rejected the IEC's pluralism, however. During the 1970s, Cuban scholars on the island tried to pressure the organization to oust some of the more politically conservative members. More recently, in 1994, several Cubans from the island boycotted the IEC's annual meeting to protest the attendance of one of their colleagues, Rolando Prats Paez, the leader of the Havana-based dissident Social Democratic Movement. Despite being rejected by some segments of the emigré community as too leftist and by some scholars in Cuba as too conservative, the IEC has endured for more than twenty-five years, primarily because of the commitment of its members. The conferences provide them with the opportunity to present their research before a supportive audience of compatriots and fellow scholars, and perhaps more importantly, the conferences provide them with the opportunity to express their *cubanía* among kindred souls. The latter is especially important to scholars based far from Miami or other emigré communities, for whom opportunities to speak in their native language and reflect on their common heritage and experience are rare. The driving force behind the organization is María Cristina Herrera, who acted as spokesperson for the organization, planned the logistics of meetings and conferences, and rallied fellow members to participate. Without her presence, the IEC would have probably disbanded after a few years. Instead, it has grown in membership, attracting a new, younger generation of Cuban American scholars, and continues to be an im-portant forum for scholars who do research on Cuba.

For the past thirty-five years, then, Cuban writers and scholars have helped to shape public and academic discourse about Cuba within their community as well as in their host society. They have articulated the concerns that emigrés had about Cuba and the United States, and about identity, nationalism, and culture. Whether consciously or unconsciously, they became spokesmen for the community, and often found themselves in the center of the ideological battles. In the process, however, they produced a rich body of work—novels, poetry, biographies, journals, anthologies, and scholarly studies—which is a record of and testimony to the experiences of more than one million people who left Cuba for the United States and ultimately made it their home.

Conclusion

Those intrigued by the community of Cuban exiles and Cuban Americans in south Florida frequently ask what will happen in Miami once there is a changing of the guard in Cuba. Will the emigrés return to their homeland? Or will thousands more Cubans immigrate to the United States? The answer is yes—to both questions. Once Fidel Castro is no longer in office (for whatever reason)—and assuming that democratic reforms are enacted—some percentage of the community will return to Cuba. The numbers are difficult to predict: a poll conducted in 1993 by Florida International University revealed that 29 percent of Cuban-born heads of households wanted to return to live permanently in Cuba, while a similar poll conducted in 1990 showed that only 14 percent would actually return.[1] Among those born or raised in the United States the percentages are probably much lower. The emigrés talk a great deal about returning to their homeland, but few will actually pack up and leave when the opportunity arises. As several interviewees told me, "Why uproot yourself twice in one lifetime? The first time was hard enough." They have invested time and hard work in the United States. They have rebuilt their lives and careers; they bought homes and raised their children here. They have developed ties to the United States in spite of their original intentions. Most do not want to start all over again, especially in a society that will undoubtedly experience social, economic, and political turmoil in the post-Castro years.

The length of time spent in the United States and family ties in the two countries are the principal factors that will influence the decision to stay or to return. For Cubans who grew up in the U.S., "returning" to Cuba would be akin to moving to a foreign country, notwithstanding the culture they claim to share with those on the island. The emigrés most likely to return will be the elderly, eager to spend their remaining years in their homeland. Also likely to return are those who feel alienated in the U.S. and have found it impossible to adapt. The majority of emigrés, however, will want to stay close to their families. Many of the first generation are now grandparents and even great-grandparents; they will not want to move too far away from their children.

Nevertheless, Cubans in south Florida will always maintain an interest and play a role in the affairs of Cuba. Cuba is closer to Miami than Tampa, Orlando, or the state capital at Tallahassee, and the interest in Cuba is as much geopolitical as cultural. South Florida, like the rest of the Caribbean, has a stake in the political and economic stability of the island, and thus Cuba will play a role in public debate on the streets of Havana USA as well as in the corridors of Tallahassee and Washington.

Travel back and forth across the Florida Straits will be guaranteed. Emigrés who remain in the U.S. will want to travel to Cuba to visit relatives, or for a vacation, or for a variety of other reasons. In much the same way that former refugees from Eastern Europe and the Baltic states are presently investing in their homelands, the more entrepreneurial among the emigrés will want to invest in or establish businesses in Cuba—both to help their former country and to increase their own fortunes. In the early 1990s, U.S. airline and shipping companies were already plotting ways to corner this new travel market. According to the *Miami Herald,* some companies were even drafting models for hydrofoils that might transport people back and forth in a couple of hours. It is conceivable that some emigrés might divide their time between the two countries, working in one country and making their homes in another, much as many Americans commute between, say, New York and Connecticut, or as others commute back and forth across the U.S.–Mexico border. The first generation's dual citizenship will facilitate this development.

Migration from Cuba will continue regardless of what happens in Cuba. In September 1994, in order to force the Cuban government to curtail the traffic of homemade rafts across the Florida Straits, the Clinton administration agreed to allow the immigration of a minimum of twenty thousand Cubans each year, not including the immediate relatives of United States citizens.[2] Even with the installation of a more democratic government, migration from Cuba will continue. Some Cubans will choose to emigrate to be reunited with their families in the United States, while others, impatient with the sluggish Cuban economy, will want to try their luck in the U.S. The number of migrants in such a scenario will depend as much on U.S. immigration policy as on the political and economic conditions in Cuba; but whatever the number, the influx of immigrants will continually revitalize Cuban identity and culture in the United States. Cuban American culture in south Florida will continue to define itself in relation to two countries and two cultures.

The most difficult challenge in the post-Castro era, both on the island and in Florida, will be learning to forgive. The exile community remains divided thirty-five years after the revolution by political differences. Emigrés are unable to forgive each other for their role (or lack thereof) in the revolution and later the counterrevolution. From the comfort of exile, they criticize their compatriots on the island for allowing the government of Fidel Castro to endure, and while they applaud the *balseros* for taking to the seas to escape Castro's Cuba, many wonder suspiciously why they didn't do it sooner. Conversely, many Cubans on the island continue to regard the emigrés as *gusanos* and cannot forgive them for exploiting, and later abandoning, their country. A great deal of cooperation (and, perhaps, time) is needed before Cuban societies on opposite sides of the Florida Straits are tolerant, peaceful, and democratic.

The Cubans of south Florida will play a major role in the civic, cultural, and political life of the area in the years to come. Their principal challenge will be to share their power base with the many different groups that call south Florida home. Over the past three decades, a growing tension— even hostility—has emerged in south Florida, the product of rapid demographic transformation and the perceived dominance of Cubans in the local economy and local politics. The 1990 U.S. census revealed that Latinos comprised 49.2 percent of Dade County's total population of 1.9 million. In the city of Miami, 62.5 percent of the population was of Latino origin; in Hialeah, 88 percent.[3] Despite a near-doubling in total population over the past thirty years, the percentage of non-Latino whites had fallen from 80 percent in 1960 to 37 percent in 1990. Such measures as the 1980 English Only amendment ultimately proved unsuccessful in controlling the Latino population (and in May 1993, voters overturned the 1980 ruling).[4] Unable to compete in a bilingual economy and angered by the cultural changes in south Florida, many non-Latino whites have moved to the counties immediately north of Dade, where they can maintain their cultural and political dominance.

The non-Latino black population has remained more rooted to the area, but blacks, too, are resentful. For thirty-five years, they have watched Cubans grow wealthier and more powerful. They resent the federal government's early assistance to the refugees—the grants and loans that helped them go to school or start small businesses, the remedial education and job retraining programs, the health benefits. Blacks resent that these non–English-speaking foreigners could receive so much while the native-born were overlooked. These benefits helped the Cubans assert their economic and political power. By 1990, three of the five members of the Miami City Commission, including the mayor, were Cuban; by contrast, only one member was African American. Blacks in Dade County have fared better economically than their counterparts elsewhere around the state—in part because of the economic transformation brought on by Cuban immigration—but many feel that they have been shut out from the most important local institutions.[5]

This resentment was obvious as early as 1968, when blacks rioted during the Republican National Convention in Miami Beach. Riots took place again in 1980, 1982, and 1989, each spurred by a specific incident involving police brutality, but each also an expression of the deep-seated resentment towards whites and Latinos.[6] In the wake of the riots the city created an antidiscrimination coalition entitled Greater Miami United to address the concerns of the various racial and ethnic communities. There are many ill feelings, however, and groups from the Nation of Islam to the Ku Klux Klan have tried to capitalize on the tension in the community.

The class, racial, ethnic, and national diversity within the Latino community is also the source of much tension. While the Cubans helped produce the economic prosperity that attracted large-scale immigration from the Caribbean and Latin America, the newer immigrants resent the Cubans' dominance in local institutions, from the Spanish-language media to city hall. Latinos complain of Cuban powerbrokers who refuse to allow others into their inner circle, of the neverending anti-Castro diatribes on the radio, and of the media's lack of sensitivity to issues that are important to them. "They think they're the only Hispanics in Miami," said one disgruntled Puerto Rican. Many of the complaints filed with the FCC in the past decade have been filed by Latinos who perceive the Cuban radio shows to be bigoted.[7] At times, Latino resentment has been expressed through violence—as in December 1990, when Puerto Ricans in the Wynwood neighborhood rioted. Like the black riots of the 1980s, the episode was a reaction to a specific case of police brutality; but it too was a manifestation of the larger ethnic and racial tensions in south Florida.[8]

Latinos also express concern about the climate of censorship in Miami, a concern shared by whites and blacks as well. Individuals who support

Fidel Castro or the Sandinistas or who favor tolerance and dialogue are branded *comunistas* and suffer discrimination, and sometimes even verbal or physical abuse. In past years, Latin American entertainers who have performed in Cuba have been banned from appearing at the annual Festival de la Calle Ocho because the organizers claim that to allow them to perform would be to risk a confrontation, endangering the two million people who attend the weeklong festivities. In December 1990, under pressure from the Cuban community, the city of Miami withdrew its official welcoming of Nelson Mandela because of his support of Fidel Castro. In January 1991, Miami city commissioners told members of the local Haitian community that they could celebrate the inauguration of their country's new president at Bayfront Park only if Fidel Castro was not invited to the inauguration in Haiti.[9] For Latinos, Haitians, and others, these incidents are just the most recent examples of the censorship in south Florida that violates their civil rights. Miami, they argue, has become a city where the needs and interests of the dominant group outweigh the needs and interests of the rest of the population.

The Cubans, however, will be forced to make concessions. While they are the largest immigrant group in south Florida, others are growing rapidly. In the early 1990s Central and South Americans, and in particular immigrants from Nicaragua and Colombia, had replaced Cubans as the fastest-growing Latino groups. Emigrés are slowly realizing that it is to their benefit to try to foster a more inclusive vision of community. Just as others accommodated them, they must now accommodate others. Hopefully, the Cuban Americans—particularly the second generation—will play a mediating and conciliatory role in community relations. As the children of emigrés, they can relate to the immigration experience of others; as Americans, they are bound to the local community and to the country that offered them safe haven. They do not share the exile generation's obsession with Cuba; rather, their energies are invested in the hybrid borderland society that produced them. It is the Cuban Americans who will ultimately help determine south Florida's future.

Notes

Introduction

1. Cuban exiles regard themselves first and foremost as Cubans forced to leave their homeland for political reasons. A Cuban American is an American of Cuban heritage. Thus it is more common for "emigrés" raised in the United States to regard themselves as Cuban Americans than it is for those who emigrated as adults, with their cultural identity already formed. However, some emigrés come to perceive themselves as Cuban Americans as well as exiles. The amount of time in the United States and the degree of adaptation are two factors that determine the development of this dual identity.

2. Joel Garreau, *The Nine Nations of North America* (New York: Avon Books, 1981).

3. Geoffrey Tomb, "City Makes World Affairs Its Business," *Miami Herald,* May 2, 1983, 1C.

Chapter 1

1. Juan M. Clark, "The Exodus from Revolutionary Cuba (1959–1974): A Sociological Analysis" (Ph.D. diss., University of Florida, 1975), 75.

2. Among the first to study the emigrés and the reasons for their disaffection were Richard R. Fagen, Richard A. Brody, and Thomas J. O'Leary, *Cubans in Exile: Disaffection and Revolution* (Stanford, California: Stanford University Press, 1968).

3. A number of works analyze the origins and consequences of the Cuban revolution. The author found the following useful: Jules R. Benjamin, *The United States and the Origins of the Cuban Revolution* (Princeton, New Jersey: Princeton University Press, 1990); Philip W. Bonsal, *Cuba, Castro, and the United States* (Pittsburgh: University of Pittsburgh Press, 1971); Jorge I. Dominguez, *Cuba: Order and Revolution* (Cambridge, Massachusetts: Harvard

University Press, 1978); Leo Huberman and Paul M. Sweezy, *Cuba: Anatomy of a Revolution* (New York: Monthly Review Press, 1961); Herbert L. Matthews, *Revolution in Cuba: An Essay in Understanding* (New York: Charles Scribner and Sons, 1975); Hugh Thomas, *The Cuban Revolution* (New York: Harper and Row, 1977); Richard E. Welch, Jr., *Response to Revolution: The United States and the Cuban Revolution, 1959–1961* (Chapel Hill: University of North Carolina Press, 1985).

4. On October 20, 1960, the State Department announced an embargo on most U.S. exports to Cuba (except medicines, medical supplies, and certain foods), in compliance with the Export Control Act, to counter the "discriminatory, aggressive, and injurious economic policies" of the Cuban government. A more comprehensive U.S. trade embargo was imposed on February 3, 1962, under the authority of section 620 (a) of the Foreign Assistance Act of 1961 (75 Stat. 445), prohibiting the importation into the United States of all goods of Cuban origin and all goods imported from or through Cuba. In May 1964, the government also issued an order requiring export licenses for sales of food and drugs to the island (previously exempted for humanitarian reasons); gift parcels became the only means of exporting these products without export licenses. The Kennedy administration hoped that the loss of income in Cuba would "reduce the capacity of the Castro regime . . . to engage in acts of aggression, subversion, or other activities endangering the security of the United States and other nations of the hemisphere." See White House Press Release, February 3, 1962, in Papers of President Kennedy, President's Office Files, Countries (Costa Rica–Cuba), Box 114a, JFK Library. A ban on travel to the island was also eventually enacted to "preserve the isolation of Cuba." See Abba P. Schwartz, *The Open Society* (New York: William Morrow and Co., 1968), 86.

5. Research Institute for Cuba and Caribbean, *The Cuban Immigration 1959–1966 and Its Impact on Miami–Dade County, Florida* (Coral Gables, Florida: Center for Advanced International Studies, University of Miami, 1967); Bryan O. Walsh, "Cubans in Miami," *America,* February 26, 1966, 286–89.

6. There is a growing literature on these earlier Cuban communities. See Susan Greenbaum, "Afro-Cubans in Exile: Tampa, Florida, 1886–1984," *Cuban Studies / Estudios Cubanos* 15 (Winter 1985): 59–72; Nancy A. Hewitt, "Cuban Women and Work: Tampa, Florida, 1895–1901" (unpublished paper presented at the meeting of the American Historical Association, Washington, D.C., December 29, 1987); Louis A. Pérez, "Cubans in Tampa: From Exiles to Immigrants, 1892–1901," *Florida Historical Quarterly* 57 (October 1978): 129–40; Gerald E. Poyo, *With All, for the Good of All: The Emergence of Popular Nationalism in the Cuban Communities of the United States, 1848–1898* (Durham, North Carolina: Duke University Press, 1989).

7. Testimony of Robert F. Hale, Director, Visa Office, Department of State, Refugees and Escapees Hearings (1961).

8. Rosario Argilagos Rodríguez, interview by the author, audiotape, October 25, 1986. Translation mine.

9. Bertha Rodríguez, interview by the author, audiotape, July 6, 1994.

10. Lutgarda Mora, interview by the author, audiotape, July 17, 1994. Translation mine.

11. Deborah Carrera, interview by the author, audiotape, July 17, 1994. Translation mine.

12. Conversation with the author, March 17, 1987. This source preferred to be unnamed in the study. Translation mine.

13. The Catholic Church had officially established the Diocese of Miami in October of 1958, and so the Cuban refugees provided the diocese with its first major challenge. For a discussion of the role the diocese played in assisting the refugees, see Michael J. McNally, *Catholicism in South Florida, 1868–1968* (Gainesville: University of Florida Press, 1982).

14. "Operations of the Cuban Refugee Emergency Center," March 28, 1961, Records of HEW, JFK Library; Refugees and Escapees Hearings (1961).

15. Tracy Voorhees, "Final Report on the Cuban Refugee Problem," *Department of State Bulletin* 44 (February 13, 1961): 220.

16. These estimates are from the Cuban Refugee Emergency Center. However, it is possible that as many as one-third of the emigrés did not register with the Center, either because they did not need financial assistance or because they preferred to rely on their own network of family and friends. See "Operations of the Cuban Refugee Emergency Center." For a poignant description in the exile press of the difficulties faced by the refugees, see "La antesala del regreso o la tumba de nuestras esperanzas," *Impresiones,* May 1962, 19–21.

17. By 1979, 55.4 percent of Cuban women sixteen years and older worked outside the home, making Cuban women the group with the highest labor force participation rate. See Lisandro Pérez, "Immigrant Economic Adjustment and Family Organization: The Cuban Success Story Reexamined," *International Migration Review* 20 (Spring 1986): 12–13. In comparison, according to the 1953 Cuban census, the last census prior to the revolution, 13.7 percent of Cuban women fourteen years and older—that is, 256,440 women—were "economically active." In Havana province, the percentage was higher—22.3 percent. República de Cuba, *Censo de población, viviendas, y electoral, informe general,* 1953.

18. "They're OK," *Newsweek,* December 4, 1961, 59.

19. "United States Assistance to Hungarian Refugees," *Department of State Bulletin* 36 (May 6, 1957): 721.

20. According to Clark, 27.9 percent of the Cubans who arrived in the first stages did not register with the CRP.

21. During the Hungarian crisis, in an effort to cut red tape and expedite the granting of political asylum, President Eisenhower asked Congress that the Emergency Refugee Relief Act be "bent, if not broken." See Schwartz, *The Open Society.* See also "The Americans and the Hungarian Story," *Saturday Review,* May 11, 1957, and "U.S. Assistance to Hungarian Refugees," 720–21.

22. This perception of the Cubans as temporary visitors was also prevalent during the first months of the Kennedy administration. See, for example, Voorhees, "Report to the President of the United States on the Cuban Refugee Problem," File "ND 19-2/CO55," Records of HEW, Box 637, JFK Library; "President Outlines Measures for Aiding Cuban Refugees," *Department of State Bulletin* 44 (February 27, 1961): 309–10; and "U.S. to Assist Refugee Cuban Scholars," *Department of State Bulletin* 44 (April 3, 1961): 490–92.

23. In his "Final Report" to President Eisenhower, Tracy Voorhees wrote: "Since so many refugees believe that this [returning to Cuba] will before long be possible, this assurance from an authoritative source that they are not losing their chance to return home is needed. It will encourage them to move for the indeterminate period to other areas and jobs, without fear." Guaranteed repatriation became the policy of the Kennedy administration as well; see White House Statement, February 3, 1961, Records of HEW, Microfilm Roll #44, JFK Library.

24. During the Kennedy administration, the Cubans continued to be "paroled" under sec. 212(d)(5) of the Immigration and Nationality Act. See Schwartz, *The Open Society*. Kennedy asked Secretary of Health, Education, and Welfare Abraham Ribicoff to conduct his own personal investigation of the emergency crisis in south Florida. Letter from John F. Kennedy to Abraham Ribicoff, January 27, 1961, Records of HEW, Microfilm Roll #44, JFK Library. See also "Report of Secretary Abraham A. Ribicoff on the Cuban Refugee Problem," February 2, 1961, Records of HEW, Microfilm Roll #44, JFK Library.

25. White House Statement, February 3, 1961, Records of HEW, JFK Library.

26. Within HEW, the Cuban Refugee Program was handled by the Social Security Administration. Aspects of the program came under the jurisdiction of the Children's Bureau, the Public Health Service, the Bureau of Family Services, and the Office of Education. Dillon S. Myer, former Commissioner of the Bureau of Indian Affairs, was appointed to direct the Cuban Refugee Program in Miami. See Memorandum from W. L. Mitchell, Commissioner of Social Security, to Dillon S. Myer, et al., February 20, 1961, Records of HEW, Microfilm Roll #44, JFK Library.

27. White House Statement, February 3, 1961, Records of HEW, JFK Library; see also "President Outlines Measures for Aiding Cuban Refugees," *Department of State Bulletin* 44 (February 27, 1961): 309–10. See also Silvia Pedraza-Bailey, *Political and Economic Migrants in America: Cubans and Mexicans* (Austin: University of Texas Press, 1985).

28. Tracy S. Voorhees, "President's Representative on Cuban Refugee Program Submits Report," *Department of State Bulletin* 44 (January 9, 1961): 46; Walsh, "Cubans in Miami." By August 31, 1961, eighty-five hundred Cuban children attended public school in Dade County. HEW provided up to 50 percent of the cost of educating Cuban children in both primary and secondary schools. See Memorandum from W. L. Mitchell to Wilbur J. Cohen, Assistant Secretary for Legislation, August 31, 1961, Records of HEW, JFK Library; Memorandum for the National Security Council Executive Committee, January 24, 1963, in File "Cuba, Security, 1963," President's Office Files, Countries, Cuba, Box 115, JFK Library; and File "ND 19-2/CO 55," Records of Government Agencies, Department of HEW, Box 637, JFK Library.

29. State Department personnel were also to assist in gathering information on both exile political activities and Castro's covert activities in the area. The Department of Defense reassigned all military attachés formerly in Havana to military installations in south Florida, and the United States Information Agency

reassigned two officers to Miami. Memorandum from George R. Marotta to McGeorge Bundy, February 3, 1961, in National Security Files, Regional Security, Box 211–220, JFK Library. See also Research Institute for Cuba and Caribbean, *The Cuban Immigration 1959–1966*, 24.

30. "Operations of the Cuban Refugee Emergency Center," March 28, 1961, Records of HEW, JFK Library. The VOLAGs were assisted in the resettlement process by the National Committee for the Resettlement of Foreign Physicians and the Community Service Division of the AFL-CIO.

31. By August 31, 1961, approximately 19 percent (7,165) of the Cuban "refugees" registered at the center, and 15 percent of those receiving assistance (or 3000 people), were permanent residents. Memorandum from Mitchell to Cohen, August 31, 1961.

32. Department of Health, Education, and Welfare, *Cuba's Children in Exile* (Washington: Government Printing Office, 1967).

33. Ramón and Leopoldina Grau, interview by Miguel Bretos, audiotape, January 19, 1987, Special Collections, Florida International University. Translation mine. Grau and his network collected American currency (which was no longer valid on the island after the breaking of diplomatic relations) and sent it to Walsh in small packages via the embassies in order to partially reimburse the church.

34. Ramón and Leopoldina Grau, interview. Polita Grau was released in 1978 and allowed to emigrate to Miami. Ramón was released in 1986 as part of Castro's prisoner release program and emigrated immediately to Miami. He met Bryan Walsh for the first time the day he arrived in Miami.

35. This information is based on interviews with three participants in Operation Peter Pan who chose to remain anonymous. Interviews were conducted September–November 1987. Similar testimonies can be found in Grupo Areíto, *Contra viento y marea* (La Habana, Cuba: Casa Las Américas, 1978).

36. During the late 1980s, many of the beneficiaries of Operación Pedro Pan held a banquet to honor Walsh, Grau Alsina, and others who facilitated their migration. Among the better-known "Peter-Panners" are former Miami City Commissioner Joe Carrollo, radio commentator Tomás Regalado, Miami Chamber of Commerce President Armando Codina, and entertainers Willie Chirino and Lissette.

37. "The Participation of the U.S. Employment Service," March 14, 1963, Records of the Department of Labor, Microfilm Roll #65, JFK Library.

38. Dr. Mirta R. Vega, telephone interview by the author, July 30, 1994. Translation mine. Dr. Vega eventually received her doctorate, became a school administrator, and designed nationally accredited language programs used in the state of Florida and throughout the country.

39. Ibid.

40. White House Statement, February 3, 1961, Records of HEW, JFK Library.

41. Report by Abraham Ribicoff in *Department of State Bulletin* 44 (April 3, 1961): 491; Memorandum from Mitchell to Cohen, August 31, 1961. See also "A Proposal to Put Education to Work to Advance Democracy," Papers of President Kennedy, President's Office Files, Countries, Cuba, Box 115, JFK

Library. The government also favored providing "training in democracy." As one Freedom House publication stated, "By training [the refugees] in the fields of democratic government, public administration, industrial and agricultural management, defense, public safety and order, public education, we can lay the foundations for a wholesome future." In "What Can We Do about Cuba?" in File "Standing Group Meeting, 6/18/63," National Security Files, Meetings and Memoranda, Box 315, JFK Library.

42. Letter from Abraham Ribicoff to W. L. Mitchell, Commissioner of Social Security, February 6, 1961, Records of HEW, JFK Library.

43. "Educational Aid for Cuban Children and Adults," Records of HEW, Microfilm Roll #47, JFK Library; "Loans to Cuban Refugee Students," *School and Society,* December 24, 1966, 476.

44. In his studies of Cuban professionals Raul Moncarz found that only 23 percent of the lawyers in his sample were able to practice their profession in the early 1970s, compared to 90 percent of Cuban architects and engineers. See "Cuban Lawyers," *International Migration* 10 (1972), and "Cuban Architects and Engineers," *International Migration* 11 (1973), both reprinted in Carlos E. Cortés, ed., *Cuban Exiles in the United States* (New York: Arno Press, 1980).

45. Ultimately, whether or not lawyers and other professionals were able to rebuild their careers in the United States depended upon a variety of factors. According to Moncarz, "occupational adapatation to the new environment [was] a function of legal status, self-employment, availability and length of retraining programs, attendance of schools or universities, state and local requirements to practice a given profession, license or higher degree in the United States, extent of ability to continue in the former profession, and the common productivity variables of age and sex." See "A Model of Professional Adaptation of Refugees: The Cuban Case in the U.S.," *International Migration* 11 (1973), reprinted in Cortés, *Cuban Exiles in the United States.*

46. Walsh, "Cubans in Miami," 287.

47. The problem lay with the state's failure to provide the appropriate funding for general assistance programs to local citizens. Federal funding was available on a three-to-one matching basis: that is, for every dollar the state appropriated for general assistance, the federal government provided three dollars for staff employment and one dollar for assistance payments. The state's elected officials, however, failed to take advantage of this program. See Marshall Wise, Speech to the Downtown Rotary Club, May 2, 1963, Records of the AFL-CIO, JFK Library.

48. Claiborne Marburgh, "Operation Simpático," *PTA Magazine,* September 1963, 31–32. The author details how, in order to help Cubans understand American traffic regulations, Dade County Parent-Teacher Associations teamed up with the Police Academy to present traffic safety courses in Spanish.

49. Refugees and Escapees Hearings (1961), 73.

50. E. M. Martin, "U.S. Outlines Policy toward Cuban Refugees," *Department of State Bulletin* 48 (June 24, 1963): 983–90.

51. Text of television documentary "Crisis Amigo," Refugees and Escapees Hearings (1961), 182.

52. By 1962, for example, Cuban refugees had repaid $122,254 and turned down $123,346 in financial assistance. Records of the Department of Labor, Microfilm Roll #65, JFK Library.

53. A number of studies have been written about the Bay of Pigs invasion. See, for example, Trumbull Higgins, *The Perfect Failure: Kennedy, Eisenhower, and the C.I.A. at the Bay of Pigs* (New York: W. W. Norton, 1987); Haynes Johnson, *The Bay of Pigs: The Leaders' Story of Brigade 2506* (New York: Dell Publishing Co., 1964); Karl Ernest Meyer and Tad Szulc, *The Cuban Invasion: The Chronicle of a Disaster* (New York: Ballantine Books, 1962); Peter Wyden, *Bay of Pigs: The Untold Story* (New York: Simon and Schuster, 1979).

54. The invasion force was named in memory of the first casualty, Carlos Rafael Santana, soldier #2506. He died while training in Central America.

55. Each brigade soldier was paid $175 a month, plus fifty dollars extra if he was married and twenty-five dollars for each dependent.

56. George Beebe, "Editors' Dilemma: To Print or Not to Print," *Miami Herald*, April 13, 1986, 4C.

57. The State Department was aware that the Castro government expected U.S. involvement. One memorandum reported: "Almost daily . . . the press carries stories, and in some cases pictures, of Cuban exiles undergoing military training at secret bases in Florida, or 'somewhere in the Caribbean,' or in Guatemala, for an invasion of Cuba. It is an open secret that the United States Government has pressured Cuban exiles to get together and that the U.S. is supporting, or at least tolerating on U.S. soil, the activities of the exiles. . . . It may be argued that all of this is supposition and none of it can be proved; but for the Latin American public—and the U.S. public, too, for that matter—it does not have to be proved." Still, the administration decided to go ahead with the planned invasion. See unsigned memorandum, March 29, 1961, in File "Cuba, General, 1/61–3/61," Papers of President Kennedy, National Security Files, Countries, Costa Rica–Cuba, Box 114a, JFK Library.

58. Isabel and Sofía Abella, interview by Rosa Abella, audiotape, January 30, 1973, Rosa Abella Audio Tape Collection, Cuban Exile Archives, University of Miami. Translation mine.

59. More than thirty years after the invasion, Cuban exiles continue to hold President Kennedy responsible for its failure, despite the conclusions of General Maxwell Taylor's report blaming the defeat on, among other factors, the failure of the CIA and other departments to adequately inform the president on all the details of the planned paramilitary strategies. The report of the Taylor commission was declassified in the 1980s. See Taylor Report, Paramilitary Study Group, Papers of President Kennedy, National Security Files, Countries, Cuba, Boxes 56–61B and 61A–61B, JFK Library.

60. Not all exiles advocated the ransom of the brigade soldiers. The Junta Revolucionaria de Liberación Nacional, a coalition of more than one hundred exile organizations, most of whom opposed the Cuban Revolutionary Council, urged that the ransom money be used to free the island once and for all, or that the money be used to free *all* political prisoners. See "¡Todos o Ningunos!" *Patria*, May 31, 1961, 4.

61. While most Latin American nations condemned the Bay of Pigs invasion, several nations also condemned Castro's ransom demands, comparing it to the Nazis' Jews-for-trucks scheme. Private groups in Uruguay, Brazil, Guatemala, Venezuela, and Nicaragua conducted their own fundraising efforts to assist in the purchase of the tractors. See File "Prisoner Exchange, 5/61–9/62," Papers of President Kennedy, National Security Files, Countries, Cuba, Box 56–61B, JFK Library.

62. "El rescate de los heroes," *Impresiones,* May 1962, 7–8.

63. Robert A. Hurwitch, interview by Francis J. Hunt DeRosa, transcript, 17 February 1967, JFK Library, 217–18.

64. Louis F. Oberdorfer, John B. Jones, and Mitchell Rogovin, "The Cuban Prisoners' Release Project," interview by Francis J. Hunt DeRosa, transcript, June 2, 1964, JFK Library. All the while the committee worked out the details of the ransom, the American Red Cross sent the Brigade soldiers "relief packages" containing instant coffee, canned meat, dry milk, a can opener, toilet paper, soap, plastic utensils, multiple vitamins, and one hundred tablets of Halazone. "Inventory of the Contents of the Packages Sent by the Red Cross" (Item 16a), Papers of President Kennedy, National Security Files, Countries, Cuba, Box 56–61B, JFK Library.

65. "Talking Points for Congressional Briefings on the Donovan Mission" (Report), Papers of President Kennedy, National Security Files, Countries, Cuba, Box 47, JFK Library.

66. The administration was careful to point out that no government funds were used, aside from administrative costs for telephone use and the like. No tax rulings were issued to contributing companies that were not already authorized by law. In order to ensure that these goods would not be sold by Cuba to other countries (a concern expressed by many companies donating goods), Cuba analysts evaluated whether the quantities requested by the Castro government could be reasonably consumed within a certain period of time; if not, comparable products were substituted. Oberdorfer, Jones, and Rogovin, interview; Hurwitch, interview.

67. Joseph F. Dolan, Assistant Deputy Attorney General, Cuban Prisoners' Release Project, interview by Francis J. Hunt DeRosa, transcript, July 8, 1964, JFK Library. The wholesale value of the shipments eventually delivered amounted to $46 million, since Castro accepted 15 percent as the calculation for charges of handling, freight, and insurance included in the $53 million total. Approximately $10 million was provided in milk, most of it from government surplus purchased by the Red Cross. See "Talking Points for Congressional Briefings on the Donovan Mission," 1.

68. Hurwitch, interview, 206–7, 218–20. See also "Talking Points for Congressional Briefings on the Donovan Mission," 3–4.

69. The Cuban government refused to allow the release of these seven because of previous "crimes against the state."

70. Twenty-one chose to return to the United States. Jack Steele, "CIA Agents Were Freed in Swap," *Washington Daily News,* April 24, 1963, in file "Prisoner Exchange, 1/63–5/63," National Security Files, Countries, Cuba, Box 56–61B, JFK Library.

71. According to the testimonies of some prisoners, Castro deliberately delayed the flights to increase the tension on the part of Kennedy administration officials waiting in Homestead. The last people to disembark from the final flight were the three brigade commanders, accompanied by James Donovan.

72. Richard W. Cull, Jr., Mario T. Noto, Richard H. Ffrench, and Robert E. Schoenenberger, interview by James A. Oesterle, transcript, December 17, 1970, JFK Library.

73. According to CIA agent (and Watergate burglar) Howard Hunt, who helped train the brigade, the soldiers' sentiments against President Kennedy were so strong that the presentation almost did not take place. See Howard Hunt, *Give Us This Day* (New Rochelle, New York: Arlington House, 1973), 221.

74. Office of the White House Press Secretary, "Remarks of the President and Mrs. John F. Kennedy . . .", December 29, 1962, in File "Standing Group Meeting, 4/23/63, Part B," in National Security Files, Meetings and Memoranda, Box 315, JFK Library.

75. Lutgarda Mora, interview.

76. A number of revisionist works were published on the tenth anniversary of the Missile Crisis and are particularly useful in understanding the crisis: James G. Blight, *On the Brink: Americans and Soviets Reexamine the Cuban Missile Crisis* (New York: Hill and Wang, 1989); Dino A. Brugioni, *Eyeball to Eyeball: The Inside Story of the Cuban Missile Crisis* (New York: Random House, 1991); Robert Smith Thompson, *The Missiles of October: The Declassified Story of John F. Kennedy and the Cuban Missile Crisis* (New York: Simon and Schuster, 1992).

77. CIA memorandum, October 24, 1962, in File "Standing Group Meetings, General, 4/63–5/63," National Security Files, Meetings and Memoranda, Box 315, JFK Library.

78. Clark, "The Exodus from Revolutionary Cuba," 75.

79. Martin, "U.S. Outlines Policy," 984.

80. In a press conference on May 5, 1961, a spokesman said: "We shall also generously fulfill our obligation to Cuban exiles among us, and we plan a series of broader measures to help them in their time of exile, to live and work in peace among us. We have particular concern for those who have suffered losses in the gallant effort of recent weeks and they will have our support." File "5/1/61–5/5/61," National Security File, McGeorge Bundy correspondence, Box 398, JFK Library. See also Records of Actions by the National Security Council, April 22, 1961, and May 5, 1961, ordering an improvement of the Cuban Refugee Program. National Security Files, Meetings and Memoranda, Box 312–313, JFK Library; and "National Security Action Memorandum No. 42," File NSAM42 "Assistance to Cuban Refugees," National Security Files, Meetings and Memoranda, Box 328–330, JFK Library.

81. "Suggested Points to Be Utilized When Answering the Main Questions and Objections on Resettlement," date unknown, Records of the Department of Labor, Microfilm Roll #65, JFK Library; "Una visita al centro de refugiados cubanos," *Impresiones,* February–March 1963, 36–39.

82. Martin, "U.S. Outlines Policy," 984.

83. Ibid., 983–90.

84. Marshall Wise, Speech to the Downtown Rotary Club, May 2, 1963, Records of the AFL-CIO, JFK Library.

85. "Castro Tells Rally Cubans Are Free to Leave Cuba," *New York Times,* September 30, 1965, 1.

86. "Why Castro Exports Cubans," *New York Times Magazine,* November 7, 1965, 30.

87. Robert M. Sayre, "Review of Movement of Cuban Refugees and Hemisphere Policy Toward Cuba," *Department of State Bulletin* 54 (May 2, 1966): 707–13.

88. Office of the White House Press Secretary, "Remarks of the President at the Signing of the Immigration Bill," October 3, 1965, in File "10/3/65," Papers of Abba P. Schwartz, Immigration Legislation, 1958, 1963–69, Box 7, JFK Library.

89. The State Department also arranged the transport of Cubans stranded at Camarioca after November 13, when the Cuban government closed the port to the emigrés' boats. As a humanitarian gesture, the U.S. government chartered three boats for "Operation Sealift" and from November 13 to 22 brought 4,598 persons to Key West. Immigration inspectors rode on each of these chartered vessels, carrying lists of persons eligible to come to the U.S. *I and N Reporter,* 18.

90. Isabel Abella, interview. Translation mine.

91. Jack Kofed, "Miami Already Has Too Many Refugees," *Miami Herald,* October 5, 1965.

92. Letter to President Johnson, October 5, 1965, National Security–Defense Files, LBJ Library.

93. Letters [1965] in the National Security–Defense Files, LBJ Library.

94. Letter to LBJ, October 13, 1965, National Security–Defense Files, LBJ Library.

95. Letter to LBJ, October 7, 1965, National Security–Defense Files, LBJ Library.

96. Letter to LBJ, no date, National Security–Defense Files, LBJ Library.

97. U.S. Cuban Refugee Program, *Training for Independence: A New Approach to the Problems of Dependency* (Washington: Social and Rehabilitation Service, 1968).

98. Preference was given to persons who had a "close family relationship to citizens or resident aliens" or who were unable to secure employment for which they were qualified because of their lack of permanent status. "Department Supports Adjustment of Status of Cuban Refugees," *Department of State Bulletin* 49 (September 5, 1966): 348–49.

99. "Permanent Resident Application Fees for Cuban Refugees Waived," *Department of State Bulletin* 49 (December 26, 1966): 967.

100. Interestingly, in recommending an adjustment act for the Cubans, the State Department issued this statement: "Passage of this bill should not and would not be taken as an indication that we believe that the Castro regime is here to stay. Our policy, which we firmly share with the other countries of the OAS, is one of opposition to the Communist regime in Cuba. Our goal and strong desire is that Cuba shall be freed from Communist domination and shall return

again to the free-world family of nations. At such time the status of Cubans as residents or parolees would in no way affect their freedom to return to their native land." "Department Supports Adjustment of Status of Cuban Refugees," *Department of State Bulletin* 55 (September 5, 1966): 348–49.

101. "New Procedures to Admit Cuban Refugees from Third Countries," *Department of State Bulletin* 54 (June 27, 1966): 1005.

102. "Suspende Castro los vuelos," *Impacto,* January 13, 1972, 5; "Vuelven de nuevo los vuelos de la libertad," *Impacto,* December 2, 1972, 7.

103. Clark, "The Exodus from Revolutionary Cuba," 75.

104. Silvia Pedraza-Bailey, "Cuba's Exiles: Portrait of a Refugee Migration," *International Migration Review* 19 (Spring 1985): 18. Clark, on the other hand, using data collected in 1962, determined that 21 percent of the Cubans who comprised the earlier arrivals (1959–62) were of the upper socioeconomic strata (having earned in Cuba more than $8,000 per year) and 56 percent were middle class (having earned $2,000–$7,999 per year). Clark, "The Exodus from Revolutionary Cuba," 235–37.

105. República de Cuba, *Censo de población,* 1953, 49.

106. Seymour Liebman, "Cuban Jewish Community in South Florida," in *American Jewish Yearbook* (New York: American Jewish Committee, 1969), 283. According to Liebman, however, no demographic study of Jewish Cubans was ever made. Dubelman estimates that only eight thousand Jews lived in Cuba prior to the revolution. See Abraham J. Dubelman, "Cuba," in *American Jewish Yearbook* (New York: American Jewish Committee, 1962), 482. See also United States Information Agency, *Cuba: A Communications Fact Book,* December 14, 1961, in File "Cuba 6/12/61–12/31/61," Papers of Arthur M. Schlesinger, Jr., White House Files, Box WH-5, JFK Library. For a discussion of Jewish migration to Cuba see Robert M. Levine, *Tropical Diaspora: The Jewish Experience in Cuba* (Gainesville: University Press of Florida, 1993). See also Jay Gayoso, "UM pasa a video la historia judía en Cuba de ayer," *El Miami Herald,* April 23, 1987, 3.

107. Alfonso Chardy, "As Jews Dwindle in Cuba, They Flourish in Miami," *Miami Herald,* September 22, 1990, 1B.

108. República de Cuba, *Censo de Población,* 1953, 48–49; Benigno E. Aguirre, "The Differential Migration of the Cuban Social Races," *Latin American Research Review* 11 (1976): 103–24. See also Lourdes Casal and Yolanda Prieto, "Black Cubans in the United States: Basic Demographic Information," in *Female Immigrants to the United States: Caribbean, Latin American, and African Experiences,* eds. Delores M. Mortimer and Roy S. Bryce-Laporte, RIIES Occasional Papers No. 2 (Washington, D.C.: Research Institute on Immigration and Ethnic Studies, Smithsonian Institution, 1981), 314–55.

109. See, for example, Ernesto G. Bermejo, "Los que quieren volver a Cuba," *Cuba Internacional,* May 1971, 55–59; and "El amargo destino de los apátridas," *Bohemia,* August 10, 1973, 74–75.

110. Aguirre, "Differential Migration of Cuban Social Races."

111. Clark, "The Exodus from Revolutionary Cuba," 128–30.

112. Rafael J. Prohías and Lourdes Casal, *The Cuban Minority in the U.S.: Preliminary Report on Need Identification and Program Evaluation, Final*

Report for Fiscal Year 1973, 2d ed. (Washington, D.C.: Cuban National Planning Council, 1974).

113. "Briefing Paper: Procedures for Admitting Refugees, Parolees, and Asylees," Miami Regional Hearing, December 4, 1979, in File "Refugees— Select Commission Papers," Box 25, Staff Offices: Domestic Policy Staff, Civil Rights and Justice, Papers of Franklin E. White, Carter Library.

Chapter 2

1. Robert L. Bowen, ed., *A Report of the Cuban-Haitian Task Force,* draft (November 1, 1980), 78, in Box 8, Records of the Cuban-Haitian Task Force, Carter Library. The number would increase slightly to 124,789 by January 30, 1981. Memo from Larry G. Willets to Wilford J. Forbush, in File "Executive Summary, 12/30/80–1/30/81," Box 21, Records of the CHTF.

2. William R. Long and Guillermo Martínez, "Castro invita al exilio a un diálogo," *El Herald,* September 7, 1978, 1.

3. John Harbron, "Castro Rules Out Exiles' Return," *Miami Herald,* March 26, 1975.

4. See Long and Martínez, "Castro invita al exilio a un diálogo"; "Castro dice que podría libertar a Matos en el futuro," *El Herald,* September 7, 1978, 3.

5. For a more detailed account of U.S.–Cuba relations during the late 1970s, see chapter 4.

6. According to Wayne Smith, former chief of the U.S. Interests Section in Havana, the Carter administration refused to acknowledge its role in the negotiations because it "feared that acknowledgement of our talks with the Cubans might send the wrong signals to countries whose cooperation we sought in opposing Cuban activities in Africa." Wayne S. Smith, *The Closest of Enemies: A Personal Account of U.S.–Cuba Relations since 1957* (New York: W. W. Norton, 1987), 146–63.

7. Helga Silva, "Cuba Selects Exiles for Castro Dialogue," *Miami News,* November 5, 1978, 1A.

8. The group was called the "Committee of the 75" because the group initially had seventy-five members, though the actual number later surpassed that.

9. Fernando Villaverde, "Llama Cuba a exilados a firmar acuerdos," *El Herald,* December 1, 1978, 1.

10. See, for example, the 1979 issues of the tabloid *Látigo* (Miami), whose motto was "Con Cuba, contra los traidores" (For Cuba, against the traitors) and the 1978–79 issues of *La Crónica.*

11. These were organizations condemned in the community because their members—mostly young, college-educated Cuban exiles—supported the revolution and the Castro government. See chapter 5 for a discussion of these organizations.

12. Gloria Gil, "Porqué decimos no al diálogo," *La Crónica,* October 10, 1978, 14–15. Translation mine.

13. Guillermo Martínez, "Exiles, Including Castro's Sister, Repeat Opposition to Cuba Talks," *Miami Herald,* October 14, 1978, 20A.

14. *La Crónica,* October 15, 1979, 23.

15. Benjamin de la Vega, "Pide sanciones la brigada para los dialogueros," *Alerta,* May 1979, 6–7. Translation mine.

16. Dan Williams, "Cigar-Maker Losing Buyers after Offering Castro a Puff," *Miami News,* November 15, 1978, 1A; "Exile Firm Targets of Bombing Tries, Shooting," *Miami Herald,* February 22, 1982, 1B.

17. "El diálogo y la desesperación de los terroristas," *Areíto* 5 (1979): 9–11.

18. Cynthia Brown, "Strong-Arming the Hispanic Press," *Columbia Journalism Review* 19 (July–August 1980): 52.

19. "138 Cuban Prisoners Reject Castro Dialogue," *Of Human Rights,* Spring 1979, 4. See also *Of Human Rights,* Spring 1980.

20. Guillermo Martínez and William R. Long, "Most Jailed Cubans Back Talks," *Miami Herald,* October 28, 1978, 1A; Villaverde, "Llama Cuba a exilados a firmar acuerdos."

21. The United States implemented a special parole program for these prisoners. Those persons who were still in prison as of August 1, 1978, and their immediate families were eligible for this program. (Persons released prior to August 1 would be eligible to apply for immigrant visas at the U.S. Interests Section in Havana.) Transportation to the United States was the responsibility of the individual prisoner, his or her family in the United States, or interested civic groups or voluntary agencies. "Information for Persons Desiring to Bring Their Relatives from Cuba to the United States" (May 1979), in File "CO38 1/20/77–1/20/81," Box 21, White House Central File, Subject File, Countries, Carter Library. See also "Castro to Free 3000, Ease Travel for Exiles," *Miami News,* November 24, 1978, 1A.

22. "Cuban Human Rights Initiatives since 1977" (9/17/79) in File "CO38 7/1/79–1/20/81," Box 21, White House Central File, Subject File, Countries, Carter Library.

23. Matos was the former military governor of the province of Camagüey. He resigned his position in 1959 in protest over the growing Communist presence in the army and the government. The Cuban government subsequently tried him for "antipatriotic and antirevolutionary conduct" and sentenced him to twenty years in prison. See also chapter 4.

24. The Americans were Lawrence Lunt, Juan Tur, Everett Jackson, and Claudio Rodríguez Morales.

25. "Exodus from Cuba," *Department of State Bulletin* 80 (July 1980): 80.

26. *La Crónica,* April 6, 1979, 10. Translation mine.

27. "Vigilancia a empleados de welfare viajan a Cuba," *La Crónica,* April 6, 1979, 16.

28. Helga Silva and Guy Gugliotta, "Journeys to Cuba Challenge Old Values," *Miami Herald,* April 8, 1979, 1A; Benjamin de la Vega, "Los vuelos: Bomba de tiempo contra Castro," *Alerta,* December 1979, 10–12.

29. Conversation with the author, Miami, March 10, 1987. Translation mine. The interviewee preferred to be unnamed.

30. The exile media that condemned the trips to Cuba had also forewarned that they would have dire consequences for the Castro government. See, for example, de la Vega, "Los Vuelos."

31. "Editorial: La posición de Cuba," *Granma*," April 13, 1980, 1. Translation mine. See also "Chronology," Records of CHTF.

32. For the Cuban interpretation of the incident see "Síntesis biográfica del soldado Pedro Ortíz Cabrera, custodio de la Misión del Perú, muerto el primero de abril," *Granma*, April 13, 1980, 1.

33. "Declaración del gobierno revolucionario de Cuba," *Granma*, April 13, 1980, 1.

34. "Exodus from Cuba," 80.

35. These accounts are based on reports from the exile news media, *Miami Herald, New York Times, Newsweek, Time,* and other periodicals, as well as on interviews with Cubans who personally witnessed the events.

36. "Editorial: La posición de Cuba."

37. "Editorial: Hay que mostrarle al imperialismo yanqui qué es Cuba," *Granma*, April 27, 1980, 9.

38. Candelaria García, interview by the author, audiotape, July 17, 1994. Translation mine.

39. "The Flight from Havana," *Newsweek*, April 28, 1980, 40.

40. "Chronology," Records of CHTF. The Carter administration also authorized $4.25 million for transportation and other costs through the Emergency Refugee and Migration Fund.

41. "The Flight from Havana," 38; "Start of a Mass Exodus," *Time*, April 28, 1980, 32.

42. See, for example, the account of Lidia González, cofounder of the Comité Humanitario de Mujeres de Cuba, in *El Nuevo Herald*, March 10, 1991, 5D.

43. Candelaria García, interview; Mirta Ojito, "Embajada de Perú: Primer paso," *El Nuevo Herald*, April 8, 1990, 1A.

44. "The Flight from Havana," 38; "Voyage from Cuba," *Time*, May 5, 1980, 43; "¡Este sí es el pueblo!" *Granma*, April 27, 1980, 1.

45. "La más grande concentración del pueblo en la historia de Cuba," *Granma*, May 11, 1980, 10. Translation mine.

46. Ibid., 10-11.

47. "Museo historico de la marcha del pueblo combatiente," *Granma*, June 9, 1980, 1.

48. Mimi Whitefield, "Cuba Recalls Boatlift with Selective Memory," *Houston Chronicle*, April 1, 1990, 25A.

49. See, for example, the May 11, 1980, issue of *Granma*.

50. "La más grande concentración del pueblo," 10.

51. Smith, *The Closest of Enemies;* "Coping with Cuba's Exodus," *Newsweek*, May 12, 1980, 60; "Carter and the Cuban Influx," *Newsweek*, May 26, 1980, 22.

52. "Chronology," Records of CHTF.

53. Ibid. See also "Sea Lift from Cuba to Key West," *Newsweek*, May 5, 1980, 59; "Voyage from Cuba," 43.

54. "Voyage from Cuba," 43.

55. "The Cuban-Haitian Task Force" (Introduction to Index), 1, in Box 1, Records of CHTF.

56. "Sea Lift from Cuba to Key West," 59.

57. Rosa Abella, "Trabajo en Opa-locka con los refugiados," audiotape, May 25, 1980, Rosa Abella Audio Tape Collection, Cuban Exile Archives, University of Miami. Translation mine.

58. Memo from William J. Beckham to Jimmy Carter, May 30, 1980, in File "6/3/80 [2]," Box 189, Staff Offices: Office of the Staff Secretary, Carter Library. See also "Cuban Refugees," *Department of State Bulletin* 80 (August 1980): 74.

59. Reinaldo Arenas, "Un largo viaje de Mariel a Nueva York," in *Necesidad de libertad: Mariel: Testimonios de un intelectual disidente* (Mexico City: Kosmos-Editorial, S.A., 1986).

60. Luisa Esquiroz, "Un peregrinaje a Cayo Hueso," *El Miami Herald,* April 11, 1987, 8.

61. Abella, "Trabajo en Opa-locka con los refugiados."

62. See File "Sponsorship File No. 1," Box 28, Records of CHTF. The participating VOLAGs were the United States Catholic Conference, the Church World Service, the United Hebrew Immigrant Aid Society, the International Rescue Committee, the World Relief Refugee Services, the American Council for Nationalities Service, the Lutheran Immigration and Refugee Service, and the Tolstoy Foundation.

63. Bowen, *Report of CHTF,* 4. On July 15, the Carter administration determined that the emergency was under control. To replace FEMA, the administration created the Cuban-Haitian Task Force, under the auspices of the State Department, to oversee the processing and resettlement of Cubans and Haitians.

64. Bowen, *Report of CHTF,* 31-36. See also Robert L. Bach, Jennifer B. Bach, and Timothy Triplett, "The Flotilla 'Entrants': Latest and Most Controversial," *Cuban Studies / Estudios Cubanos* 11/12 (July 1981-January 1982), 35.

65. Néstor Almendros and Orlando Jiménez-Leal, *Conducta impropia* (Madrid: Editorial Playor, 1984); Candelaria García, interview.

66. Abella, "Trabajo en Opa-locka con los refugiados."

67. Candelaria García, interview.

68. Memorandum, Christian Holmes to Eugene Eidenberg, 8/28/80, in Folder "White House I," Box 10, Records of CHTF. See also File "Sponsorship File No. 1," Box 28, Records of CHTF.

69. Bowen, *Report of CHTF,* 56-58. Some of the individuals diagnosed as mentally retarded were later found to be "illiterates who were depressed and withdrawn," while some diagnosed as psychotic or otherwise mentally ill were found to be faking their illnesses in order to leave the stressful environment of the camps.

70. Bowen, *Report of CHTF,* 55; Thomas D. Boswell, Manuel Rivero, and Guarioné M. Díaz, eds., *Bibliography for the Mariel-Cuban Diaspora,* Paper no. 7 (Gainesville: Center for Latin American Studies, the University of Florida, 1988), 3.

71. Cited in File "Events, [n.d.]," Box 21, Records of CHTF; File "Homosexuals File No. 1," Box 22, Records of CHTF; Bowen, *Report of CHTF*, 58–59. According to the Immigration and Naturalization Act of 1952, the United States could expel aliens with "a sexual deviation or mental defect." In August 1979, the Public Health Service determined that homosexuality per se would no longer be considered a mental disease or defect. Nonetheless, on September 9, 1980, the Justice Department determined that homosexuals would be excluded—but "solely upon the voluntary admission by the alien that he or she is homosexual."

72. Text of speech, Box 22, Staff Offices: Domestic Policy Staff, Civil Rights and Justice, Papers of Franklin E. White, Carter Library.

73. "Exodus from Cuba," 80.

74. A sample of letters protesting Mariel and American immigration policy are available in File "ND16/CO38 1/20/77–1/20/81," Box ND-42, White House Central File, Subject File: National Security–Defense, Carter Library.

75. Richard Morin, "Deluge Adds to Fear in Uneasy Miami," *Miami Herald*, December 8, 1980, 11.

76. "The Cuban Tide Is a Flood," *Newsweek*, May 19, 1980, 29.

77. "White House Statement on Cuban Refugees, May 14, 1980," in File "Cuban Refugees, 1980," Box 1, Staff Offices: Office of Hispanic Affairs, Papers of Armando Rendon, Carter Library.

78. On May 8, at the invitation of the Costa Rican government, representatives from twenty-two nations and seven international organizations met in San José to discuss the migration from Cuba. All twenty-two nations pledged to assist the United States in resettling the Cubans.

79. "White House Statement on Cuban Refugees, May 14, 1980." See also Memorandum for President Carter from Jack Watson, May 15, 1980, Box 1, Records of CHTF. Also see Thomas O. Enders, "Cuban and Haitian Migration," *Department of State Bulletin* 81 (October 1981): 78; Victor Palmieri, "Cuban Refugees," *Department of State Bulletin* 80 (August 1980): 73–75.

80. Mario A. Rivera, "The Cuban and Haitian Influxes of 1980 and the American Response: Retrospect and Prospect," November 1980, in Box 12, Records of CHTF.

81. Civil fines were secured by the seizure of the boat itself by the Customs Department. See Memorandum from Paul R. Michel to Victor Palmieri and David Aaron, August 19, 1980, in File "Cuban Refugees," Box 35, Records of CHTF.

82. File "Entrants vs. Refugees," Box 21, Records of CHTF.

83. Boswell, Rivero, and Díaz, *Bibliography*, 1–22. Heriberto Dixon has written that the percentage of blacks and mulattoes might have been as high as 40 percent; mulattoes were hard to classify. "Undoubtedly," he writes, "many of the lighter mulattoes will attempt to 'pass' for white in the United States." See "The Cuban-American Counterpoint: Black Cubans in the United States," *Dialectical Anthropology* 13 (1988): 227–39; and Dixon's "Who Ever Heard of a Black Cuban?" *Afro-Hispanic Review* 1 (September 1982): 10–12.

84. Bowen, *Report of CHTF*, 70; Boswell, Rivero, and Díaz, *Bibliography*, 5.

85. See Bach, Bach, and Triplett, "Flotilla 'Entrants' "; Gastón A. Fernández, "The Flotilla Entrants: Are They Different?" *Cuban Studies / Estudios Cubanos* 11/12 (July 1981–January 1982): 49–54; Alejandro Portes, Juan M. Clark, and Robert D. Manning, "After Mariel: A Survey of the Resettlement Experiences of 1980 Cuban Refugees in Miami," *Cuban Studies / Estudios Cubanos* 15 (Summer 1985): 37–59; Bowen, *Report of CHTF,* 70–71.

86. Portes, Clark, and Manning, "After Mariel," 45–46; Bowen, *Report of CHTF* 70–71.

87. In order to be considered a refugee under section 207 of the Immigration and Nationality Act (as amended by the Refugee Act of 1980), a group of individuals had to be designated by the president as "of special humanitarian concern to the United States" following consultations with Congress. These individuals had to be identified abroad and cleared for transportation to the United States. Aliens who came to the U.S. outside the established refugee admission procedures could have their claims adjudicated on a case-by-case basis under section 208 of the law. On May 2, Eugene Eidenberg officially announced that the Cuban arrivals would not be classified as refugees nor would they be eligible for benefits under the Refugee Act of 1980 (P.L. 96-212).

For a discussion of the refugees' motivations for coming to the United States, see, for example, Portes, Clark, and Manning, "After Mariel," 42. Of their sample of 514 Cubans in the Miami metropolitan area, 80.1 percent emigrated for political reasons, 12.3 percent cited family reasons, 3.7 cited economic reasons, and 3.9 percent said they were forcibly expelled.

88. The Cubans were temporarily admitted into the United States under section 212(d) (5) of the Immigration and Nationality Act for a sixty-day period so that security checks could be made and applications for asylum processed. The authorization was renewable every sixty days pending a decision on their status. On June 20, the administration announced a special designation for the Cubans and Haitians who entered the U.S. during this period: "Cuban-Haitian entrant (status pending)." Cubans who had arrived in the U.S. from April 21 to June 19 fell into this category, as well as all Haitians who were in INS proceedings as of June 19. Those who arrived later were to be evaluated for asylum in accordance with the Refugee Act of 1980, though the June 19 cutoff date was later extended by the president to October 10, 1980. On July 31, legislation was introduced that enabled the Cuban-Haitian entrants to apply for permanent resident status after living in the U.S. for two years and qualified them for limited social services.

89. File "ST9 2/1/80–1/20/81," Box ST-7, White House Central Files, Subject File: States-Territories, Carter Library.

90. Financial assistance to the Cubans and Haitians was authorized by section 2(c) of the Migration and Refugee Assistance Act, which is not limited to refugees. While the Cubans and Haitians did not qualify for resettlement assistance, they were eligible for food stamps under 7 U.S.C. 2015(f).

91. File "Attitudes of Americans", Box 19, Records of CHTF.

92. "Miami File No. 3," Box 22, Records of CHTF.

93. Telegram from Eugene Eidenberg to Governor Carlos Romero Barceló in File "White House [2]," Box 10, Records of CHTF. For a sample of the protest letters recieved from Puerto Rican residents see folder "Cuban Refugees,

8/15/80–11/28/80," Box 2, Staff Offices: Office of Hispanic Affairs, Papers of Miriam Cruz, Carter Library.

94. The civil suits were: Wilfredo Marquez Colon et al. v. James Carter et al.; Jorge Colon et al. v. James Carter; and Commonwealth of Puerto Rico v. Edmund S. Muskie et al. See File "Bohen, F. M. Chronological File, 11/21/80–12/9/80," Box 10, Records of CHTF. In order to get around these suits as well as the cease-and-desist order from the Environmental Control Board, Carter issued an executive order exempting Fort Allen from the local pollution control requirements and the laws enumerated in the lawsuits. A federal court ruled that Fort Allen was exempt from the National Environmental Policy Act but upheld the injunction until the Supreme Court ruling. See File "Background Info, Cities, Awareness Tour," Box 19, Records of CHTF.

95. The riots occurred at Eglin, Fort Indiantown Gap, and Fort Chaffee. At Indiantown, five hundred military police had to be flown in to restore order. "The Refugees: Rebels with a Cause," *Newsweek*, June 16, 1980, 30–31.

96. Mark Neilsen, "'Bad Press' Creates Difficulties in Resettling Cuban Refugees," *National Catholic Reporter*, August 15, 1980, 22.

97. Bowen, *Report of CHTF*, 55.

98. "The Cuban Conundrum," *Newsweek*, September 29, 1980, 21.

99. In a letter to Rep. Claude Pepper asking for financial assistance to increase the police force, City Manager Richard Fosmoen warned that from sixteen hundred to five thousand Cubans were roaming the streets. In Box 6, Records of CHTF. See also Mirta Ojito and Ivan Román, "Exito y progreso de los refugiados," *El Nuevo Herald*, April 21, 1990, 1D.

100. Rivera, "The Cuban and Haitian Influxes," A15–16. On September 16, the Cuban government announced that all those who hijacked planes to Cuba would face "drastic penal measures" and would be extradited. Two days later, two Cubans hijacked a plane to Havana and the Cuban government acted on its pledge. Hijackings to Cuba stopped—at least for the next few years.

101. Memo from Christian Holmes, Director of the CHTF, to Eugene Eidenberg, November 3, 1980, Box 10, Records of CHTF.

102. Bach, Bach, and Triplett, "Flotilla 'Entrants,'" 33–38.

103. File "Background Info, Cities for Awareness Tour," Box 19, Records of CHTF.

104. File "May 1, 1980", Box 1, Records of the CHTF.

105. Memorandum from Esteban Torres to Jack Watson, April 29, 1980, in Box 17, Staff Offices: Special Assistant to the President: Esteban Torres, Carter Library. The *Miami Herald* and the *Miami News* frequently reported on Cuban intelligence efforts. See, for example, "Castro's Spies Prowl Miami, Defector Says," *Miami News*, December 18, 1971; Joe Crankshaw, "500 Castro Agents Operate in Miami, Witness Testifies," *Miami Herald*, August 19, 1976; and Jim McGee, "Exiles Wage Silent War with Castro's Spies," *Miami Herald*, June 19, 1983.

106. See *Granma* from April to July 1980.

107. By the end of September, eighty-nine Cuban entrants had petitioned the U.S. government to be allowed to return to Cuba. File "Third Country Position", Box 28, Records of CHTF.

108. An estimated one thousand were unaccompanied minors, and these were particularly vulnerable to institutional and physical abuse. The Cuban American Legal Defense Fund filed a lawsuit for the release of 293 minors at Fort McCoy, many of whom had been raped. The lawsuit led to increased security measures at the camps and the segregation of minors. File "White House I," Box 10, Records of CHTF.

109. File "Third Country Position," Box 28, Records of CHTF.

110. Bowen, *Report of CHTF,* 71.

111. File "Repatriation and Deportation," Box 27, Records of CHTF. See also Memorandum from Frank White to Stuart Eizenstat, June 6, 1980, in File 4, Box 24, Staff Offices: Domestic Policy Staff, Civil Rights and Justice, Papers of Franklin E. White, Carter Library.

112. Carla Anne Robbins, "South Florida's Melting Pot About to Boil," *Business Week,* February 4, 1985, 86-87.

113. Frederic Tasker, "Anti-Bilingualism Approved in Dade County," *Miami Herald,* November 5, 1980, 1A.

114. William E. Schmidt, "Detaining Cubans Exacts Rising Toll," *New York Times,* March 10, 1986, 1.

115. Ronald Smothers, "Their Crimes Vary, but Most Cubans Are Serving Sentences of Frustration," *New York Times,* November 30, 1987, B11.

116. Schmidt, "Detaining Cubans." See also the testimony of Rep. John Lewis of Georgia for an account of the conditions he found at the Atlanta penitentiary. Mariel Hearings (1988).

117. Gary Leshaw, "Final Story of Marielitos Isn't Written," *Atlanta Journal and Constitution,* April 21, 1990, A15.

118. Jacquelyn Swearingen, "Rights Groups Urge OAS to Seek Hearings for Mariel Detainees," *Miami Herald,* April 16, 1987, 19A.

119. Fred Grimm, "Judge Refuses to Imprison Cuban Refugee," *Miami Herald,* April 23, 1987, 19A.

120. *Miami Herald,* December 1, 1987, 1A.

121. Lindsey Gruson, "Cuban Inmates in Louisiana Free All 26 Hostages," *New York Times,* November 30, 1987, 1.

122. Mariel Hearings (1988); Fred Grimm and Mirta Ojito, "Problema de detenidos del Mariel no recibe solución," *El Nuevo Herald,* April 22, 1990, 14A. In late August 1991, thirty-one Cubans at Talladega Penitentiary again took prison employees hostage. All thirty-one men surrendered a week later, however, and were subsequently deported.

123. Double Exposure / TV Latina, *Miami-Havana* (London: Channel 4 Television, 1992), documentary.

124. See, for example, Luis Feldstein Soto's article "No se prevé otro Mariel," *El Miami Herald,* April 12, 1987, 1.

125. Roberto Fabricio, "Mariel Boatlift Still Raising Waves of Fear," *Miami Herald,* May 28, 1983, 1B. For federal recommendations, see File "Mariel II", Box 12, Records of CHTF.

126. Ana E. Santiago, "Bajo revisión plan de emergencia ante otro Mariel," *El Nuevo Herald,* May 25, 1991. For a discussion of the *balseros'* motivations for coming to the U.S. see Lizette Alvarez, "Exodo cubano: De asunto político a económico," *El Nuevo Herald,* April 21, 1991, 1A.

127. "Cubans Raft to the U.S. in Soaring Numbers," *Houston Chronicle,*
August 18, 1994, 1A, 12A.

128. The antigovernment demonstrations were prompted by rumors that a
boat was sailing to Havana to take them to Florida. Hundreds of people gathered
on the waterfront boulevard known as el Malecon. Some carried signs and
chanted antigovernment slogans; others smashed windows and threw stones at
riot police. Castro blamed the United States for the incident because of its policy
of welcoming the *balseros.* Mimi Whitefield and Fabiola Santiago, "Threat of
Cuba Immigrant Wave Puts U.S. on Alert," *Houston Chronicle,* August 7, 1994,
29A; "Cubans Urged to Ignore Castro's Threat of Exodus," *Houston Chronicle,*
August 7, 1994, 29A; "Cubans Will Be Detained," *Houston Chronicle,* August
19, 1994, 1A, 18A.

129. "U.S.-Cuba Joint Communique on Migration," *U.S. Department of
State Dispatch* 5, no. 37 (September 12, 1994), 603.

Chapter 3

1. Milton Gordon, *Assimilation in American Life* (New York: Oxford
University Press, 1964). Gordon discusses theories of assimilation, including the
concepts of anglo-conformity, the melting pot, and cultural pluralism.

2. Rafael J. Prohías and Lourdes Casal were the first to report this situation
in *The Cuban Minority in the U.S.: Preliminary Report on Need Identification
and Program Evaluation,* 2d ed. (Washington, D.C.: Cuban National Planning
Council, 1974). The census data was reported in Thomas D. Boswell and James
R. Curtis, *The Cuban-American Experience: Culture, Images, and Perspectives*
(Totowa, New Jersey: Rowman and Allanheld, 1983). The 1980 census data
does not include the Cubans of Mariel.

3. Lisandro Pérez, "Cubans in the United States," *Annals of the American Academy of Political and Social Science* 487 (September 1986): 130. This
figure does not include the Cubans who arrived during the Mariel boatlift.

4. These figures were provided by the Metro–Dade County Planning
Department, Research Division. According to the 1990 census, the total Latino
population in Dade County was 953,407. Cubans comprised 59 percent of this
number.

5. See, for example, Eleanor Rogg's "The Influence of a Strong Refugee
Community on the Economic Adjustment of Its Members," in Carlos E. Cortés,
ed., *Cuban Exiles in the United States* (New York: Arno Press, 1980). Here and
in other studies, Rogg concludes that the existence of a strong Cuban community in West New York, New Jersey, favorably influenced the adjustment of
its members by "providing a comparison referent which does not demean the
refugees' sense of self-worth as well as by providing psycho-social strength and
satisfactions to its members."

6. These figures were provided by the Census Bureau, Planning Commission, Hudson County, New Jersey. According to the 1990 census, the
population of Union City was 58,013. There were 43,869 Hispanics (or 75.6%
of the population); of these, 15,084 were Cuban. The total population of West

New York, New Jersey, was 38,125. Of this number, 27,930 were Hispanic. Cubans totaled 12,502. See also Evelyn Nieves, "Union City and Miami: A Sisterhood Born of Cuban Roots," *The New York Times,* November 30, 1992, B1.

7. F. Peirce Eichelberger, "The Cubans in Miami: Residential Movement and Ethnic Group Differentiation," (Master's thesis, University of Cincinnati, 1974), 49; cited in Boswell and Curtis, *The Cuban-American Experience.*

8. Boswell and Curtis, *The Cuban-American Experience,* 78–79.

9. One such bank was Republic National. Through the initiative of its Cuban emigré director Luis Botifoll, the bank granted small loans (up to thirty thousand dollars) on the basis of character. Botifoll eventually was appointed chairman of the board, and today Republic National Bank is Miami's largest Hispanic-owned bank. See Hector Cantu, "Building a Bridge to Success," *Hispanic Business,* September 1993, 16.

10. María Cristina García, "Adapting to Exile: Cuban Women in the United States, 1959–1973," *Latino Studies Journal* 2 (Spring 1991).

11. Everett C. Parker, "Miami: Test for the Churches," *Christian Century* 78 (October 18, 1961): 1241–42.

12. The *Miami Herald* reported in its November 16, 1980, issue that over thirty thousand non-Latin whites left Dade County between 1970 and 1980.

13. The Cuban National Planning Council reported that 91.9 percent of Cubans in Miami in 1977 spoke only Spanish at home and an additional 4 percent spoke mostly Spanish. See Guarioné Díaz, *Evaluation and Identification of Policy Issues in the Cuban Community* (Miami: Cuban American Planning Council, 1980). This data is also presented in Max J. Castro, "The Politics of Language in Miami," in Guillermo J. Grenier and Alex Stepick, eds., *Miami Now! Immigration, Ethnicity and Social Change* (Gainesville: University Press of Florida, 1992), 112.

14. Details of the study, conducted by the Strategy Research Corporation in 1984, are reported in Castro, "The Politics of Language in Miami," 111–12.

15. "Curso de historia de Cuba para mayores de 60 años," *Diario las Américas,* August 17, 1974. Translation mine.

16. See "Drogas y orgias sexuales: efectos del libertinaje," *¡Fe!,* October 1, 1972, 9, for an example of the many articles published in exile periodicals reflecting this fear.

17. McNally, *Catholicism in South Florida,* 153.

18. "El Colegio Belén en el exilio," *Impresiones,* February–March 1964, 55.

19. "Rekindling Memories of Motherland," *Miami Herald,* July 27, 1983, 1B.

20. Aida Serra de Madrazo, founder of the Municipio de Regla, telephone interview by the author, 11 November 1986. Translation mine. See also "La tarea municipalista," *Cubanacan: Asociación de Villaclareños en el Exilio,* September 1978, 2; "Los municipios y la causa de Cuba," *RECE,* August 1966, 1.

21. For example, a February 1971 letter from the directorate of the Association of Villaclareños in Exile states, "The lyceums and clubs that the Cubans in exile organized to lead the wars of independence, which liberated us from Spain's tutelage, are now duplicated in the Cuban municipalities in exile."

Translation mine. Cuban Exile Archives, University of Miami. The February 24, 1968, issue of *La Nación* (published by the Cuban Municipalities in Exile, and not to be confused with the political tabloid by the same name) says, "No other [organization] could represent as completely the true essence of the Cuban nation." Translation mine.

22. *Miami Herald,* October 7, 1974.

23. For a brief history of Cuban theater in the United States see the introduction to Rodolfo J. Cortina, ed., *Cuban American Theater* (Houston: Arte Público Press, 1991), 7-18. For an analysis of Cuban theater in the U.S. prior to 1940, see Nicolás Kanellos, *A History of Hispanic Theater in the United States: Origins to 1940* (Austin: University of Texas Press, 1990).

24. These include the National Association of Cuban Industrialists, National College of Cuban Pharmacists in Exile, National College of Cuban Lawyers in Exile, Cuban Medical Association in Exile, Cuban Nurses Association in Exile, Association of Cuban Dentists in Exile, Association of Cuban Veterinary Doctors in Exile, College of Cuban Journalists in Exile, National College of Cuban Teachers in Exile, and Association of Cuban Accountants in Exile, among many others. Most notable among the Cuban labor unions was the Federation of Telephone Workers of Cuba in Exile.

25. Seymour Liebman, "Cuban Jewish Community in South Florida," in *American Jewish Yearbook* (New York: American Jewish Committee, 1969), 243. For a discussion of the Chevet Achim and other Jewish organizations in Cuba, see Levine, *Tropical Diaspora.*

26. Chief among the Cuban holidays are *el veinte de mayo,* commemorating the day Cuba officially became a republic; *el diez de octubre,* commemorating the beginning of the Ten Years' War against Spain in 1868; and *el veinticuatro de febrero,* commemorating the beginning of the 1895 war against Spain, which ultimately brought independence.

27. As Richard Handler and Jocelyn Linnekin have written, "To do something because it is traditional is already to reinterpret, and hence to change it." See "Tradition, Genuine or Spurious," *Journal of American Folklore* 97 (1984): 273-88. See also Edward Shils, "Tradition," *Comparative Studies in Society and History* 13 (1971): 122-59; and Eric Hobsbawm and Terence Ranger, eds., *The Invention of Tradition* (Cambridge: Cambridge University Press, 1992).

28. *Santería* has become the subject of several studies in the past ten years. I include two here: Joseph Murphy, *Santería: An African Religion in America* (Boston: Beacon Press, 1988); Migene González-Wippler, *Santería, the Religion: A Legacy of Faith, Rites, and Magic* (New York: Harmony Books, 1989).

29. Joan Biskupic, "Animal Sacrifice Ban Tests Religion Rights," *Washington Post,* November 1, 1992, A1.

30. Author Roberto G. Fernández is known for his comical depictions of *quinceañeras* in such works as *Raining Backwards* (Houston: Arte Público Press, 1988) and *La vida es un special* (Miami: Ediciones Universal, 1981). See chapter 5. For examples of the "new" *quinceañeras* see back issues of the Miami-based newspaper *Diario las Américas,* particularly from the 1970s.

31. The symbolism at the Three Kings Day Parade was particularly powerful. At one parade attended by the author, one float portrayed Cuba as a young

child, wrapped in a Cuban flag, with her hands and feet in chains; another presented the Cuban flag with a stake (holding a Soviet flag) through its star.

32. McNally, *Catholicism in South Florida,* 157.

33. "Emotivo rosario viviente en el Bayfront Park," *Impresiones,* June 6, 1961, 7. Translation mine.

34. In 1868, after the first successful battles of the Ten Years' War (1868–78), General Carlos Manuel de Céspedes journeyed to the sanctuary of El Cobre to present his battle sword to la Virgen in gratitude. Other revolutionary heroes, including Ignacio Agramonte and Antonio Maceo, were also known for their acts of devotion to la Virgen. To celebrate their final victory in 1898, General Calixto García ordered a thanksgiving mass at El Cobre. Many years later, in 1915, the Cuban veterans of the war of independence officially requested that Pope Benedict XV declare la Virgen de la Caridad the spiritual patron of Cuba.

35. The statue, a duplicate of the original statue in the Sanctuary of El Cobre, was taken out of Cuba via the Panamanian Embassy in Havana. The statue was housed at first in one of the children's camps of Operation Peter Pan, then in San Juan Bosco Church in Little Havana. Beginning in 1967, the statue was displayed in a temporary chapel on Biscayne Bay, until it was finally transferred to the Ermita, which was completed in 1973. The only time the statue of la Virgen de la Caridad del Cobre is taken out of the Ermita is on September 8 for a religious procession. An exception was made during the visit of Pope John Paul II to Miami in September 1987, when the statue was transferred to the Pope's temporary residence.

36. "Marian Shrine for Miami Urged," *The Voice,* September 16, 1966, 1, 14.

37. Hilda Inclán, "Batista's Influence Seen Lingering," *Miami News,* August 7, 1973, 14A.

38. Ernesto Montaner, "La unidad imposible," *Patria,* February 14, 1961, 1.

39. Thomas, *The Cuban Revolution,* 355.

40. "Quevedo en Miami . . . a buscarlo!" *Cuba Libre,* October 28, 1960. Translation mine.

41. "Mensaje," *Página,* May 20, 1971.

42. For a declaration of principles of Cuban workers in Cuba and exile, see *Trabajo,* March 8, 1968, 4–5.

43. Editorial, *Comandos L,* August 1965, 2. Translation mine.

44. *Guerra* (New York), August 13, 1976, 3. Translation mine.

45. Armando García Sifredo, "El privilegio de ser Cubano," *La Nación,* December 17, 1976, 2. Translation mine.

46. The Cuban *Zig-Zag* incurred the wrath of Fidel Castro when it published one particular caricature of him. He attacked the periodical in his weekly speech, prompting the burning of thousands of copies by Castro supporters. The Castro government eventually tried to enlist the magazine's director to its cause, but Rosenada opted to defect to the United States. *Zig-Zag* continued publishing for a few more weeks under a new staff, but the magazine never regained its former popularity and eventually folded. See *Impresiones,* December 1963–January 1964, 66–68.

47. Andrew St. George, "The War of Wits," *Parade,* August 7, 1966.

48. Geoffrey Tomb, "Roberto Suárez Named Miami Herald President," *Miami Herald,* June 20, 1990, 1A.

49. Heberto Padilla, "La radio en Miami," *El Miami Herald,* January 2, 1986, 5. Translation mine.

50. Fabiola Santiago, "Emisoras hispanas ejercen gran influencia en Miami," *El Herald,* June 22, 1986, 1, 8.

51. In *The Miami Herald,* March 22, 1986. See also Santiago, "Emisoras hispanas"; *Miami Herald,* December 9, 1987, 1B; and "Patriotism or Journalism?" (Miami: WTVJ, "Montage," first aired May 4, 1986).

52. Jay Ducassi, "Stations Seldom Face Libel Suits or FCC Action," *Miami Herald,* June 22, 1986, 2B.

53. Fabiola Santiago, "Pennsylvania Station Owns Top-Rated Spanish Station," *Miami Herald,* June 22, 1986, 2B.

54. Joel Achenbach, "Cuban Radio Plays by Its Own Broadcasting Rules," *Miami Herald,* May 22, 1985, 1B.

55. *Miami Herald,* November 7, 1986, 17D.

56. Among the first to write about the Cuban economic enclave were sociologists Alejandro Portes and Robert L. Bach. They defined the economic enclave as "a distinctive economic formation, characterized by the spatial concentration of immigrants who organize a variety of enterprises to serve their own ethnic market and the general population." According to Portes and Bach, the enclave economy allowed Cubans to avoid the economic disadvantages that usually accompany segregation. See Alejandro Portes and Robert L. Bach, *Latin Journey: Cuban and Mexican Immigrants in the United States* (Berkeley and Los Angeles: University of California Press, 1985), and Alejandro Portes, "The Social Origins of the Cuban Enclave Economy of Miami," *Sociological Perspectives* 30 (October 1987): 340–71. A study by Portes and Jensen found that ethnic enterprises were effective avenues for economic mobility, particularly for men; although few women were self-employed, they earned higher incomes working within the enclave economy. See Alejandro Portes and Leif Jensen, "The Enclave and the Entrants: Patterns of Ethnic Enterprise in Miami before and after Mariel," *American Sociological Review* 54 (December 1989): 929–49.

For another interpretation of the enclave economy, and more specifically the role of Cubans in the U.S. labor movement, see Guillermo J. Grenier, "The Cuban American Labor Movement in Dade County: An Emerging Immigrant Working Class," in Grenier and Stepick, eds., *Miami Now!* 133–59. Grenier explores the role class-based organizations such as labor unions have played in fostering group solidarity and group consciousness.

57. "Cuban and Haitian Arrivals: Crisis and Response," June 30, 1980, 6, in File "ND16/CO38 1/20/77–1/20/81," Box ND-42, White House Central File, Subject File: National Security–Defense, Carter Library. See also Carlos Arboleya, *The Cuban Community, 1980: Coming of Age as History Repeats Itself* (Miami, 1980).

58. Carlos Arboleya, *El impacto cubano en la Florida* (Miami, 1985). Arboleya, former president and CEO of Barnett Bank, Miami, periodically published reports on the Cuban community in south Florida. Arboleya's report also included the following statistics for Dade County: over 4,500 Cuban

doctors, 500 lawyers, 17 bank presidents and 390 vice presidents, and 25,000 garment workers. See also "Dade Latin Businesses Top U.S.," *Miami Herald,* October 23, 1986, 1A.

59. In 1990, the median family income for Cubans was $33,504, which was higher than the median family income for Latinos in the U.S. ($27,972) but lower than the median national income ($37,403). 18.5 percent of Cubans had four or more years of college education, as compared to 9.7 percent for Latinos and 23.7 percent for the nation as a whole. 21.6 percent of Cuban males and 20 percent of Cuban females were professionals or executives (as compared to the national averages of 26.3 and 27.2 percent). See Alejandro Portes, "¿Quienes somos? ¿Qué pensamos? Los cubanos en Estados Unidos en la década de los noventas," *Cuban Affairs / Asuntos Cubanos* 1, no. 1 (Spring 1994): 5.

For an analysis of the 1980 census, see Lisandro Pérez, "The Cuban Population of the United States: The Results of the 1980 U.S. Census of Population," *Cuban Studies / Estudios Cubanos* 15 (Summer 1985): 1–18; Joan Moore and Harry Pachón, *Hispanics in the United States* (Englewood Cliffs, New Jersey: Prentice-Hall, 1985), 69–78. The 1980 census did not include the Cubans who arrived during the Mariel boatlift.

60. Lisandro Pérez, "Immigrant Economic Adjustment and Family Organization: The Cuban Success Story Re-examined," *International Migration Review* 20 (Spring 1986): 4–20. See also Pérez, "The Cuban Population of the United States," 8–9. The 1980 census revealed that more Cuban women worked outside the home than any other group, 55.4 percent as compared to the national average of 49.9 percent. For an analysis of Cuban women's roles in the economic, political, and cultural affairs of the community, see García, "Adapting to Exile." For an economic analysis see Myra Marx Ferree, "Employment without Liberation: Cuban Women in the U.S.," *Social Science Quarterly* 60 (January 1979): 35–50. See also Dorita Roca Mariña, "A Theoretical Discussion of What Changes and What Stays the Same in Cuban Immigrant Families," in José Szapocznik and María Cristina Herrera, eds., *Cuban Americans: Acculturation, Adjustment, and the Family* (Washington: The National Coalition of Hispanic Mental Health and Human Services Organization, 1978).

61. Pérez, "Immigrant Economic Adjustment." See also Portes and Jensen, "The Enclave and the Entrants."

62. Portes and Jensen found that 34 percent of their Mariel respondents (excluding the self-employed) were working for Cuban-owned firms. See Portes and Jensen, "The Enclave and the Entrants."

63. Arboleya, *The Cuban Community, 1980.* See also Raymond A. Mohl, "An Ethnic 'Boiling Pot': Cubans and Haitians in Miami," *Journal of Ethnic Studies* 13 (Summer 1985): 51–74.

64. "To Miami, Refugees Spell P-R-O-S-P-E-R-I-T-Y," *Business Week,* November 3, 1962, 92; "Cuban Refugees Write a U.S. Success Story," *Business Week,* January 11, 1969, 84.

65. In his article "Immigrant Economic Adjustment and Family Organization," Lisandro Pérez challenges the "myth of the golden exile." He concludes that comparisons of economic achievement between Hispanic groups are inconclusive because they ignore the differences in the structural conditions

within which economic adjustment takes place. See also Alejandro Portes, "Dilemmas of a Golden Exile: Integration of Cuban Refugee Families in Milwaukee," *American Sociological Review* 34 (August 1969): 505–18.

66. In 1990, 16.9 percent of Cuban Americans lived in poverty, as compared to 13.5 percent of the general population; Portes, "¿Quienes somos?" 5. See also note 60.

67. Alfonso Chardy, "'Invisible Exiles': Black Cubans Don't Find Their Niche in Miami," *Houston Chronicle,* September 12, 1993, 24A.

68. "Temas," *Impacto,* March 11, 1972. Translation mine. The concerns of the Cuban working class are articulated in the exile newspapers *El Trabajador, Trabajo,* and *Impacto.*

69. "Editorial," *Cubanacan: Asociación de Villaclareños en el Exilio,* 9, no. 106 (January 1975), 1. Translation mine.

70. Editorial, *Martiano,* November 1972, 2. Translation mine.

71. "Temas," *Impacto,* May 20, 1973, 2. Translation mine.

72. "Are We to Become Citizens?" *Antorcha,* January 1968, 5.

73. Founded in 1967, Abdala took its name from a fable by the nineteenth-century independence leader José Martí. Abdala, a prince from the imaginary land of Nuvia, renounces all material comforts and pleasures in order to defend his nation. Prince Abdala ultimately dies for his beliefs.

74. "Entre dos banderas," *Antorcha,* April 1973, 2. Translation mine.

75. Editorial, *Antorcha,* October 1969, 1. Translation mine.

76. Editorial, *Antorcha,* December 1969, 1. Translation mine.

77. Roberto Fabricio, "The Cuban Americans: Fifteen Years Later," *Tropic Magazine (Miami Herald),* July 14, 1974, 30–36.

78. Miguel Pérez, "10,000 New Americans Is Exile Group's Goal," *Miami Herald,* November 24, 1975, 8B; George Volsky, "Cuban Exiles Now Seek U.S. Citizenship," *New York Times,* July 4, 1976, 19; Helga Silva, "The Cuban Exiles: Landmarks of an Era," *Miami Herald,* April 8, 1979, 22A.

79. Arboleya, *The Cuban Community, 1980,* 3.

80. Roberto Fabricio, "Cubans at Home, but Homesick," *Miami Herald,* October 29, 1972, 1B.

81. Humberto Cruz, "Dade Cubans Won't Return, Study Shows," *Miami Herald,* June 10, 1974. The *Herald* published part of a study by sociologists Juan Clark and Manuel Mendoza of Miami-Dade Community College. Clark and Mendoza conducted interviews with 151 Dade Cubans fifty-five years or older—the group most likely to have failed to adapt to life in the United States—and less than half of these stated that they would return to Cuba if Castro were overthrown.

82. Alejandro Portes and Rafael Mozo, "The Political Adaptation Process of Cubans and Other Ethnic Minorities in the United States: A Preliminary Analysis," *International Migration Review* 19 (March 1985): 35–63.

83. Metro–Dade County, Board of County Commissioners, Resolution no. R.-502-73; Chuck Gómez, "In Cases of Emergency, Latins Can Lose Out," *Miami Herald,* June 3, 1974, 1A.

84. Resolution no. R.-502-73, as cited in Castro, "The Politics of Language in Miami," 116.

85. Carlos Harrison, "Mariel Refugees Still Feel Isolated, Study Says," *Miami Herald,* January 13, 1987, 3B; Derek Reveron, "Se disipó el temor de que refugiados fueran carga," *El Nuevo Herald,* April 22, 1990, 4B.

86. Helga Silva provides a fascinating account of the accommodation of these children into the Dade County school system in *The Children of Mariel: Cuban Refugee Children in South Florida Schools* (Washington: Cuban American National Foundation, 1985).

87. Guillermo Martínez, "The Children of Mariel Turn School into Success Story," *Miami Herald,* January 15, 1987, 27A.

88. Ana E. Santiago, "¿Volverían a Cuba los de Mariel?" *El Nuevo Herald,* April 22, 1990, 1A.

89. Ibid., 15A.

90. Luisa Esquiroz, "Un peregrinaje a Cayo Hueso," *El Miami Herald,* April 11, 1987, 8.

91. Isabel Castellanos, "The Use of English and Spanish among Cubans in Miami," *Cuban Studies / Estudios Cubanos* 20 (1990): 49–63. Castellanos concludes, however, that Spanish will continue to be as important as English in Dade County because of the number of Spanish-speaking immigrants who continue to settle in south Florida each year and the high volume of tourists from Latin America.

92. Bertha Rodríguez, interview.

93. Silvia Pérez, conversation with the author, Miami, 10 November 1986. Translation mine.

Chapter 4

1. See, for example, Carlos A. Forment, "Political Practice and the Rise of an Ethnic Enclave," *Theory and Society* 18 (January 1989): 47–81; and Alejandro Portes and Alex Stepick, *City on the Edge: The Transformation of Miami* (Berkeley: University of California Press, 1993).

2. Cited in Portes, "¿Quienes somos?" 5.

3. As early as 1960, exile periodicals reported the activities of the guerrilla fighters and the Cuban underground. See, for example, "El Escambray: Territorio libre en la Cuba fidelista," *Bohemia Libre,* October 9, 1960.

4. Citing presidential proclamation No. 3004 and Section 215 of the Immigration and Nationality Act (66 Stat. 190), Secretary of State Christian Herter (who replaced John Foster Dulles) authorized law enforcement agencies to detain any persons leaving the United States for Cuba to engage in activities for the purpose of "starting or furthering civil strife in that country." See Memorandum dated November 1, 1959, in File "Cuba, General, 1/63," National Security Files, Countries, Cuba, Box 37A–38, JFK Library. As early as 1958, a U.S. federal grand jury indicted former Cuban president Carlos Prío Socarrás for planning arms deliveries to Cuba in violation of the U.S. Neutrality Act. See Thomas, *The Cuban Revolution,* 194.

5. The U.S. government, however, never officially referred to it as a "provisional government." As late as March 22, 1961, a State Department spokesman declared that the establishment of a provisional government in the

U.S. without federal permission violated U.S. sovereignty and international law, and that no such consent had been granted to the Cuban refugees. Unsigned memorandum, March 29, 1961, in File "Cuba, General, 1/61–3/61," National Security Files, Countries, Costa Rica–Cuba, Box 114a, JFK Library.

6. Interestingly, in June 1960 the Cuban exile newspaper *Cuba Libre* claimed to be the propaganda vehicle for twenty-three of those political organizations.

7. Members of Batista's army were the only men in exile to have military experience, and they rose quickly to positions of leadership in the invasion force.

8. See, for example, the November 18, November 25, and December 9, 1960, issues of *Cuba Libre.*

9. Unsigned Memorandum, March 29, 1961, in File "Cuba, General 1/61–3/61," Files, Countries, Costa Rica–Cuba, Box 114a, JFK Library.

10. Ibid.

11. Two-thirds of the nineteen members who comprised the first cabinet were either in prison or in exile. See U.S. Department of State, *Cuba* (Washington: Government Printing Office, 1961).

12. Ray and the MRP were reportedly opposed to joining the CRC because of the presence of old guard politicians such as Hevia and Varona as well as because of the organization's ties to the CIA. Realizing that U.S. involvement improved its chances for success, however, the MRP finally joined after agreeing with the former Frente members on several key points in the CRC platform. Some of the key provisions in the platform included (1) general elections within eighteen months; (2) agrarian reform; (3) return of confiscated assets except those regarded as necessary for the national interest, with owners receiving proper reimbursement; (4) low-cost housing; (5) elimination of state control of labor; and (6) free enterprise and private ownership.

13. Felipe Pazos had resigned as first president of the National Bank and was replaced by Che Guevara. Col. Ramón Barquín was a military attaché in France and Spain for the revolutionary government before his defection. Raul Chibás was a prominent leader of the Orthodox Party; his brother, Eduardo, head of the party before his untimely death, was reportedly one of Castro's personal heroes. Various exile newspapers, among them *Cuba Libre* and *Patria,* condemned the members of the CRC. A February 14, 1961, editorial in the pro-Batista tabloid *Patria,* for example, warned that political unity in the exile community was impossible because of the extremes in ideology. The Batistianos could never forgive the *arrepentidos* (repentants). The editor, Ernesto Montaner, warned that the war against Castro was also a war against his friends and followers, including the *arrepentidos.*

14. While Fidel Castro ridiculed the CRC, calling it the Council of Worms, he was reportedly concerned about Ray's inclusion, since it foiled his attempts to link the Council completely to the old guard. Memorandum for the President from Arthur Schlesinger, Jr., March 31, 1961, in File "Cuba, General, 1/61–3/61," President's Office Files, Countries, Costa Rica–Cuba, Box 114a, JFK Library. See also Thomas, *The Cuban Revolution,* 581.

15. Memorandum from Arthur M. Schlesinger, Jr., to Tracy Barnes, March 29, 1961, in File "Cuba, General, 1/61–3/61," National Security Files, Countries, Cuba, Box 35A–36, JFK Library.

16. National Security Action Memorandum No. 43, April 25, 1961, National Security Files, Meetings and Memoranda, Box 328–330, JFK Library. According to CIA operative Howard Hunt, there were an estimated two hundred G-2 agents operating in the Miami area in the early 1960s. See Hunt, *Give Us This Day*, 60.

17. Assassination attempts were considered. A 1975 Senate investigation on alleged assassination plots involving foreign leaders revealed evidence of at least eight different CIA plots to assassinate Fidel Castro from 1960 to 1965.

18. These activities included maintaining support within the exile community. Toward this end the CRC published a periodical called *Cuba Nueva* (1962–63), which articulated the political views of the CRC and kept the community informed about developments within Cuba. The CRC also continued to try to garner international support for its government in exile.

19. The government's official line regarding the recruitment program was that it was "a means of helping [Cuban refugees] adjust to the United States." The Department of Defense was disappointed with the response in the exile community, however. The number of volunteers was initially high, but when recruits realized that they were not being trained to invade Cuba, most dropped out. The program was terminated on June 30, 1962. Upon their release from Cuban prisons, between four hundred and five hundred members of Brigade 2506 joined the U.S. army, two hundred as officers. One of them, former brigade commander Erneido Oliva, ultimately rose to the rank of Brigadier General of the National Guard. National Security Action Memorandum No. 43; Memorandum for the President from Robert McNamara, June 6, 1961, and from Roswell Gilpatric, January 31, 1962, in File "NSAM #54," National Security Files, Meetings and Memoranda, Box 330, JFK Library. See also Memorandum for the National Security Council Executive Committee, January 24, 1963, in File "Cuba, Security, 1963," President's Office Files, Countries, Cuba, Box 115; and Transcript of Press Conference, April 3, 1963, in File "Standing Group Meetings, General, 4/63–5/63," in National Security Files, Meetings and Memoranda, Box 315, JFK Library.

20. Press conference, December 31, 1962, in File "Standing Group Meeting, 4/23/63, Part B," in National Security Files, Meetings and Memoranda, Box 315, JFK Library. Records of the Missile Crisis made available for the first time in January 1992 reveal that Kennedy's pledge was contingent upon Castro's behavior in the Western hemisphere. Kennedy warned that any "aggressive actions" by Castro would provoke a response from the United States. See Thompson, *The Missiles of October*; Robert Pear, "The Cuba Missile Crisis: Kennedy Left a Loophole," *New York Times*, January 7, 1992, A5.

21. Summary Record of NSC Standing Group Meeting no. 9/63, July 9, 1963, in National Security Files, Meetings and Memoranda, Box 315, JFK Library. For a sample of responses to inquiries from private citizens, see File "ND 19-2/CO 55," Records of HEW, Box 637, JFK Library.

22. Report No. 165 (August 23, 1963), in Central Intelligence Agency, Foreign Broadcast Information Service, Daily Reports, Latin America, Box 33, JFK Library.

23. U.S. corporations lost an estimated $1.1 billion in property as a result of the nationalization programs of the revolutionary government and the break-

down in U.S.–Cuba relations. These corporations stood to profit from Castro's overthrow and pressured the U.S. government to take a tougher line towards Cuba. Transcript of interview of Robert Hurwitch (Office of Cuban Affairs, Department of State), by John Plank, May 4, 1964, JFK Library.

24. The DRE is one of the older rebel groups, founded in 1957 during the anti-Batista struggles. It disbanded temporarily in 1959. The DRE that operated in exile was reestablished in Havana on February 5, 1960, and had representatives in various cities throughout Latin America. For a history of the organization, see "Inicio de nuestra lucha," *Trinchera*, February 10, 1963, 7.

25. "Ataque," *Trinchera*, September 6, 1962, 3; Al Burt, "El ataque comando de Manuel Salvat," *El Miami Herald*, June 11, 1980.

26. In "Comandos L," No. 105-117222 (subsection A), Records of the FBI.

27. José Ignacio Rivero, "¿Hasta cuando?" *Impresiones*, February–March 1963, 4. Translation mine.

28. Edited transcripts of Cuban news broadcasts, Central Intelligence Agency, Foreign Broadcast Information Service, Daily Reports, Latin America, Box 33, JFK Library.

29. In "Comandos L," No. 105-117222 (section 1) and "Comandos L," No. 105-117222 (subsection A), Records of the Federal Bureau of Investigation.

30. Statement, March 30, 1963, in File "Standing Group Meeting, 4/23/63, Part A," in National Security Files, Meetings and Memoranda, Box 315, JFK Library. See also Notes by Dean Rusk and Edward Martin, March 19, 1963, in File "Cuba, General, 1/63–3/63," in President's Office Files, Countries, Cuba, Box 115; and transcript of Press Conference, April 3, 1963, in File "Standing Group Meetings, General, 4/63–5/63," in National Security File, Meetings and Memoranda, Box 315, JFK Library.

31. Transcript of interview of Robert Hurwitch, Office of Cuban Affairs, Department of State, by John Plank, April 24, 1964, JFK Library.

32. In "Comandos L," No. 105-117222 (subsection A), Records of the FBI.

33. In "Comandos L," No. 105-117222 (section 2), Records of the FBI.

34. Martin, "U.S. Outlines Policy," 983–90; "Major Cuban Exile Organizations [1962]," in File "Cuba, 11/1/62–12/29/62," Papers of Arthur M. Schlesinger, Jr., White House Files, Box WH-5, JFK Library; Al Burt, "Cubans Split, Action Could Unite Them," *Miami Herald*, March 11, 1963, 8A. See also interdepartmental memos, 1966 National Security Files (Latin America–Cuba), LBJ Library.

35. See, for example, the November 18, 1960, issue of exile tabloid *Cuba Libre*, which was the first to use the term.

36. See *Miami Herald*, April 19, 1963, 1A; "Another Cuban Fiasco?" *U.S. News and World Report*, April 29, 1963, 33–36; and "A Refugee Leader Blames U.S. for 'Broken Promise,'" *U.S. News and World Report*, April 29, 1963, 65–67.

37. Press Statement by the Department of State, April 15, 1963, in File "Standing Group Meeting, 4/23/63, Part A," in National Security Files, Meetings and Memoranda, Box 315, JFK Library.

38. A letter sent to President Kennedy by the Association of Cuban Magistrates in Exile prompted a telegram from the State Department urging them

to dissolve at once, since the formation of a government-in-exile was a violation of the "sovereignty and territory of the United States." Telegram, October 7, 1961, in File "Cuba 6/12/61-12/31/61," Papers of Arthur M. Schlesinger, Jr., White House Files, Box WH-5, JFK Library.

39. The group also claimed to have air-dropped over one hundred thousand copies of García Kohly's platform over Cuba. CCMJ Platform, in File "Cuba, General, 1/62-8/62," in National Security File, Countries, Cuba, Box 36, JFK Library.

40. In "MRR" (subsection A), Records of the FBI.

41. In "MRR" (section 3), Records of the FBI.

42. Undated letter from Ted Clifton to Mr. O'Donnell, in File "4/22/61-4/30/61" in President's Office Files, Countries, Costa Rica-Cuba, Box 114a, JFK Library. See also Hurwitch interview of April 24, 1964, JFK Library; and Hunt, *Give Us This Day*, 83-84.

43. Thomas, *The Cuban Revolution*, 695; William Ryan, "Exile Splits Confuse Issues," *Miami News*, April 17, 1963, 1A.

44. Editorial in *Guerra*, February 22, 1964, 1. Translation mine.

45. See, for example, the disdain the group RECE had for Vietnam War protestors, as shown in the August 1967 issue of their tabloid, *RECE*.

46. See the memoirs of former CIA operatives published during the 1970s and 1980s—for example, Bradley Earl Ayers, *The War That Never Was: An Insider's Account of CIA Covert Operations against Cuba* (New York: Bobbs-Merrill, 1976); Hunt, *Give Us This Day;* and Ralph W. McGehee, *Deadly Deceits: My Twenty-Five Years in the CIA* (New York: Sheridan Square Publications, 1983). See also John Prados, *Presidents' Secret Wars: CIA and Pentagon Covert Operations since WWII* (New York: William Morrow and Co., 1986); and Harry Rositzke, *The CIA's Secret Operations: Espionage, Counterespionage, and Covert Actions* (New York: Reader's Digest Press, 1977).

47. CIA cable dated July 20, 1964, in National Security File, Latin America-Cuba, Box 22, LBJ Library.

48. Telegram, RECE to LBJ, March 8, 1966, National Security-Defense Files, Box 22, LBJ Library; "Debe actuarse en Cuba con la misma energía que en Vietnam," *Impacto*, May 20, 1972.

49. Five members of Alpha 66, for example, were given nine-month suspended jail sentences and two years' probation by a U.S. district court for trying to supply Cuban guerrillas with rifles stolen from the Colt Industries plant in Hartford, Connecticut. They were also ordered to pay Colt $265 for each stolen rifle. See *Miami News*, May 4, 1971.

50. In "Comandos L," No. 105-117222 (section 1), Records of the FBI.

51. Press release from the Comité Pro-Referendum, National Security-Defense Files, Latin America-Cuba, Box 22, LBJ Library. See also Don Bohning, "Cuban Exiles Choose—Meet the Leaders in Worldwide Vote," *Miami Herald*, May 24, 1964, 6B. Votes were counted by the Service Bureau Corporation, a subsidiary of IBM, and the results were certified by a local judge.

52. "Realiza el RECE censo militar a través de todo el mundo," *RECE*, November 1964, 4.

53. *RECE*, April 1965.

54. "¡Cubano ayuda a la guerra!" *RECE*, July 1966, 2; *RECE*, April 1969.

55. See *RECE*, December 1965; "Comandos L," No. 105-117222 (section 6), Records of the FBI.

56. *RECE*, December 1965. Translation mine.

57. Myles R. R. Frechette, "Cuban-Soviet Impact on the Western Hemisphere," *Department of State Bulletin* 80 (July 1980): 79–80.

58. *Miami Herald*, December 29, 1975.

59. Roberto Fabricio, "Torch Ruins Show Rising Exile Anger," *Miami Herald*, October 13, 1974, 1B; Roberto Fabricio, "Exiles Protest Lifting of Cuba Sanctions," *Miami Herald*, November 4, 1974, 1B; Roberto Fabricio, "Cubans' OAS Protest Cooled by Downpour," *Miami Herald*, May 11, 1975, 1D.

60. "El exilio pide relaciones entre Cuba y Estados Unidos," *Areíto* 5, nos. 19–20 (1979): 7–8; "10 mil exiliados piden Carter reanude relaciones con Cuba," *El Mundo*, June 25, 1979, 8.

61. See, for example, the *Miami Herald*, April 2, 1975, July 23, 1975, and August 22, 1978.

62. Editorial in *Martiano*, n.d. Translation mine.

63. Carlos López-Oña, Jr., "Los traidores," *Antorcha*, July 1970, 4. Translation mine.

64. The shipment of food and medicine to Cuba was always hotly debated in the community. See, for example, *¡Fe!*, December 15, 1972, 1. Even burial in Cuba—which was allowed beginning in 1979—was strongly discouraged because such arrangements benefitted the Cuban government financially. Ana E. Santiago, "Más restos cubanos llevados a la isla," *El Nuevo Herald*, April 4, 1991, 1A, 4A.

65. "Desde la cárcel denuncia La Cova al exilio Cubano," *La Nación*, October 15, 1976, 14. Translation mine.

66. "Exiles Say They Planted Bomb on Cuban Airliner," *New York Times*, July 16, 1976, 8; "Terrorism Charged to Cubans in Testimony by Miami Police," *New York Times*, August 23, 1976, 12; "Nine Cuban Refugees Go on Trial in Miami Tomorrow, Putting Focus on Terrorists' Activity in South Florida," *New York Times*, November 28, 1976, 35. See also *Cuba Update* (Center for Cuban Studies) 1, no. 1 (April 1980).

67. See chapter 2 for a discussion of the *diálogo*.

68. Jay Clarke, "Cubans in Miami Fearful," *Washington Post*, May 23, 1976, E1.

69. Edna Buchanan, "Foes Stalked Slain Exile," *Miami Herald*, February 23, 1974, 1B; "Acusa Nieves de agresión a líder pragmatista," *¡Fe!*, April 7, 1973, 3; "No permitiremos que juege con Cuba un puñado de traidores," *¡Fe!*, June 15, 1973, 2. See also Internal Security Hearings, 1976, 615.

70. Hilda Inclán, "Six Cuban Exiles Marked for Death by 'Zero,'" *Miami Herald*, April 25, 1974; "Dara plazo a Torriente," *¡Fe!*, February 24, 1973, 7; "Torriente es el farsante mas grande que ha parido este exilio corrompido y timorato," *¡Fe!*, May 19, 1973, 10.

71. "Nine Cuban Refugees Go on Trial in Miami Tomorrow, Putting Focus on Terrorists' Activities in South Florida," *New York Times*, November 28, 1976, 35.

72. José Ignacio Lasaga, "El terrorismo en Miami," *Krisis* 1 (Spring 1976): 23, 30. Translation mine.

73. On August 31, 1977, a group of men claiming to represent the Brigade 2506 Veterans Association announced that they would continue "all kinds of actions to fight against the communist tyranny."

74. Hilda Inclán, "I Am Not Afraid," *Nuestro,* April 1977, 46–47; Benjamin de la Vega, "Estrepitosa caida de la WQBA en el survey de la Arbitron," *Alerta,* August 1980; Larry Rohter, "Dissenting Voice Fights to Stay on Air," *New York Times,* March 2, 1993, A14. As a side note, Milián organized the first Three Kings Day parade in Little Havana in 1971. See *Miami Herald,* January 7, 1975, 1B.

75. Internal Security Hearings (1976), 615–16.

76. Ibid., 632, 651.

77. Ibid., 652. Letelier, ambassador to the U.S. during Salvador Allende's government, was a vocal critic of the Pinochet military regime. Cuban militants claimed that he was a subversive furthering the cause of international communism. See *El Imparcial,* May 7, 1981, 1.

78. For a sample of newspaper articles dealing with this topic see "El espionaje del G-2 en Miami," *Bohemia Libre,* November 13, 1960, 83; "Lleno el exilio de agentes G-2," *Patria,* July 25, 1961, 4; "Castro Spies Prowl Miami, Defector Says," *Miami News,* December 18, 1971; Joe Crankshaw, "500 Castro Agents Operate in Miami, Witness Testifies," *Miami Herald,* August 19, 1976; Jim McGee, "Exiles Wage Silent War with Castro Spies," *Miami Herald,* June 19, 1983, 1A. Cuban exile newspapers claimed that the number of spies in Miami was much larger than that supposed by local authorities. One exile newspaper, for example, claimed that as many as seventy-five hundred Cuban spies operated in south Florida. See *Látigo,* January 1979, 10. Most newspapers never explained how they arrived at these figures. The tabloid *Patria* published pictures of suspected G-2 police hiding in exile. See also "Aumento alarmante de infiltrados," *Impacto,* December 30, 1971, 1.

79. McGee, "Exiles Wage Silent War with Castro Spies."

80. For example, a 1974 interview by Prensa Latina with defector Carlos Rivero Collado (a former *brigadista* and the son of Andrés Rivero Agüero, Batista's chosen successor) discussed his work with the Pragmatistas and the Cuban Nationalist Movement. A Radio Havana interview with 1976 defector Manuel de Armas discussed the alleged involvement of the group Abdala in the assassination of exile leader Rolando Masferrer. Internal Security Hearings (1976) 626–27, 631–32, 649–56.

81. For one such interpretation see Lasaga, "El terrorismo en Miami." See also *El Clarín,* May 27, 1976.

82. In 1990 and 1991, the FBI arrested two more Cubans connected to the plot. Two former Chilean military officials remain in hiding at the time of writing. In July 1991, the Chilean Supreme Court reopened the Letelier case. See Gloria Marina, "Five Cubans and an American Figure in the Letelier Case," *Miami Herald,* May 6, 1978, 11A; and "A investigación aspecto chileno del caso Letelier," *El Nuevo Herald,* September 24, 1990, 1A.

83. Many in the exile community did not understand why Americans were making such a fuss about Watergate, and they continued to support President

Nixon in his "struggle against subversion." See Frank Calzón, "El exilio cubano y la crisis norteamericana," *¡Cuba Va!* 1 (Winter 1974): 3–5; Pedro Moreno, "Watergate y los cubanos," *Joven Cuba* 1 (February 1974): 11–12; Roberto Fabricio, "Watergate Had Ironic Twists for Cubans," *Miami Herald,* June 12, 1982, 1B.

84. *Guerra* (New York), November 19, 1976, 3. Translation mine. See also the August/September 1973 issue of *Abdala,* in which the editors pay tribute to a young Cuban who died while putting together a bomb in his Paris hotel room: "From a very young age he was attracted by his patriotic duty. . . ."

85. Gaston Baquero, "No hay mas alternativa que la violencia," reprinted in *Impacto,* October 14, 1972, 5. Translation mine.

86. *El Imparcial,* May 7, 1981.

87. Internal Security Hearings (1976), 636–37.

88. *La Crónica,* October 10, 1978, 18.

89. Federación de Organizaciones Cubanas de Illinois, "Petition to the United States Department of Justice," Box 17, Staff Offices, Papers of Esteban Torres, Carter Library.

90. Merrill Collett, "Absuelto Bosch en Venezuela," *El Herald,* July 22, 1986, 1A.

91. Reinaldo Ramos, "Exiliados reflexionan sobre Orlando Bosch," *El Herald,* July 27, 1986, 1, 3. Translation mine.

92. Letter to the editor, *Miami Herald,* April 2, 1983, 16A.

93. Genie N. L. Stowers, "Political Participation, Ethnicity, and Class Status: The Case of Cubans in Miami," *Ethnic Groups* 8 (1990): 76–77; Eleanor Meyer Rogg and Rosemary Santana Cooney, *The Adaptation and Adjustment of Cubans: West New York, New Jersey,* Monograph No. 5 (New York: Hispanic Research Center, Fordham University, 1980), 18; Thomas D. Boswell and James R. Curtis, *The Cuban American Experience* (Totowa, New Jersey: Rowman and Allanheld, 1983), 174.

94. See, for example, "Hay coexistencia si triunfan los Democratas," *Impacto,* December 17, 1971. Ironically, it was under the Republican administrations of Reagan and Bush that Cubans were denied refugee status and even deported.

95. María de los Angeles Torres, "From Exiles to Minorities: The Politics of Cuban Americans," in F. Chris García, ed., *Latinos and the Political System* (Notre Dame, Indiana: University of Notre Dame Press, 1988), 81–98.

96. Advertisement for the Cuban American National Foundation in *Girón,* June 1982, 4.

97. Lourdes Meluzá, "La Causa: Exiles Redirect Their Efforts," *Miami Herald,* April 13, 1986, 6C.

98. Elizabeth A. Palmer, "Exiles Talk of PACs and Power, Not Another Bay of Pigs," *Congressional Quarterly Weekly Report,* June 23, 1990, 1933; John Spicer Nichols, "The Power of the Anti-Fidel Lobby," *Nation,* October 24, 1988, 389.

99. Nichols, "The Power of the Anti-Fidel Lobby," 390.

100. *Girón,* January–March 1983, 1.

101. The Cuban government offered more menacing critiques: Castro threatened to interfere with the regular broadcasts of several hundred U.S. radio stations, and briefly disrupted commercial broadcasts as far away as Utah and Iowa as a "test and demonstration." John Spicer Nichols, "Broadcast Wars," *NACLA Report on the Americas* 24, no. 3 (November 1990): 32.

102. "Second Thoughts on Radio Martí," *New York Times,* March 22, 1986, 26.

103. Ibid. Castro's AIDS "containment program," however, includes isolating individuals who test positive for the HIV virus.

104. See, for example, Fabiola Santiago, "Exito de fuga alentó a 5 Cubanos," *El Miami Herald,* May 23, 1986, 1, 8.

105. *El Herald,* May 17, 1987, 22-23.

106. Excerpt from letter from Ricardo Bofill to Ernesto Betancourt, director of Radio Martí, published in Dick Capen, "All Share in Radio Martí's Goal," *Miami Herald,* October 4, 1987, 3C.

107. Nichols, "Broadcast Wars," 30-31.

108. R. A. Zaldivar, "Cabildeo cubano cosecha frutos," *El Herald,* August 11, 1986, 1, 6.

109. Jon Nordheimer, "Cuban American Leader Builds a Foundation of Power beyond Miami," *New York Times,* July 12, 1986, 6.

110. One of CANF's most notable losses was Frank Calzón, who drafted the original idea for the foundation while a graduate student at Georgetown University and served as its executive director from 1981 to 1987. Another loss was Ernesto Betancourt, director of Radio Martí, who resigned from the station in 1990 because of personal differences with Mas Canosa. The annual turnover among employees at the station was estimated at over 25 percent. See John Spicer Nichols, "Mas Canosa's Pork Barrel," *NACLA Report on the Americas* 24, no. 3 (November 1990): 34.

111. *Miami Herald,* August 13, 1987, 29A.

112. Sergio López-Miró, "The Cernuda Affair," *Miami Herald,* May 9, 1989, 26A.

113. Celia W. Dugger and Heather Dewar, "Federal Agents Seize Art Brought from Cuba," *Miami Herald,* May 6, 1989, 1B; Carlos Alberto Montaner, "Ramón Cernuda, Cuban Art, and a 'Moral Lynching,'" *Miami Herald,* May 20, 1989, 30A; Elizabeth Hanly, "The Cuban Museum Crisis, or Fear and Loathing in Miami," *Art in America* 80 (February 1991): 31-35; Margarita F. Ruiz and Santiago Morales, "One Museum, Two Visions, No Easy Solutions," *Miami Herald,* April 25, 1991.

114. Christopher Marquis, "Cuba Studies Plan Angers Profs," *Miami Herald,* May 2, 1989, 2B.

115. Larry Rohter, "Miami Leaders Are Condemned by Rights Unit," *New York Times,* August 19, 1992, A18; Larry Rohter, "When a City Newspaper Is the Enemy," *New York Times,* March 19, 1992, A16.

116. Rohter, "Miami Leaders."

117. Ibid.

118. *Miami Herald,* December 10, 1987, 7C. See also *El Herald,* May 17, 1987, 22-23.

119. *Fundación*, special issue, 1991; *Fundación* 2, no. 7 (1992).

120. Meluzá, "La Causa: Exiles Redirect Their Efforts."

121. Paid announcement signed by Huber Matos appearing in *New York Times*, August 23, 1981, 22.

122. "Análisis del artículo del New York Times," *CID*, October 1983, 31; Luis Feldstein Soto, "La Causa Abandons Violence," *Miami Herald*, February 21, 1988, 1B, 4B; Huber Matos, "Preparamos al pueblo de Cuba para la libertad que ha de vivir," *CID*, December 1983, 27–28; *La Crónica*, October 30, 1979, 2.

123. Jo Thomas, "Freed Cuban Tells of Time Spent in a 'Concrete Box' Underground," *Of Human Rights*, Spring 1980, 1.

124. Arnaldo Ramos Yániz, "Por qué ataca José Ignacio Rivero a Huber Matos?" *Alerta*, February 1980, 31–32.

125. José Ignacio Rivero, "Huber Matos y su Congreso," *El Imparcial*, August 27, 1981, 2 (reprinted from the *Diario Las Américas*). Translation mine.

126. Ramos Yániz, "Por qué ataca José Ignacio Rivero a Huber Matos?"

127. "Entrevista a Carlos Alberto Montaner," *CID*, December 20, 1981, 18. Translation mine.

128. Cover, *Guanimar (Municipio de Alquizar)*, October–November 1984. Translation mine.

129. Front page picture, *El Imparcial*, August 6, 1981. Translation mine.

130. Herald survey cited in *Areíto* 9 (1984): 4–5.

131. Fabiola Santiago, "Emisoras hispanas ejercen gran influencia en Miami," *El Herald*, June 22, 1986, 1.

132. *Diario Las Américas*, January 19, 1982, 2B. These camps were also the subject of a news story by Ralph Renick of Channel 4 (WCKT) in Miami.

133. Joseph B. Treaster, "A Cuban American 'Advisor' Tells of Combat with Nicaraguan Rebels," *New York Times*, December 22, 1986, A19.

134. Feldstein Soto, "Hispanics Laud Reagan in Iran-Contra Dealings," *Miami Herald*, December 3, 1986, 1B.

135. Charles Whited, "Pat Buchanan Still Spouting Bold Invective," *Miami Herald*, December 11, 1986, 1C.

136. Frank Greeve and Miguel Pérez, "Seventeen Years Later: Still Thousands of Political Prisoners in Cuba," *Of Human Rights*, January 1977, 7–9.

137. "Presos Políticos," *El Herald*, June 8, 1986, 1, 4.

138. Charles Greenfield, "Armando Valladares: Twenty-Two Years of Solitude," *Nuestro*, December 1983, 14–18; Liz Balmaseda, "The Ironic Diplomacy of Armando Valladares," *Miami Herald*, October 7, 1990, 1H; and "'Brush Telegraph' Tells News of Prisoners," *Of Human Rights*, Spring 1978, 1. See also *Of Human Rights*, Spring 1980, 1.

139. Unidades Militares de Ayuda a la Producción, or Military Units for Assistance in Production.

140. Guillermo Cabrera Infante, "El preso político desconocido," *El Herald*, September 30, 1986, 5.

141. The only book discussing the experience of women political prisoners is Esther Pilar Mora Morales, *La verdad sobre el presidio político de mujeres en la Cuba castrista* (Miami: Revista Ideal, n.d.).

142. Mirta Ojito, "Martha Frayde: Testigo de la historia," *El Nuevo Herald*, August 25, 1990, 1D. See also *Conducta impropia: Un film de Néstor Almendros y Orlando Jiménez-Leal* (Madrid: Editorial Playor, 1985).

143. *Miami Herald*, June 29, 1984, 15A. The Americans had been accused of various crimes, including drug smuggling and espionage.

144. "Presos Políticos," 1, 4.

145. Editorial, *Miami Herald*, October 17, 1985, 2B.

146. Tom Bowman, "Castro Denies Exit Visas to 48 at the Last Minute," *Miami Herald*, December 17, 1986, 1A.

147. Greenfield, "Armando Valladares," 17.

148. Peter Slevin, "Cuba y EU intercambian insultos y acusaciones en foro de Ginebra," *El Miami Herald*, March 7, 1987, 1.

149. Peter Slevin, "Cuba Wins on Rights Vote," *Miami Herald*, March 12, 1987, 1A.

150. *El Nuevo Herald*, February 11, 1988, 1A.

151. Luciano García, "Ayuno pidiendo condenar a Castro," *El Nuevo Herald*, March 1, 1988, 1C; see also *El Nuevo Herald*, March 6, 1988, 1C.

152. Peter Slevin, "U.S., Cuba Find Compromise," *Miami Herald*, March 11, 1988, 1A.

153. Aryeh Neier, "Cuba: The Human Rights Show," *New York Review of Books*, June 15, 1989, 33-35.

154. These include the Cuban Committee for Human Rights, the Cuban Commission for Human Rights and National Reconciliation, the Martí Committee for Human Rights, the Human Rights Party, the Movement for Democratic Integration, and the "Green Path" Eco-Pacifist Movement. See Mimi Whitefield, "No 'Havana Spring' for Cuban Dissidents," *Miami Herald*, June 4, 1990, 1A; Balmaseda, "The Ironic Diplomacy of Armando Valladares"; Editorials in *Miami Herald*, July 2, 1990, July 19, 1990, July 21, 1990, February 9, 1991, February 25, 1991.

Eleven human rights activists were jailed for trying to meet with the UN delegation in 1988, and demonstrators were arrested during Mikhail Gorbachev's visit in April 1989. Others have been arrested for sharing their views with the foreign press. See Christopher Marquis, "Cuban Repression Is Rising, OAS Told," *Miami Herald*, October 3, 1990, 21A.

155. Ana E. Santiago, "Informe sobre Cuba circulará anticipadamente," *El Nuevo Herald*, November 30, 1990, 1A; "Cuba en la mirilla de Amnistía Internacional," *El Nuevo Herald*, February 3, 1991, 4A.

156. Argentina's favorable vote was the first time any Latin American member of the commission had voted against Cuba. Mexico and Brazil, longtime supporters of Cuba, abstained. Voting with Cuba were the Soviet Union, the Ukraine, Iraq, Ethiopia, and China.

157. Mirta Ojito, "U.N. Commission Votes to Send Human Rights Monitor to Cuba," *Miami Herald*, March 7, 1991, 1.

158. For a copy of CANF's plans for a transitional government see *Fundación* 2, no. 10 (n.d.).

159. The Orthodox Party, for example, began publishing a monthly bulletin

called *La Ortodoxia* to renew public support. The Christian Democratic Party also began publishing a monthly bulletin in late 1990.

160. "Declaración de Arcos Bergnes," *El Nuevo Herald*, June 16, 1990, 8A.

161. Pablo Alfonso, "Valladares califica de traición plan de Arcos," *El Nuevo Herald*, June 12, 1990, 1a (translation mine); "Declaración de A. Valladares," *El Nuevo Herald*, June 16, 1990, 1A; Balmaseda, "The Ironic Diplomacy of Armando Valladares."

162. Following these meetings, the Soviet press had only praise for the emigrés, whom they called "an entrepreneurial lot." Soon after, the Soviet airline Aeroflot chose Miami as the hub for its Latin American flights. See Sandra Dibble, "Soviet Visitors Excite Exiles," *Miami Herald*, May 26, 1990, 2B; Alfonso Chardy, "News from Moscow: Miami Cubans Are OK," *Miami Herald*, September 29, 1990, 1A; Alfonso Chardy, "Exiles Plan Talks on Cuba in Moscow," *Miami Herald*, October 15, 1990, 1A.

163. The text of the document appears in "En aras de la unidad," *Fundación* 1, no. 3 (n.d.): 5-7.

164. Alfonso Chardy, "Cuban Vice-President Apparently Misspoke about Talks with Exiles," *Miami Herald*, October 28, 1990, 1B; Alfonso Chardy, "Cuban Exile Groups Wield Increasing Clout," *Miami Herald*, November 4, 1990, 1B. In 1994, the Cuban Democratic Platform voted to ask the U.S. government to partially lift the trade embargo against Cuba, allowing the transfer of food, medicines, and medical equipment. In "A pesar de todo, no todo está perdido," *Contrapunto*, June 1994, 30.

165. Pablo Alfonso, "Exiliados proponen anexión de Cuba a EU," *El Nuevo Herald*, February 5, 1991, 4A.

166. William M. LeoGrande, "A Party Divided and Paralyzed," *Nation*, October 24, 1988, 395-97.

167. Iván Román, "Hope for Speedy End to Castro Era Fading, Poll Shows," *Miami Herald*, May 9, 1991, 1B. A survey by FIU professors showed that Cubans have a "wide variety of opinions on what steps should be taken." These opinions ranged from hard-core conservative—a military invasion by U.S. troops—to the liberal idea that negotiations should be conducted and greater freedom of travel from the island be allowed. See David Hancock, "Radio Station Protesters Pelted with Eggs," *Miami Herald*, April 19, 1991.

168. Editorial, *Palenque*, Spring 1993, 3. Translation mine.

169. The sending of food and medicine to Cuba via third countries was always hotly debated in the community. See, for example, *¡Fe!*, December 15, 1972, 1, and "Telegram to Senator George McGovern, June 6, 1977," in White House Central Files–Foreign Affairs, Box Fo-30, Carter Library. Even burial in Cuba—which was allowed beginning in 1979—was strongly discouraged because such arrangements benefitted the Cuban government financially. Ana E. Santiago, "Más restos cubanos llevados a la isla," *El Nuevo Herald*, April 4, 1991, 1A, 4A.

170. Ana E. Santiago, "Riña entre cubanos por envíos a la isla," *El Nuevo Herald*, April 19, 1991, 1B.

171. Larry Rohter, "As Crisis in Cuba Worsens, Unity of Exiles Is Crumbling," *New York Times*, October 6, 1993, 1.

172. Stephanie Griffith, "New Rules Put Cubans on the Spot," *Washington Post,* August 15, 1993, B5.

173. *El Nuevo Herald,* April 18, 1991, 1B.

174. Rohter, "As Crisis Worsens," 1; "Welcome to Cuban Affairs," *Cuban Affairs / Asuntos Cubanos* 1, no. 1 (Spring 1994): 2. In February 1994, the CCD decided to support several bills in Congress that favored the partial or complete lifting of the U.S. trade embargo against Cuba. The most comprehensive, the Rangel bill, introduced by Rep. Charles B. Rangel (D–NY) on April 29, 1993, called for the repeal of the Cuban Democracy Act and all previous statutes that imposed the embargo against Cuba.

175. A summary of the CCD's first year of activities can be found in *Cuban Affairs/Asuntos Cubanos* 1, no. 2-3 (Summer-Fall 1994).

176. Juan Carlos Coto, "Nuevo emisora radial enfurece a exiliados," *El Nuevo Herald,* March 28, 1991, 1B.

177. Howard French, "Clinton Choice for Latin Post Stirs Feud between Two Groups," *New York Times,* January 27, 1993, A2; Steven A. Holmes, "Clinton Fills Post for Latin America," *New York Times,* March 2, 1993, A13.

178. The conference was titled "La Nación y la Emigración." The meetings at the Presidential Palace between the Cuban Americans and Fidel Castro were secretly videotaped by someone in the Cuban government and released to the press. The edited eleven-minute tape caused an uproar in the community, since it showed the participants laughing and shaking hands with Castro. One participant, former Democratic congressional candidate Magda Montiel Davis (who had run against Ileana Ros-Lehtinen), was shown kissing Castro and calling him *maestro* (teacher). Montiel Davis received death threats, and her offices were boycotted.

Why the Cuban government released the tape to the press is the subject of much conjecture. One popular theory is that conservatives in the Cuban government wished to block change; another theory proposed that, knowing that some Cubans would react violently, the Cuban government wished to focus more negative attention on the exile community. The news magazine *Contrapunto,* published in Miami, dedicated an entire issue (June 1994) to the conference and the reaction of the emigré community. See also William Booth, "Cuban American Exiles Court Castro, and Trouble," *Washington Post,* April 28, 1994, A3; Howard French, "Havana Woos Exiles, Easing Visits and Dangling Financial Carrot," *New York Times,* April 25, 1994, A9.

Chapter 5

1. Related to the author by Guillermo Cabrera Infante at the Miami International Book Fair, 1986.

2. Reinaldo Arenas, "La represión (intelectual) en Cuba," in *Necesidad de Libertad* 43; Heberto Padilla, "Los Cubanos y la cultura," *El Herald,* November 9, 1985, 5.

3. Charles Greenfield, "Writing in Exile: A Portrait of Guillermo Cabrera Infante, Cuba's Foremost Novelist and Critic," *Nuestro,* October 1982, 24.

252 NOTES TO PAGES 171–80

4. For more on these writers see Nicolás Kanellos, ed., *Biographical Dictionary of Hispanic Literature in the United States* (Westport, Connecticut: Greenwood Press, 1989); Naomi E. Lindstrom, "Cuban American and Continental Puerto Rican Literature," in *Sourcebook of Hispanic Culture in the United States,* ed. David William Foster (Chicago: American Library Association, 1982), 225.

5. Roberto G. Fernández, *Raining Backwards* (Houston: Arte Público Press, 1988), 11.

6. Ibid., 36.

7. Omar Torres, *Fallen Angels Sing* (Houston: Arte Público Press, 1991), 32, 60.

8. Ibid., 65.

9. Elías Miguel Muñoz, *Crazy Love* (Houston: Arte Público Press, 1989), 111–12.

10. Virgil Suárez, *Latin Jazz* (New York: Simon and Schuster, 1989), 12.

11. Elías Miguel Muñoz, "Grandfather," in *Cuban American Writers: Los Atrevidos,* ed. Carolina Hospital (Princeton: Ediciones Ellas / Linden Lane Press, 1988), 145.

12. Fernández, *Raining Backwards,* 85.

13. Ibid., 47.

14. Leopoldo M. Hernández, *Martínez,* in *Cuban American Theater,* ed. Cortina, 26.

15. Ibid., 25.

16. Ibid., 28.

17. Carolina Hospital, "The Old Order," in *Paradise Lost or Gained? The Literature of Hispanic Exile,* ed. Fernando Alegría and Jorge Ruffinelli (Houston: Arte Público Press, 1990), 106.

18. Ibid., 107.

19. Miguel González-Pando, *Once upon a Time,* in *Cuban American Theater,* ed. Cortina, 239–78.

20. Iván Acosta, *El super* (Miami: Ediciones Universal, 1982), 69. Translation mine.

21. Ibid.

22. Roberto G. Fernández, *La Montaña Rusa* (Houston: Arte Público Press, 1985), 80.

23. Fernández, *Raining Backwards,* 87–88.

24. Acosta, *El super,* 23–24.

25. Torres, *Fallen Angels Sing,* 74.

26. Acosta, *El super,* 26.

27. Fernández, *Raining Backwards,* 86.

28. Torres, *Fallen Angels Sing,* 83–84.

29. Ibid., 88.

30. Uva Clavijo, *With All and for the Good of All,* in *Cuban American Theater,* ed. Cortina, 169.

31. Ibid.

32. Ibid., 181.

33. Ibid., 170.

34. Ibid., 170–71.

35. Ibid., 174.

36. Torres, *Fallen Angels Sing*, 14.

37. Silvia Burunat, "Lourdes Casal," in *Biographical Dictionary of Hispanic Literature*, ed. Kanellos, 53. Translation by Burunat.

38. Gustavo Pérez-Firmat, "Home," *Bilingual Review* (1980): 171.

39. Lourdes Casal, untitled poem, in *Itinerario ideológico: Antología de Lourdes Casal*, ed. María Cristina Herrera and Leonel Antonio de la Cuesta (Miami: Instituto de Estudios Cubanos, 1982), 127. Translation mine.

40. Leonel Antonio de la Cuesta, "Perfil biográfico," *Itinerario Ideológico*, 3–8.

41. Flora González Mandri, "El regreso," in *Paradise Lost or Gained?*, ed. Alegría and Ruffinelli, 38–60. "El regreso" is excerpted from González Mandri's memoirs entitled *Una casa que rueda*.

42. Ibid., 51. Translation mine.

43. Ibid., 59–60.

44. Ibid., 41.

45. René R. Alomá, *A Little Something to Ease the Pain*, in *Cuban American Theater*, ed. Cortina, 202.

46. Margarita Engle, *Singing to Cuba* (Houston: Arte Público Press, 1993), 152.

47. Ibid., 79–80.

48. Ibid., 153–54.

49. Cristina García, *Dreaming in Cuban* (New York: Alfred A. Knopf, 1992), 117.

50. Ibid., 235–36.

51. Fernández, *Raining Backwards*, 199.

52. Elías Miguel Muñoz, "Little Sister Born in This Land," in *Cuban American Writers*, ed. Hospital, 146.

53. Critic Eliana S. Rivero has written that the emergence of bilingual texts "signals for them an established conscientization of minority status. . . . the political consciousness of being 'dual' or 'other' is clearly expressed at the linguistic level." See Eliana S. Rivero, "(Re)Writing Sugarcane Memories: Cuban Americans and Literature," in *Paradise Lost or Found?* ed. Alegría and Ruffinelli, 173.

54. Gustavo Pérez-Firmat, "Dedication," quoted in *Cuban American Writers*, ed. Hospital, 158. From Pérez-Firmat, *Bilingual Blues* (Tempe, Ariz.: Bilingual Press / Editorial Bilingüe, 1995). Reprinted by permission of Bilingual Press.

55. Fernández, *Raining Backwards*, 78–79.

56. Ibid., 153.

57. Maida Watson, "The Search for Identity in the Theater of Three Cuban American Female Dramatists," *Bilingual Review* 16 (May–December 1991): 193.

58. Dolores Prida, *Savings*, in *Beautiful Señoritas and Other Plays* (Houston: Arte Público Press, 1991), 69–116.

59. Dolores Prida, *Beautiful Señoritas*, 20–21.

60. Dolores Prida, *Coser y cantar*, in *Beautiful Señoritas*, 66.

61. Fernández, *La Montaña Rusa*, 143. Translation mine.
62. Ibid.
63. Muñoz, *Crazy Love*, 11.
64. Ibid., 48.
65. Ibid.
66. Ibid., 16.
67. Elías Miguel Muñoz, *The Greatest Performance* (Houston: Arte Público Press, 1991), 149.
68. This tendency to dismiss the work of Cuban emigrés persisted into the 1980s. Literary critic and poet Carolina Hospital wrote that of the thirteen articles published in Latin American journals between 1978 and 1982 exploring Latin American creativity in exile, the work of Cuban exiles was mentioned only four times. See "Los hijos del exilio cubano y su literatura," *Explicación de textos literarios* 15, no. 2 (1986-87): 103-15.
69. In 1971, Heberto Padilla, one of Cuba's foremost poets and novelists, was arrested by the state police, tortured, and forced to confess to a series of crimes. Only three years earlier, Padilla had been awarded UNEAC's literary prize, the country's highest literary honor, for *Fuera del juego* (Sent off the field). His outspokenness and his maverick style, however, earned him the contempt of several high government officials. He frequently maligned the mediocrity of Cuban writing under the revolution and criticized Cuban authors for their docility, and by 1970 his work came under attack. *Verde Olivo*, the official newspaper of the Cuban Army, accused him of writing "soft literary pieces that were a blend of pornography and antirevolutionary ideas."
   Following Padilla's arrest, thirty-three European and Latin American intellectuals, including Jean-Paul Sartre, Simone de Beauvoir, Mario Vargas Llosa, Carlos Fuentes, and Julio Cortázar, sent a protest letter to Fidel Castro, which was published in *Le Monde* on April 9, 1971. Castro's response came a few weeks later, during his closing remarks at the First National Congress of Education and Culture in Havana. Calling them "bourgeois intellectuals," "shameless pseudo-leftists," "CIA agents," and "agents of imperialism," Castro officially severed ties with these intellectuals and warned them that they were no longer welcome in Cuba. In May 1971 the intellectuals responded with yet another letter, this one signed by sixty writers. The second letter was much more blunt, comparing Padilla's mistreatment to "the most sordid moments of the Stalinist era." See Juan Goytisolo, "Twenty-Six Rue de Bievre," *Partisan Review* 51 (1984): 680-91; "Primera carta de los intelectuales europeos y latinoamericanos a Fidel Castro," reprinted in Arenas, *Necesidad de libertad*, 235; "Discurso de clausura del Primer Congreso Nacional de Educación y Cultura, 30 de abril de 1971," reprinted in Arenas, *Necesidad de libertad*, 236-39.
70. Told to the author by Néstor Almendros at the screening of *Nadie escuchaba*, Museum of Fine Arts, Houston, Texas, June 1988.
71. In 1964, the Cuban government established the UMAP camps to "rehabilitate" homosexuals, prostitutes, and other "undesirables". In Almendros and Jiménez-Leal, *Conducta impropia*, 32, 142.
72. Participants in these congresses stressed that they were dissidents; they did not reject the revolution, but rather what the revolution had become. They

perceived themselves as the true liberals of Cuba, hoping to steer their country away from a "fascism of the left." To call attention to human rights abuses in Cuba, each congress had a president-in-absentia, an empty chair symbolizing the absence of a well-known political prisoner. Past "presidents" included Armando Valladares, Jorge Valls, Angel Cuadra, and Eloy Gutiérrez Menoyo. See, for example, "Gran evento de los intelectuales cubanos libres," *CID*, June 1986, 14–15.

73. "Declaración de apoyo a intelectuales cubanos," *El Nuevo Herald*, June 24, 1991; Pablo Alfonso, "Writers in Cuba Issue Public Call for Democracy," *Miami Herald*, May 31, 1991, 1A; Pablo Alfonso and Evelyn Larrubia, "Datos de los firmantes," *El Nuevo Herald*, June 24, 1991.

74. Greenfield, "Writing in Exile," 22.

75. Arenas, "La represión (intelectual) en Cuba," 43. Translation mine.

76. Reinaldo Arenas y Roberto Valero, "Carta abierta a ediciones del norte," *CID*, March 31, 1982, 15.

77. "Denuncia: Escritores al servicio de Castro," *CID*, September 1982, 3. See also Irene Rostagno, "Fifty Years of Looking South: The Promotion and Reception of Latin American Literature in the United States" (Ph.D. diss., University of Texas at Austin, 1984), 172.

78. "Denuncia," 3.

79. "Carta abierta a Joseph Papp," *Revista Mariel* 2 (Summer 1984): 35. Translation mine.

80. Norma Niurka, "Llena teatro de N.Y. obra de Miami," *El Herald*, August 30, 1986, 1C.

81. Heberto Padilla, "¿Muerte o resurección de SIBI?" *El Herald*, April 5, 1986, 5.

82. "Aid for Cuban Artists," *Nuestro*, January–February 1982, 11.

83. Jon Nordheimer, "Tempest in Miami over Playwright," *New York Times*, May 10, 1986, 6.

84. Roger Lowenstein, "Miami Vise: The Herald Is Wooing Cuban Readers, but It Risks Loss of Anglos," *Wall Street Journal*, March 5, 1987, 1.

85. Letter to the editor from Carlos M. Luis in *El Herald*, May 11, 1986, 10. Translation mine.

86. Carlos M. Luis, "La Dolores y sus heraldos," *Mariel Magazine* 1, no. 1 (1986): 20.

87. The museum was founded in 1974 as a "museum-without-walls." It sponsored historical exhibits on Cuban history as well as exhibitions of Cuban art and material culture at various locations throughout Dade County. It maintained offices at the Little Havana Community Center. In 1982, after acquiring a permanent collection of art and artifacts, the museum leased from the city of Miami a former fire station in Little Havana, which was renovated and converted into an exhibition space. "Brief History of the Cuban Museum," in Inauguration Catalogue, Cuban Museum of Art and Culture, October 10, 1982.

88. These artists were Manuel Mendive, Mariano Rodríguez, Raúl Martínez, and Carmelo. This second auction coincided with an exhibition of donated Cuban paintings that included works by Wilfredo Lam and Raúl Martínez, artists who supported the revolution.

89. According to one journalist, the controversy really began when a prominent Cuban exile, previewing the collection to be auctioned, recognized one of the paintings as the former property of her family. Enraged, she then used her influence to launch a campaign against the museum. See Hanly, "The Cuban Museum Crisis."

90. Cernuda is the representative in Miami of the Coordinated Organizations of Human Rights in Cuba (CODEHU).

91. Celia W. Dugger and Heather Dewar, "Federal Agents Seize Art Brought from Cuba," *Miami Herald,* May 6, 1989, 1B; Sergio-López Miró, "The Cernuda Affair," *Miami Herald,* May 9, 1989, 26A; Carlos Alberto Montaner, "Ramón Cernuda, Cuban Art, and a 'Moral Lynching,'" *Miami Herald,* May 20, 1989, 30A. In 1991, the U.S. Treasury Department exempted artworks from the general U.S. trade embargo against Cuba. See Mimi Whitefield, "EU abre las puertas a obras de arte de Cuba," *El Nuevo Herald,* May 28, 1991. For Cernuda's account of these events see "Culture and Politics in Cuban Miami: Marifeli Pérez-Stable Interviews Ramón Cernuda," *Culturefront* (New York Council for the Humanities), 2, no. 1 (Winter 1993): 20–23.

92. Cynthia Corzo, "Museo cubano gana pleito a Miami," *El Nuevo Herald,* May 22, 1992. Among the reasons cited by the city for evicting the *museo* were: (1) the institution did not have insurance; (2) the directors had not retired peacefully from the premises when their contract expired; (3) the museum had sold artwork in violation of its city contract; (4) the directors of the museum had personally profited from their tenure with the museum; and (5) the museum posed a danger to the community because of the controversy it engendered. For a first-hand account of both sides of the "war"—the Rescue Committee and the Cuban Museum's board—see essays by Margarita F. Ruiz and Santiago Morales, under the headline "One Museum, Two Visions, No Easy Solutions," *Miami Herald,* April 25, 1991.

93. *Joven Cuba* 3 (January 1974): 3–4. Translation mine.

94. "Documento-Respuesta," *¡Cuba Va!* 1 (Winter 1974): 30–32.

95. Editorial, *Krisis* 1, no. 2 (Summer 1975): 1. Translation mine.

96. José Prince, "Revista nueva generación," *Antorcha,* September 1969, 8. Translation mine.

97. *¡Cuba Va!* 1, no. 1 (Autumn 1974): 1.

98. "Nuestra carta de ciudadanía cultural, 1981" (editorial), *Areíto* 7, no. 27 (1981): 96. Translation mine.

99. *Krisis* 1, no. 2 (Summer 1975): 1.

100. Related to the author by Marifeli Pérez-Stable, a former board member of *Areíto.* See also Leonel Antonio de la Cuesta, "Perfil biográfico," 3–8.

101. Editorial, *Areíto* 9, no. 36 (1984): 4–5.

102. Ibid.; see also "Nuestra carta," 95–97.

103. "Nuestra carta," 96.

104. Grupo Areíto, *Contra viento y marea* (La Habana, Cuba: Casa las Américas, 1978), 14. Translation mine.

105. Uva Clavijo, "Respuesta de los estudiantes cubanos a Areíto," *Diario las Américas,* July 23, 1974, 5. See also "Documento-respuesta," in *¡Cuba Va!* 1, no. 1 (Autumn 1974): 30–32.

106. Editorial, *Abdala*, April 1978, 3; translation mine. For another example of exile press reaction see "¿Quién es Lourdes Casal?" *Impacto*, October 3, 1973, 3.

107. Editorial, *Areíto* 1, no. 4 (January–March 1975): 3.

108. "La verdad sobre Lezama Lima," *CID*, September 1984, 26.

109. Henry Maurer, "With the Venceremos in Cuba," *Nation*, July 2, 1977, 6–10; Sandra Levinson and Carol Brightman, *Venceremos Brigade: Young Americans Sharing the Life and Work of Revolutionary Cuba* (New York: Simon and Schuster, 1971).

110. Editorial, *Areíto* 4, nos. 3–4 (Spring 1978): 2–3.

111. Barbara Gutierrez and Jay Ducassi, "City, Exiles Attack Pro-Castro Brigade," *Miami Herald*, October 29, 1982, 1C. The incident set off yet another round of debate in Miami on a recurring theme: the politicization of culture and the climate of censorship in Miami. Around the same time that the Maceo Brigade was condemned, the City Commission also voted to donate ten thousand dollars to the paramilitary group Alpha 66 to assist in the renovation of its headquarters. Letters to the *Miami Herald* criticized the commissioners for condemning the Maceo Brigade while at the same time supporting a political organization "that sends its cadre to infiltrate Cuba and cause hardship for the people by sabotaging the economy." They also protested the lack of freedom of expression in Miami. "What exists now in the Cuban community is officially sanctioned terrorism," wrote one resident, "where people who don't agree with the prevailing views are physically attacked when they try to present their opinions publicly." A number of emigrés wrote the *Herald*, some to explain their opposition to the Brigada and others to assert the constitutional right of the brigade members to say whatever they wanted wherever they wanted. The former compared their response to that of Jews confronted with anti-Semitism or blacks confronted with overt racism. *Herald* columnist Roberto Fabricio wrote that the press conference "was comparable to the Ku Klux Klan holding a press conference in the South Bronx, Harlem, or Liberty City, defending White supremacy." Letter from Humberto Pérez, Military Chief of Alpha 66, *El Herald*, November 9, 1982, 4; "In Defense of Miami's Antonio Maceo Brigade" (letters to the editor), *Miami Herald*, November 5, 1982, 22A; Roberto Fabricio, "Maceo Brigade Like KKK to Cuban Exiles," *Miami Herald*, October 30, 1982, 1B.

112. *Cuban Studies Newsletter*, December 1970, 1.

113. María Cristina Herrera, interview by the author, audiotape, Coral Gables, Florida, March 19, 1987. Translation mine.

114. Ibid.

115. Letter from María Cristina Herrera to the *Miami Herald*, August 12, 1984, 2E.

Conclusion

1. Deborah Sontag, "The Lasting Exile of Cuban Spirits," *New York Times*, September 11, 1994, 1E.

2. "U.S.–Cuba Joint Communiqué on Migration," *U.S. Department of State Dispatch* 5, no. 37 (September 12, 1994), 603.

3. Richard Wallace, "South Florida Grows to Latin Beat," *Miami Herald,* March 6, 1991, 1A; Sandra Dibble, "New Exiles Flocking to Dade," *Miami Herald,* April 11, 1987, 1D; Celia W. Dugger, "Latin Influx, Crime Prompt 'Flight' North," *Miami Herald,* May 3, 1987, 1B.

4. "Dade County Commission Repeals English-Only Law," *New York Times,* May 19, 1993.

5. Sergio López-Miró, ". . . While Hispanics Become the Area's Scapegoats," *Miami Herald,* October 11, 1990, 27A.

6. Jeffrey Schmalz, "Disorder Erupts Again in Miami on Second Night after Fatal Shooting," *New York Times,* January 18, 1989, 1; Jeffrey Schmalz, "Miami Mayor Apologizes to Police for Actions at Scene of Disorder," *New York Times,* January 19, 1989, 1.

7. Jay Ducassi, "Stations Seldom Face Libel Suits or FCC Action," *Miami Herald,* June 22, 1986, 2B.

8. Steven A. Holmes, "Miami Melting Pot Proves Explosive," *New York Times,* December 9, 1990, E4.

9. Nancy San Martín, "Castro Clause on Inaugural Upsets City's Haitian Leaders," *Miami Herald,* January 31, 1991, 3B.

Select Bibliography

Much of the research for this study was conducted in Miami. Three libraries were particularly helpful. The archives at the University of Miami's Otto G. Richter Library hold a vast collection of periodicals, letters, documents, artifacts, photographs, and memorabilia relating to the postrevolutionary Cuban migration. The Cuban exile periodical collection alone contains over seven hundred titles, most published in Dade County but others published in Cuban communities around the United States and abroad. More than any other source, the periodicals collected here provide greater insight into the political, social, civic, economic, artistic, and religious life of the emigrés in south Florida than any other source. Archivist Esperanza B. de Varona has catalogued these periodicals in annotated form in her bibliography, *Cuban Exile Periodicals at the University of Miami* (1987). The Richter library is also a repository for most secondary materials relating to Cubans in the United States.

The Miami–Dade Public Library has on microfilm the two major English-language newspapers published in Dade County during this thirty-five-year period, the *Miami Herald* (and *El Nuevo Herald*) and the *Miami News*. Just as the Cuban periodicals help to reveal the issues and concerns important to the emigré community, the *Herald* and the *News* provide insight into the concerns of non-Cubans. These newspapers give a fairly detailed account of the Cubans' accommodation to south Florida, as well as the evolution of ethnic relations.

The Special Collections department at Florida International University in University Park houses a small but growing collection of materials related to the Cuban exile experience. These include a few taped interviews, newspapers, photographs, and assorted memorabilia.

Other materials important to this study were found in various presidential libraries. The John F. Kennedy Library in Boston contains records of the early years of the Cuban Refugee Program as well as information on the Bay of Pigs invasion, the Missile Crisis, and the CIA's "secret war" against the Castro government in the early 1960s. The Lyndon Baines Johnson Presidential Library in Austin contains valuable information on the freedom flights of 1965–73, and the National Security–Defense Files contain letters, telegrams, reports, and documents concerning the exiles' political and paramilitary activities in south Florida. The Jimmy Carter Library in Atlanta holds the records of the Cuban-Haitian Task Force and the attempts by the Carter administration to normalize diplomatic and trade relations with the Castro government in the late 1970s.

The Nettie Lee Benson Latin American Collection at the University of Texas at Austin houses some secondary materials relating to Cubans and to other Latino immigrant groups in the United States. Included in its periodical collection is the Miami-based *Diario las Américas*. Until the publication of *El Herald* in 1976, the *Diario* was the most widely read Spanish-language newspaper in south Florida, and in the 1990s it continues to have one of the largest circulations of any newspaper or tabloid in south Florida (and in Puerto Rico). It serves as an important forum and source of information for the Cuban and Latino community.

The following bibliography lists some of the primary and secondary sources important to this study. The dates listed for the periodicals are the issues used as reference, not the lifespan of the periodicals.

Newspapers

Diario Las Américas, Miami, 1973–85.
Granma, Havana, 1980.
Miami Herald, 1959–94.
El Herald, 1976–87; *El Nuevo Herald*, 1987–94.
Miami News, 1962–86.

Cuban Exile Newspapers, Tabloids, and News Magazines

Abdala, Elizabeth, New Jersey, 1971.
Actualidad, Miami, 1970.
Ahora, New York, 1963.
Alerta, Miami, 1970–78.
Alpha, Miami, 1979.
Antorcha, Coral Gables, Florida, 1968–74.
Aplausos, New Jersey, 1974–81.
Bohemia Libre, Caracas, Venezuela, 1960–69.
Boletín Informativo de las Fuerzas Armadas Constitucionales de Cuba en el Exilio, Miami, 1965.
Boletín Internacional de Noticias, Miami, 1962–69.
Boletín Partido Demócrata Cristiano, Miami, 1991–92.
Boletín Semanal Informativo, Coral Gables, Florida, 1960–62.
Candilejas, Miami, 1965–72.
Centinela de la Libertad, Miami, 1963–65.
CID, Miami, 1981–85.

El Clarín, New York, New Jersey, and Miami, 1963–68.
Comandos L, Miami, 1965–66.
Conciencia, Caracas, Venezuela, 1961–64.
Contrapunto, Miami, 1994.
El Correo de New Orleans, 1964.
La Crónica, San Juan, Puerto Rico, 1978–79.
Cruzada, Miami, 1961–62.
Cuba Democrática, Miami, 1962.
La Cuba de Ayer, Miami, 1978.
Cuba en Marcha, Boston, 1967.
Cuba Espera, Miami, 1972.
Cuba Laboral, Miami, 1964–67.
Cuba Libre, Miami, 1968.
Cuba Libre (Organo de la Insurrección Cubana), Miami, 1961–62.
Cuba Nueva (Consejo Revolucionario Cubano), Miami, 1962–63.
Cuba Nueva (Organo de Orientación y Combate de las Fuerzas Nacionalistas, Revolucionarias, y Democraticas del Pueblo Cubano), Miami, 1966.
Cuban Affairs / Asuntos Cubanos, Princeton, 1994.
Cuban Report, Miami, 1962.
Cubanacán: Asociación de Villaclareños en el Exilio, Miami, 1966–78.
El Cubano Libre, West New York, New Jersey, 1977–86.
El Día, Miami, 1970–71.
Denuncia, Miami, 1962.
Despertar News, New Jersey, 1976–86.
Dignidad, Miami, 1962–64.
El Dominicano (Municipio de Santo Domingo), Miami, 1976, 1978.
DRE Internacional, Miami, 1964.
El Expreso de Miami, 1976.
¡Fe!, Miami, 1972–73.
El Fénix, San Juan, 1968–75.
Fragua, Miami, 1990–92.
Fundación, Miami, 1991–92.
Girón, Miami, 1965–83, 1984–86.
Guanimar (Municipio de Alquizar), 1967–69, 1972–77, 1983–85.
Guerra, Miami, 1964.
Guerra, New York, 1968–76.
El Gusano, Miami, 1966–67.
Impacto, Miami, 1971–73.
El Imparcial, Miami, 1981–84.
Impresiones, Miami, 1961–64.
Información, Houston, 1980–86.
Información Católica Cubana, Miami, 1962–65.
Látigo, Miami, 1978–79.
Liberación, Hialeah, Florida, 1984.
La Lucha, Miami, 1967.
Martiano (Partido Revolucionario Martiano), Miami, 1972–73.

El Mundo, Wilmington, Delaware, 1960–62.
La Nación, Miami, 1976–86.
La Nación (Municipios Cubanos en el Exilio), Miami, 1968–69.
La Ortodoxia, Miami, 1992.
Página, Miami, 1971–77.
Palenque, Miami, 1990–93.
Patria, Miami, 1959–86.
La Prensa de Miami, 1965–69.
Pro-Cuba, West Palm Beach, 1967–68, 1978–93.
El Pueblo, New York, 1960.
Raíces, Hialeah, Florida, 1979.
La Razón, Union City, New Jersey, 1985.
RECE, Miami, 1964–76.
Réplica, Miami, 1963–85.
Revista Ideal, Miami, 1971–80.
Sig-Sag, Union City, New Jersey, 1979.
Trabajo, Miami, 1968–69.
El Trabajador, Miami, 1977–80.
Tridente, Miami, 1963–64.
Trinchera, Miami, 1961–64.
Vanguardia, New York, 1968.
La Voz Libre, Los Angeles, 1981.
Zig-Zag, Miami, 1961–74, 1981–85, 1989.

Cuban Exile Journals and Literary Magazines

Alacrán Azul, Miami, 1970–71.
Areíto, New York, 1975–84.
Cuadernos Desterrados, Miami, 1964–66.
Cuadernos del Hombre Libre, Miami, 1966–67.
Cuban Studies / Estudios Cubanos, Pittsburgh, 1975–89.
¡Cuba Va!, Miami, 1974.
Exilio, New York, 1965–73.
El Gato Tuerto, San Francisco, 1985.
Joven Cuba, New York, 1974–76.
Krisis, Miami, 1975–79.
Linden Lane Magazine, Princeton, New Jersey, 1982–90.
Mariel Magazine, Miami, 1986.
Nueva Generación, Miami and New York, 1965–79.
Punto y Aparte, Miami, 1973.
Reunión, Coral Gables, Florida, 1975–83.
Revista Mariel, New York, 1983–85.

Special Collections

Cuban Exile Archives, Richter Library, University of Miami, Coral Gables, Florida.

Cuban Exile History Archives, Florida International University, Miami, Florida.
Records of the Federal Bureau of Investigation, 1961–1967. Department of Justice, Washington, D.C.
Jimmy Carter Presidential Library, Atlanta, Georgia.
  Records of the Cuban-Haitian Task Force.
  Staff Offices: Records of the Domestic Policy Staff, Civil Rights and Justice.
  Staff Offices: Records of Special Assistant to the President, Esteban Torres.
  Staff Offices: Records of the Office of Hispanic Affairs. Papers of Gilbert Colón.
  Staff Offices: Records of Office of Hispanic Affairs. Papers of Miriam Cruz.
  Staff Offices: Records of Office of Hispanic Affairs. Papers of Armando Rendón.
  White House Central File, Subject File, Countries.
  White House Central File, Subject File, National Security–Defense.
  White House Central File, Subject File, Federal Government–Organizations.
  White House Central File, Subject File, Foreign Affairs.
  White House Central File, Subject File, Judicial-Legal Matters.
  White House Central File, Subject File, States-Territories.
John F. Kennedy Presidential Library, Boston, Massachusetts.
  Papers of Abba P. Schwartz.
  Papers of Arthur M. Schlesinger, Jr.
  Papers of President Kennedy, National Security Files.
  Papers of President Kennedy, President's Office Files, Departments and Agencies.
  Records of the AFL-CIO.
  Records of the Central Intelligence Agency, Foreign Broadcast Information Service.
  Records of the Department of Commerce.
  Records of the Department of Health, Education, and Welfare.
  Records of the Housing and Home Finance Agency.
  Records of the Department of Justice.
  Records of the Department of Labor.
Lyndon Baines Johnson Presidential Library, Austin, Texas.
  National Security–Defense Files. Latin America–Cuba.

Newsletters and Bulletins

Cuba Update, Center for Cuban Studies, New York, 1980.
Cuban Affairs / Asuntos Cubanos, Cuban Committee for Democracy, Princeton, New Jersey, 1994.
Cuban Studies Newsletter, University of Pittsburgh Center for International Studies, 1970–74.

Cuban Update, Cuban American National Foundation, Washington, D.C., 1985–86.
Department of State Bulletin, 1956–81.

Census Schedules

República de Cuba. *Censo de población, viviendas, y electoral, informe general,* 1953.
Bureau of the Census, United States Department of Commerce. *Census of the General Population.* 1970, 1980, and 1990 editions.

Reports

Bowen, Robert L., ed. *A Report of the Cuban-Haitian Task Force.* Washington: Government Printing Office, 1980.
Hernández, Andrés R., ed. *The Cuban Minority in the U.S.: Final Report on Need Identification and Program Evaluation.* Washington: Cuban National Planning Council, 1974.
Prohías, Rafael J., and Casal, Lourdes, eds. *The Cuban Minority in the U.S.: Preliminary Report on Need Identification and Program Evaluation, Final Report for Fiscal Year 1973.* 2d ed. Washington: Cuban National Planning Council, 1974.
U.S. Cuban Refugee Program. *Training for Independence: A New Approach to the Problems of Dependency.* Washington: Social and Rehabilitation Service, 1961.
U.S. Department of State. *Cuba.* Washington: Government Printing Office, 1961.
Unzueta, Silvia M. *The Mariel Exodus: A Year in Retrospect.* Miami: Office of the County Manager, April 1981.
Voorhees, Tracy S. *Report to the President of the United States on the Cuban Refugee Problem.* Washington: Government Printing Office, 1961.

Government Hearings

U.S. Senate Committee of the Judiciary. *Hearings before a Subcommittee to Investigate Problems Connected with Refugees and Escapees.* 87th Cong., 1st sess., 1961.
U.S. House Committee of the Judiciary. *Hearings before a Subcommittee to Investigate Problems Connected with Refugees and Escapees.* 88th Cong., 1st sess., 1963.
U.S. Senate Committee of the Judiciary. *Hearings Before the Subcommittee to Investigate the Administration of the Internal Security Act and Other Internal Security Laws.* 89th Cong., 2d sess., 1963.

U.S. House Committee on Appropriations. *Hearings to Determine Foreign Assistance and Related Agencies Appropriations for 1965.* 88th Cong., 2d sess., 1964.
U.S. House Committee of the Judiciary. *Adjusting the Status of Cuban Refugees to That of Lawful Permanent Residents of the United States, Report to Accompany H.R. 15183.* 89th Cong., 2d sess., 1966.
U.S. Senate Committee of the Judiciary. *Hearings before the Select Committee to Study Governmental Operations with Respect to Intelligence Operations.* 94th Cong., 1st sess., 1975.
U.S. Senate Committee of the Judiciary. *Hearings before the Subcommittee to Investigate the Administration of the Internal Security Act and Other Internal Security Laws.* 94th Cong., 2d sess., 1976.
U.S. House Committee of the Judiciary. *Hearings before the Subcommittee on Courts, Civil Liberties, and the Administration of Justice on the Mariel Cuban Detainees—Events Preceding and Following the November 1987 Riots.* 100th Cong., 2d sess., 1988.

Books, Articles, and Dissertations

Aaron, Harold Robert. "The Seizure of Political Power in Cuba, 1956–59." Ph.D. diss., Georgetown University, 1964.
Acosta, Iván. *El super.* Miami: Ediciones Universal, 1982.
———. *Un cubiche en la luna: Tres obras teatrales,* Houston: Arte Público Press, 1989.
Aguirre, Benigno E. "The Differential Migration of the Cuban Social Races." *Latin American Research Review* 11 (1976): 103–24.
"Aid for Cuban Artists." *Nuestro,* January-February 1982, 11.
"Aid to Cuban Refugees: Refugee Problems." *America,* February 1961, 655–56.
Alegría, Fernando, and Jorge Ruffinelli, eds. *Paradise Lost or Gained? The Literature of Hispanic Exile.* Houston: Arte Público Press, 1990.
Alexander, T. "Those Amazing Cuban Emigrés." *Fortune,* October 1966, 144–49.
Almendros, Néstor. *A Man with a Camera.* Translated by Rachel Phillips Belash. New York: Farrar, Straus & Giroux, 1984.
Almendros, Néstor, and Jorge Ulla. "Cuba vista por dos cineastas" (PBS interview, translated by Vicente Echerri), *Linden Lane Magazine,* October-December 1990, 38–39.
Almendros, Néstor, and Orlando Jiménez-Leal. *Conducta impropia: Un film de Néstor Almendros y Orlando Jiménez-Leal.* Madrid: Editorial Playor, 1985.
"Another Cuban Fiasco?" *U.S. News and World Report,* April 29, 1963, 33–36.
Arenas, Reinaldo. *Necesidad de libertad: Mariel: Testimonios de un intelectual disidente.* Mexico City: Kosmos-Editorial, S.A., 1986.
Ayers, Bradley Earl. *The War That Never Was: An Insider's Account of CIA Covert Operations against Cuba.* New York: Bobbs-Merrill, 1976.

Azicri, Max. "The Politics of Exile: Trends and Dynamics of Political Change among Cuban-Americans." *Cuban Studies / Estudios Cubanos* 11/12 (July 1981–January 1982): 55–73.

Bach, Robert L. "The New Cuban Immigrants: Their Background and Prospects." *Monthly Labor Review* 103 (1980): 39–46.

———. "The New Cuban Exodus: Political and Economic Motivations." *Caribbean Review* 11 (Winter 1982) 22–25, 58–60.

———. "Socialist Construction and Cuban Emigration: Exploration into Mariel." *Cuban Studies / Estudios Cubanos* 15 (Summer 1985): 19–36.

Bach, Robert L., Jennifer B. Bach, and Timothy Triplett. "The Flotilla 'Entrants': Latest and Most Controversial." *Cuban Studies / Estudios Cubanos* 11/12 (July 1981–January 1982): 29–48.

"Backlash in Miami." *Newsweek*, March 17, 1975, 32.

Baloyra, Enrique. "Making Waves: A View of the Cuban Community in the U.S.," *Cuban Studies / Estudios Cubanos* 11/12 (July 1981–January 1982): 76–78.

Balseiro, José Agustín, ed. *Presencia hispánica en la Florida*. Miami: Ediciones Universal, 1976.

Bender, Lynn Darrell. "The Cuban Exiles: An Analytical Sketch." *Journal of Latin American Studies* 5 (1973): 271–78.

———. *The Politics of Hostility: Castro's Revolution and United States Policy*. Hato Rey, Puerto Rico: Interamerican University Press, 1975.

Benitez, Tomás. "The Impact of the Cuban Community upon Dade County." Master's thesis, Georgetown University, 1970.

Benjamin, Jules R. *The United States and the Origins of the Cuban Revolution: An Empire of Liberty in an Age of National Liberation*. Princeton, New Jersey: Princeton University Press, 1990.

Bermejo, Ernesto G. "Los que quieren volver a Cuba." *Cuba Internacional*, May 1971, 56–59.

Biskupic, Joan. "Animal Sacrifice Ban Tests Religion Rights." *Washington Post*, November 1, 1992, A1.

Blight, James G. *On the Brink: Americans and Soviets Reexamine the Cuban Missile Crisis*. New York: Hill and Wang, 1989.

"Bomb Blast Shatters 100 Capital Windows." *New York Times*, September 8, 1977, 22.

Bonsal, Philip W. *Cuba, Castro, and the United States*. Pittsburgh: University of Pittsburgh Press, 1971.

Booth, William. "Cuban American Exiles Court Castro, and Trouble." *Washington Post*, April 28, 1994, A3.

Boswell, Thomas D., and James R. Curtis. *The Cuban-American Experience: Culture, Images, and Perspectives*. Totowa, New Jersey: Rowman and Allanheld, 1983.

Boswell, Thomas D., and Manuel Rivero. "Cubans in America: A Minority Group Comes of Age." *Focus*, April 1985, 2–9.

Boswell, Thomas D., Manuel Rivero, and Guarioné Díaz, eds. *Bibliography for the Mariel-Cuban Diaspora*. Paper no. 7. Gainesville: Center for Latin American Studies, the University of Florida, 1988.

Brenner, Philip. "The Thirty-Year War." *NACLA Report on the Americas* 24, no. 3 (November 1990): 17–20.

Brooke, James. "Exiled Cuban Writers Relish Liberty." *New York Times,* August 22, 1984, 1.

Brown, Cynthia. "Strong-Arming the Hispanic Press." *Columbia Journalism Review* 19 (July-August 1980): 51–54.

Brugioni, Dino A. *Eyeball to Eyeball: The Inside Story of the Cuban Missile Crisis.* New York: Random House, 1991.

Buckley, William F. "Brave Cubans Behind Bars." *New York Post,* June 7, 1979, 2.

Burt, Al. "Cuban Exiles: The Mirage of Havana." *Nation,* January 25, 1965, 76–79.

———. "Miami: The Cuban Flavor." *Nation,* March 8, 1971, 299–302.

Cabrera Infante, Guillermo. *Three Trapped Tigers.* Translated by Donald Gardner and Suzanne Jill Levine. New York: Avon Books, 1985.

Calzón, Frank. "LULAC's Mission to Havana." *Cuban Update* (Spring 1985), 1–4.

Cantu, Hector. "Building a Bridge to Success." *Hispanic Business,* September 1993, 16.

Carbonell, Néstor T. *And the Russians Stayed: The Sovietization of Cuba.* New York: William Morrow and Co., 1989.

"Carter and the Cuban Influx." *Newsweek,* May 26, 1980, 22–31.

Casal, Lourdes. "Memories of a Black Cuban Childhood." *Nuestro,* April 1978, 61–62.

———. "Cubans in the United States: Their Impact on U.S.–Cuba Relations." In *Revolutionary Cuba in the World Arena,* edited by M. Weinstein, 109–36. Philadelphia: Institute for the Study of Human Issues, 1979.

Casal, Lourdes, and Andres Hernández. "Cubans in the U.S.: A Survey of the Literature." *Cuban Studies / Estudios Cubanos* 5 (July 1975): 25–51.

Casal, Lourdes, and Yolanda Prieto. "Black Cubans in the United States: Basic Demographic Information." In *Female Immigrants to the United States: Caribbean, Latin American, and African Experiences,* edited by Delores M. Mortimer and Roy S. Bryce-LaPorte, 314–55. RIIES Occasional Papers no. 2. Washington, D.C.: Research Institute on Immigration and Ethnic Studies, Smithsonian Institution, 1981.

Castellanos, Isabel. "The Use of English and Spanish among Cubans in Miami." *Cuban Studies / Estudios Cubanos* 20 (1990): 49–63.

"Castro's Crime Bomb." *U.S. News and World Report,* January 16, 1984, 27–30.

"Castro Tells Rally Cubans Are Free to Leave Cuba." *New York Times,* September 30, 1965, 1.

Castro Hidalgo, Orlando. *Spy for Fidel.* Miami: E. A. Seemann, 1971.

Clark, Juan M. "The Exodus from Revolutionary Cuba (1959–1974): A Sociological Analysis." Ph.D. diss., University of Florida, 1975.

———. *The Cuban Exodus: Background, Evolution, Impact.* Miami: Union of Cubans in Exile, 1977.

Clark, Juan M., José Ignacio Lasaga, and Rose S. Reque. *The 1980 Mariel Exodus: An Assessment and Prospects.* Washington, D.C.: Council for Interamerican Security, 1981.

Clarke, Jay. "Cubans in Miami Fearful." *Washington Post,* May 23, 1976, E1.

"Coming: New Effort to Topple Castro?" *U.S. News and World Report.* May 11, 1964, 39.

"Coping with Cuba's Exodus." *Newsweek,* May 12, 1980, 60–63.

Cortés, Carlos E., ed. *Cuban Exiles in the United States.* New York: Arno Press, 1980.

——, ed. *The Cuban Experience in the United States.* New York: Arno Press, 1980.

——, ed. *Cuban Refugee Programs.* New York: Arno Press, 1980.

Cortina, Rodolfo J., ed. *Cuban American Theater.* Houston: Arte Público Press, 1991.

Coser, Lewis A. *Refugee Scholars in America.* New Haven: Yale University Press, 1984.

Coto, Juan Carlos. "Nueva emisora radial enfurece a exiliados." *El Nuevo Herald,* March 28, 1991, 1B.

"The Cuban Conundrum." *Newsweek,* September 29, 1980, 23–24.

"Cuban Exiles in Paris Tell of Prison Torture." *New York Times,* April 15, 1986, 7A.

"Cuban Exodus Resumes." *America,* January 1, 1966, 3.

"Cuban Refugees." *Saturday Evening Post,* April 8, 1961, 79.

"Cuban Refugees Write a U.S. Success Story." *Business Week,* October 16, 1969, 84.

"Cuban Success Story in the U.S." *U.S. News and World Report,* March 20, 1967, 104–6.

"Cubans Take Off on SBA Test Run." *Business Week,* June 21, 1969, 41.

"Cuban Tide Is a Flood." *Newsweek,* May 19, 1980, 28–29.

"Cubans Vote with Their Feet." *Newsweek,* April 21, 1980, 53.

"Cuba's New Refugees Get Jobs Fast." *Business Week,* March 12, 1966, 69.

Curtis, James R. "Miami's Little Havana: Yard Shrines, Cult Religion and Landscape." In *Rituals and Ceremonies in Popular Culture,* edited by Ray B. Browne, 105–19. Bowling Green: Bowling Green University Popular Press, 1980.

de Varona, Esperanza B. *Cuban Exile Periodicals at the University of Miami Library: An Annotated Bibliography.* Seminar on the Acquisition of Latin American Library Materials (SALALM) no. 19. Madison: University of Wisconsin Press, 1987.

Díaz, Guarioné. *Evaluation and Identification of Policy Issues in the Cuban Community.* Miami: Cuban American Planning Council, 1980.

Díaz-Briquets, Sergio, and Lisandro Pérez. *Cuba: The Demography of Revolution.* Washington, D.C.: Population Reference Bureau, 1981.

Dixon, Heriberto. "Who Ever Heard of a Black Cuban?" *Afro-Hispanic Review* 1 (September 1982): 10–12.

———. "The Cuban-American Counterpoint: Black Cubans in the United States." *Dialectical Anthropology* 13 (1988): 227–39.

Dominguez, Jorge I. *Cuba: Order and Revolution.* Cambridge, Massachusetts: Harvard University Press, 1978.

———. "U.S. Immigration Policies Towards Cuba." In *Western Hemisphere Immigration and United States Foreign Policy,* edited by Christopher Mitchell, 31–88. Pittsburgh: Pennsylvania State Press, 1992.

Draper, Theodore. "Castro's Cuba: A Revolution Betrayed?" *Encounter,* March 1961, 6–23.

———. "Cuba and U.S. Policy." *New Leader,* June 5, 1961, 3–34.

———. *Castro's Revolution: Myths and Realities.* New York: Frederick A. Praeger, 1962.

Dubelman, Abraham. "Cuba." *American Jewish Yearbook,* 481–85. New York: American Jewish Committee, 1962.

Egerton, John. *Cubans in Miami: A Third Dimension in Racial and Cultural Relations.* Nashville, Tennessee: Race Relations Information Center, 1969.

"El amargo destino de los apátridas." *Bohemia,* August 10, 1973, 74–75.

"End of the Freedom Flights." *Time,* September 1971, 34.

Engle, Margarita. *Singing to Cuba.* Houston: Arte Público Press, 1993.

Esteve, Himilce. *El exilio cubano en Puerto Rico: Su impacto político-social, 1959–1983.* San Juan, Puerto Rico: Editorial Raíces, 1984.

"Exiles, Inc." *Newsweek,* April 3, 1961, 51.

"Exiles Say They Planted Bomb on Cuban Airliner." *New York Times,* July 16, 1976, 8.

"Exodus from Hungary." *Christian Century* 73 (December 19, 1956): 1471.

Fabricio, Roberto. "The Cuban Americans: Fifteen Years Later." *Tropic Magazine,* July 14, 1974, 30–36.

Fagen, Richard R., Richard A. Brody, and Thomas J. O'Leary. *Cubans in Exile: Disaffection and Revolution.* Stanford, California: Stanford University Press, 1968.

Fernández, Gastón A. "The Flotilla Entrants: Are They Different?" *Cuban Studies / Estudios Cubanos* 11/12 (July 1981–January 1982): 49–54.

———. "The Freedom Flotilla: A Legitimacy Crisis of Cuban Socialism?" *Journal of Interamerican Studies and World Affairs* 24 (May 1982): 183–209.

———. "Conflicting Interpretations of the Freedom Flotilla Entrants." *Cuban Studies / Estudios Cubanos* 14 (Winter 1984): 49–51.

Fernández, Gastón, and León Narváez. "Bibliography of Cuban Immigration/Adaptation to the United States." *Cuban Studies / Estudios Cubanos* 15 (Summer 1985): 61–72.

Fernández, Roberto G. *La vida es un special.* Miami: Ediciones Universal, 1981.

———. *La montaña rusa.* Houston: Arte Público Press, 1985.

———. *Raining Backwards.* Houston: Arte Público Press, 1988.

Ferree, Myra Marx. "Employment without Liberation: Cuban Women in the U.S." *Social Science Quarterly* 60 (January 1979): 35–50.

"Flight from Havana." *Newsweek*, April 28, 1980, 38–40.

Forment, Carlos A. "Political Practice and the Rise of an Ethnic Enclave." *Theory and Society* 18 (January 1989): 47–81.

Frankel, Max. "Journey of Inquiry into Castro's Cuba." *New York Times Magazine*, January 22, 1961, 8.

Franqui, Carlos. *Family Portrait with Fidel*. New York: Vintage Books, 1984.

"Freedom Flotilla." *Time*, May 19, 1980, 16.

Freedman, Anne B. "In the Fishbowl." *Nuestro*, May 1979, 14.

French, Howard. "Clinton Choice for Latin Post Stirs Feud Between Two Groups." *New York Times*, January 27, 1993, A2.

———. "Havana Woos Exiles, Easing Visits and Dangling Financial Carrot," *New York Times*, April 25, 1994, A9.

Gallagher, Patrick L. "The Cuban Exile: A Socio-Political Analysis." Ph.D. diss., St. Louis University, 1974.

García, Cristina. *Dreaming in Cuban*. New York: Alfred A. Knopf, 1992.

García, María Cristina. "Cuban Exiles and Cuban Americans: A History of an Immigrant Community in South Florida." Ph.D. diss., University of Texas at Austin, 1991.

———. "Adapting to Exile: Cuban Women in the United States, 1959–1973." *Latino Studies Journal* 2 (Spring 1991).

Garreau, Joel. *The Nine Nations of North America*. New York: Avon Books, 1981.

Gilder, George. *The Spirit of Enterprise*. New York: Simon and Schuster, 1984.

González, María E. "Six Out of Cuba: Artists of the Mariel Boatlift." *Marquee*, February-March 1983, 40–46.

Gordon, Milton. *Assimilation in American Life*. New York: Oxford University Press, 1964.

Goytisolo, Juan. "Twenty-Six Rue de Bievre." *Partisan Review* 51 (1984): 680–91.

Greenbaum, Susan D. "Afro-Cubans in Exile: Tampa, Florida, 1886–1984." *Cuban Studies / Estudios Cubanos* 15 (Winter 1985): 59–72.

Greenfield, Charles. "Cuba's Matriarch of Letters: Lydia Cabrera." *Nuestro*, September 1982, 14–17.

———. "Writing in Exile: A Portrait of Guillermo Cabrera Infante, Cuba's Foremost Novelist and Critic." *Nuestro*, October 1982, 22–24.

———. "Cuban Theater in Exile: Miami's Little Broadway." *Nuestro*, November 1982, 36–38.

———. "Armando Valladares: Twenty-Two Years of Solitude." *Nuestro*, December 1983, 14–18.

———. "Life Imitating Art: A Profile of Reynaldo Arenas." *Nuestro*, June-July 1985, 40–42.

Grenier, Guillermo J., and Alex Stepick, eds. *Miami Now! Immigration, Ethnicity and Social Change*. Gainesville: University Press of Florida, 1992.

Griffith, Stephanie. "New Rules Put Cubans on the Spot," *Washington Post,* August 15, 1993, B5.

Grupo Areíto. *Contra viento y marea.* La Habana, Cuba: Casa Las Américas, 1978.

Gruson, Lindsey. "Cuban Inmates in Louisiana Free All 26 Hostages." *New York Times,* November 30, 1987, 1.

Guernica, Antonio. "Cuba: A Personal Journey." *Nuestro,* September 1984, 53.

Guillén, Ligia. "Homenaje a la Virgen de la Caridad." *La voz católica,* August 30, 1985, 1.

Haines, David W., ed. *Refugees in the United States: A Reference Handbook.* Westport, Connecticut: Greenwood Press, 1985.

Handler, Richard, and Jocelyn Linnekin. "Tradition, Genuine or Spurious." *Journal of American Folklore* 97 (1984): 273–88.

Herrera, Maria Cristina, and Leonel Antonio de la Cuesta, eds. *Itinerario ideológico: Antología de Lourdes Casal.* Miami: Instituto de Estudios Cubanos, 1982.

Higgins, Trumbull. *The Perfect Failure: Kennedy, Eisenhower, and the C.I.A. at the Bay of Pigs.* New York: W. W. Norton, 1987.

"Hispanic Power at the Polls." *Newsweek,* July 14, 1983, 23.

Hobsbawm, Eric, and Terence Ranger, eds. *The Invention of Tradition.* Cambridge: Cambridge University Press, 1992.

Holmes, Steven A. "Clinton Fills Post for Latin America." *New York Times,* March 2, 1993, A13.

Horowitz, Irving Louis. "The Cuba Lobby: Supplying Rope to a Mortgaged Revolution." *Washington Review of Strategic and International Studies* (July 1978): 58–71.

Horowitz, Irving Louis, ed. *Cuban Communism.* 2d ed. New Brunswick, New Jersey: Transaction Books, 1972.

Hospital, Carolina. "Los hijos del exilio cubano y su literatura." *Explicación de textos literarios* 15 (1986–87): 103–15.

———, ed. *Cuban American Writers: Los Atrevidos.* Princeton: Ediciones Ellas / Linden Lane Press, 1988.

Howe, Marvin. "For Cuban Chinese, the Twain Meet." *New York Times,* June 17, 1985, 8.

Huberman, Leo, and Paul M. Sweezy. *Cuba: Anatomy of a Revolution.* New York: Monthly Review Press, 1961.

"Huge Throng in Marine Stadium to Honor Lady of Cobre Tonight." *Catholic Voice,* September 8, 1972, 1.

Hunt, Howard. *Give Us This Day.* New Rochelle, New York: Arlington House, 1973.

Inclán, Hilda. "I Am Not Afraid." *Nuestro,* April 1977, 46–47.

"International Law Luncheon Features Felipe Rivero." *The Slip Sheet* (University of Miami Law School), December 7, 1967, 1.

"Iowa, Sí! Training Programs for Spanish Teachers." *Newsweek,* August 1963, 75.

"It's Your Turn in the Sun." *Time,* October 16, 1978, 48.

Jacoby, Susan. "Miami Sí, Cuba No." *New York Times Magazine*, September 29, 1974.

Johnson, Haynes. *The Bay of Pigs: The Leaders' Story of Brigade 2506*. New York: Dell Publishing Co., 1964.

Kanellos, Nicolás. *A History of Hispanic Theater in the United States: Origins to 1940*. Austin: University of Texas Press, 1990.

———, ed. *Biographical Dictionary of Hispanic Literature in the United States*. Westport, Connecticut: Greenwood Press, 1989.

Kunz, E. F. "The Refugee in Flight: Kinetic Models and Forms of Displacement." *International Migration Review* 7 (Summer 1973): 125–46.

LeoGrande, William M. "A Party Divided and Paralyzed." *Nation*, October 24, 1988, 395–97.

Leshaw, Gary. "Final Story on Marielitos Isn't Written." *Atlanta Journal and Constitution*, April 21, 1990, A15.

Levine, Barry. "Sources of Ethnic Identity for Latin Florida: Cubans in Miami." *Caribbean Review* 8 (January-March 1979): 30–33.

Levine, Robert M. *Tropical Diaspora: The Jewish Experience in Cuba*. Gainesville: University Press of Florida, 1993.

Levinson, Sandra, and Carol Brightman. *Venceremos Brigade: Young Americans Sharing the Life and Work of Revolutionary Cuba*. New York: Simon and Schuster, 1971.

Liebman, Seymour. "Cuban Jewish Community in South Florida." In *American Jewish Yearbook*, 238–46. New York: American Jewish Committee, 1969.

Lindstrom, Naomi E. "Cuban American and Continental Puerto Rican Literature." In *Sourcebook of Hispanic Culture in the United States*, edited by David William Foster, 221–45. Chicago: American Library Association, 1982.

Llanes, José. *Cuban Americans: Masters of Survival*. Cambridge, Massachusetts: Abt Books, 1982.

"Loans to Cuban Refugee Students." *School and Society*, December 24, 1966, 476.

Loescher, Gil, and John A. Scanlan. *Calculated Kindness: Refugees and America's Half-Open Door, 1945 to the Present*. New York: Free Press, 1986.

Lowenstein, Roger. "Miami Vise: The *Herald* Is Wooing Cuban Readers, but It Risks Loss of Anglos." *Wall Street Journal*, March 5, 1987, 1.

Mackey, William Francis, and Nieda von Beebe. *Bilingual Schools for a Bicultural Community: Miami's Adaptation to the Cuban Refugees*. Rowley, Massachusetts: Newbury House Publishers, 1977.

Marburgh, Claiborne. "Operation Simpático." *PTA Magazine*, September 1963, 31–32.

Marchetti, Victor, and John D. Marks. *The CIA and the Cult of Intelligence*. New York: Alfred A. Knopf, 1974.

"Marian Shrine for Miami Urged." *Catholic Voice*, September 16, 1966, 1.

Masud-Piloto, Felix. *With Open Arms: Cuban Migration to the United States.* New York: Rowman and Littlefield, 1988.

Massey, Douglas S., and Kathleen M. Schnabel. "Recent Trends in Hispanic Immigration to the United States." *International Migration Review* 17 (Summer 1983): 212–44.

Matthews, Herbert L. *The Cuban Story.* New York: George Braziller, 1961.

———. *Revolution in Cuba: An Essay in Understanding.* New York: Charles Scribner's Sons, 1975.

Maurer, Henry. "With the Venceremos in Cuba." *Nation,* July 2, 1977, 6–10.

McCoy, Clyde B., and Diana H. Gonzalez. *Cuban Immigration and Immigrants in Florida and the United States: Implications for Immigration Policy.* BEBR Monograph no. 3. Gainesville, Florida: Bureau of Economic and Business Research, University of Florida, 1985.

McDowell, Edwin. "For Cuban Author, Liberty Is Sweet." *New York Times,* July 22, 1986, C15.

McGehee, Ralph W. *Deadly Deceits: My Twenty-Five Years in the CIA.* New York: Sheridan Square Publications, 1983.

McNally, Michael J. *Catholicism in South Florida, 1868–1968.* Gainesville: University of Florida Press, 1982.

Medina, Pablo. *Exiled Memories: A Cuban Childhood.* Austin: University of Texas Press, 1990.

Mejías-Rentas, Antonio. "Hispanic Vote in Chicago—A Message Missed." *Hispanic Link,* April 24, 1983.

Meyer, Karl Ernest, and Tad Szulc. *The Cuban Invasion: The Chronicle of a Disaster.* New York: Ballantine Books, 1962.

"Miami Museum Defies City's Order to Vacate." *New York Times,* April 2, 1991, 19.

"Miami: New Hispanic Power Base in the U.S." *U.S. News and World Report,* February 19, 1979, 69.

"Miami: No Place Like It." *Time,* November 12, 1965, 37.

"Miami Plans to Evict Cuban Art Museum from City Building." *New York Times,* April 1, 1991, 7.

"Miami Recoils." *The Economist,* December 22, 1984, 15–16.

"Miami's Angry Cubans." *Newsweek,* September 1, 1975, 55.

"Miami's Black Violence." *Newsweek,* July 28, 1980, 41.

Mohl, Raymond A. "An Ethnic 'Boiling Pot': Cubans and Haitians in Miami." *Journal of Ethnic Studies* 13 (Summer 1985): 51–74.

Montaner, Carlos Alberto. "The Roots of Anti-Americanism in Cuba." *Caribbean Review* 13 (Spring 1984): 13–16, 42–46.

Moore, Joan, and Harry Pachón. *Hispanics in the United States.* Englewood Cliffs, New Jersey: Prentice-Hall, 1985.

Mora Morales, Esther Pilar. *La verdad sobre el presidio político de mujeres en la Cuba castrista.* Miami: Revista Ideal, n.d.

Muñoz, Elías Miguel. *Los viajes de Orlando Cachumbambé.* Miami: Ediciones Universal, 1984.

———. *Crazy Love.* Houston: Arte Público Press, 1989.

———. *The Greatest Performance*. Houston: Arte Público Press, 1991.
Nazario, Sonia L. "Yanqui Sí: After a Long Holdout, Cubans in Miami Take a Role in U.S. Politics." *Wall Street Journal*, June 7, 1983, 1.
Neilsen, Mark. "Bad Press Creates Difficulties in Resettling Cuban Refugees." *National Catholic Reporter* 16 (August 15, 1980): 22–23.
"New Flight from Castro: New Headache for the U.S." *U.S. News and World Report*, October 25, 1965, 56.
Nichols, John Spicer. "A Communications Perspective on Radio Martí." *Cuban Studies / Estudios Cubanos* 14 (Summer 1984): 35–46.
———. "Broadcast Wars." *NACLA Report on the Americas* 24, no. 3 (November 1990): 30–33.
———. "Mas Canosa's Pork Barrel." *NACLA Report on the Americas* 24, no. 3 (November 1990): 34.
———. "The Power of the Anti-Fidel Lobby." *Nation*, October 24, 1988, 389–92.
"Nine Cuban Refugees Go on Trial in Miami Tomorrow, Putting Focus on Terrorist Activity in South Florida." *New York Times*, November 28, 1976, 35.
Nordheimer, Jon. "Cuban American Leader Builds a Foundation of Power beyond Miami." *New York Times*, July 12, 1986, 6.
———. "Tempest in Miami over Playwright." *New York Times*, May 10, 1986, 6.
Oettinger, Katherine Brownell. "Services to Unaccompanied Cuban Refugee Children in the United States." *Social Service Review* 36 (December 1962): 377–84.
"Operation Airlift." *Newsweek*, July 31, 1961, 47.
Padilla, Felix M. "On the Nature of Latino Ethnicity," *Social Science Quarterly* 65 (June 1984): 651–64.
Padilla, Heberto. *Heroes Are Grazing in My Garden*. Translated by Andrew Hurley. New York: Farrar, Straus & Giroux, 1984.
———. *Self Portrait of the Other*. Translated by Alexander Coleman. New York: Farrar, Straus & Giroux, 1990.
Parker, Everett C. "Miami's Real-Life Drama." *Christian Century*, 78 (October 11, 1961), 1209–10.
———. "Miami: Test for the Churches." *Christian Century*, 78 (October 18, 1961): 1241–42.
———. "Help for Cuban Refugees." *Christian Century*, 78 (November 22, 1961): 1390–91.
Pear, Robert. "The Cuba Missile Crisis: Kennedy Left a Loophole." *New York Times*, January 7, 1992, A5.
Pedraza-Bailey, Silvia. *Political and Economic Migrants in America: Cubans and Mexicans*. Austin: University of Texas Press, 1985.
———. "Cuba's Exiles: Portrait of a Refugee Migration." *International Migration Review* 19 (Spring 1985): 4–34.
Pérez, Lisandro. "The Cuban Population of the United States: The Results of the 1980 U.S. Census of Population," *Cuban Studies / Estudios Cubanos* 15 (Summer 1985): 1–18.

————. "Immigrant Economic Adjustment and Family Organization: The Cuban Success Story Reexamined." *International Migration Review* 20 (Spring 1986): 4–20.

————. "Cubans in the United States." *Annals of the American Academy of Political and Social Science* 487 (September 1986): 126–37.

Pérez, Louis A. "Cubans in Tampa: From Exiles to Immigrants, 1892–1901." *Florida Historical Quarterly* 57 (October 1978): 129–40.

Persons, Albert C. *Bay of Pigs: A Firsthand Account of the Mission by a U.S. Pilot in Support of the Cuban Invasion Force in 1961.* Jefferson, North Carolina: McFarland and Co., 1990.

Peterson, Mark. "The Flotilla Entrants: Social Psychological Perspectives on their Employment." *Cuban Studies / Estudios Cubanos* 12 (July 1982): 81–85.

Portes, Alejandro. "Dilemmas of a Golden Exile: Integration of Cuban Refugee Families in Milwaukee," *American Sociological Review* 34 (August 1969): 505–18.

————. "The Social Origins of the Cuban Enclave Economy of Miami." *Sociological Perspectives* 30 (October 1987): 340–71.

Portes, Alejandro, and Robert L. Bach. "Immigrant Earnings: Cuban and Mexican Immigrants in the United States." *International Migration Review* 14 (Fall 1980): 315–41.

————. *Latin Journey: Cuban and Mexican Immigrants in the United States.* Berkeley and Los Angeles: University of California Press, 1985.

Portes, Alejandro, Juan M. Clark, and Robert L. Bach. "The New Wave: A Statistical Profile of Recent Cuban Exiles to the United States." *Cuban Studies / Estudios Cubanos* 7 (1977).

Portes, Alejandro, Juan M. Clark, and Robert D. Manning. "After Mariel: A Survey of the Resettlement Experiences of 1980 Cuban Refugees in Miami." *Cuban Studies / Estudios Cubanos* 15 (Summer 1985): 37–59.

Portes, Alejandro, and Leif Jensen. "The Enclave and the Entrants: Patterns of Ethnic Enterprise in Miami before and after Mariel." *American Sociological Review* 54 (December 1989): 929–49.

Portes, Alejandro, and Rafael Mozo. "The Political Adaptation Process of Cubans and Other Ethnic Minorities in the United States: A Preliminary Analysis." *International Migration Review* 19 (March 1985): 35–63.

Portes, Alejandro, and Alex Stepick. *City on the Edge: The Transformation of Miami.* Berkeley and Los Angeles: University of California Press, 1993.

Poyo, Gerald E. *With All and for the Good of All: The Emergence of Popular Nationalism in the Cuban Communities of the United States, 1848–1898.* Durham, North Carolina: Duke University Press, 1989.

Prados, John. *Presidents' Secret Wars: CIA and Pentagon Covert Operations since WWII.* New York: William Morrow and Co., 1986.

Prida, Dolores. "After Castro's Invitation." *Nuestro,* October 1978, 46–47.

————. *Beautiful Señoritas and Other Plays.* Houston: Arte Público Press, 1991.

Prieto, Yolanda. "Reinterpreting an Immigration Success Story: Cuban Women, Work, and Change in a New Jersey Community." Ph.D. diss., Rutgers University, 1984.

————. "Cuban Women in the U.S. Labor Force: Perspectives on the Nature of Change." *Cuban Studies / Estudios Cubanos* 17 (1987): 73–91.

————. "Apuntes preliminares sobre la incorporación de la mujer cubana a la fuerza laboral en los Estados Unidos." *Areíto* 6 (1980): 23–25.

"Protestants to Aid Catholic Refugee." *Christian Century*, May 29, 1963, 702.

"Refugee Gulags." *Nation*, December 12, 1981, 628–29.

"Refugee Leader Blames U.S. for 'Broken Promise.'" *U.S. News and World Report*, April 29, 1963, 65–67.

"Refugees from Castro." *The Economist*, December 22, 1962, 1205.

"The Refugees: Rebels with a Cause." *Newsweek*, June 16, 1980, 30–31.

Richmond, Marie LaLiberté. *Immigrant Adaptation and Family Structure among Cubans in Miami, Florida*. New York: Arno Press, 1980.

Ripoll, Carlos. *The Heresy of Words in Cuba*. Perspectives on Freedom, no. 4. New York: Freedom House, 1985.

Robbins, Carla Anne. *The Cuban Threat*. New York: McGraw-Hill, 1983.

————. "South Florida's Melting Pot About to Boil." *Business Week*, February 4, 1985, 86–87.

Rogg, Eleanor Meyer. *The Assimilation of Cuban Exiles: The Role of Community and Class*. New York: Aberdeen Press, 1974.

Rogg, Eleanor Meyer, and Rosemary Santana Cooney. *The Adaptation and Adjustment of Cubans, West New York, New Jersey*. Monograph no. 5. New York: Hispanic Research Center, Fordham University, 1980.

Rohter, Larry. "When a City Newspaper Is the Enemy." *New York Times*, March 19, 1992, A16.

————. "Miami Leaders Are Condemned by Rights Unit." *New York Times*, August 19, 1992, A18.

————. "Cuban Exiles Try to Stop PBS Show." *New York Times*, October 13, 1992, A15.

————. "A Rising Cuban-American Leader: Statesmen to Some, Bully to Others." *New York Times*, October 29, 1992, A18.

————. "Dissenting Voice Fights to Stay on Air." *New York Times*, March 2, 1993, A14.

————. "As Crisis in Cuba Worsens, Unity of Exiles Is Crumbling." *New York Times*, October 6, 1993, 1.

Rositzke, Harry. *The CIA's Secret Operations: Espionage, Counterespionage, and Covert Action*. New York: Reader's Digest Press, 1977.

Rostagno, Irene. "Fifty Years of Looking South: The Promotion and Reception of Latin American Literature in the United States." Ph.D. diss., University of Texas at Austin, 1984.

Rothchild, John. "The Cuban Connection and the Gringo Press." *Columbia Journalism Review* 23 (September-October 1984): 48–51.

Said, Abdul Aziz, ed. *Ethnicity and U.S. Foreign Policy*. New York: Praeger, 1977.

Schmidt, William E. "Detaining Cubans Exacts Rising Toll." *New York Times,* March 10, 1986, 1.
Schwartz, Abba P. *The Open Society.* New York: William Morrow and Co., 1968.
"Sea Lift from Cuba to Key West." *Newsweek,* May 5, 1980, 59–60.
"Second Thoughts on Radio Martí." *New York Times,* March 22, 1986, 26.
Shils, Edward. "Tradition." *Comparative Studies in Society and History* 13 (1971): 122–59.
Silva, Helga. *The Children of Mariel: Cuban Refugee Children in South Florida Schools.* Washington, D.C.: Cuban American National Foundation, 1985.
Smith, Vern E. "In the Flotilla at Mariel." *Newsweek,* May 12, 1980, 63.
Smith, Wayne S. *The Closest of Enemies: A Personal Account of U.S.–Cuba Relations since 1957.* New York: W. W. Norton, 1987.
Smothers, Ronald. "Their Crimes Vary, but Most Cubans Are Serving Sentences of Frustration." *New York Times,* November 30, 1987, B11.
Soler, Frank. "The Miami Connection." *Caribbean Review* 3 (October-December 1974): 4–5.
"Spain's Cuban Refugees." *Christian Century,* October 24, 1973, 1047.
"Start of a Mass Exodus." *Time,* April 28, 1980, 32.
St. George, Andrew. "The War of Wits." *Parade,* August 7, 1966, 1.
Stowers, Genie N. L. "Political Participation, Ethnicity, and Class Status: The Case of Cubans in Miami." *Ethnic Groups* 8 (1990): 73–90.
Suárez, Virgil. *Latin Jazz.* New York: Simon and Schuster, 1989.
———. *Welcome to the Oasis and Other Stories.* Houston: Arte Público Press, 1992.
Suchlicki, Jaime. *Cuba: From Columbus to Castro.* New York: Charles Scribner and Sons, 1974.
Sullivan, Teresa A. "The Occupational Prestige of Women Immigrants: A Comparison of Cubans and Mexicans," *International Migration Review* 18 (Winter 1984): 1045–61.
Szapocznik, José, and María Cristina Herrera, eds. *Cuban Americans: Acculturation, Adjustment, and the Family.* Washington, D.C.: The National Coalition of Hispanic Mental Health and Human Services Organization, 1978.
Szulc, Tad. "'Guerra' Still the Word in Miami." *New York Times Magazine,* July 5, 1964, 9.
———. *Fidel: A Critical Portrait.* New York: William Morrow and Co., 1986.
———. "Nicaragua, an Echo of the Bay of Pigs." *New York Times,* March 16, 1986, 25.
"Terrorism Charged to Cubans in Testimony by Miami Police." *New York Times,* August 23, 1976, 12.
"They're O.K." *Newsweek,* December 4, 1961, 59.
Thomas, Hugh. *The Cuban Revolution.* New York: Harper and Row, 1977.
Thomas, John F. "Cuban Refugees in the United States," *International Migration Review* 1 (Spring 1967): 46–57.

Thompson, Robert Smith. *The Missiles of October: The Declassified Story of John F. Kennedy and the Cuban Missile Crisis.* New York: Simon and Schuster, 1992.

"Three Days of Black Rage in Miami." *Newsweek,* June 2, 1980, 34.

"Three Plead Guilty in Blast at Mission." *New York Times,* February 8, 1986, 31.

Tift, Susan. "Working Hard Against an Image." *Time,* September 12, 1983, 24–25.

"To Miami, Refugees Spell Prosperity." *Business Week,* November 23, 1962, 94.

Torres, María de los Angeles. "From Exiles to Minorities: The Politics of Cuban Americans". In *Latinos and the Political System,* edited by F. Chris García. Notre Dame, Indiana: University of Notre Dame Press, 1988.

———. "Working Against the Miami Myth." *Nation,* October 24, 1988, 392–94.

Torres, Omar. *Fallen Angels Sing.* Houston: Arte Público Press, 1991.

Treaster, Joseph B. "A Cuban American 'Advisor' Tells of Combat with Nicaraguan Rebels." *New York Times,* December 22, 1986, A19.

———. "In the Bushes of Florida, Cuban 'Brigade' Tries to Keep Flame Alive." *New York Times,* December 26, 1986, A14.

"Two in Miami Seeking Cubans for Angola; FBI Plans Inquiry." *New York Times,* January 4, 1976, 20.

Ulla, Jorge, Lawrence Ott, and Miñuca Villaverde. *Dos films de Mariel: El éxodo cubano de 1980.* Madrid: Editorial Playor, 1986.

"U.S. Changes Policy on Cuban Refugees." *Christian Century,* January 22, 1964, 100–101.

Valladares, Armando. *Against All Hope.* Translated by Andrew Hurley. New York: Alfred A. Knopf, 1986.

———. *Prisionero de Castro.* Barcelona: Editorial Planeta, S.A., 1982.

Valls, Jorge. *Twenty Years and Forty Days.* New York: Americas Watch, 1986.

Vila, José Jorge, and Guillermo Zalamea-Arenas. *Exilio.* Miami: Editorial AIP, 1967.

Volsky, George. "U.S. Cuban Refugee Program Split by Reports of Director's Political Activity." *New York Times,* May 10, 1976, 16.

———. "Cuban Exiles Now Seek U.S. Citizenship." *New York Times,* July 4, 1976, 19.

———. "Contra Supporter Describes His Role." *New York Times,* January 4, 1987, 8L.

"Voyage from Cuba." *Time,* May 5, 1980, 43.

Walsh, Bryan O. "Cubans in Miami." *America,* February 26, 1966, 286–89.

———. "Cuban Refugee Children." *Journal of Inter-American Studies and World Affairs* 13 (July-October 1971): 378–415.

Watson, Maida. "The Search for Identity in the Theater of Three Cuban American Female Dramatists." *Bilingual Review* 16 (May-December 1991): 188–96.

Welch, Richard E., Jr. *Response to Revolution: The United States and the Cuban Revolution, 1959–1961*. Chapel Hill: University of North Carolina Press, 1985.

"Whatever Happened to the Cuban Airlifts?" *U.S. News and World Report*, July 28, 1969, 6.

"When Cuban Exiles Broke Loose in Washington." *U.S. News and World Report*, August 3, 1964, 8.

Whitefield, Mimi. "Cuba Recalls Boatlift with Selective Memory." *Houston Chronicle*, April 1, 1990, 25A.

Whitefield, Mimi, and Fabiola Santiago. "Threat of Cuba Immigrant Wave Puts U.S. on Alert." *Houston Chronicle*, August 7, 1994, 29A.

"Why Castro Exports Cubans." *New York Times Magazine*, November 7, 1965, 30.

Wong, Francisco R. "The Political Behavior of Cuban Migrants." Ph.D. diss., University of Michigan, 1974.

Wyden, Peter. *Bay of Pigs: The Untold Story*. New York: Simon and Schuster, 1979.

Yearley, C. K. "Cubans in Miami: An Uncertain Status." *Commonweal*, November 19, 1965, 210–11.

Zaldivar, Raquel Puig. "Freedom to Suffer." *Nuestro*, March 1980, 14–15.

Index

Tamiami Park, 62
Tampa (Florida), 16
Teatro Avance, 194
Teatro Bellas Artes, 90
Teatro Nuevo, 197
television stations, 108. *See also* radio
    stations; Spanish-language news me-
    dia
tent cities, 63
terrorism. *See* militant extremists
theater, 90, 93, 163
Thomas, John F., 37, 45
Three Kings Day parade, 96, 234n.31
Torch of Friendship, 138
Torres, Omar, 173, 174, 178, 181
Trabajo, 102
Tractors for Freedom Committee, 32
Training for Independence. See *Aprenda
    y Supérese*
Trinchera, 102
Triple A (Frente Nacional Democrático),
    124. *See also* counterrevolutionary
    activities; Cuban exile politics
T.V. Martí, 149, 163

Ulla, Jorge, 158, 192
Union City (New Jersey), 85, 232n.6
Unión de Mujeres, 134
United Nations, 133, 143; Commission
    on Human Rights, 160, 161–162,
    163, 249n.156
United States Coast Guard, 38, 60, 61,
    67, 78, 130, 136
United States Information Agency
    (USIA), 28
University of Florida, 28, 112
University of Havana, 28
University of Miami, 26, 27, 28, 31, 90,
    112, 123

Valerio, Andrés, 117
Valerio, Pedro, 157
Valero, Roberto, 117, 193, 195

Valladares, Armando, 157, 160–161,
    164, 192
Valladares, Martha, 157–158
Valls, Jorge, 157, 159, 192
Varela, Félix, 94
Vargas Llosa, Mario, 105, 157
variety shows, 93
Varona, Manuel Antonio, 124, 131
Vega, Mirta R., 26–27, 217n.38
Venceremos Brigade, 203
Victoria, Carlos, 169
La vida es un special, 173
Vietnam, 40, 134, 243n.45
Virgen de la Caridad del Cobre, 87, 98–
    99, 235nn.34,35
visa waivers, 16, 24
Voluntary Relief Agencies (VOLAGs),
    19, 23, 45, 62, 63, 156, 157,
    227n.62
Voorhees, Tracy, 21

Walsh, Bryan O., 24–25, 217nn.34,36
Watergate, 143, 245n.83
West New York (New Jersey), 85,
    232n.6
With All and for the Good of All, 179–
    180
Women: chaperoning of, 95; in Cuban
    American literature, 188–191; as hu-
    man rights activists, 157, 158, 161;
    employment of, 20, 26, 87, 101,
    109, 215n.17, 236n.56, 237n.60;
    entrepreneurship of, 87; in exile poli-
    tics, 133–134; periodicals for, 101; as
    political prisoners, 159; targeted by
    popular media, 189
writers. *See* artists and writers

YUCAS. *See* Cuban exiles, second gener-
    ation of

Zig-Zag, 104, 235n.46

Compositor: Braun-Brumfield, Inc.
Text: 10/13 Galliard
Display: Galliard
Printer and Binder: Braun-Brumfield, Inc.